THE ART OF DOLLS

1700 - 1940

By Madeline Osborne Merrill

Photographs By Richard Merrill
Edited By Estelle L. Johnston

Published By  Hobby House Press, Inc.
Cumberland, Maryland 21502

42513

Additional Copies of this book may be purchased at $35.00
from
HOBBY HOUSE PRESS, INC.
900 Frederick Street
Cumberland, Maryland 21502
or from your favorite bookstore or dealer.
Please add $2.00 per copy postage.

Library of Congress Catalog Number: 85-060436

Printed in the United States of America
ISBN: 0-87588-231-5

Table of Contents

Acknowledgements

The enthusiastic acceptance by collectors of the information found in the first three *Handbook of Collectible Dolls* stimulated and encouraged us to combine their content with extensive new doll material gathered since 1977. This work has resulted in *The Art of Dolls 1700-1940*, a large comprehensive book which includes a major color section.

Our grateful thanks are re-extended to the many collectors all over the United States, who, over the years, have made their dolls and their knowledge available for text and photographs. In particular, appreciation goes to our fellow members of The Doll Collectors of America, Inc. (DCA) who have been most generous. Many worthwhile contributions have also been made by members of The Doll Study Club of Boston, Inc. and The Granite State Doll Club of New Hampshire. Additionally, many museums have made their resources available for our purposes. The confidence of others in our care of their dolls while in our hands for study and photography has been amazing — especially that of a collector in Florida who, although not knowing us personally, sent a valuable doll for our use.

The untimely death of the author in 1981 left a mass of text, 1100 black and white photographs and 200 in color to be assembled, collated, and laid out in book form. Consideration of the qualifications possessed by knowledgeable collectors lead to the choice of Estelle L. Johnston to act as editor. Estelle Johnston joined the DCA in 1972 and had been a friend and consulting correspondent over the years with Madeline Merrill. The form in which *The Art of Dolls 1700-1940* is found today is largely the result of her efforts in behalf of the author's family and Hobby House Press, Inc. For this service I am deeply appreciative.

Richard Merrill

About The Author
Madeline O. Merrill 1907-1981

Madeline Merrill's awareness of old dolls as being collectible originated in the early 1940s while she was a member of a class in rug hooking. The rug hooking instructor dealt in antiques and had a few dolls on display. Having two young daughters at the time, Madeline thought they might become interested in the type of dolls little girls had played with in earlier years. Her first purchase was a wax-over, squash head with a red woolen dress, for which, she admitted much later, she had paid $30.00.

Madeline became acquainted with other doll collectors in the eastern Massachusetts area, and was soon invited to join The Doll Collectors of America, Inc. (DCA), the pioneer doll Club in the United States. She became a member of DCA in April of 1949. On that same day, Nellie W. Perkins of Albany, New York, joined DCA also. The two women became good friends, having in common a deep interest in the origin and manufacture of antique dolls, and the mechanical and artistic skills needed for their refurbishing and restoration.

As willing participants in the activities of DCA, Madeline Merrill and Nellie Perkins served as co-editors of the 1964 and 1967 editions of the DCA Manuals. The DCA bi-monthly Bulletin for members was inaugurated in 1966 and Madeline served as its first editor. She was President of DCA from 1967-1969, and during her term of office the first three day Annual Meeting of DCA was held in Rockport, Massachusetts to which location DCA has returned each year since.

She was a member of The Granite State Doll Club of New Hampshire, affiliated with The United Federation of Doll Clubs.

While on a trip to England with Nellie Perkins in 1968, after their experience gained in editing two DCA Manuals, the idea of publishing a concise, compact book to aid novice collectors in identifying and evaluating their dolls was formed. On their return to the United States, a three-way verbal agreement was reached between Madeline Merrill, Nellie Perkins, and Richard Merrill to contribute their various skills equally, to finance the publication equally, and to share the profits equally if any accrued. This verbal agreement held in satisfaction to all until the death of Nellie Perkins in 1975. The first *Handbook of Collectible Dolls* was published in 1969, and with later additions, grew to three volumes as last printed in 1977.

Over the years Madeline Merrill and her husband gave many illustrated programs on old dolls before historical societies, women's clubs, and various other doll clubs. She researched and wrote articles on antique type dolls which were printed in such publications as *Doll Reader,*™ *The DCA Bulletin, Doll News, Maine Antique Digest, Spinning Wheel,* and several regional convention booklets of The United Federation of Doll Clubs. A three installment review of "American Made Dolls" was published by *Doll Reader,*™ posthumously, in 1982. At the time of her death, Madeline was Honorary Curator of Dolls at The Essex Institute in Salem, Massachusetts. She also wrote continually on genealogical matters, and had served her term as Regent of The Boston Tea Party Chapter of the Daughters of the American Revolution (DAR).

Her own collection of dolls grew slowly and achieved only modest proportions as measured by present day standards of numbers. But the quality, costuming, and overall general condition of her dolls remain second to none.

Her first love and principal interest began and remained with the early woodens, papier mâchés, poured waxes, good chinas, and the better bisques of pre World War I days.

Madeline Osborne Merrill passed away on August 22, 1981. She had worked steadily for many months on the text and revisions of this publication. Her work was left about 85% completed. I have finished the task to the best of my ability. At the risk of appearing too personally involved, may I dedicate this book to her memory?

Richard Merrill

Editor's Word

This book contains a truly extraordinary collection of photographs of an unusually wide range of dolls. For the convenience of the reader the standard chronological format has been largely followed, using the actual or probable dates of manufacture as a guide. However, to avoid the long jumps in time in covering any one group of dolls, the photographs have been divided into dolls primarily of the 19th century and those of the 20th century. While many bisques continued to be produced in the same molds in the early part of the 20th century, one can observe a stylistic change in the over all conception of dolls — child dolls not only captured the market but tended towards greater realism in many different materials. The price of this move to realism was often the loss of romance.

It is, of course, not possible in many cases to draw a clear line between the two centuries, so the division has been made on the preponderence of dolls in each type that fall in either century. In categorizing dolls by the material primarily of the head, wooden dolls are clearly some of the earliest — although papier mâché-like and cloth dolls of the 17th and 18th century are rarely found. As we move into the 19th century the overlapping of time frames makes the ordering necessarily somewhat arbitrary, but there has been an effort to place some of the smaller categories such as cloth squarely in their own periods for comparative appreciation.

Dolls of similar types, as far as possible, have been placed on the same page or surrounding pages for easy study and comparison. Also, dolls with bonnets or hats molded in the same material as the head appear in their appropriate materials of wax, china, bisque, etc. rather than in a mixed group of their own. The color photographs have been arranged to fall between the categories they cover and to provide additional visual information with cross-referencing to the more comprehensive data in the black-and-white counterparts.

I believe the Merrills' intent to provide a useful reference book has been accomplished.

Estelle Johnston

Foreword

The Art of Dolls 1700-1940 is intended as a useful guide and reference for newer collectors attempting a comprehensive selection of antique and collectible dolls, and as support and enjoyment for those whose collections are presently well established.

The content of *The Art of Dolls 1700-1940* represents a revision and up-grading of text and photographs, and a re-editing of the entire material of the final three *Handbooks of Collectible Dolls* as last published by Merrill & Perkins in 1977. New material, a color section, and photographs of approximately three hundred dolls gathered by Madeline and Richard Merrill since that time and never before published have been added.

The age range of dolls covered by *The Art of Dolls 1700-1940* extends from the earliest play dolls commonly found, notably the early woodens of the Queen Anne era, so-called, of the 1750-1825s, through the many fine woodens, waxes, papier mâchés, chinas, cloths, etc. of the 1825-1900 period. Included also is the full range of the fine bisque and parian dolls from the 1860s through World War I. These are covered in detail. Additionally, coverage is provided in the field of good compositions, woodens, cloth, and dolls of other materials, especially those made in America between World War I and World War II. Such dolls are establishing a place for themselves in comprehensive collections of antique and collectible dolls.

The later era of plastics and vinyls, together with the special interest in the work of modern doll artists, and the reproduction of antique dolls, must be left for attention by other more qualified authorities.

Wooden Dolls - 19th Century and Earlier

Much research has been done and many articles published on wooden dolls. For an excellent reference see *Doll Collectors Manual 1964* by The Doll Collectors of America, Inc.

Wooden dolls are most interesting and are assets to any collection.

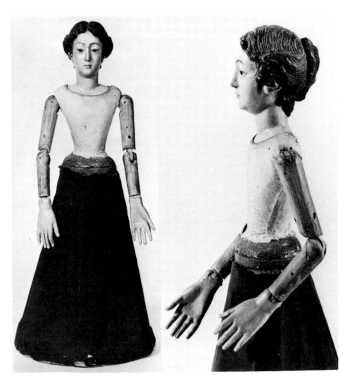

1. EARLY WOODEN SKIRT-CAGE FIGURE
Period: Early 18th century, possibly late 17th century.
Body: All wooden.
Remarks: A 20" (50.8cm) finely carved wooden head and torso mounted on a skirt cage. Hair styling is deeply carved in the wood. Face has pupilless set-in glass eyes, and facial features are painted over a thin coat of gesso. Much conjecture as to country of origin, whether French, Flemish, Spanish, or Italian, as well as to original usage. Certainly not used as a childs play doll, but possibly an adult collecting form displaying elaborately made fashionable gowns of the era or as a church figure. *Merrill Collection.*

Wood was one of the materials used in the earliest days of doll making, and, to a limited extent, is still used by present day doll makers. Throughout the entire period, there is great variation in the detail and workmanship of these dolls.

Mass production brought an end to the fine, handmade wooden dolls of the 18th and early 19th century. Workmanship cheapened until, by the end of the 19th century, only an inexpensive pegged-wooden of inferior construction was available - one that may still be purchased.

2. ALL WOODEN CRECHE DOLL - FULLY JOINTED
Period: 18th century or earlier.
Body: All wooden; fully jointed.
Remarks: Beautiful all wooden 16½" (41.9cm) hand carved creche doll. Enameled over gesso head has set-in glass eyes; open-closed mouth with tiny teeth; elaborately carved and decorated coiffure. Hands match complexion in color. Lower legs have painted on shoes and stockings. Made in many sizes to represent the various figures commonly found around the Christmas crib. The earlier wooden and wax creche dolls are of more interest than the later ones of clay and terra cotta. *Collection of Bertha Hanscom.*

1

3. HAND CARVED WOODEN CHURCH FIGURE
Period: 18th century.
Body: Wire frame wrapped in jute-like material; carved wooden arms and legs.
Remarks: 20" (50.8cm) exquisitely carved wooden church doll. Expressive face is enameled over gesso; set-in glass eyes; delicately carved hands; bare feet, clad in sandals. *Merrill Collection.*

4. CHURCH FIGURE WITH MOURNFUL MEIN
Period: Late 18th and early 19th century.
Body: Wire frame wrapped in jute-like material; carved wooden lower limbs.
Remarks: 19" (48.3cm) church figure with head of terra cotta. Expressive face, with mournful mein, has upraised glass eyes and gaping mouth showing molded tongue and small upper teeth. Wears gold trimmed black silk dress. Hand carved arms and legs are of wood with enamel over gesso finish.

Note: It is of interest that the head is of terra cotta while the lower limbs are of wood. These parts are generally of the same material. *Collection of Mrs. Eugenia Shorrock.*

5. CRECHE FIGURES IN TERRA COTTA
Period: Late 18th to mid-19th century.
Body: Wire frame wrapped in jute-like material; molded terra cotta limbs.
Remarks: The first three dolls at left - shepherd, madonna, angel - are of the late 18th century. They have inset glass eyes, expressive faces, and are delicately modeled and painted. The last two at right, representing villagers, are of the mid-19th century. They have painted eyes and lack the fine workmanship of the earlier dolls. Their clothes are lined with Italian printed paper. All dolls shown are of terra cotta. *Merrill Collection.*

6. MID-18th CENTURY "QUEEN ANNE" DOLL

Period: Circa 1750.

Body: All wooden; legs, jointed at knees and hips, are wooden pegged; wooden arms, held in bent position by
  wires, are attached to shoulders by cloth.

Remarks: 21" (53.3cm) mid-18th century *Queen Anne* doll. Documentation reads: "This doll was dressed The Year 1752." The gilt
and bejewelled watch, suspended from chatelaine, is inscribed, "E. Booth London." Doll, in original glass-topped box, was found in
London. She has set-in, pupilless glass eyes with stylized lashes and brows. Wears cap on her light brown wig of fine human hair. This
type doll, referred to as *Queen Anne* was made during the reigns of the British monarchs - Mary, Anne and the Georges. It might more
properly be called "Mary-Anne-Georgian." *Collection of Miss Zelda Cushner.*

3

7. 18th CENTURY "QUEEN ANNE" DOLL

Period: Mid-18th century.

Body: Wooden with crudely jointed wooden legs; nailed-on arms of rolled linen.

Remarks: 19" (48.3cm) *Queen Anne* wooden doll showing variation in shape of head and shoulders. Full face, with brightly painted cheeks, has set-in pupilless glass eyes; typical dotted brows and lashes; human hair wig.

BELOW:

8. MID-18th CENTURY WOODEN DOLL

Period: Circa 1750.

Body: Wood; pegged wooden legs; cloth hung wooden arms.

Remarks: The well defined features, bulging glass eyes, pointed chin, carved ears and rounded bosom of this 16" (40.6cm) *Queen Anne*-type doll testify as to her early date. These characteristics are lacking in later dolls of this type. The painted over gesso head has the typical dotted eyelashes and brows. Wig is of flax. Dressed in old brocade. *Merrill Collection.*

20. EARLY 19th CENTURY PEGGED WOODEN DOLLS
Period: Early part of 19th century.
Body: Fully pointed all wooden; wood pegged.
Remarks: A group of small, all jointed wooden dolls ranging in height from 1" (2.5cm) to 7" (17.8cm). Dolls have painted heads, forearms and legs. The 5" (12.7cm) size, with its painted yellow comb, a favorite of the young Princess Victoria, is sometimes referred to as the *Queen Victoria* wooden doll. Very small dolls of this type are referred to as *penny woodens. Merrill Collection.*

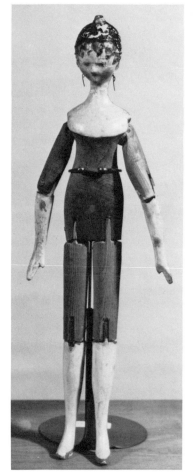

22. WOODEN DOLL OF THE EMPIRE PERIOD
Period: Early 19th century.
Body: High waisted, all wooden; jointed and wood pegged.
Remarks: A 13" (33cm) all wooden, jointed doll with high waist of the Empire period. Contemporary with the so-called *Queen Victoria* dolls. She has painted features and wears wooden comb in hair. A unique feature is the painted wooden earrings.

24. WOMAN AND CHILD SHELL-DRESSED DOLLS
Period: Early 19th century.
Body: All wooden; jointed and pegged.
Remarks: Two shell dolls, 5¾" (14.7cm) and 4½" (11.5cm) high.
As with most dolls in this category, the heads are of molded
plaster on jointed, wooden bodies. Woman holds spray of shell
flowers, girl carries a shell tray of colorful wares of same
material. The statement that these early, wooden bodied, shell-
dressed dolls originated in Brittany is generally accepted. *Merrill
Collection.*

23. CHILD DOLL DRESSED IN SHELLS
Period: Early 19th century.
Body: All wooden; jointed and pegged.
Remarks: 2½" (6.9cm) pegged wooden doll dressed in costume
completely covered with shells. So-called *shell dolls*, come in
many sizes and forms and are believed to have been brought from
Brittany in Southern France by 19th century tourists making the
"Grand Tour" of Europe. *Merrill Collection.*

**25. ELONGATED VARIANT OF PEGGED WOODEN
DOLL**
Period: 1835.
Body: All wooden; jointed and pegged.
Remarks: The elongated wooden body plus molded plaster head
combine in making this 12" (30.5cm) wooden doll rare and
unique. Features are painted, hair has clustered curls at sides and
Apollo knot on top. Dolls with this style hairdo almost
invariably have heads of papier mâché mounted on cloth or
leather bodies with wooden arms and legs. *Merrill Collection.*

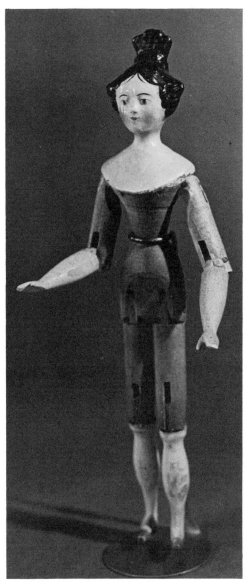

26. WOODEN DOLL WITH APOLLO KNOT
Period: Circa 1835.
Body: All wooden; jointed and pegged.
Remarks: A 7¾" (19.8cm) pegged wooden doll with molded head of plaster. Features are painted and hair is done with Apollo knot and cluster of curls at sides. Doll heads with this style hairdo are generally of papier mâché.

27. WOODEN PEGGED DOLLS WITH MOLDED PLASTER HEADS
Period: Second quarter of 19th century.
Body: All wooden; pegged.
Remarks: The distinguishing feature of the two dolls shown is their molded plaster heads in contrast to the all wooden generally found with this type doll
Left: 5½" (14.0cm) pegged wooden doll with molded plaster head and hat. Rare. Painted features include blue eyes. Long black curls fall low on shoulders. Molded hat, resembling a crown, has white rolled rim, blue sides, bright red top. Wears lace trimmed dress with train.
Right: 5¼" (13.4cm) doll has molded hat; earrings; and unusual hairdo.
At the present time, pegged wooden dolls with molded plaster heads are rarer than those of all wood - perhaps because of their fragile nature, not too many survived. Doll on right: *Merrill Collection.*

28. EARLY PEGGED WOODEN DOLL WITH WIG
Period: Early 19th century.
Body: All wooden; pegged joints.
Remarks: *Distinguishing feature:* black painted spot on head with removable real hair wig. Head is painted over layer of gesso. Doll has finely painted red sandals. All original - found in London.

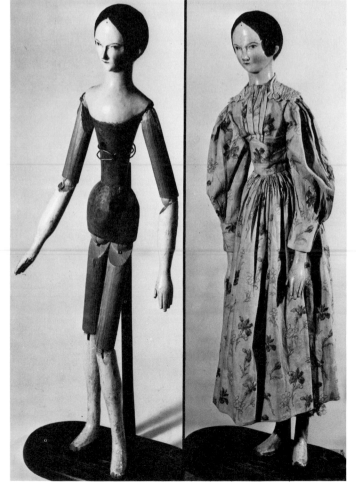

29. EARLY 19th CENTURY WOODEN DOLL
Period: Early 19th century.
Body: All wooden.
Remarks: Very finely carved all wooden doll - dressed and undressed - showing eight ball and socket joints; typical of early 19th century wooden dolls. This doll has painted eyes and hair style of 1835-40. Original condition - 30" (76.2cm) in height.

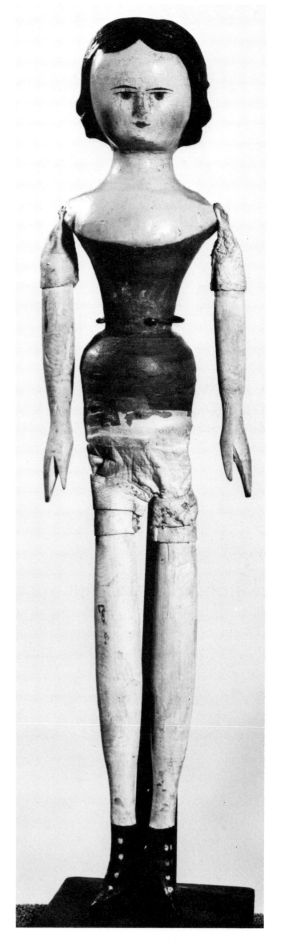

ABOVE:

30. PEGGED WOODEN DOLL WITH CARVED SIDE CURLS

Period: Early 19th century.

Body: Fully jointed all wooden; wooden pegged.

Remarks: All original 10" (25.4cm) jointed wooden doll whose black painted hair has carved curls at sides and bun in back. Painted features include blue eyes and rosy cheeks. Body construction type of era. Documented as of 1790 but almost certainly of later date. *Merrill Collection.*

BELOW:

31. WOODEN DOLL OF 1830s

Period: Circa 1830.

Body: All wooden; jointed and wooden pegged.

Remarks: 6¼" (15.8cm) all wooden doll with hairdo of 1830s; bun on crown of head and carved wooden curls at sides. She has painted features and is in excellent condition. *Collection of Mrs. John M. Park, Jr.*

RIGHT:

32. WOODEN DOLL WITH RED TORSO

Period: Second half of 19th century.

Body: All wooden with kidskin joinings. Torso painted red.

Remarks: Old wooden doll with carved hairdo of the 1840s. Made in Bohemia. Also found with blonde coloring and in sizes up to 20" (50.8cm) to 24" (61cm). *Merrill Collection.*

Note: See "Folk Toys - Les Jouet Populaire" (Orbis, Prague, 1952).

No 11 Natalie Avenue
Walton Park.
Melrose Highlands
Massachusetts
U. S. A.

To whom it may
concern -

This doll is named
Jemima, Rennie,
Sawyer. She was
sent to the writer
from Edinburg
Scotland during
The Summer of
Nineteen hundred

and eight. (1908)
She crossed on the
Cunard steamer
"Ivernia" and was
brought to me by two
sisters of the sender,
Miss J. M. Rennie
of Edinburg Scotland.
This is what is
called a Dutch doll
and they were much
used during the
early part of the
nineteenth Century.

but are very seldom
seen in these days.
(Mrs) Nellie. Tolman. Sawyer
Thursday July 20th
1908.

P. S. Please preserve
this doll.

34. ALL WOODEN DOLL WITH MOLDED COMPOSITION FACE

Period: 1840s.

Body: All wooden with eight hemispherical joints; typical of early 19th century dolls.

Remarks: The face mask of this rare 14" (35.6cm) wooden doll is of molded composition. The curls, applied to the back of the head, are apparently of the same material. She has set-in opaque black glass eyes and painted features. Lower limbs are painted as are the blue slippers.

35. SO-CALLED "DUTCH" WOODEN DOLL IN PERIOD COSTUME

Period: Mid-19th century.

Body: All wooden; jointed.

Remarks: 21" (53.3cm) so-called *Dutch* or *Blockhead* wooden doll made in Gröden Tal. Painted features include black hair. Brown printed cotton dress and straw bonnet are of the 1840 period.

OPPOSITE PAGE:
33. SO-CALLED "DUTCH" WOODEN DOLL

Period: Mid-19th century.

Body: All wooden; jointed.

Remarks: A 13" (33cm) *Dutch*, (a corruption of *Deutsch*) doll of the mid-19th century, documented as to date. Made in Gröden Tal. Good construction; ball joints at shoulders and hips. Tongue and groove joints at elbows and knees. The note reproduced beside photo of doll was found folded up in the silk reticule seen hanging from the dolls arm. *Merrill Collection.*

36. FINELY CARVED WOODEN SHOULDERHEAD
Period: Early 19th century.
Body: Cloth with wooden limbs.
Remarks: Fine and early doll, 30" (76.2cm) in height, with artistically carved wooden head; hollowed shoulders. Well finished head has painted features including large, brown eyes. Center parted hair falls low on shoulders in large, loose curls. A large and unusual wooden doll of high quality.

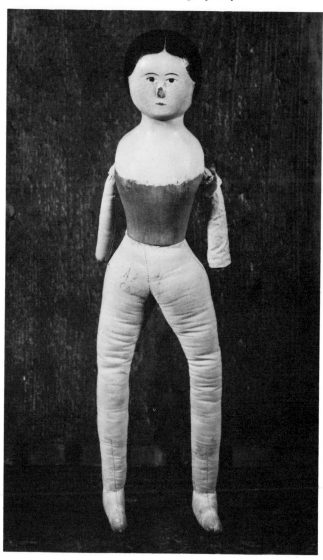

38. NAIVE WOODEN DOLL
Period: Last half of 19th century.
Body: Head and torso of wood; arms and lower body of cloth.
Remarks: A simply crafted, 20" (50.8cm) doll with upper body of the skittle-shaped, all wooden dolls made in Sonneburg. Painted head and torso were turned from one piece of wood. Cloth arms hang from a hole bored through the shoulders. Lower half of body is entirely of cloth. An interesting doll with unusual body. *Merrill Collection.*

LEFT:

37. HAND CARVED WOODEN SHOULDERHEAD
Period: Early 19th century.
Body: Cloth with leather arms.
Remarks: American primitive doll, 23" (58.4cm) in height, with hand carved wooden head of pine; hollowed shoulders. Head glued to stuffed cotton body. Doll has painted features; came from a Maine coastal town. *Merrill Collection.*

16

RIGHT:
39. BLACK DOLL BY JOEL ELLIS, MADE IN SPRINGFIELD, VERMONT

Period: 1873-74.

Body: All wooden; fully jointed; hands and feet of metal.

Remarks: 12" (30.5cm) wooden jointed doll patented by Joel Ellis of the Co-operative Manufacturing Co., Springfield, Vermont- referred to as a *Springfield Doll.* Mold of doll is same as that of white dolls by Joel Ellis. Brown coloring gives it special interest. Mouth painted to show a row of tiny white teeth. Legs have painted white stockings and black boots.

BELOW:
40. WOODEN DOLLS, MADE IN SPRINGFIELD, VERMONT

Period: 1870s through 1880s.

Body: All wooden; fully jointed; hands and feet of metal

Remarks: *Springfield* wooden jointed dolls named for town of manufacture - Springfield, Vermont.

Left: Doll patented in 1873 by Joel Ellis. Made in 12" (30.5cm), 15" (38.1cm) and 18" (45.7cm) sizes.

Right: Rare black doll patented by Mason & Taylor in 1881. Other manufacturers in Springfield, Vermont, made similar dolls for a short period of time. Doll on left: *Merrill Collection.*

BELOW RIGHT:
41. MARTIN PATENT WOODEN DOLL, MADE IN SPRINGFIELD, VERMONT

Period: 1879.

Body: All hardwood; fully jointed; hands and feet of pewter.

Remarks: 11½" (29.2cm) wooden jointed doll made by the Jointed Doll Company of Springfield, Vermont, under Patent #214,830 granted to Frank D. Martin on April 29, 1879. This patent covered an improved method of constructing the knee and elbow joints to allow greater movement, and included the unique manner of fastening the joints by means of metal rivets. Swivel neck head is of molded composition over a wooden core. *Collection of Shirley Sanborn.*

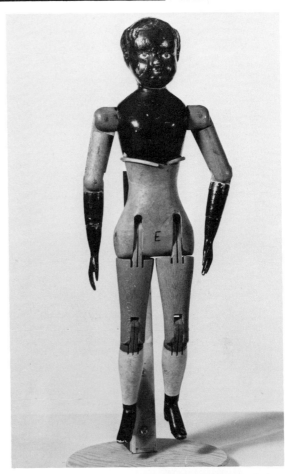

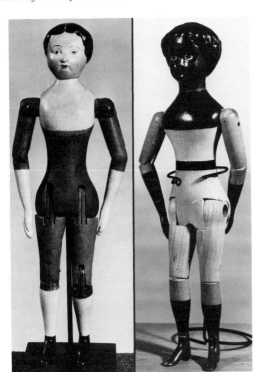

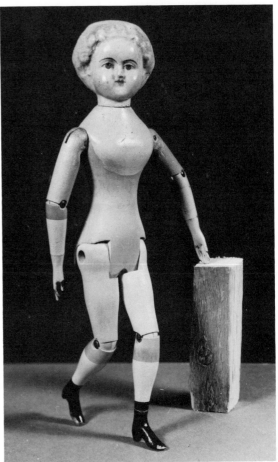

42. WITCH OR WIZARD DOLL BY MASON & TAYLOR

Period: 1881.

Body: All wooden; jointed at shoulders and hips.
  Metal feet with upturned toes.

Remarks: Seldom seen, 9¾" (24.9cm) Oriental character doll by
Mason & Taylor of Springfield, Vermont. Differs greatly from
other dolls by this concern. The rather crudely painted head is of
molded composition over a wooden core and a toggle arrange-
ment in the neck allows for an imaginary decapitation. *Witch* or
Wizard dolls were factory dressed in printed cotton kimonos.
Merrill Collection.

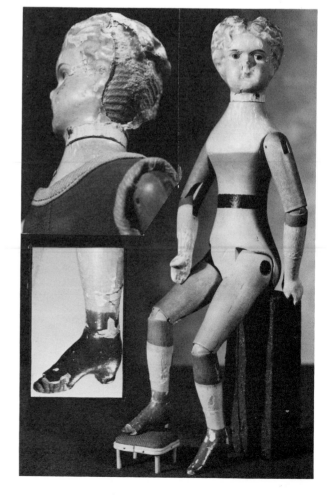

**43. WOODEN SPRINGFIELD DOLL WITH
       COMPOSITION HANDS AND FEET**

Period: Circa 1880.

Body: All wooden; fully jointed; hands and feet of
  composition molded over wooden core.

Remarks: 11½" (29.2cm) wooden doll attributed to Mason &
Taylor and made at the Jointed Doll Company of Springfield,
Vermont. It has Johnson patented head and Sanders patented
joints. Head, hands and feet are molded over a wooden core (see
inserts). It is highly unusual to find hands and feet done in this
manner. They are generally of metal. *Merrill Collection.*

Dolls of Papier-Mâché and Composition - 19th Century

The term "papier-mâché" is applied to that material which is made of paper (powdered or torn bits) and paste (sometimes more of a plaster of paris binding medium). When molded and hardened it is most durable.

Fine doll heads have been made in this manner since the 18th century.

These dolls may have painted or glass eyes; molded or real hair; and are generally of German or French make.

In the later period (1850-1900) it is sometimes difficult to determine whether a doll should be termed "papier mâché" or "composition." The latter, no doubt, being basically papier mâché with additives.

44. DIRECTOIRE PAPIER MÂCHÉ DOLLS
Period: 1804-1815.
Body: Wood; short arms nailed to stick-like bodies.
Remarks: Three very rare and fragile dolls with papier mâché or plaster heads. Standing 9" (22.9cm), 12" (30.5cm), and 11" (27.9cm) respectively. Painted features are rather crudely drawn, giving a saucy expression. Wisps of human hair still remain beneath glued-on bonnet on doll on right. Originally made as inexpensive playthings of the Directoire period. Dolls all original in every respect. Costumes of gauze and paper. *Courtesy of The Essex Institute, Salem, Massachusetts.*

45. EARLY FRENCH DOLL OF CARTON MOULE

Period: First quarter of 19th century.

Body: Head, torso, upper legs of carton moule; molded in one piece; cloth hung arms of wood; lower legs of linen.

Remarks: Rare and fragile 9½" (24.2cm) carton moule doll with painted head and human hair wig. Wears pink cotton dress with gilt paper trim, pink paper bonnet, and white paper petticoat - all original. Cloth sleeves are lined with French newsprint. Came mounted on circular wooden base. Few of these rather flimsy dolls exist. *Merrill Collection.*

46. BRITTANY SHELL DOLLS WITH HEADS OF MOLDED CARTON

Period: Early 19th century.

Body: Wooden; pegged to rectangular wooden bases.

Remarks: 9½" (24.2cm) and 10" (25.4cm) dolls from Brittany with well molded and painted carton moule heads; crudely carved wooden hands. Man's wig of human hair. They are colorfully costumed in small, sand sprinkled, red and white shells. Also decorated with and carry flowers. Large for their type, they are remarkably well preserved and extremely rare. *Merrill Collection.*

60. EARLY BLACK PAPIER MÂCHÉ DOLL
Period: Mid-19th century.
Body: Narrow waisted black leather with black
   wooden limbs.
Remarks: 13" (33cm) black doll whose extremely well modeled
head has ethnic features including tightly curled hair. Gold
colored earrings and necklace are painted on. Black dolls are
considered rare. *Merrill Collection.*

ABOVE:
62. PAPIER MÂCHÉ JOCKEY WITH MOLDED CAP
Period: Third quarter of 19th century.
Body: Leather with wooden limbs.
Remarks: 7" (17.8cm) papier mâché jockey with molded-on red
cap, yellow band, black visor. Black painted wooden legs, cuffed
with orange paper, serve as riding boots. Doll is pantless. Lower
portion of white leather body substitutes for riding breeches.
Harper's Bazar of 1867 carried a Christmas ad of Althof,
Bergmann & Co. in which the shown doll appeared. *Collection of
Bertha Hanscom.*

LEFT:
61. BONNETTED PAPIER MÂCHÉ DOLL
Period: Circa 1840.
Body: Kid with wooden limbs.
Remarks: 15" (38.1cm) demure, smiling doll with slightly
dropped head. Molded blue bonnet has painted white crisscrossed
trim in front and four white stars on crown. Black painted hair is
brush marked around face. Brown painted eyes. This type doll
seldom found with bonnet.

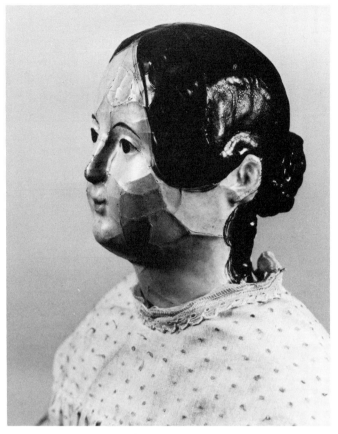

63. PAPIER MÂCHÉ HEAD - CIRCA 1840
Period: Second quarter of 19th century.
Body: Cloth with leather arms.
Remarks: 21" (53.3cm) papier mâché doll with unusual modeling. Black molded hair is drawn under exposed ears to bun in back. 1840 period. Painted features. Similar heads may be found in other sizes. This type head was also made in china.

64. PAPIER MÂCHÉ DOLL - CIRCA 1840
Period: Circa 1840.
Body: All cloth.
Remarks: 25" (63.5cm) early papier mâché doll with painted features including blue eyes. Black painted hairdo has molded bun in back plus two molded and brushmarked single curls behind each ear. *Merrill Collection.*

65. EARLY 19th CENTURY PAPIER MÂCHÉ DOLL
Period: Second quarter of 19th century.
Body: Leather with wooden limbs.
Remarks: 24" (61cm) beautifully modeled papier mâché doll whose expressive face has brown painted eyes and rosy cheeks. The brushmarked hair, drawn behind well exposed ears, falls low on shoulders in eight deeply sculptured curls. This type doll is more often found in smaller sizes. *Merrill Collection.*

LEFT:

66. PAPIER MÂCHÉ DOLL - CIRCA 1840
Period: Circa 1840s.
Body: Leather with wooden limbs.
Remarks: 17" (43.2cm) early papier mâché doll in excellent original condition. Brown painted eyes; rosy cheeks. Unusual styling of hair exposes back of ears only. Molded hair has thick, shoulder length curls at sides and braided bun at back.

68. EARLY PAPIER MÂCHÉ DOLL WITH LONG CURLS
Period: Second quarter of 19th century.
Body: All cloth.
Remarks: 28" (71.1cm) papier mâché, long molded brushmarked curls (8) from center part; finely stroked brows; upper and lower painted lashes; upper lid has prominent modeling. Large dark milk glass stationary eyes. *Unusual feature:* open mouth with two upper and two lower broad, square teeth. In addition the cloth body has been attached to the head in a most unusual way; the lower edge of the shoulder plate is sewn to a strip of linen cloth through 48 small sew holes and the linen is sewn to the hand stitched body. *Collection of Lorna Lieberman.*

LEFT:

67. Papier Mâché Doll - Circa 1840
Period: Circa 1840s.
Body: All leather.
Remarks: 19½" (49.6cm) papier mâché doll with bright blue painted eyes and rosy cheeks. A finely modeled doll with unusual hairdo - braided bun on upper back of head plus brushmarked curls falling low behind exposed ears.

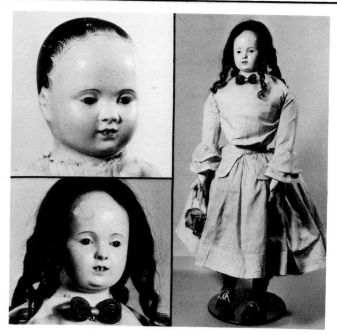

69. FRENCH PAPIER MÂCHÉ DOLL
Period: Second quarter of 19th century.
Body: Well shaped pink kid leather body with
    long stiff arms and legs, exaggerated derriere.
Remarks: 32" (81.3cm) doll has set-in glass eyes; open mouth
with two upper and two lower teeth of split bamboo. Painted hair
but furnished with a black human hair wig nailed to pate. *Merrill
Collection.*

70. FRENCH PAPIER MÂCHÉ DOLL
Period: Second quarter of the 19th century.
Body: Well shaped white kidskin body; stiff arms
    and legs; no joints.
Remarks: 30" (76.2cm) doll with set-in glass eyes; closed mouth;
wearing wig of black human hair nailed on over black painted
pate. *Merrill Collection.*

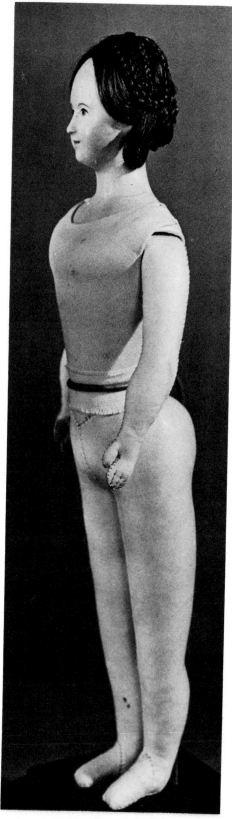

**71. FRENCH PAPIER MÂCHÉ DOLL WITH ALL
LEATHER BODY**
Period: Mid-19th century.
Body: All leather.
Remarks: 13½" (34.3cm) French doll with usually found body;
all pink leather. Well shaped, it has small waist and long,
unjointed limbs. Papier mâché head has painted features and
human hair wig. *Merrill Collection.*

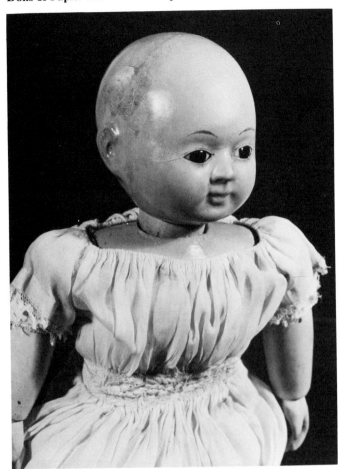

LEFT:

72. MOTSCHMANN-TYPE BABY DOLL

Period: Mid-19th century.

Body: Torso of papier mâché and twill; arms and legs of wood with upper sections of cloth; hands and feet of composition; string suspended.

Remarks: 15" (38.1cm) all original Motschmann-type baby doll with swivel joint at neck. The papier mâché head has baby hair indicated at back of head and over ears; set-in glass eyes. Squeak box in midriff. Similar to Motschmann doll patented in Germany in 1857. This type doll may also be found waxed. See page 62. Wears original baby clothes.

73. PAPIER MÂCHÉ DOLL ON PINK LEATHER BODY

Period: Mid-19th century.

Body: Well shaped pink leather body; no joints.

Remarks: 15" (38.1cm) French papier mâché doll with painted features, including blue eyes. The fine human hair wig is inserted in slit on top of head, giving appearance of center part. *Collection of Mrs. Elmer Morley.*

LEFT:

74. "PRE-GREINER" DOLLS

Period: Mid-19th century.

Body: Cloth with leather or cloth arms.

Remarks: Two early dolls with identical papier mâché heads of the pre-Greiner type.

Left: 23" (58.4cm) doll with small waist; long brown leather arms.

Right: 21½" (54.6cm) doll with thick waist; short cloth arms with stitched-in fingers.

These dolls were made when it was possible to buy heads alone to mount on home made bodies. The dolls shown illustrate the differences in body proportions when dolls were fashioned in this manner. *Merrill Collection.*

76. "PRE-GREINER" DOLL - CIRCA 1840
Period: Second quarter of 19th century.
Body: Cloth with leather arms.
Remarks: 32" (81.3cm) papier mâché doll called *pre-Greiner* as it was made before the patented Greiner of 1858. Fine papier mâché head with set-in glass eyes. Resembles the Greiner patented doll. Comes in various sizes. Unmarked.

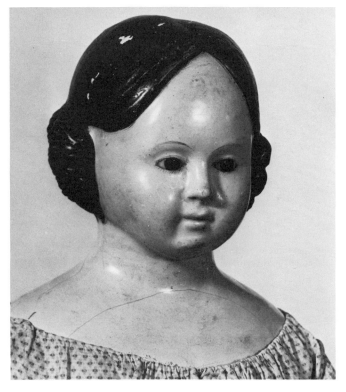

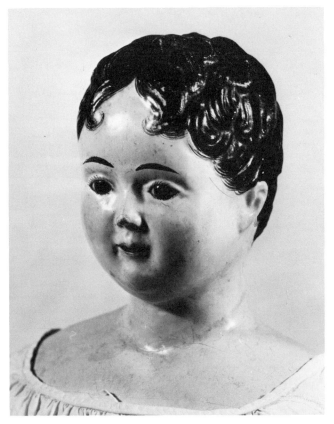

**75. FRENCH PAPIER MÂCHÉ DOLL WITH
        MOLDED HAIRDO**
Period: Second quarter of 19th century.
Body: Well shaped pink leather body with long, stiff arms and legs; no joints.
Remarks: 28" (71.1cm) fine, early papier mâché doll with molded, brushmarked hair as opposed to smooth painted pates of same type dolls shown on page 29. Doll has set-in pupilless glass eyes; open mouth with inserted teeth of bamboo. A very desirable doll. *Merrill Collection.*

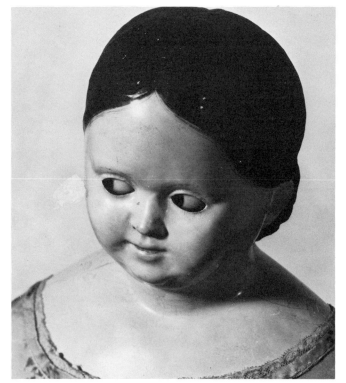

77. FLIRTY-EYED PAPIER MÂCHÉ DOLL
Period: Second quarter of 19th century.
Body: Cloth with leather arms.
Remarks: Large, early papier mâché doll. Plain hairdo with ears exposed. Glass eyes move from side to side.

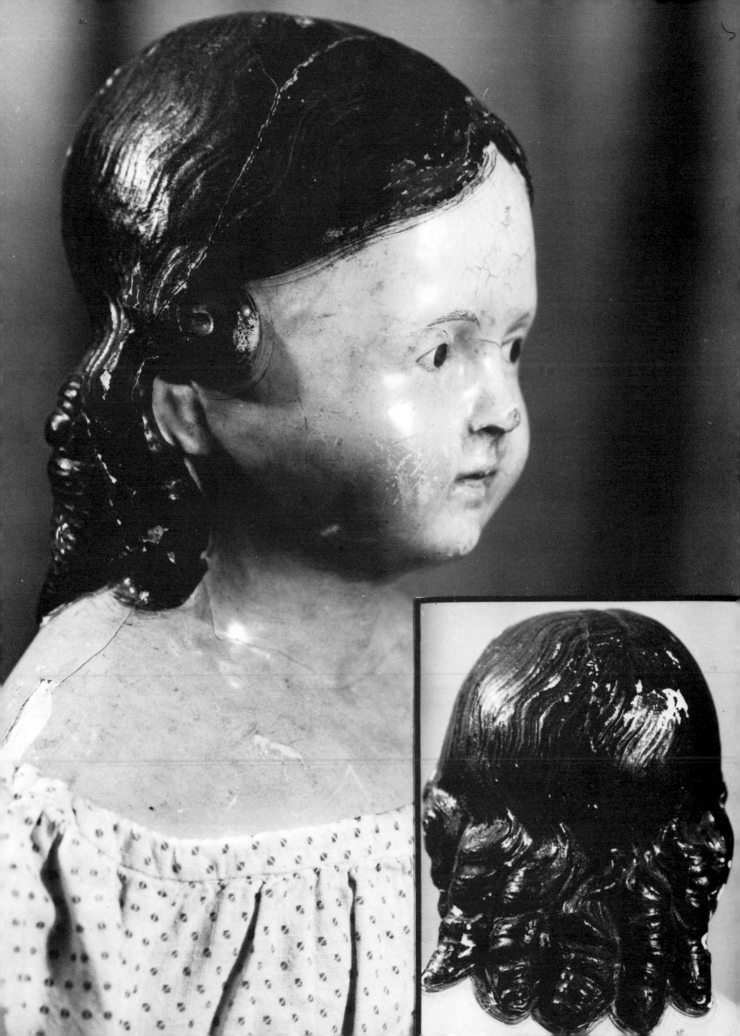

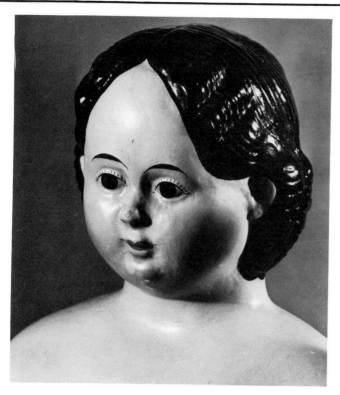

79. GREINER DOLL - PATENTED 1858
Period: Third quarter of 19th century.
Body: Cloth with leather arms.
Remarks: First patented doll in America. A papier mâché doll head made by Ludwig Greiner of Philadelphia in 1858; bears label on back of shoulders. Doll has painted eyes, comes in various sizes and coloring. The Greiner patent was extended in 1872 and dolls made under this later patent are so marked.

80. BLONDE GREINER DOLL - 1872 PATENT
Period: Third quarter of 19th century.
Body: Cloth with leather arms.
Remarks: Papier mâché doll head made under the 1872 extended patent of Ludwig Greiner of Philadelphia. So labeled on back shoulders. This doll usually found as a brunette. Dolls manufactured under this patent found in various molds. The Greiner firm closed in 1883. *Merrill Collection.*

OPPOSITE PAGE:
**78. EARLY PAPIER MÂCHÉ DOLL WITH CURLS
LOW ON SHOULDERS**
Period: Second quarter of 19th century.
Body: All cloth.
Remarks: Early, 28" (71.1cm) papier mâché doll whose brush-marked hair, exposing ears, has seven loose curls falling low on shoulders (see illustration). The short necked, full faced head has brown painted eyes, feathered brows and rosy cheeks. *Merrill Collection.*

81. GREINER DOLL - 1872 PATENT
Period: Third quarter of 19th century.
Body: Cloth with leather arms.
Remarks: A 19" (48.3cm) doll with papier mâché head made under the 1872 patent of Ludwig Greiner of Philadelphia. So labeled on back shoulders. Patent extended in 1872. Doll shown above has unusual molding of the black painted hair. Blue painted eyes. Greiner dolls, blonde and brunette, were made in various molds and sizes. *Merrill Collection.*

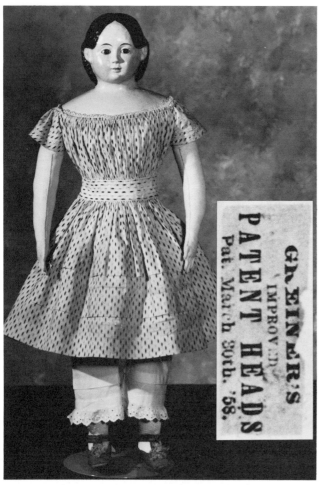

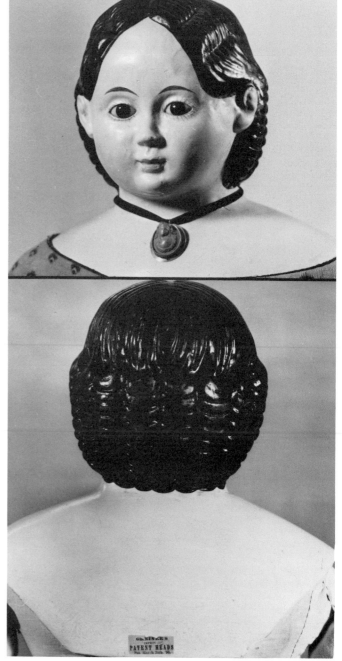

82. GLASS-EYED DOLL BY GREINER - BEARING
IMPROVED PATENT HEADS LABEL
Period: Patented 1858.
Body: Cloth with leather arms; marked #13.
Remarks: All original, labelled, 30" (76.2cm), Greiner patented
doll with glass eyes; painted upper and lower lashes; molded hair
with ten vertical curls. *Merrill Collection.*

83. Close-up of papier mâché head by Greiner with inset glass
eyes - so rare that some state such heads were never made. *Merrill*
Collection.

84. PAPIER MÂCHÉ DOLL WITH BLACK BAND IN HAIR

Period: Third quarter of 19th century.
Body: Cloth with leather arms.
Remarks: 25" (63.5cm) doll with well finished head. Features, including blue eyes, are painted. Molded blonde hair, short and simply styled, is brushed away from face and exposes ears. Back curls are held in place by a black painted band. Unmarked. *Collection of The Essex Institute, Salem, Massachusetts.*

BELOW:

85. PAPIER MÂCHÉ HEAD - HAIR STYLED AS A YOUNG GIRL

Period: Third quarter of 19th century.
Body: Kid with wooden arms and legs. Blue paper bands around leather to wooden joinings.
Remarks: 11" (27.9cm) doll similar to Illustration 84. *Merrill Collection.*

86. HATTED PAPIER MÂCHÉ BOY DOLL
Period: Third quarter of 19th century.
Body: Cloth with gussets at knees and upper back
legs; leather hands.
Remarks: 14½" (36.9cm) hatted boy with head of papier mâché.
Painted features include blue eyes and brush marked black hair.
Blue molded-on Scandinavian styled cap, with red and white
tassel, is decorated with red and yellow sprays. *Merrill Collection.*

87. COMPOSITION DOLL BY LERCH & CO.
Period: Late 1860s.
Body: Cloth with leather arms.
Remarks: 24" (61cm) rarely seen doll whose molded and painted
composition head includes blue eyes and black hair. Marked on
back shoulders: "Lerch & Co.,//Manufacturers//No. 6." Made
by Philip Lerch of Philadelphia, Pennsylvania. Doll heads may
also be found with label printed: "Lerch and Klag//Manu-
facturers//Philadelphia, Pa." *Collection of Jessie F. Parsons.*

36

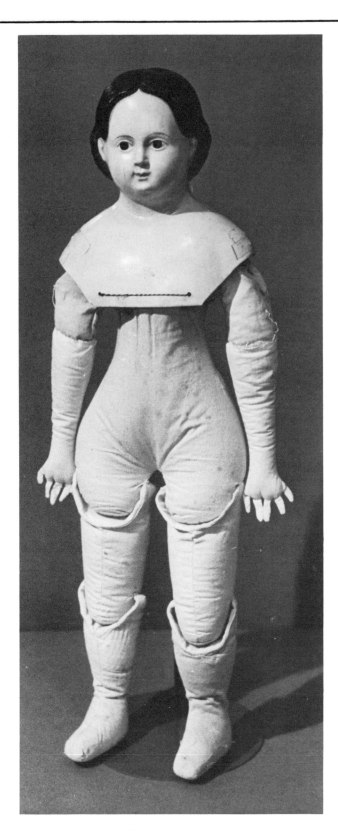

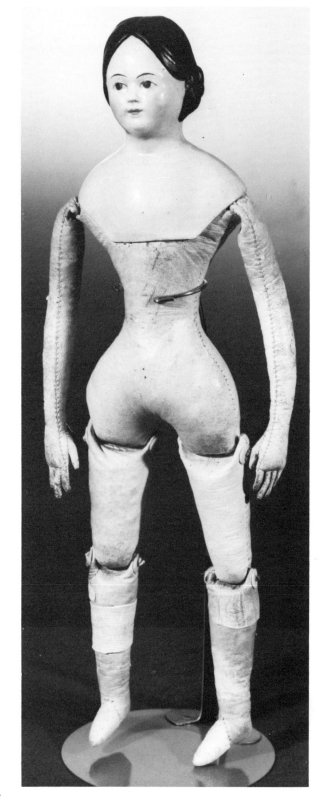

88. PAPIER MÂCHÉ HEAD ON ROBINSON-TYPE BODY
Period: Last half of 19th century.
Body: All cloth; jointed at hips and knees.
Remarks: 24" (61cm) doll with fine, mid-19th century papier mâché head. Features are painted, including blue eyes, and black molded hair exposes ears. Apparently homemade, the cloth body, with cardboard lined joints, is of the type patented by Sarah Robinson in 1883. Head possibly earlier than body. *Collection of Lorna S. Lieberman.*

89. PAPIER MÂCHÉ HEAD ON ROBINSON-TYPE BODY
Period: Last half of 19th century.
Body: Leather; jointed at hips and knees.
Remarks: 14½" (36.9cm) doll with fine, early papier mâché head. Painted blue eyes; black molded hair; exposed ears. Interesting leather body is of the type patented by Sarah Robinson in 1883. Note method of connecting knee and hip joints - tightly drawn threads running between bone buttons. Head possibly earlier than body.

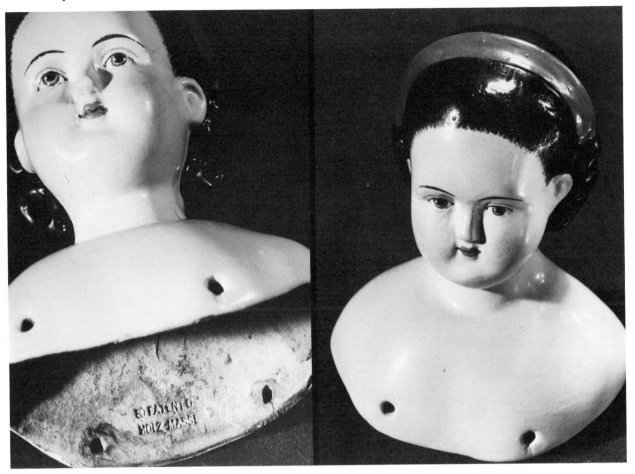

ABOVE:

90. COMPOSITION DOLL WITH DRESSEL "HOLZ MASSE" MARK

Period: Last quarter of 19th century.
Body: Cloth with composition arms.
Remarks: 4" (10.2cm) composition head with painted features, including blue eyes. Molded brown hair, with ears exposed, has brush marks in front, loose curls in back, and red painted band on top. Marked (see illustration): "ED Patent DE// Holz Masse." Distributed by the German firm of Cuno & Otto Dressel. Holz Masse may be translated as wood pulp. *Collection of Mrs. Elmer Morley.*

91. COMPOSITION DOLL WITH DRESSEL "HOLTZ MASSE" MARK

Period: Last quarter of 19th century.
Body: Cloth with composition limbs.
Remarks: Fine and original example of composition head, bearing "Holtz Masse" trademark of the Cuno & Otto Dressel firm of Germany. The well painted head, with blue eyes, has feathered brows; blonde hair; and a varnish coat in excellent state of preservation. This company handled dolls of many different materials by various makers. The Dressel family had long associations in the doll business.

92. PAPIER MÂCHÉ DOLL BY JUDGE & EARLY

Period: 1875.

Body: Cloth with leather arms.

Remarks: A rare 22½" (57.2cm) blonde papier mâché doll. Black banded hairdo has ten vertical curls falling low on shoulders. Painted pale blue eyes; pierced ears. Made by Edward S. Judge of Baltimore, Maryland and Philadelphia, Pennsylvania. Labeled on back shoulders: "Judge & Early//No. 5//Patd. July 27, 1875." *Collection of Mrs. Louise H. Lund.*

BELOW:

93. COMPOSITION DOLL LABELLED "A.W."

Period: Last quarter of 19th century.

Body: Cloth with leather arms.

Remarks: 17" (43.2cm) doll whose composition head has blue painted eyes with lower lashes only, molded black hair, exposed ears. Marked (see insert): "A.W.//Ser. A/3" on back shoulders. Made by the German firm of Adolf Wislizenus. This doll was also made by blonde coloring.

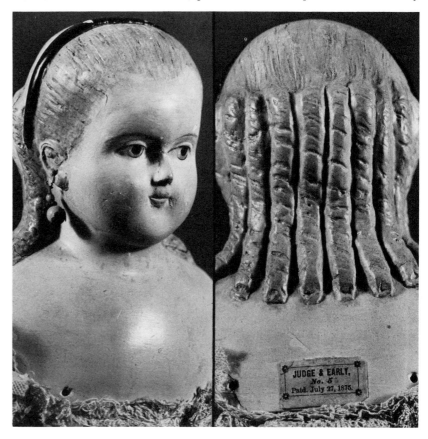

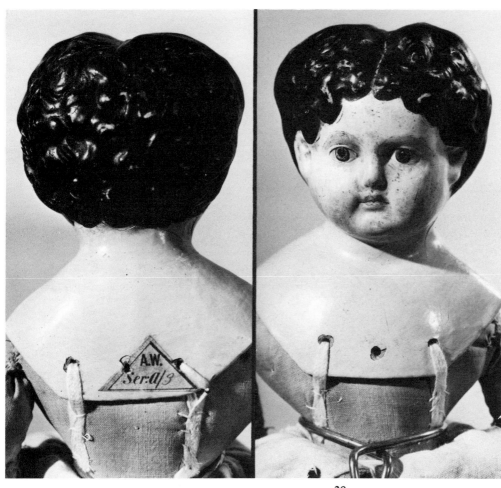

ABOVE LEFT:

94. BLACK HAIR DOLL - MARKED "SUPERIOR"
Period: Third quarter of 19th century.
Body: Cloth with leather arms.
Remarks: This often found *Superior* doll has well painted features and sweet expression. Distinguishing characteristic of these dolls: a row of tiny black dashes denoting lower eyelashes. The 25" (63.5cm) doll shown has dark brown eyes; well defined brows; black hair with brushmarks outlining curls. Made in various sizes; brunette and blonde.

ABOVE RIGHT:

95. BLONDE DOLL - MARKED "SUPERIOR"
Period: Third quarter of 19th century.
Body: Cloth with leather arms.
Remarks: 31" (78.7cm) doll head with *Superior* label on back of shoulders. Although often referred to as a papier mâché head, this very thick material might well be called composition. Contemporary with American made Griener dolls. Found with blonde hair and blue eyes, or black hair and brown eyes. *Merrill Collection.*

LEFT:

96. COMPOSITION DOLL LABELLED "NO. 2015"
Period: Last quarter of 19th century.
Body: Cloth with leather arms.
Remarks: 26" (66cm) composition doll with blonde molded hair; blue painted eyes with lower lashes only; exposed ears. Printed label on back shoulders reads: "No. 2015/7" (see insert). Number 2015 is often part of the M & S mark found on Superior doll heads.

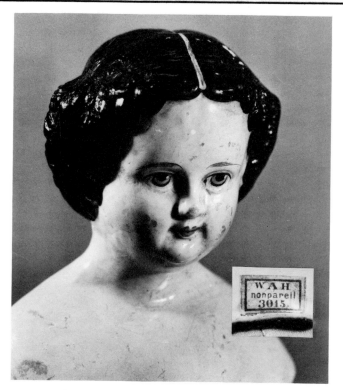

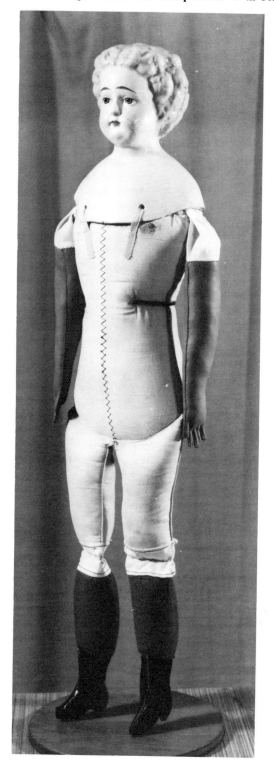

97. COMPOSITION DOLL MARKED "W A H//NONPAREIL"

Period: Last quarter of 19th century.

Body: Cloth with leather arms; sewed-on blue leather boots.

Remarks: 18" (45.7cm) composition doll strongly resembling the doll marked "Superior" on page 40. Doll has well painted features with molded black hair. Also made with blonde coloring. Marked by paper label in back of shoulders (see insert): "W A H//Nonpareil//3015."

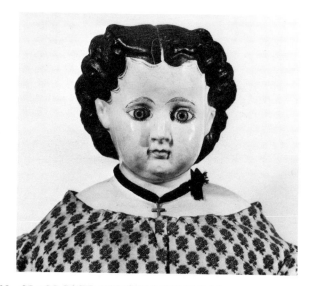

98. GLASS-EYED COMPOSITION DOLL

Period: Last quarter of 19th century.

Body: Cloth with leather arms.

Remarks: 30" (76.2cm) composition doll with unusual feature -set-in glass eyes. This type generally has painted eyes. The molded hairdo is edged with fine brushmarks; eyebrows are feathered; upper and lower lashes indicated. Doll is of the period and similar to dolls marked "Superior" and "W A H Nonpareil." *Courtesy of The Essex Institute, Salem, Massachusetts.*

99. COMPOSITION HEADED DOLL ON COMMERCIALLY MADE BODY

Period: 1880s.

Body: Cloth with leather arms; imitation leather boots.

Remarks: 26" (66cm) doll whose well made composition head has blue painted eyes; closed mouth; molded blonde hair. Colorful cloth body has red vertical zig-zag stitching on front of torso, red stitched knee joints, bright red cotton legs and imitation leather boots. Unmarked. Inside head still retains fragments of the *Boston Journal* of Tuesday morning, January 9, 1882. *Merrill Collection.*

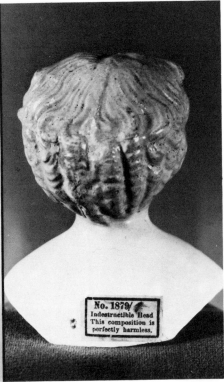

100. DOLL WITH "INDESTRUCTIBLE" COMPOSITION HEAD

Period: Last quarter of 20th century.
Body: Cloth with leather arms and sewed-on blue leather boots.
Remarks: 13" (33cm) doll whose composition head has painted features and blonde molded hair. Labeled on back shoulders: "No. 1879/1//Indestructible Head//This composition is//perfectly harmless." Maker unknown. *Collection of Zelda H. Cushner.*

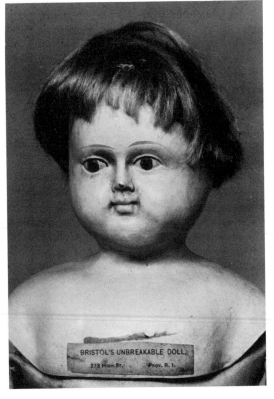

101. COMPOSITION DOLL WITH UNUSUAL HAIR STYLE

Period: Last quarter of 19th century.
Body: Cloth with leather arms.
Remarks: 24" (61cm) composition doll with unusual hair style - horizontal rather than vertical curls. This styling used only in front; back hair has row of customary up and down curls. Doll is of good quality with well painted features; blue eyes; blonde hair. Unmarked.

102. BRISTOL'S UNBREAKABLE DOLL

Period: 1886-1900.
Body: Leather.
Remarks: Few examples of this doll exist. Although the molded composition head shown here is on a leather body, it is probable that many were fitted to cloth bodies. She has painted features and a human hair wig. Early records mention an Emma L. Bristol as a doll maker in Providence, Rhode Island. The label reads: "BRISTOL'S UNBREAKABLE DOLL//273 High St., Prov., R.I." *Collection of The Margaret Woodbury Strong Museum.*

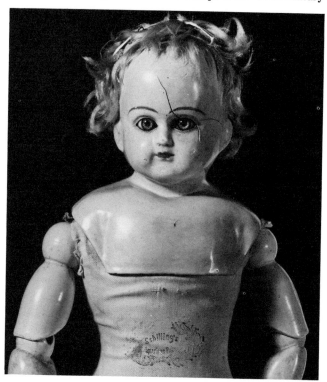

104. "AMERICAN PET" COMPOSITION DOLL BY SCHILLING

Period: 1880s.

Body: Cotton twill with composition legs; arms of wood and composition; elastic strung through wooden tube in shoulders.

Remarks: 17" (43.2cm) quality composition doll made by the Schilling firm of Germany who obtained, in 1884, a U.S. patent on shown arms. Stamped on body within fancy scroll is "Schilling's//American Pet." The shown doll has stationary glass eyes; light mohair wig; the slightly turned head is well modeled with excellent finish.

105. COMPOSITION DOLL BY SCHILLING

Period: Late 19th and early 20th century.

Body: Cloth with composition limbs.

Remarks: Well made 23" (58.4cm) composition doll by F. M. Schilling Co. of Sonneburg, Germany. Bears distinctive "angel" trademark. Doll has original lambs wool wig, and is glass eyed. Baby dolls, some with "papa" and "mama" voice boxes, were also made by this firm. Trademark was, at times, stamped only on the chemise which might account for so many unmarked Schilling dolls. *Merrill Collection.*

103. GLASS-EYED COMPOSITION DOLL

Period: Late 19th century.

Body: Cloth with leather arms; sewed-on leather boots.

Remarks: Typical composition head of period with set-in glass eyes and hair wig. Head mounted on late 19th century commercially made cloth body with leather arms; striped cotton stockings; and sewed-on leather boots. All original.

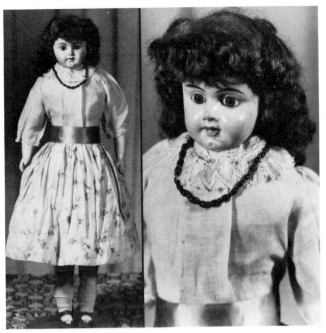

106. COMPOSITION HEAD DOLL

Period: Late 19th century.

Body: Cloth with composition forearms and lower legs.

Remarks: 31" (78.7cm) doll with nicely molded composition head. Mold marks run up through center of chest and face, over pate and down through center of back shoulders. Straw-stuffed cloth body. Set, blue paperweight eyes. Well drawn features with finely drawn eyelashes and eyebrows. Excellent uncracked finish. Dressed with portions of original costumes. *Merrill Collection.*

108. COMPOSITION BABY WITH MOVABLE CRYING MOUTH

Period: Last quarter of 19th century.

Body: Cloth with composition limbs.

Remarks: 14" (35.6cm) baby with bellows in torso. When pressed, baby cries while lower jaw opens exposing tiny painted-in teeth. The smoothly finished composition head has stationary glass eyes and the remains of a light mohair wig. An unusual crying baby.

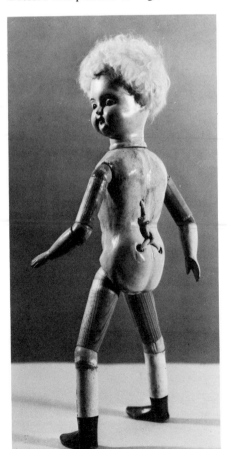

LEFT:

107. COMPOSITION DOLL WITH UNUSUAL BODY

Period: Late 19th century.

Body: Composition torso with jointed wooden limbs; elastic strung through holes provided in lower back (see illustration).

Remarks: 14" (35.6cm) flange-necked composition doll with painted features; set-in glass eyes; lambskn wig. Both the body and method of stringing are unusual. *Collection of Miss Elma B. Fuller.*

RIGHT:

109. PAPIER MÂCHÉ BONNETTED DOLL WITH MOLDED-ON CLOTHING

Period: Late 19th and early 20th century.

Body: All papier mâché; jointed at neck and shoulders.

Remarks: 12" (30.5cm) papier mâché bonnetted doll with added feature of molded-on clothing. Socket head, with painted features, has molded-on white bonnet with red band. Clothing of like color is decorated in pink and red. Black painted slippers. *Collection of Mrs. Nancy Shurtleff.*

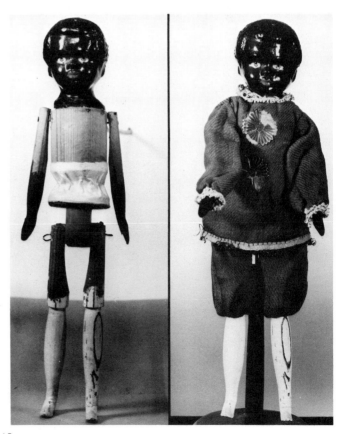

ABOVE:

110. BLACK PAPIER MÂCHÉ DOLL
Period: Late 19th and early 20th century.
Body: Black cloth with composition limbs.
Remarks: Small, cheaply made but appealing black papier mâché doll. When bellows in body are pressed, the doll squeaks and sticks out her tongue.

ABOVE RIGHT:

111. BLACK COMPOSITION DOLL - HIGHLY GLAZED
Period: Last quarter of 19th century.
Body: Cloth with black leather arms.
Remarks: 16" (40.6cm) black doll with head highly glazed - inside and out. At first glance resembles china. Composition head appears to be made of finely ground wood. Mold resembles those of era; with four sew holes for attaching to body. The head is bald and has painted features. An unusual doll - all original. Unmarked. *Merrill Collection.*

RIGHT:

112. BLACK PAPIER MÂCHÉ BOY DOLL
Period: Late 19th century.
Body: Wooden; jointed at hips and shoulders;
  bellows in torso.
Remarks: 9" (22.9cm), all original black boy doll whose papier mâché head has well defined and painted ethnic features. "Squeaks" when bellows in body is pressed downward. Wears red, yellow and blue costume with lace and gilt paper trim. Being black and a boy gives added interest to this doll. *Merrill Collection.*

113. PROSOPOTROPE - A FOUR FACED DOLL

Period: 1866+.

Body: None mentioned; probably cloth.

Remarks: An extremely rare 6" (15.2cm) tall hatted shoulder head containing a vertically revolving sphere, which as rotated reveals four different faces. This example is formed of a hard composition with brightly painted features and decoration. A few *prosopotropes* have been found with a wax-over coating. The unusual design of this doll's head is based on a patent obtained by Dominico Checkeni of New Haven, Connecticut in 1866. New Haven directories of the time list Checkeni as a toymaker, as was the name of Ozias Morse. The printed labels found pasted inside the shoulders states the dolls were "Manufactured and sold by Ozias Morse of West Acton, Massachusetts. Sole agent for the patentees." The intricate design of the four piece molds required to form the faces and shoulders and the skill required for assembly and decoration indicate a manufactory of some sophistication. Just where and by whom the heads were really manufactured remains unresolved. Perhaps Ozias Morse was a traveling sales representative who sold the heads along with other toys while on the road. *Collection of Virginia Olsen.*

Wax Dolls - 19th Century

Wax has been used to make dolls from ancient to modern times.

They were much in demand in the 1800s but their popularity had waned by the end of that century. Very few continued to be made in the 20th century.

Wax dolls vary greatly in quality and are difficult to date accurately, as few were marked.

There are three general types:
1. Poured wax.
2. Poured wax with plaster or other reinforcement.
3. Wax-over pressed cardboard, papier mâché, or composition.

Note: The latter type (#3) is the one most commonly found.

Most realistic and beautiful are the poured wax dolls made during the second and third quarters of the 19th century by such famous doll making families as Montanari and Pierrotti of London.

Wax dolls were also produced in Germany during the same period and to some extent in France.

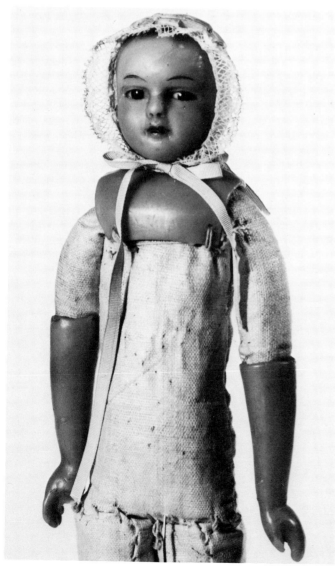

115. WAX-OVER-COMPOSITION DOLL WITH 1838 DOCUMENTATION

Period: Second quarter of 19th century.
Body: Cloth with pink kidskin arms.
Remarks: 20" (50.8cm) doll in unplayed with condition. Elaborately gowned, its wax-over-composition head has inset glass eyes and mohair wig with bow of tulle. Wears original dress of mull with laced, white satin bodice. Although purchased in Paris in 1838, the doll is probably of German origin. *Collection of The Essex Institute, Salem, Massachusetts.*

114. WIRE-EYED POURED WAX BABY DOLL

Period: First quarter of 19th century.
Body: Cloth with poured wax arms.
Remarks: 12½" (31.8cm) poured wax doll whose glass-eyes open and shut by raising and lowering a wire which protrudes from lower front of torso. A most unusual doll as this type is generally made in wax-over-composition or papier mâché. It strongly resembles the English wax dolls of the period.

117. WIRE-EYED WAX DOLL IN PATRIOTIC COSTUME
Period: Circa 1850.
Body: Cloth with kid arms.
Remarks: 18½" (47cm) wax-over-composition doll with brown mohair wig; glass eyes operated by wire. Dress of white tarleton trimmed with red ribbon. Apron of alternate stripes of red and white ribbon. Bodice of blue silk with white embroidered stars. Blue velvet hat trimmed with red, white and blue ribbons plus side rosettes of red and white ribbons. Blue silk shoes; embroidered white stockings. Costume completely original. *Courtesy of The Margaret Woodbury Strong Museum.*

116. ENGLISH WAX DOLL IN SCOTISH COSTUME
Period: Mid-19th century.
Body: Cloth with brown leather arms.
Remarks: A 15" (38.1cm) wax-over papier mâché doll dressed in Scottish costume. The pale wax face has painted features; stationary brown pupilless glass eyes; mohair wig. The leather arms on this particular doll are unusually good in proportion - dolls of this type generally have arms that are much too short. Early dolls may often be found in foreign costume. *Courtesy of The Essex Institute, Salem, Massachusetts.*

118. WAX-OVER PAPIER MÂCHÉ DOLLS

Period: Second and third quarters of 19th century.

Body: Cloth with leather arms.

Remarks: A large pair of wax-over papier mâché (pressed cardboard) dolls - white in complexion color. They may also come with wire eyes; operated by a wire protruding from midsection of body. Leather arms come in various colors. Very similar pink toned wax-over papier mâché dolls, having better definition in molding, were made simultaneously in Germany. The illustrated dolls are called *English Wax*.

Left: 28" (71.1cm) wax doll with glued on wig of human hair; stationary brown, pupilless, glass eyes; brown leather arms; painted features.

Right: 29" (73.7cm) wax doll with hair inserted in slit on head; stationary brown glass eyes; dark blue leather arms; painted features. Doll on right: *Merrill Collection.*

119. ENGLISH WAX DOLL - CASED

Period: Mid-19th century.

Body: Cloth with blue leather arms.

Remarks: A glass-topped box, with wire loop for hanging, containing 13" (33cm) English wax doll in pristine condition; two small all-wax dolls; artificial flowers. Box is wallpaper lined and backed with 1850 Punch's Almanac. Dolls of this era are occasionally found encased in this manner. Their history is uncertain. Erroneously referred to as "graveyard" dolls. Used as a wall hanging - possibly as a memorial to a child. *Merrill Collection.*

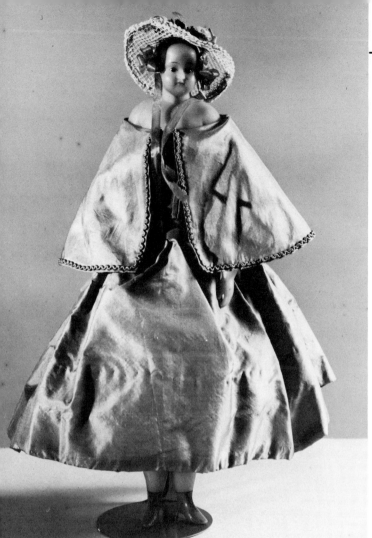

120. POURED WAX DOLL - ALL ORIGINAL
Period: Mid-19th century.
Body: Cloth with poured wax limbs.
Remarks: 12" (30.5cm) poured wax doll in pristine condition. The well modeled head, with deep shoulders; has black beady eyes; black painted hair. Blue silk dress, with matching cape, has tight bodice and full skirt. Flower decorated hat of silk mesh has ribbon rosettes and ties. Poured wax legs have vermillion painted boots. *Collection of Mrs. Elmer Morley.*

121. WAX PEDLAR DOLL - ENGLISH
Period: Circa 1840.
Body: Cloth with wax arms and shoes.
Remarks: 11" (27.9cm) wax pedlar doll with molded character face of old lady with beady eyes, set-in tiny teeth, gray mohair wig. Wears traditional costume of 19th century London street vendors; red wool hooded cape, black silk bonnet over white lace cap. Carries tray of tiny wares - infinite in variety. Doll, costume and wares completely original. For pedlar doll of leather see page 149, Illustration 340. *Merrill Collection.*

122. QUEEN VICTORIA PORTRAIT DOLL IN POURED WAX

Period: Mid-19th century.
Body: Cloth with poured wax arms.
Remarks: Rare, 22" (55.9cm) poured wax portrait doll of the young Queen Victoria. Deep ivory toned head has parted lips with painted-in teeth, stationary blue glass eyes, light brown human hair wig. White satin gown is topped by ermine-trimmed, red velvet cape. Crown of red velvet is trimmed with gold braid. *Collection of The Rhode Island Historical Society, Providence, Rhode Island.*

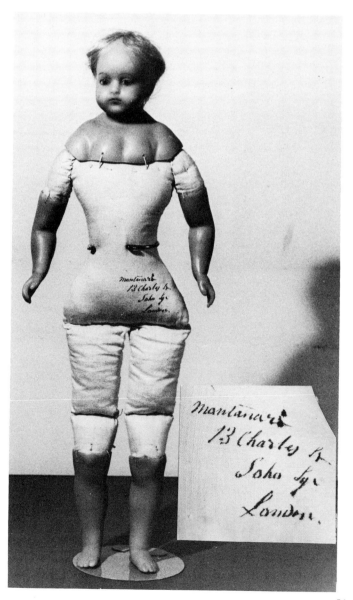

123. MARKED, POURED WAX BABY DOLL BY MONTANARI

Period: Third quarter of 19th century.
Body: Cloth with hollow, poured wax limbs.
Remarks: 20" (50.8cm) baby doll with side turned, poured wax head. Delicately tinted, it has inset blue glass eyes and inserted hair, brows and lashes. Came dressed in long baby dress and embroidered flannel petticoat. Marked in ink on torso: "Montanari//13 Charles St//Soho Sqr//London." Although many dolls of this type are attributed to Montanari, seldom is one found marked. *Collection of The Quincy Homestead. Courtesy of The Massachusetts Society of Colonial Dames.*

124. MONTANARI TYPE POURED WAX DOLL
Period: Third quarter of 19th century.
Body: Cloth with hollow wax limbs.
Remarks: 23" (58.4cm) unmarked poured wax doll with hairs singly inserted in thick wax head. *Unusual feature:* sleeping rather than stationary glass eyes. A Montanari type - probably made by one of the well known families of London wax doll makers. Documented as gift to a child in the 1860s. *Merrill Collection.*

125. POURED WAX DOLL - MONTANARI TYPE
Period: Third quarter of 19th century.
Body: Cloth with hollow wax arms and legs.
Remarks: 19½" (49.6cm) unmarked, poured wax doll with set-in hair and eyelashes. Stationary blue glass eyes. A Montanari type. Doll dressed in one of three original costumes. Came in wooden box designed to hold her.

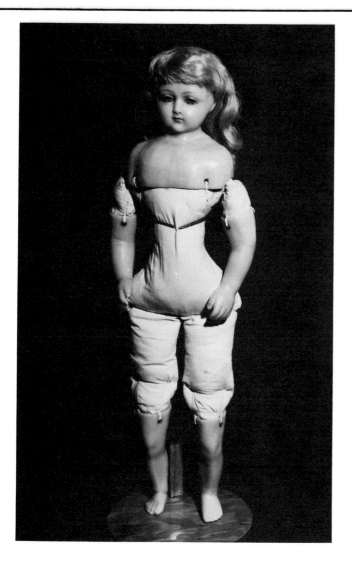

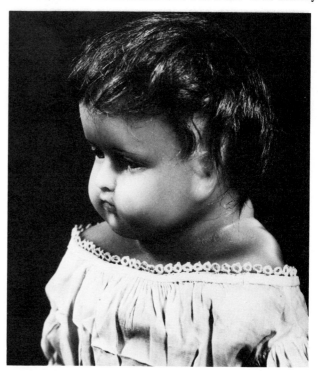

127. WAX BABY DOLL BY PIEROTTI
Period: Third quarter of 19th century.
Body: Cloth with hollow; molded wax limbs.
Remarks: Poured wax baby doll with glass eyes and inserted hair. Marked on back of head with maker's name "Pierotti." Made in London by one of the famous families who produced exquisite poured wax dolls which were most realistic.

126. WAX CHILD DOLL BY PIEROTTI
Period: Third quarter of 19th century.
Body: Cloth with hollow, poured wax limbs.
Remarks: 21" (53.3cm) child doll with poured wax head. Sensitively modeled, it has inset blue glass eyes; painted brows; inserted hair and lashes. Holes, with metal grommets, allow for sewing limbs to body. Marked on back of head with its London maker's name "Pierotti."

128. POURED WAX DOLL BY CHARLES MARSH OF LONDON
Period: Last quarter of 19th century.
Body: Cloth with poured wax limbs.
Remarks: 19" (48.3cm) doll with poured wax head. Stationary blue glass eyes have inserted lashes, painted brows. Flowing blonde hair was affixed to doll's head by embedding tufts of mohair into wax scalp. Warranty and trademark of Charles Marsh of London stamped on front of body (see illustration). Marked wax dolls are rarely found. *Collection of Miss Zelda H. Cushner.*

OPPOSITE PAGE:
129. POURED WAX DOLL - EAST INDIAN LADY
Period: Last half of 19th century.
Body: Brown cloth with hollow, poured wax limbs.
Remarks: 16½" (41.9cm) brown poured wax doll molded and dressed to represent an East Indian lady. Inserted hair; stationary glass eyes; pierced ears. Earrings, necklaces, bracelets and rings of brightly colored beads and pearls. Head encircled with twisted strands of small gold beads. Red dress trimmed with bands of gold and silver ribbon. The illustrated doll is of the Montanari type. *Collection of Miss Zelda H. Cushner.*

130. UNMARKED, POURED WAX TODDLER
Period: Third quarter of 19th century.
Body: Cloth with hollow, poured wax limbs.
Remarks: 15" (38.1cm) unmarked, poured wax child or baby (toddler) doll with inserted hair, brows and lashes. Head, of sweet expression, is slightly turned, delicately tinted, and has set-in blue glass eyes. *Merrill Collection.*

RIGHT:
132. LONDON RAG BABY
Period: 1865 to end of 19th century.
Body: All cloth.
Remarks: 14" (35.6cm) baby with gauze covered facial mask of wax. Painted features include bright blue eyes, almost glass-like in appearance. A popular and inexpensive doll made during the last half of the 19th century. Came in various sizes. Made in London and sold fully dressed. Due to its perishable nature, few of these dolls have survived. *Courtesy of The Essex Institute, Salem Massachusetts.*

131. WAX-OVER-COMPOSITION ORIENTAL FEATURED DOLL - WIRE-EYED
Period: Second quarter of 19th century.
Body: Motschmann type - see page 30.
Remarks: 10" (25.4cm) wax-over-composition doll with oriental features. Well modeled head has glass eyes that move by raising and lowering of wire protruding from back of torso. Wears original costume; faded yellow silk with gold braid trim. Brown velvet cap, with red crocheted top, has small bell attached. German made.

RIGHT:

133. BLONDE WAX-OVER PAPIER MÂCHÉ DOLL

Period: Third quarter of 19th century.

Body: Cloth with leather arms; or cloth with composition or wooden limbs.

Remarks: Early wax-over papier mâché doll with blonde hairdo molded so as to expose ears. Stationary glass eyes. Very similar in mold to the papier mâché dolls of the period.

BELOW:

134. BOY HATTED DOLL IN WAX-OVER-COMPOSITION

Period: Third quarter of 19th century.

Body: Cloth with wooden limbs.

Remarks: Small 9" (22.9cm) wax-over-composition boy doll - all original. Wears molded white hat banded in red. Painted wooden legs have brown stockings and black boots. *Merrill Collection.*

BELOW:

135. LADY WITH PAINTED LINES ON WAXED COIFFURE

Period: Third quarter of 19th century.

Body: Cloth with wooden limbs.

Remarks: 19" (48.3cm) all original, wax-over-composition doll whose adult shaped face has pupilless glass eyes and molded blonde hair with back comb. *Unusual feature:* lines, detailing hairdo, are painted on top of wax coating - a method often used on lips and eyebrows but seldom on hair. *Collection of Mrs. Fidelia Lence.*

137. WIRE-EYED WAX-OVER-COMPOSITION DOLL
Period: Third quarter of 19th century.
Body: Cloth with wooden limbs.
Remarks: Referred to as *squash* or *pumpkin* head, this 19"
(48.3cm) wax-over-composition doll has two rare features for her
type:
1. Mouse colored hair.
2. Wire-eyes. Eyes that open and shut by raising and lowering
   wire which protrudes from lower torso.
Dolls of this type generally come with blonde molded hair and
stationary glass eyes. The illustrated doll is unique - wire eyes are
found in earlier dolls. See pages 47 and 55. *Merrill Collection.*

136. WAX-OVER-COMPOSITION DOLL
Period: Third quarter of 19th century.
Body: Cloth with wooden limbs.
Remarks: 22" (55.9cm) wax-over-composition doll with pupilless glass eyes; painted features; molded blonde hair with black
ribbon. Called squash or pumpkin head. Note wooden limbs
which place doll in 1850-60 era.
Note: This old wax doll purchased in 1946 by Madeline
Merrill was the first doll of her collection, for which she, later on
and reluctantly, admitted to having paid $30.00. *Merrill Col-
lection.*

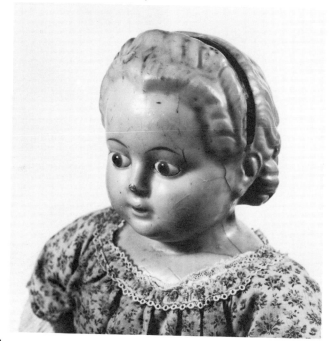

RIGHT:
138. "POP-EYED" WAX-OVER-COMPOSITION DOLL
Period: Third quarter of 19th century.
Body: Cloth with wax-over-composition limbs.
Remarks: 28" (71.1cm) wax-over-composition doll with pompadour hairdo; banded in black. Note large, staring, blown glass
eyes - characteristic of the so-called *pop-eyed* wax dolls.

140. HATTED WAX-OVER-COMPOSITION DOLL
Period: Third quarter of 19th century.
Body: Cloth with wooden arms.
Remarks: 11½" (29.2cm) wax-over-composition hatted doll with set-in glass eyes; pierced ears. Partial mohair wig is attached to head below rim of waxed hat. Yellow hat, with green and red band, has brown, red and green molded plumes. *Collection of Mrs. Elmer Morley.*

139. HATTED WAX-OVER-COMPOSITION DOLL
Period: Third quarter of 19th century.
Body: Cloth with wooden limbs.
Remarks: 15" (38.1cm) wax-over-composition hatted doll whose wooden arms and legs indicate a doll of the mid-19th century. Wears a molded black hat with mauve brim and pink plume. *Merrill Collection.*

RIGHT:
141. HATTED WAX-OVER-COMPOSITION DOLL
Period: Third quarter of 19th century.
Body: Cloth with wooden limbs.
Remarks: 22" (55.9cm) wax-over-composition hatted doll with pupilless glass eyes, blonde molded hair. Green molded-on hat, with red band, is topped by large molded plume. *Collection of The Rhode Island Historical Society, Providence, Rhode Island.*

142. HATTED WAX-OVER-COMPOSITION DOLL
Period: Third quarter of 19th century.
Body: Cloth with wooden arms.
Remarks: The molded pink bonnet of this 20" (50.8cm) wax-over-composition doll is decorated with molded-on and painted sprigs of flowers. Glued to the head, below the bonnet rim, are remnants of blonde mohair curls. Doll shown front and rear. Rear view shows snood, with gilt paper decoration, held in place by inserting into slot just below bonnet edge. *Courtesy of The Essex Institute, Salem, Massachusetts.*

143. BLUE SCARF DOLL IN WAX-OVER-COMPOSITION
Period: Third quarter of 19th century.
Body: Cloth with waxed composition limbs.
Remarks: 16½" (41.9cm) wax-over-composition doll with painted features, glass eyes and molded blue scarf draped over molded blonde hair. A rarity in the field of wax dolls. The blue scarf doll as generally known is one of great beauty made of parian. See page 177. *Collection of Miss Zelda H. Cushner.*

144. HATTED DOLL IN WAX-OVER-COMPOSITION
Period: Third quarter of 19th century.
Body: Cloth with composition arms and booted legs.
Remarks: Unusual 20" (50.8cm) hatted doll with molded-on waxed hat; trimmed with velvet, ostrich plume and gold edging. Mohair ringlets are tacked to the waxed head below the hat. Cobalt blue pupilless eyes; and well modeled limbs. *Merrill Collection.*

145. HATTED WAX IN KATE GREENAWAY STYLE
Period: Third quarter of 19th century.
Body: Cloth with composition limbs.
Remarks: Wax-over-composition hatted doll. Molded bonnet with red ribbon and bow in Kate Greenaway style.

146. WAX LADY DOLL - DRESSED AS BRIDE
Period: Circa 1870-1880.
Body: Cloth with wax-over-composition limbs.
Remarks: 15" (38.1cm) wax-over-composition doll with applied blonde wig; sleeping eyes; brightly colored cheeks. Wears fancy bridal dress of net trimmed with blonde lace and small bunches of flowers. White net veil caught to green and white coronet. White heeled boots. Original costume. *Courtesy of The Margaret Woodbury Strong Museum.*

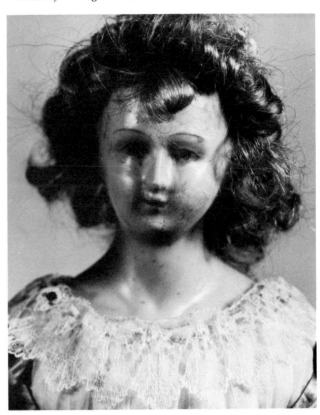

147. WAX DOLL WITH PAINTED EYES
Period: Circa 1860-1865.
Body: Cloth with leather arms.
Remarks: 19" (48.3cm) wax-over-composition doll with painted features and human hair wig. Note brown painted eyes - unusual. Wax dolls almost always come with glass eyes. Wears original, simple type dress.

LEFT:
148. WAX-OVER PAPIER MÂCHÉ LADY DOLL
Period: Third quarter of 19th century.
Body: Cloth with composition arms and legs.
Remarks: Rare 24" (61cm), slim-waisted wax-over-composition lady - possibly a portrait doll. Head, with patrician features, is slightly turned and has smiling mouth with painted upper teeth; large blue glass eyes; upswept blonde mohair wig. *Unusual features:* molded blouse with applied lace trim. Wrist length yellow painted gloves. *Collection of Miss Zelda H. Cushner.*

60

149. SWIVEL-NECKED LADY DOLL IN WAX-OVER-COMPOSITION

Period: Circa 1875.
Body: Cloth with waxed composition arms.
Remarks: 16½" (41.9cm) lady doll whose wax-over-composition head swivels on an unwaxed composition shoulder piece; molded and painted to represent a high necked blouse. Cloth collar is set-on. Head has stationary blue glass eyes; pierced ears; light mohair wig. Swivel-necked dolls in wax are considered rare. *Collection of Mrs. Germaine L. Bachand.*

150. WAX LADY WITH MOLDED GLOVES
Period: Circa 1880.
Body: Glazed cotton with composition legs and
    lightly waxed arms.
Remarks: 20" (50.8cm) adult featured, poured wax doll with blue inset glass eyes and elaborately styled mohair wig. Wears original blown glass earrings. Red trimmed, yellow gloves are molded on the hands. Molded brown and black boots are topped by white knitted stockings and gilt trimmed pink garters. Wears original factory made percale chemise. *Collection of Estelle Johnston.*

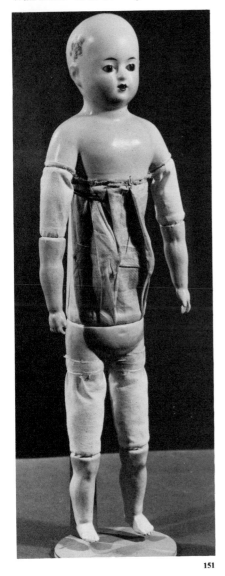

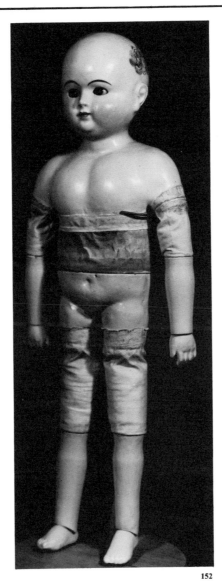

151

152

153

151. MOTSCHMANN-TYPE DOLL - VARIANT
Period: Third quarter of 19th century.
Body: Torso of papier mâché with inserted voice box; twill covered. One piece composition limbs differ from jointed ones generally found on this type doll.
Remarks: 20" (50.8cm) wax-over papier mâché baby doll of Motschmann type. Hair indicated under wax; stationary blue glass eyes; open mouth with teeth. Differs from contemporaries in operation of voice box. Cries "mama" and "papa" by pushing in on either of two wooden levers. Usual method - downward compression of bellows.

152. WAX-OVER PAPIER MÂCHÉ BABY DOLL
Period: Third quarter of 19th century.
Body: Torso of papier mâché with inserted bellows and squeak box; arms and legs of wood with upper sections of cloth; hands and feet of composition; string suspended.

Remarks: 23" (58.4cm) wax-over papier mâché baby doll with sleeping eyes; hair indicated under wax. Bellows in midriff for crying. May also be found with stationary eyes; head that is separate and movable on shoulders; and with open mouth and teeth. Similar to the Motschmann doll patented in Germany in 1857. This doll may also be found not waxed. *Merrill Collection.*

153. MOTSCHMANN-TYPE BABY DOLL WITH KICKING AND CRYING MECHANISM
Period: Third quarter of 19th century.
Body: Key-wound mechanism within cloth-covered cardboard torso; composition limbs.
Remarks: Wax-over papier mâché doll of Motschmann-type. Made to represent a baby with wispy painted curls at sides of head. When clock works mechanism is set in motion, baby moves head from side to side; raises and lowers limbs and cries "mama" and "papa." Body construction and action is much like that found in a French bisque doll by Jules Steiner.

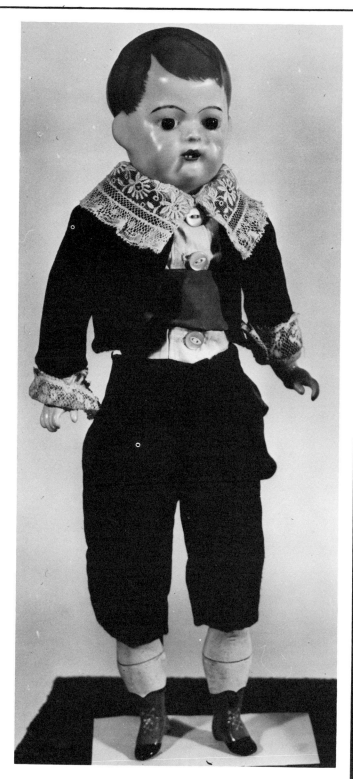

154. BOY DOLL IN WAX-OVER-COMPOSITION
Period: Third quarter of 19th century.
Body: Cloth with composition limbs.
Remarks: 18" (45.7cm) wax-over-composition boy doll with painted hair, glass eyes, and open mouth with set-in teeth. Same model may have closed mouth. A good quality doll throughout. The arms and legs are of better workmanship than generally found in dolls of this type. Made in Germany. The head of the illustrated doll is lined with German printed paper. *Merrill Collection.*

155. TWO-FACED, SWIVEL-NECKED LADY DOLL IN WAX-OVER-COMPOSITION
Period: Circa 1875.
Body: Cloth with waxed composition arms.
Remarks: 18" (45.7cm) two-faced lady doll in wax-over-composition. Head has two swivels; one at neck for exposing faces, other at top of head for rotation of wig. Awake face has set-in glass eyes; sleeping face is completely waxed. Wears original costume with train - comparable to those of French dolls of period. *Merrill Collection.*

156. WAX-OVER-COMPOSITION DOLL ON SCHMITT-TYPE BODY

Period: Last quarter of 19th century.
Body: Jointed composition, elastic strung.
Remarks: 17" (43.2cm) doll with flanged head of wax-over-composition; set-in glass eyes; mohair wig. Body appears to be by French firm of Schmitt whose dolls generally have heads of bisque. Illustrated doll unmarked. *Collection of Nancy Shurtleff.*

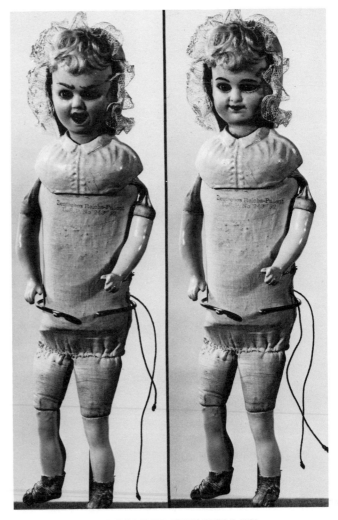

157. TWO FACED POURED WAX DOLL BY BARTENSTEIN

Period: Circa 1880.
Body: Cardboard cylinder, housing mechanism, is cloth covered; bare feet, legs and arms are of composition.
Remarks: A 13" (33cm) movable double faced doll of poured wax. Operates by pull strings which cause baby to cry as the head revolves within the papier mâché cap. A smiling and crying face alternately appears, as illustrated. Has decalcomania eyebrows and is found with blue or brown glass eyes. Made by Fritz Bartenstein of Germany. Patented in both Germany and the United States. (U.S. Patent #243,752 - July 5, 1881.) Patent often printed on front of cloth body. *Merrill Collection.*

158. WAX-OVER-COMPOSITION DOLL

Period: 1870-1890.
Body: Straw stuffed cloth body; composition arms and legs.
Remarks: 21" (53.3cm) wax-over-composition head. Pupilless, cobalt blue sleep eyes. Dressed in original underwear and fine copperplate print cotton dress. This doll given to Madeline Merrill in 1950 by Miss Grace C. Hunt of Saugus, Massachusetts, who received it as a gift at Christmas in 1879. Copy of old tintype shows Miss Hunt at the age of four in 1880 with her doll in its' carriage. *Merrill Collection.*

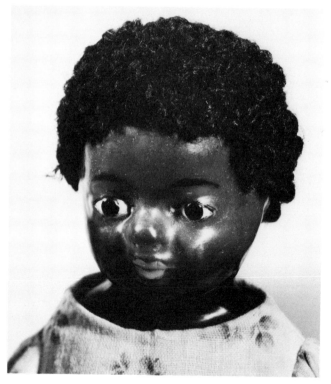

159. WAX-OVER PAPIER MÂCHÉ CLOWN

Period: Late 19th century.
Body: Wooden with wooden limbs.
Remarks: 12" (30.5cm) mechanical clown doll with wax-over papier mâché head. All original. When bellows in chest is pressed, the doll squeaks, blinks eyes, and clashes cymbals. *Merrill Collection.*

160. BLACK WAX-OVER-COMPOSITION DOLL

Period: Last quarter of 19th century.
Body: Cloth with composition limbs.
Remarks: Occasionally found Black wax-over-composition doll with stationary glass eyes and black lambskin wig. Wears heeled composition boots of the period. Dolls of this type found in many sizes. *Merrill Collection.*

161. POURED WAX DOLL WITH COMBINATION WIG
Period: Last quarter of 19th century.
Body: Cloth with kid arms.
Remarks: 18" (45.7cm) poured wax doll head with plaster reinforcement; a more durable head than the earlier poured wax ones that lacked this feature. Doll has sleeping eyes. Two methods of hair application are used - hair imbedded in tufts around face combined with a glued-on partial wig. *Merrill Collection.*

163. DOLL OF POURED WAX - WITH SET-IN TEETH
Period: Last quarter of 19th century.
Body: Cloth with wax-over-composition limbs.
Remarks: Fine quality poured wax head; turned to one side. Brown sleeping eyes; fine light mohair wig. *Unusual feature:* open mouth with set-in porcelain teeth. Dolls of this mold are generally found with closed mouth.

LEFT:
162. POURED WAX DOLL WITH SLEEP EYES
Period: Second quarter of 19th century.
Body: Cloth body; straw stuffed with composition arms and legs.
Remarks: 17" (43.2cm) doll with poured wax shoulder head and glass sleep eyes. Human hair wig tacked onto pate. Composition forearms waxed-over. Molded composition boots brightly decorated, with high buttons on side. Doll is dressed in completely original net over foundation costume. *Merrill Collection.*

RIGHT:
164. WAX-OVER-COMPOSITION DOLL ON LEATHER BODY

Period: Last quarter of 19th century.
Body: All leather.
Remarks: 21½" (54.6cm) all original doll with wax-over-composition head on all leather body. Set-in blue glass eyes; pierced ears; mohair wig. Occasionally good quality wax dolls are found on this type body. Wears pale blue and pink lace-trimmed satin dress with matching straw hat. *Collection of Mrs. Elmer Morley.*

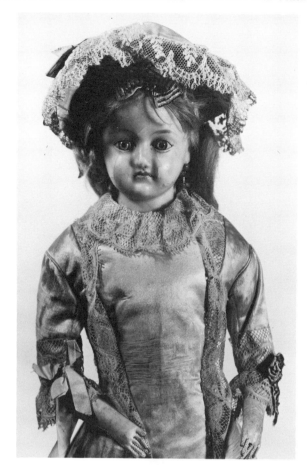

165. POURED WAX DOLL WITH SIDE-TURNED HEAD

Period: Last quarter of 19th century.
Body: Cloth with leather arms.
Remarks: 21" (53.3cm) doll with pink tinted, poured wax head; side-turned. Of fine quality, characteristic of her type, she has brown sleeping eyes; closed mouth and blonde mohair wig. *Merrill Collection.*

RIGHT:
166. POURED WAX DOLL WITH PLASTER REINFORCEMENT

Period: Last quarter of 19th century.
Body: Cloth with wax-over-composition arms; composition legs with stocking covering; and molded boots with gilt and silk tassel trim.
Remarks: Fine quality poured wax doll with plaster reinforcement in head; blown glass eyes; pierced ears; mohair wig. All original.

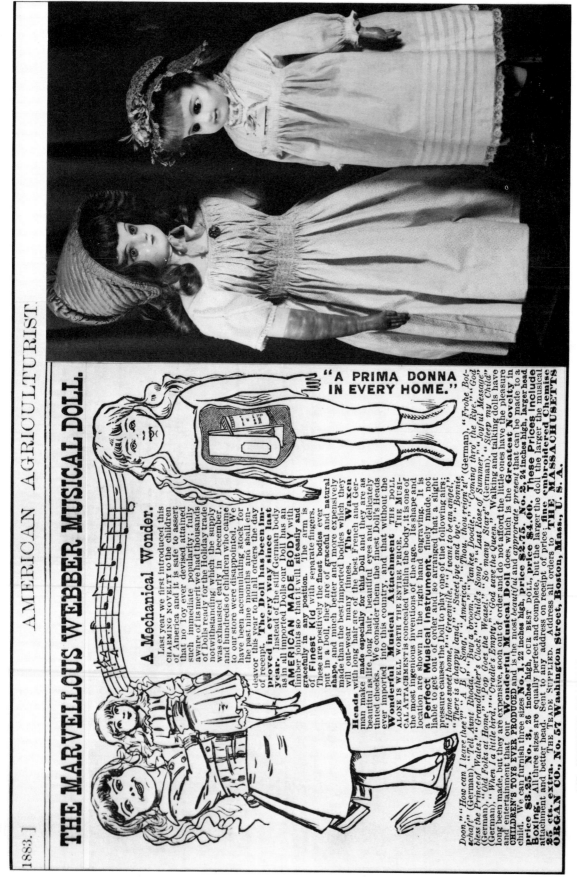

tune doll plays are printed on cloth body. Pressure on bellows in doll's chest causes organ within to play one of several tunes provided by manufacturer. 26" (66cm) doll at left plays "Sleep My Child;" 22" (55.9cm) doll at right plays "I Sing Greenville." Wax-over-composition heads, of finest German and French manufacture, have stationary glass eyes and human hair wigs. *Merrill Collection.*

167. WEBBER SINGING DOLLS IN WAX-OVER-COMPOSITION

Period: Patented 1882.

Body: Cloth with leather arms.

Remarks: *The Marvelous Webber Singing Doll* patented in United States and foreign countries by William Webber of Medford, Massachusetts and distributed by the Massachusetts Organ Company of Boston. Inventor's name, patent dates and

168. VARIATIONS IN WIGS ON WAX DOLLS

Period: Late 19th century.
Body: Cloth with composition limbs.
Remarks: Cheaply made wax-over-composition dolls, showing types of hairdos created by laying mohair over molded bumps of head.
Left: Center part of hairdo between parallel bumps.
Right: Pompadour hairdo with bump across front of head. *Merrill Collection.*

BELOW:

169. POURED WAX DOLL WITH JOINTED COMPOSITION BODY

Period: Last quarter of 19th century.
Body: Composition; elastic strung.
Remarks: The tinted, poured wax head of this 10" (25.4cm) doll is fitted over a cylindrical wooden neck piece which projects from the body. She has set-in glass eyes and curly mohair wig. The body construction is most unusual; flange-necked head on a ball jointed, elastic-strung composition body. Wax heads are generally of the shoulder type, mounted on cloth or leather bodies. Illustrated doll unmarked. *Merrill Collection.*

BELOW RIGHT:

170. ALL WAX DOLL

Period: Last quarter of 19th century.
Body: All wax with movable arms, elastic strung at shoulders.
Remarks: 7½" (19.1cm) molded wax doll. Unusual. Except for movable arms, much like *Frozen Charlottes* (see page 133). Painted features; blonde mohair wig; inset blue glass eyes. Molded and painted socks and boots. (One hand and part of boots missing). Inside of doll is hollow from top of head to upper legs. *Collection of Mrs. Frank Maitland.*

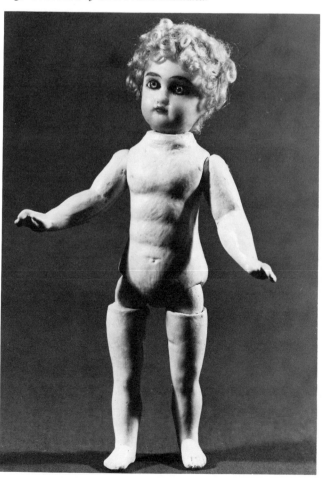

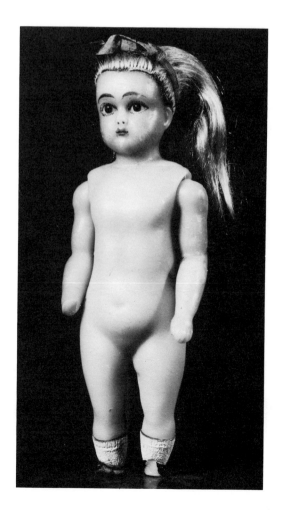

China Dolls - 19th Century

China - a term given to glazed ceramic heads as compared to unglazed. Produced by carrying one step beyond biscuit stage (see Bisque classification).

Dolls of this category are usually found with molded black hair, occasionally with blonde hair, and very rarely with dark brown hair. A rarity is a bald headed china doll wearing a wig. Extremely rare is a doll having china head, legs, and arms on a pegged wooden body, or a doll with sleeping glass eyes operated by means of a wire.

Some details denoting unusual china dolls would be:
1. Flesh toned china.
2. Depth in modeling of features and hairdo.
3. Any unusual hairdo - i.e., touches of lustre, snoods, ribbons, trim, or any other decoration.
4. Brushmarks around face.
5. Brown painted eyes - considered rare in this category.
6. Set-in glass eyes - extremely rare.

Seldom is any identification mark found on china doll heads.

Heads are sometimes found on crude homemade bodies.

Of help in dating china dolls are the following:
1. Hair style of period.
2. Flat soled shoes used up to about 1860.
3. Heeled boots and bulbous legs of later period.

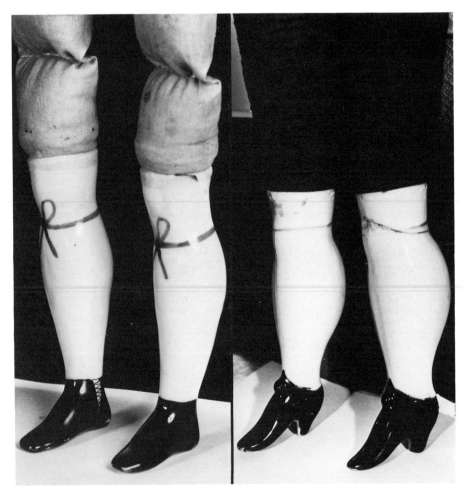

171. EXAMPLES OF CHINA LEGS
Left: Close-up of flat-soled shoes found on pre-Civil War (1860) china dolls. Not all dolls of this period have china limbs, as heads were often mounted on cloth bodies with leather arms.
Right: Close-up of bulbous legs with heeled boots. Type often found on post-Civil War dolls. *Merrill Collection.*

(Continued on page 87).

20" (50.8cm) carved wooden church figure. See Page 1, Illustration 1.

16"(40.6cm) Queen Anne type. See Page 4, Illustration 8.

21" (53.3cm) Queen Anne type. See Page 6, Illustration 13.

OPPOSITE PAGE:

Left: 12" (30.5cm). Pupilless black set-in glass eyes. Dotted eyelashes and eyebrows. Cloth hands and feet. Appears to be original dress and bonnet. **Center:** 10" (25.4cm). Black painted eyes. Eyelashes and eyebrows are dotted with fine lines drawn through. Five finger wooden arms, and wooden legs attached to torso like this. **Right:** 8" (20.3cm). Brown painted eyes and brown dotted eyelashes and eyebrows. Twisted cloth arms and legs. Original dress and mob cap. See Pages 6 and 7.

CLOCKWISE:

18" (45.7cm) cloth doll named for owner, Content Phillips of Lynn, Massachusetts in about 1785-90. White cloth body, blonde human hair wig, lace cap with blue satin ribbon, 2 white linen petticoats, off white linen dress hand-stamped in brown floral design, white silk fichu, blue ribbon at neck and waist; white knit stockings, blue satin shoes, one blue garter. Pocket watch hung from neck on string, white kid gloves. *Lynn Historical Society.*

26" (66.0cm) wooden Empire doll. Ball joint at waist. See page 8, illustration 19.

9½" (24.2cm) and 10" (25.4cm) pair of carton-type dolls dressed in shells suggesting male and female costumes of Brittany. See Page 20, Illustration 46.

RIGHT:
5¼" (13.4cm) wooden doll with so-called alien head of molded plaster-like material (often found in early 'papier mâché' heads) with molded hat and long braid. See Page 11, Illustration 27 right.

12" (30.5cm) wooden doll with molded alien head. See Page 10, Illustration 25.

TOP LEFT:
23" (58.4cm) poured wax doll of the English type with inserted hair and unusual sleeping glass eyes. See Page 52, Illustration 124.

TOP:
Left: 19" (48.3cm) wax-over-composition with wire eyes. **Right:** 22" (55.9cm) wax-over-composition doll of more usual type. See Page 57.

LEFT:
18" (45.7cm) poured wax doll with plaster reinforcement in head, sleeping glass eyes, and glued wig with inserted hair around face for more natural hairline. See Page 66, Illustration 161.

OPPOSITE PAGE:
28" (71.1cm) English wax-over-papier-mâché doll with original clothes. Photographed with a display of accessories from a somewhat later period.

ABOVE:
An interesting group of unusual
chinas on jointed wood bodies. See
Page 80.

Marked Danish head of the Royal
Copenhagen Manufactory. See Page
88, Illustration 174.

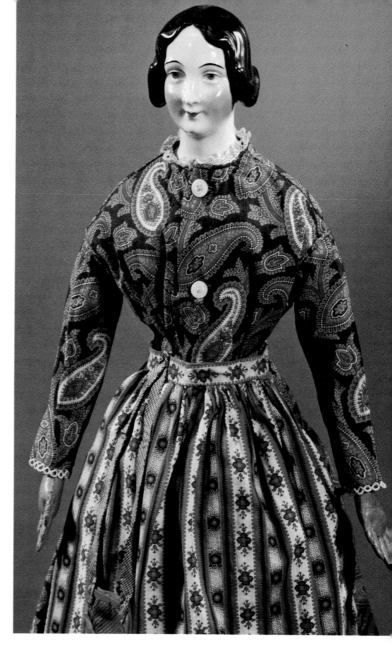

TOP LEFT:
5½" (14.0cm) pink toned, brown hair KPM shoulderhead both above with usual Orb & Scepter mark and KPM. See Page 90, Illustration 180.

TOP RIGHT:
20" (50.8cm) KPM china. Cloth body, leather arms, no ears showing. See Page 89, Illustration 178.

LEFT:
20" (50.8cm) pink toned china, head and shoulder view. Ears showing, dark brown tint to hair. See Page 90, Illustration 181.

OPPOSITE PAGE:
Two glass eyed chinas. **Left:** hairstyle also found in papier mâché. See similar doll, Page 105, Illustration 209. **Right:** See Page 90, Illustration 218.

ABOVE:
20" (50.8cm) china doll of unusual mold. See Page 99, Illustration 201.

22" (55.9cm) china tan dress, red trim. Ears showing, brush marks. See Page 109, Illustration 226.

ABOVE:
20" (50.8cm) china with molded snood trimmed with lustre-touched frill and bunch of grapes. See Page 116, Illustration 245.

Two later 19th century china dolls. **Left:** similar doll on Page 112. **Right:** type referred to as "lowbrow" made over a period extending into the 20th century.

(Continued from page 70).

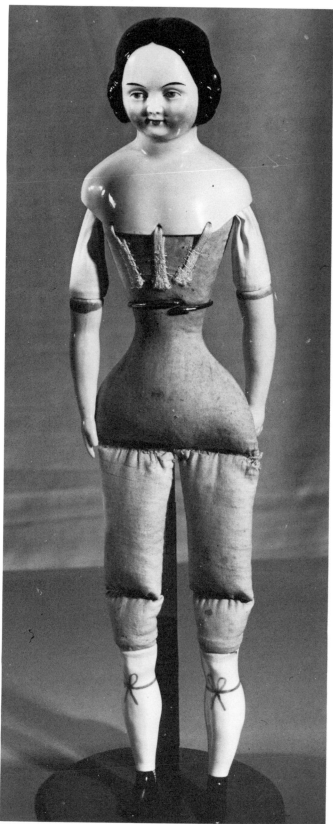

173. EXAMPLE OF LATE CHINA DOLL WITH CHINA LIMBS

Period: Late 19th century.

Body: Typical cloth with late china limbs.

Remarks: Illustration shows a correctly assembled doll of the late 19th century. Note cupped hands and bulbous legs with high heeled boots. *Merrill Collection.*

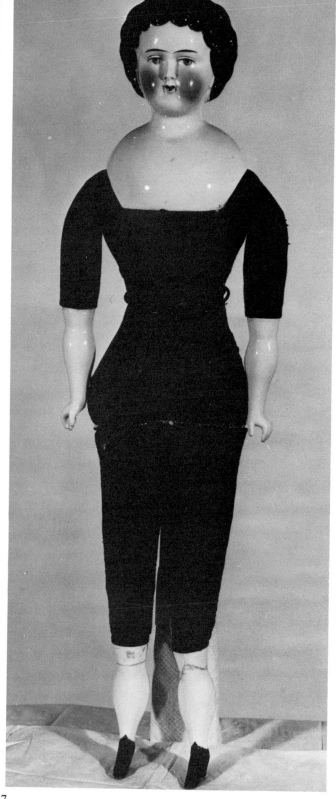

172. EXAMPLE OF EARLY CHINA DOLL WITH CHINA LIMBS

Period: Mid—19th century.

Body: Typical cloth with early china limbs.

Remarks: Illustration shows an example of a correctly assembled china doll of the mid-19th century. Note the slim type arms and flat soled shoes. Head, with dimples, unusual. *Merrill Collection.*

174. CHINA HEAD BY ROYAL COPENHAGEN
Period: 1840s.
Body: All cloth or cloth with leather arms.
Remarks: 4¼" (10.9cm) fine and early china doll head with creamy complexion and painted features. Brown molded hair, with center part, is drawn over exposed ears to large, coiled bun in back. Behind each ear falls a single, brushmarked curl. Underside of shoulder has three vertical lines and dot in blue (see insert); a mark of the Royal Copenhagen Manufactory of Denmark. Dolls by this maker are extremely rare. *Merrill Collection.*

BELOW:
175. CHINA HEAD BY JACOB PETIT
Period: Second quarter of 19th century.
Body: All cloth; cloth with leather arms; or all leather.
Remarks: Deep pink-toned porcelain doll head; 7" (17.8cm) in height. Rare and early. Has dark blue painted eyes with upper lashes only; brown painted pate to receive hair wig. Marked (in blue) under glaze on inside of left shoulders: "10 10 J P." Made in France by Jacob Petit who obtained, in 1843, a patent for making porcelain doll heads.

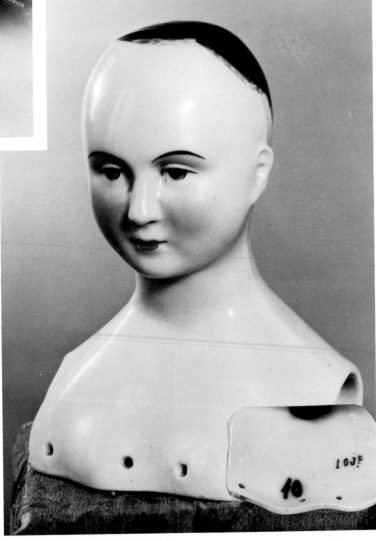

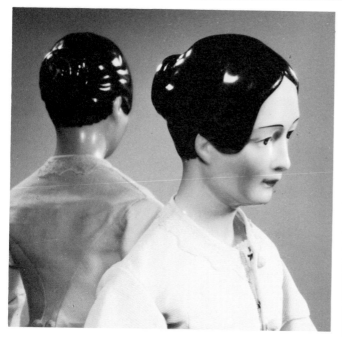

176. EARLY, BROWN HAIRED CHINA DOLL
Period: 1840.
Body: Cloth with china limbs.
Remarks: Sensitively modeled 19½" (49.6cm) china doll with a portrait like quality to its pink toned china head. An aristocratic lady with slim face, long neck and deep shoulders. Eyes are painted blue and ears exposed. Center parted brown hair is drawn to a braided bun in back. Brushmarks edge hair line at nape of neck. Unusual.

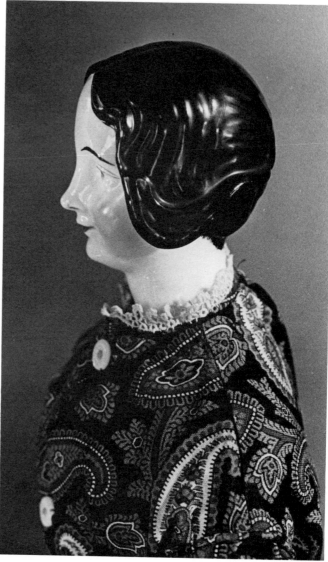

178. K.P.M. MARKED CHINA DOLL BY KÖNIGLICHE PORZELLAN MANUFACTUR OF BERLIN
Period: Mid-19th century.
Body: Cloth with leather arms.
Remarks: 20" (50.8cm) doll whose marked (K.P.M.) head is of white rather than the usual pink toned china used by this firm. Of distinctive mold and expression, the head has painted features and its brown molded hair, minus usual bun in back, is brushmarked at back and loosely waved over ears in front. *Merrill Collection.*

LEFT:
177. LADY CHINA DOLL - BY K.P.M.
Period: Mid-19th century.
Body: Cloth with leather arms.
Remarks: Rare and beautiful pink-toned china head with mark of K.P.M. (Berlin) porcelain factory. Painted blue eyes and brown hair. Hair is molded in loops over ears and drawn to braided bun in back. Note long, slender neck and extremely well modeled contours of bust and shoulders. *Collection of Mrs. J. Newton Barrows.*

179. CHINA DOLL HEAD MARKED "K.P.M."
Period: Mid-19th century.
Body: Cloth with leather arms.
Remarks: 4½" (11.5cm) china head of a lady doll bearing two marks of the Königliche Porzellan Manufactur of Berlin - red orb and blue eagle over initials K.P.M. The head is pink toned and the black molded hair is minus a bun in back which is not too unusual with this particular head. Dolls bearing the marks of fine porcelain manufacturers such as K.P.M. are highly regarded and extremely scarce. *Merrill Collection.*

180. BROWN HAIR CHINA DOLL - MARKED "K.P.M."
Period: Mid-19th century.
Body: Cloth with leather arms.
Remarks: 5" (12.7cm) head of lady doll bearing, on underside of shoulder, the red orb mark of the Königliche Porzellan Manufactur of Berlin over the initials K.P.M. An expressive, early porcelain head, deep pink in tone, and having hair painted brown rather than the usual black. Molded hair is minus the usual bun in back as is the case with head shown on page 89, Illustration 178. *Merrill Collection.*

181. 1840-1850 PERIOD BROWN HAIRED CHINA DOLL
Period: Mid-19th century.
Body: Cloth with leather arms.
Remarks: 21" (53.3cm) pink molded china doll with brown molded hair drawn under exposed ears to bun in back. In rare instances, brown haired dolls similar to the one shown have been found with the marks of the Royal Copenhagen Manufactory of Denmark. This type head may also be found in papier mâché. *Merrill Collection.*

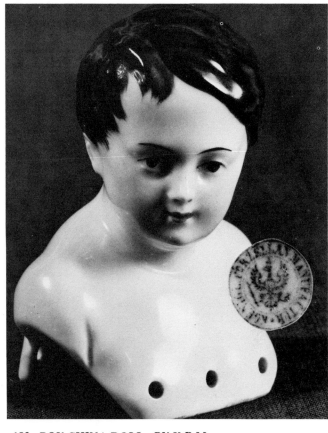

182. BOY CHINA DOLL - BY K.P.M.
Period: Mid-19th century.
Body: Cloth with leather arms.
Remarks: Rare china boy doll with mark of the Königliche Porzellan Manufactur, the state owned porcelain factory at Berlin, beneath glaze on underside of shoulder (see insert). Referred to as K.P.M. An exquisite doll with well shaped contours, molded hair with brushmarks, deep blue painted eyes.

183. BOY CHINA DOLL - MARKED K.P.M.
Period: Mid-19th century.
Body: Cloth with leather arms.
Remarks: 21½" (54.6cm) pink-toned china boy doll with brown molded hair and blue painted eyes. Under the glaze, on inside of front shoulder, are two marks of the Königliche Porzellan Manufactur of Berlin: brown crossed swords and dark blue eagle over initials K.P.M. Other than hair style, note resemblance to K.P.M. doll shown on page 89.

WOODFORD & MERRILL'S
FANCY STORE,
309 Washington Street,
BOSTON.

185A.   185B.

OPPOSITE PAGE:

184. BOY CHINA DOLL - MARKED K.P.M.
Period: Mid-19th century.
Body: Cloth with leather arms.
Remarks: 19" (48.3cm) boy doll whose pink-toned china head bears the red orb and blue eagle marks of Königliche Porzellan Manufactur of Berlin (K.P.M.) Sticker on chest printed: "From Woodford & Merrill's//Fancy Store//309 Washington Street//Boston." Of particular interest is his complete, finely made, inner and outer clothing. *Colletion of The Essex Institute, Salem, Massachusetts.*

185A. EARLY CHINA DOLL WITH LEATHER BODY
Period: Mid-19th century.
Body: Pink leather.
Remarks: Doll with boyish hairdo; brushmarks around face; painted eyes. China is pink in tone with high lustre.

185B. PAIR OF SHELL DRESSED DOLLS WITH HEADS OF CHINA
Period: Mid-19th century.
Body: Cloth with china limbs.
Remarks: 6¾" (17.2cm) and 6" (15.2cm) pair of early china headed dolls intricately dressed in shells. They have brushmarked hair and the man's complexion is pink toned. Note that hands and fingers of man are covered with shells - highly unusual. It is rare to find shell dolls with heads of china. Most have wooden or plaster heads on jointed wooden bodies. They were shell dolls dressed in Brittany. Shell dolls: *Merrill Collection.*

186. BOY CHINA DOLL
Period: Mid-19th century.
Body: Cloth with leather arms.
Remarks: The china head of this 10" (25.4cm) boy is very white in tone. Features, including light blue eyes, are delicately painted. Smooth black hair is deeply brushmarked. Boy dolls are uncommon.

186.

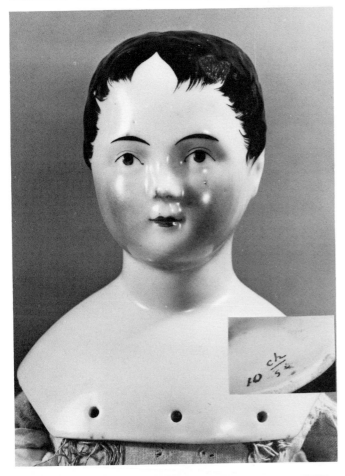

187. CHINA BOY DOLL WITH BRUSHMARKED HAIR
Period: 1840-1850.
Body: Cloth with elbow length kid-covered
  wooden arms.
Remarks: Slim faced doll with boyish hairdo; completely brushmarked around head. China is pink in tone with highly colored cheeks. Painted features include blue eyes. Note black markings on under side of shoulders (see insert). Occasionally found on early china heads.

189. ROYAL COPENHAGEN CHINA HEAD ON PEGGED WOODEN BODY
Period: Second quarter of 19th century.
Remarks: 16½" (41.9cm) doll with china head and limbs on articulated, pegged-wooden body (unusual as this type doll is generally small in size). Super-rare because of flesh tinted head, brown hair and mark (3 vertical lines with dot) of the Royal Copenhagen Manufactory. A highly glazed, beautifully modeled head with painted blue eyes. Hair, with white center part, is drawn around exposed ears to coil in back. Both china hands are in relaxed, extended position. China boots, with slight heels are painted black with yellow soles.

LEFT:
188. BOY CHINA DOLL
Period: Mid-19th century.
Body: Cloth with leather arms.
Remarks: 19½" (49.6cm) china headed boy doll with well defined black molded hair; blue painted eyes. Unusual. Boy dolls are of much interest due to relative scarcity. *Collection of Mrs. Fidelia Lence.*

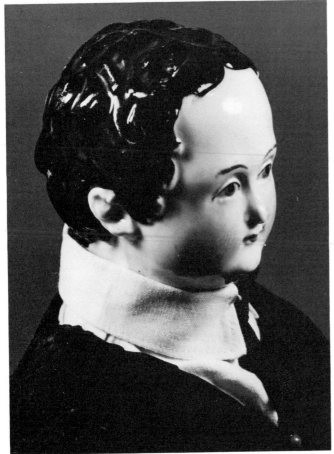

190. CHINA DOLLS WITH PEGGED WOODEN BODIES
Period: Second quarter of 19th century.
Body: Wooden pegged with china limbs.
Remarks: Two examples of china headed dolls on pegged-wooden bodies with china limbs.
Left: 5" (12.7cm) doll whose pink toned head is mounted on a dowel projecting from body.
Right: 7¼" (18.5cm) doll whose china head is attached to body by wooden pegs; two in front, one in back. Hairdo of 1840 period, exposed ears with braided bun in back. *Merrill Collection.*

BELOW LEFT:
191. CHINA DOLL WITH PEGGED WOODEN BODY
Period: Second quarter of 19th century.
Body: Wooden pegged with china limbs.
Remarks: 16" (40.6cm) china headed doll on articulated pegged-wooden body with china limbs. A deep shouldered, beautifully modeled head with painted blue eyes; black hair with nine long vertical curls. Unusually large size.

   Note: left hand in relaxed, extended position; right one clenched with hole pierced from front to back. China slippers, with slight heels, are painted vermillion with yellow soles. *Merrill Collection.*

BELOW RIGHT:
192. CHINA DOLL WITH PEGGED WOODEN BODY
Period: Second quarter of 19th century.
Body: Pegged wooden with china limbs.
Remarks: 10½" (26.7cm) well proportioned, high quality doll whose pink-toned china head; pegged to a wooden body; has painted blue eyes; highly colored cheeks. Black molded hair, drawn behind exposed ears, falls low on shoulders in five long curls. A rare doll dressed in early gauze costume, trimmed in gold colored, metallic lace. *Merrill Collection.*

193. CHINA DOLL REPRESENTING YOUNG MAN
Period: 1840s.
Body: Cloth with china limbs.
Remarks: Rare and early 25" (63.5cm) man doll whose creamy toned china head has slim face, long neck and deep shoulders. Brushmarked hair, with side part, is black with brown overtones. Doll has a portrait like quality and is original in all respects. Finely detailed costume includes plush collared coat and striped velvet pants.

194. YOUNG MAN CHINA DOLL - CREDITED TO MEISSEN
Period: Mid-19th century.
Body: Cloth with leather arms.
Remarks: Delicately tinted, 18" (45.7cm) man doll whose highly glazed, white-toned china head has blue painted eyes; feathered brows; pink tinted cheeks and ears. Finely drawn, light brown hair lines give further definition to the molded blonde hair. A rare head - credited to Meissen. *Collection of The Rhode Island Historical Society, Providence, Rhode Island.*

195. CHINA DOLL WITH MOLDED BACK COMB IN TORTOISE SHELL COLORS
Period: Circa 1840.
Body: Cloth with china limbs.
Remarks: Rare and early 25" (63.5cm) doll with deep shouldered, pink-toned china head. Black molded hair, with center part, is smoothly looped over ears in front. In back, a large, molded "tortoise shell" comb holds a double braided coronet in place.

196. CHINA DOLL WITH UNCOLORED, MOLDED BACK COMB
Period: Circa 1840.
Body: Cloth with leather arms.
Remarks: 6" (15.2cm) china doll head with painted features, highly colored cheeks. Black molded hair, with center part, is smoothly looped over ears in front. In back, an uncolored comb is encircled by a single braided coil.

197. BROWN HAIRED AND BROWN EYED CHINA DOLL
Period: Mid-19th century.
Body: Cloth with china limbs.
Remarks: 24" (61cm) early china doll with two rare features; dark brown hair and brown painted eyes. Center parted hair, in soft waves, is looped over ears and drawn to large braided bun in back.

LEFT:
198. PINK-TONED CHINA DOLL WITH LONG VERTICAL CURLS

Period: Circa 1840.
Body: Cloth with leather arms.
Remarks: Early pink-toned china, 10" (25.4cm) in height, whose long, vertical curls end in undercut ledge. The head, with long, sloping shoulders, has painted blue eyes; black hair. Occasionally found with brown painted eyes. This particular mold is sometimes referred to as *Sophia Smith. Merrill Collection.*

199. BLACK HAIRED CHINA OF UNUSUAL MOLD

Period: Second quarter of 19th century.
Body: Cloth with wrist-length china hands; sewn-on leather boots.
Remarks: 21" (53.3cm) rare doll with Germanic featured china head. Mold believed to have been made for German domestic trade rather than for export. Creamy toned face has pale blue painted eyes; rosy tinted cheeks and chin. Black molded hairdo has fifteen curls ending in sharp ledge just below ears. Wears an elaborate and original Black Forest costume. Doll purchased in Germany.

200. PINK-TONED CHINA DOLL WITH LONG VERTICAL CURLS - VARIANT

Period: Mid-19th century.
Body: Cloth with china arms.
Remarks: 22" (55.9cm) deep pink-toned china doll of unusual mold. The highly glazed head has painted blue eyes (highlighted); nostrils indicated by red circles; thirteen vertical curls ending in undercut ledge. A large doll for her type.

201. CHINA DOLL WITH DIMPLES

Period: Mid-19th century.

Body: Cloth with leather arms; or cloth with china limbs.

Remarks: Unusual 20" (50.8cm) china doll with dimples; pink-toned complexion; blue painted eyes; and smiling mouth. See page 87 for body. *Merrill Collection.*

202. PINK-TONED CHINA DOLL

Period: Mid-19th century.

Body: Cloth with leather arms; or cloth with china limbs.

Remarks: Pink-toned china doll having painted blue eyes and high coloring. Plain hairdo has eleven well modeled vertical curls. *Merrill Collection.*

203. PINK-TONED CHINA DOLL WITH MATCHING CHINA ARMS AND BAREFOOT LEGS

Period: Mid-19th century.

Body: Combination cloth and leather with china limbs.

Remarks: Several features denoting a rare doll are combined in this 12" (30.5cm) pink-toned china doll. Note seldom seen bare feet. She is beautifully modeled - even to the round of throat and contours of back shoulders. The turned head, on unusually deep shoulders, has painted brown eyes and black hair. Under the glaze, on inside of shoulders, is marked the letter "G" in black script. Possibly the mark of the Gera factory of Germany which was originally owned by the Greiner family.

204. CHINA DOLL WITH HIGH FOREHEAD
Period: Mid-19th century.
Body: Cloth with leather arms; or cloth with china
   limbs.
Remarks: Early china doll with high forehead and sloping
shoulders. *Merrill Collection.*

BELOW:
206. CHINA DOLL IN ORIGINAL QUAKER DRESS
Period: Mid-19th century.
Body: Cloth with red leather arms.
Remarks: 20" (50.8cm) doll in original, extremely well made
Quaker garb. Dress and bonnet are of gray sateen, underwear
and kerchief of white linen. The pink-toned china head, with blue
painted eyes and black molded hair, is typical of the period.
Collection of The Essex Institute, Salem, Massachusetts.

205. CHINA DOLL WITH DEEP PINK COMPLEXION
Period: Mid-19th century.
Body: Cloth with leather arms.
Remarks: 21" (53.3cm) doll whose deep pink-toned china head
has painted blue eyes, slightly parted lips and highly colored
cheeks. Smoothly molded hair, with white center part, ends in
fourteen well modeled vertical curls. Deep pink-toned complexions
on china dolls are considered exceptional. *Collection of Lorna S.
Lieberman.*

207. DOLL AND WARDROBE OF 1854

Period: 1854.

Body: Cloth with leather arms.

Remarks: The pink-toned china head of this 22" (55.9cm) doll has center parted black hair with twelve vertical curls, blue painted eyes and rosy cheeks. Doll and wardrobe were a birthday gift to a child in 1854. A note to this effect still accompanies the doll. The clothing is of great interest as it illustrates in detail what was worn by girls of that period. The doll wears a brown printed cotton dress; faded red stockings and pale green shoes. Underwear consists of a chemise, hemstitched and tucked petticoats and drawers. Additional clothing shown:

Top (from left to right): white cotton nightcap; straw hat with ribbon trim; wool cape trimmed with lace and ribbon bands; checked silk apron; cotton print dress with puffed sleeves.

Bottom (from left to right): cotton nightgown; wool, polka dotted dress; white cross-bar-red cotton cape with tasselled hood. *Merrill Collection.*

The following note came with Selina Little's doll.
Boston, Mass. Nov. 27, 1854

My Dear Little Fanny

The bearer of this note, Mable Lee, is an orphan, whom your cousins, the Hoopers, found one day. She was very naked, though not very poor, as her plumpness will show. So they concluded to bring her to our house and make her a suit of clothes; after doing this, they could think of no home so agreeable to the young girl, as your own dear mother's house in Greenwood Avenue.

She is not to take the place of the other little girl there, but to help her pass her time agreeably. Perhaps when it is cloudy and cold, she will make sunshine for a little while. If she fails to do this, I advise if she is naughty or cross at all, that you put her into some dark corner or drawer till she is herself again.

May your birthdays all be happy ones, my dear!
From your loving Aunt,
Priscilla Langdon Hooper

208. CHINA DOLL WITH BROWN EYES
Period: Mid-19th century.
Body: Cloth with cloth or leather arms.
Remarks: Pink-toned china doll with brown painted eyes; exposed ears; feathered eyebrows; painted lashes. Very fine modeling. Sloping shoulders indicative of an early doll. *Merrill Collection.*

209. GLASS EYED CHINA DOLL MARKED INSIDE BACK SHOULDERS
Period: Mid-19th century.
Body: Cloth with leather arms.
Remarks: 16½" (41.9cm) pink-toned china doll with set-in black pupilless glass eyes; painted upper and lower lashes; exposed ears. Under the glaze, on inside of back shoulders, is marked the letter "G" in black script - plus incised number 106. See pages 99 and 106 for china dolls with identical "G" mark. *Merrill Collection.*

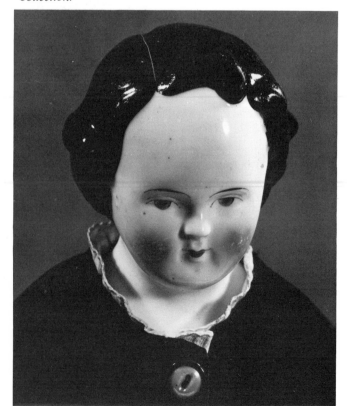

210. CHINA DOLL WITH SIDE PARTED HAIR
Period: Mid-19th century.
Body: Cloth with leather arms; or cloth with china limbs.
Remarks: 21" (53.3cm) china headed doll with dark blue painted eyes; rosy cheeks. Dressed as a boy, in brown, velvet jacket and trousers. *Unusual feature:* hair parted on side rather than in middle. *Merrill Collection.*

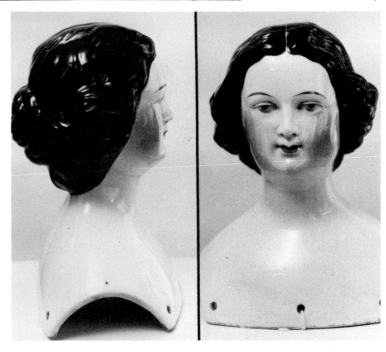

211. CHINA DOLL WITH CURLS LOW ON SHOULDERS
Period: Mid-19th century.
Body: Cloth with leather arms.
Remarks: 11" (27.9cm) pink-toned china doll whose hairdo, exposing ears, has eight long curls falling low on shoulders. Indicative of early doll. Arms are made of pink leather rather than the usual white. *Merrill Collection.*

212. "JENNY LIND" CHINA HEAD - VARIANT
Period: Mid-19th century.
Body: Cloth with leather arms.
Remarks: Front and side view of a highly glazed so-called *Jenny Lind* china head - 6" (15.2cm) in height. Differs from usual in its finely detailed modeling. Wavy hair, brushmarked at sides, is drawn to bun in back. Painting of face includes rosy cheeks, blue eyes, brown eyebrows.

213. "JENNY LIND" CHINA DOLL
Period: Mid-19th century.
Body: Cloth with leather arms.
Remarks: So-called *Jenny Lind* china doll. Found in several sizes. Nice modeling of features. Black molded hairdo is drawn to pug in back.

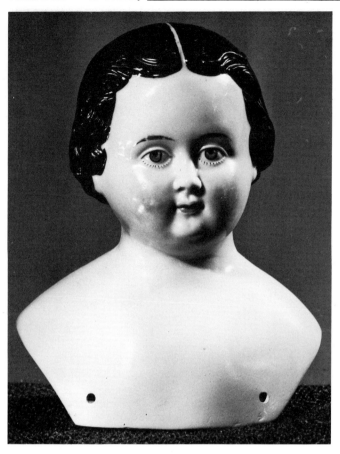

214. CHINA DOLL WITH PAINTED EYELASHES
Period: Mid-19th century.
Body: Cloth with leather arms.
Remarks: Doll with fine modeling and detail. *Unusual feature:* painted lower lashes - not commonly found on china dolls. Blue painted eyes.

215. BROWN EYED CHINA DOLL WITH UNUSUAL HAIR LINE
Period: Mid-19th century.
Body: All cloth.
Remarks: 16" (40.6cm) doll whose fine china head has brown painted eyes with lower lashes only; exposed ears; back swept hair with vertical curls ringing neck. Painting of hair line around face is very unusual. *Collection of Mrs. Fidelia Lence.*

216. MID-19th CENTURY CHINA DOLL
Period: Mid-19th century.
Body: Cloth with leather arms.
Remarks: 23" (58.4cm) early china doll with brown painted eyes; exposed ears; ten vertical curls ringing head. The mold of this china head, even to number of curls (10), is practically identical to that of the Greiner patented head of papier mâché. *Courtesy of Mrs. Russell E. Smith.*

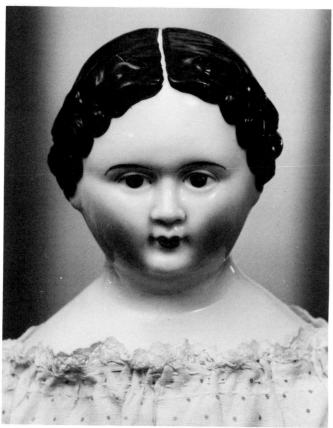

217. BROWN EYED CHINA DOLL
Period: Mid-19th century.
Body: All cloth.
Remarks: 16" (40.6cm) doll whose china head has highlighted, brown painted eyes. Considered unusual in a china doll. *Merrill Collection.*

218. GLASS-EYED CHINA DOLL
Period: Mid-19th century.
Body: Cloth with leather arms.
Remarks: 21" (53.3cm) doll with set-in brown glass eyes; well modeled features; fine detail; painted lashes. Considered rare. *Merrill Collection.*

219. WIGGED, GLASS EYED CHINA DOLL MARKED INSIDE BACK SHOULDERS

Period: Mid-19th century.
Body: Cloth with leather arms.
Remarks: 19" (48.3cm) pink-toned china doll with set-in blue glass eyes; painted upper and lower lashes; slit in head to receive wig. Under the glaze, on inside of back shoulders, is marked the letter "G" in black script (see insert).

220. WIGGED, GLASS EYED CHINA DOLL - VARIANT

Period: Mid-19th century.
Body: Cloth with leather arms.
Remarks: 13" (33cm) doll whose china head is glazed on the face and shoulders only; the glaze following an incised hair line. Unglazed back of head is cut away under the wig - a feature common to bisque but rare in china dolls. She has set-in blue glass eyes, rosy cheeks and human hair wig. *Collection of The Essex Institute, Salem, Massachusetts.*

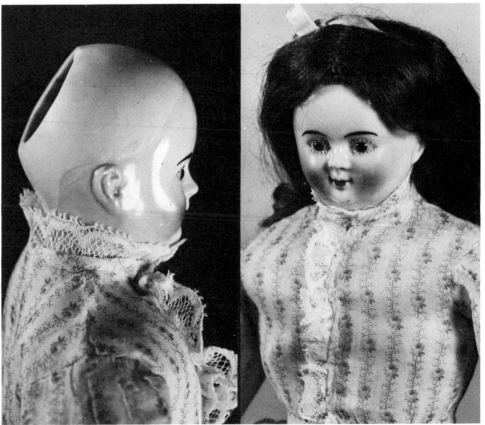

LEFT:
231. EARLY CHINA DOLL - UNMARKED
Period: Mid-19th century.
Body: All cloth.
Remarks: Rare and early unmarked doll whose deep pink-toned head is 5½" (14cm) in height. Exceptional in detail, it has highly colored cheeks, up-raised blue painted eyes. Streaked and shaded light brown hair has loosely molded curls around head. Note four rather than the usual three sew holes for attaching head to body.

232. CHINA DOLL OF UNUSUAL MOLD
Period: Mid-19th century.
Body: All leather.
Remarks: 26" (66cm) doll with deep shouldered, Germanic featured china head. Mold believed to have been made for German domestic trade rather than for export. Dimpled face, slightly pink in tone, has brightly colored cheeks, painted blue eyes. Waving, swept back hair ends in ten large, vertical curls. Wears original clothes. Bought from a family in Tubingen, Germany.

LEFT:
233. BLONDE CHINA DOLL WITH UPSWEPT HAIR
Period: Third quarter of 19th century.
Body: Cloth with leather arms; or cloth with china
limbs.
Remarks: A highly glazed china head of superior quality. The upswept molded hairdo, banded in black, has two rows of flat ringlets in front and six vertical curls in back.

LEFT:
234. CHINA DOLL WITH SNOOD
Period: Mid-19th century.
Body: Cloth with leather arms.
Remarks: Hairdo (of the period) has snood, band, and bows trimmed with gold. A fine and early 18" (45.7cm) china doll with painted blue eyes and brushmarks around face. *Merrill Collection.*

235. SMALL CHINA DOLL WITH SNOOD
Period: Mid-19th century.
Body: Cloth with china limbs.
Remarks: 5¾" (14.7cm) china doll - smaller version. Band, bows and snood of the period hairdo are touched with gold. Note larger doll has leather arms on cloth body as opposed to illustrated doll which has china limbs. Smaller dolls have great appeal for many collectors.

LEFT:
236. CHINA DOLL WITH SNOOD - VARIANT
Period: Mid-19th century.
Body: Cloth with leather arms.
Remarks: Fairly plain hairdo with snood outlined in gold. Brushmarks all around face. 15" (38cm) interesting china doll with delicate coloring and painted blue eyes. *Merrill Collection.*

237. BLONDE CHINA DOLL WITH SNOOD
Period: Third quarter of 19th century.
Body: Cloth with leather arms.
Remarks: 13" (33cm) china doll whose black snood is held in place by gold edged band, of blue with matching bows. *Merrill Collection.*

238. CHINA DOLL WITH DECORATED SNOOD
Period: Third quarter of 19th century.
Body: Cloth with china limbs.
Remarks: 18" (45.7cm) china doll with gold trimmed snood caught in decorated band of lavender lustre. Molded hair, with white center part, has fine brushmarks around face. Rare and fine. *Collection of Mrs. Louise H. Lund.*

113

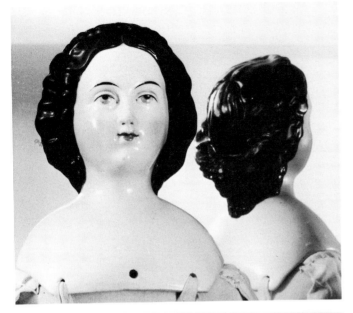

239. "JENNY LIND" TYPE CHINA DOLL

Period: Mid-19th century.
Body: Cloth with leather, or cloth with china limbs.
Remarks: White toned china head of this 23" (58.4cm) doll has blue painted eyes with molded lids. Black molded hair has flat, circular braid on top, rolls at sides, three low hanging curls at nape of neck. Shown in front and rear views.

241. BROWN EYED CHINA DOLL IN HISTORIC DRESS

Period: Mid-19th century.
Body: Cloth with leather arms.
Remarks: 19½" (49.6cm) creamy complexioned china headed doll with brown painted eyes. Brushmarked hair is drawn to a braid encircled bun in back (see insert). *Added importance:* pale blue taffeta dress is documented as "Made from dress and trimmings worn by Madam Adams (wife of John Adams, 2nd President of United States) A.D. 1785 at the Court of St. James." *Collection of The Quincy Homestead. Courtesy of The Massachusetts Society of Colonial Dames.*

240. CHINA DOLL WITH MOLDED BRAID ENCIRCLING HEAD

Period: Mid-19th century.
Body: Cloth with leather arms.
Remarks: 15" (38.1cm) slim faced; long necked; early china doll. Black molded hair has braid encircling head, held by double bow in back. *Collection of Miss Zelda Cushner.*

242. EARLY CHINA HEAD
Period: Mid-19th century.
Body: Cloth with leather arms.
Remarks: Extremely rare hairdo with single curl behind each exposed ear. Braid and comb modeled over massed curls in back. Note long neck and sloping shoulders found on early dolls.

243. CHINA DOLL WITH LOW HANGING SNOOD
Period: Mid-19th century.
Body: Cloth with leather arms, or cloth with china limbs.
Remarks: 14" (35.6cm) china headed doll with painted blue eyes, rosy cheeks. Upswept, deeply sculptured hair is caught in a low hanging snood. Brushmarks line face. Ears exposed. A finely detailed doll shown in front and rear views.

244. CHINA DOLL HEAD WITH SNOOD AND SIDE CURLS
Period: Mid-19th century.
Body: Cloth with leather arms.
Remarks: Large and beautiful 9" (22.9cm) china doll head. Long necked and finely featured. Brushmarked hair, with center part, has shoulder length curls at each side of head and tassel decorated snood in back. Snood, white tassels and matching bow show touches of gold. Note lack of sew holes for attaching head to body. Unusual and very lovely.

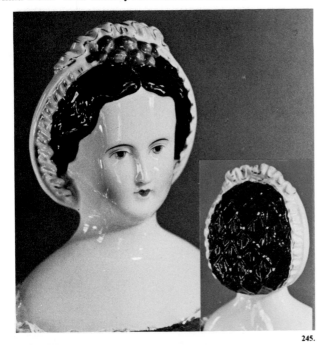

245.

246.

247.

248.

245. CHINA DOLL WITH DECORATED FRILL-TRIMMED SNOOD

Period: Mid-19th century.
Body: Cloth with china limbs.
Remarks: The china head of this 20" (50.8cm) doll has a frill-trimmed, lustre touched, grape decorated band holding a molded snood in place. Complexion is white in tone and the features, including blue eyes, are painted. This head, in smaller size, may be found on the autoperipatetikos or walking doll. *Merrill Collection.*

246. CHINA DOLL WITH HEAVY, BLACK SNOOD

Period: Mid-19th century.
Body: Cloth with leather arms.
Remarks: 6" (15.2cm) rare china head. Deeply modeled light brown hair is brushmarked at sides and dressed to expose ears. Heavily modeled black snood, with standing ruffle on top, holds center parted, side braided hair in place. Very unusual.

247. CHINA DOLL WITH FANCY HAIRDO

Period: Third quarter of 19th century.
Body: Cloth with leather arms.
Remarks: An exceptional 16" (40.6cm) brown haired china doll with blue painted eyes and elaborate hairdo. Heavy braids, on either side of face, are brought to braided flat bun in back. Molded beads, entwined at sides, add to the fancy hair styling. Fine brushmarks edge the face. May also be found with blonde hair. *Collection of Miss Zelda H. Cushner.*

248. UNUSUAL TRIMMED CHINA DOLL

Period: Mid-19th century.
Body: Cloth with leather arms.
Remarks: China doll with hairdo low on shoulders; wears molded blouse with touches of blue and lustre. *Merrill Collection.*

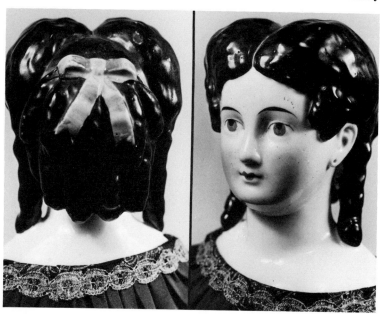

249. CHINA DOLL WITH EXCEPTIONALLY MODELED HAIR

Period: Circa 1860s.
Body: Cloth with china limbs.
Remarks: 20½" (52.1cm) doll whose china head has painted features and pierced ears. Center parted brown molded hair has two small curls above and a long, free standing curl behind each ear. Note the separation between neck and curls. Back hair is bunched in long curls; tied with a blue molded bow. Very rare. *Collection of The Margaret Woodbury Strong Museum, Rochester, New York. Photograph by Barbara W. Jendrick.*

250. CHINA DOLL WITH MOLDED BEADS IN HAIR

Period: Third quarter of 19th century.
Body: Cloth with leather arms.
Remarks: 20" (50.8cm) pink-toned china doll whose brush-marked hair, with puffs and waves, is drawn to a low bun in back of neck. Black molded beads hold side hair in place. The long slim face has painted eyes. An unusual doll - shown in front and back views.

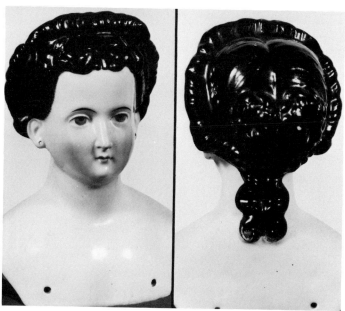

251. CHINA DOLL WITH FANCY HAIRDO

Period: Third quarter of 19th century.
Body: All cloth or cloth with leather arms.
Remarks: Large, 7½" (19.1cm) china head with finely molded features, deep blue painted eyes, pierced ears. Banded and brushmarked hair, with center part, has long rolls at top and sides, double coils in back, and two loose curls at nape of neck. *Collection of Mrs. Fidelia Lence.*

252

253

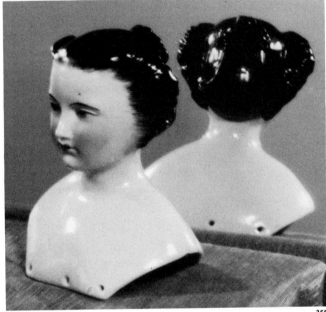

254

255

252. LARGE CHINA HEAD WITH UNCOLORED FLOWERS MOLDED IN HAIR

Period: 1840-1850.
Body: Cloth with white leather arms.
Remarks: 7" (17.8cm) long necked china doll head whose pink toned coloring tapers to white at edge of high rounded bust. Exposed ears are pierced. Two curls fall from large, loosely braided bun on back of head. Uncolored morning glories decorate sides of hair behind ears. An early, fine porcelain head - heavy in weight.

253. LARGE CHINA HEAD WITH COLORED FLOWERS IN HAIR

Period: 1840-1850.
Body: Cloth with white leather arms.
Remarks: 6" (15.2cm) china head with pink-toned complexion; painted blue eyes; brown eyebrows. Brushmarked hair, dark brown in color, has single curl falling from braided bun on back of head. Blue, pink and orange morning glories decorate both sides of hair behind the ears.

254. CHINA DOLL WITH SINGULAR COIFFURE

Period: Circa 1860s.
Body: Cloth with china limbs.
Remarks: 17" (43.2cm) adult faced china doll with unusually high coloring; blue painted eyes; long, slim neck and sloping shoulders. Brushmarked black painted hair has two gold bands on top and massed curls in back. Behind each ear, and falling low on shoulders, are two long, single curls.

255. CHINA DOLL WITH BRUSHMARKED, UPSWEPT HAIR

Period: Mid-19th century.
Body: Cloth with leather arms.
Remarks: 6" (15.2cm) china head with large, blue painted eyes and highly colored cheeks. Brushmarked, upswept hair is rolled high at sides and widely looped to molded bow in back. An early, high quality doll.

LEFT:
256. FRENCH CHINA DOLL - BRUNETTE
Period: Third quarter of 19th century.
Body: All leather.
Remarks: 17" (43.2cm) French china doll; brunette rather than the usual blonde. Rosy cheeked shoulder head has brown glass eyes; feathered brows and lashes; dark brown human hair wig. Although illegible, oval mark on body (shown in illustration) is probably that of Mlle. Rohmer of Paris. *Collection of Mrs. Fidelia Lence.*

257. CHINA DOLL - MARKED "ROHMER"
Period: Third quarter of 19th century.
Body: Leather with china arms.
Remarks: 17" (43.2cm) choice, marked, French china doll. The highly glazed head has dark blue stationary glass eyes; feathered brows and finely drawn-on lashes. Blonde mohair wig. Bears the mark of French doll maker Mlle. Rohmer of Paris.

LEFT:
258. CHINA DOLL - FRENCH TYPE
Period: Third quarter of 19th century.
Body: All leather.
Remarks: 11" (27.9cm) choice china doll. The highly glazed head has painted blue eyes; finely drawn lashes; feathered brows. Fine, blonde mohair wig covers bald china pate. Typical of French china dolls of the period. *Courtesy of The Essex Institute, Salem, Massachusetts.*

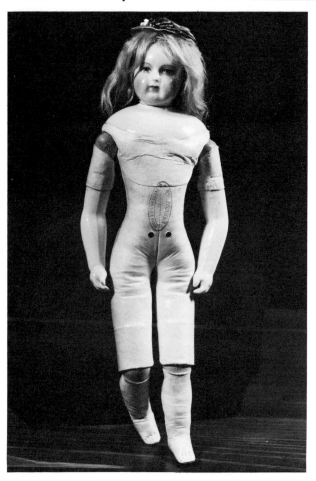

259. CHINA DOLL - MARKED "MME ROHMER"
Period: Third quarter of 19th century.
Body: Leather with wooden joints at shoulders
and knees; china arms.
Remarks: 13½" (34.3cm) china doll. Flange-necked head swivels on shoulder piece. Delicately painted features; blue painted eyes; blonde mohair wig. Doll photographed to show mark and body construction. Note two eyelet holes below mark - typical. Marked in oval: "Mme. Rohmer//Brevite SGDGA Paris." *Collection of Mrs. Elmer Morley.*

260. CHINA DOLL - MARKED ROHMER
Period: Third quarter of 19th century.
Body: Leather with pink porcelain arms; upper
arms of wood, leather covered.
Remarks: 13" (33cm) pink-toned china doll with flange necked head which swivels on matching shoulder plate. The highly glazed head is delicately colored. Painted blue eyes; light colored fur wig. Bears mark of the French doll maker Mme. Rohmer.

261. FRENCH CHINA DOLL -
UNMARKED
Period: Third quarter of 19th century.
Body: Leather with gussetted joints and
long porcelain arms.
Remarks: 18" (45.7cm) doll whose highly glazed porcelain head has blue set-in glass eyes; rosy cheeks; finely drawn brows and lashes; mohair wig. Unmarked. This type luxury doll was assembled in Paris by "Maison (Mlle. Calixte Huret) Huret" and Mme. Rohmer. *Merrill Collection.*

262. CHINA DOLL BY HURET WITH GUTTA PERCHA BODY

Period: Third quarter of 19th century.

Body: Original gutta percha body replaced by one of cloth and leather. However, doll still retains original gutta percha arms.

Remarks: 16" (40.6cm) doll by Huret of Paris. Fine china head has blue painted eyes; feathered brows; light mohair wig. Still remaining from crumpled, original body of gutta percha is the 1855 Napoleon III stamp and Huret mark. *Collection of The Rhode Island Historical Society, Providence, Rhode Island.*

263. CHINA DOLL BY HURET

Period: Third quarter of 19th century.

Body: All leather.

Remarks: 15" (38.1cm) Huret child doll with stationary shoulder head; large blue painted eyes; delicately tinted face; finely drawn brows and lashes; light mohair wig. Marked (with Napoleon III stamp - 1855): "Brevet D'Inv: SGDG//Maison Huret//Boulevard Montmarte, 22//Paris." *Collection of Mrs. Louise H. Lund.*

264. CHINA DOLL WITH MOLDED-ON PILLBOX
Period: Third quarter of 19th century.
Body: Cloth with china limbs.
Remarks: 16" (40.6cm) china doll whose white molded-on pillbox has black edging, blue top and small flowers at center front. Turned head has blue painted eyes; exposed ears and light brown, shoulder length curls. Top of the molded-on pillbox as well as the curls are matte finished. *Collection of Shirley F. Sanborn.*

265. CHINA HATTED DOLL
Period: Third quarter of 19th century.
Body: Cloth with leather arms.
Remarks: Large, well modeled hatted doll in china; 20½" (52.1cm) in height. Hat, in dull finish, has purple top and lustre decorated band. Side turned head has blue painted eyes; exposed ears; long yellow curls falling low on shoulders. Hatted dolls in china are considered rare. *Collection of Mrs. Fidelia Lence.*

122

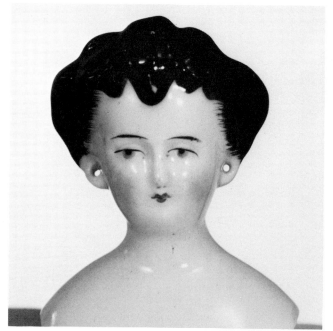

266.

267.

268.

269.

266. CHINA DOLL WITH PIERCED EARS
Period: Third quarter of 19th century.
Body: Cloth with leather arms or cloth with china
limbs.
Remarks: China lady doll with added feature - pierced ears. A
small head (3¼"[8.3cm]) with painted blue eyes and brushmarks
at sides of face. Black molded hair has cluster of curls on
forehead and massed curls on lower back of head.
267. "DAGMAR" CHINA DOLL
Period: Third quarter of 19th century.
Body: Cloth with leather arms; or cloth with china
limbs.
Remarks: Aristocratic china lady called *Dagmar*. This beautifully molded doll also comes in blonde coloring as well as
brunette. Note brushmarks around face. In addition to cluster of
curls on forehead, the hair has a band holding massed curls in
back. This same doll may also be found in parian.

268. CHINA DOLL WITH UPSWEPT HAIRDO
Period: Mid-19th century.
Body: Cloth with leather arms; or cloth with china
limbs.
Remarks: Of special interest is the rare hairdo with exposed ears
and brushmarks around face. An unusual and interesting china
doll.
269. CHINA DOLL WITH SPILL CURLS
Period: Third quarter of 19th century.
Body: Cloth with china limbs.
Remarks: 13½" (34.3cm) china doll with painted features,
including blue eyes. Massed curls, spilling low over shoulders
and forehead, are held in place on top of head by black molded
band. Ears are exposed and brushmarks edge the forehead and
temples. *Collection of Mrs. Elmer Morley.*

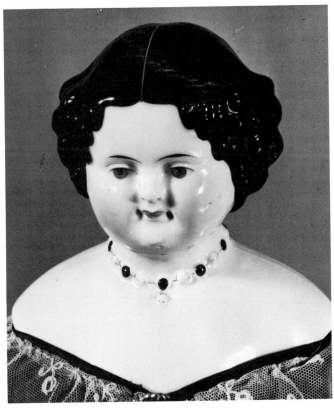

LEFT:
270. CHINA DOLL WITH HIGH FOREHEAD
Period: Third quarter of 19th century.
Body: Cloth with leather arms; or cloth with china limbs.
Remarks: Doll with very high forehead and different facial expression. Good modeling. 21" (53.3cm). *Merrill Collection.*

271. CHINA DOLL WITH MOLDED NECKLACE
Period: Mid-19th century.
Body: Cloth with leather arms.
Remarks: 21" (53.3cm) black haired china doll with painted blue eyes. Exceptional feature - molded-in necklace of plain and colored beads. Very rarely, this doll is found in parian. *Merrill Collection.*

LEFT:
272. CHINA DOLL WITH MOLDED NECKLACE - VARIANT
Period: Mid-19th century.
Body: Cloth with leather arms.
Remarks: 14" (35.6cm) china headed doll whose plain white bodice is edged by a blue and gold molded necklace. Bodice contrasts sharply with the deep pink coloring of the face and neck. A unique doll of her type. *Collection of Dorothy P. Burton.*

273.

274.

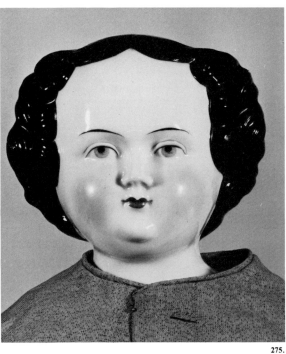

275.

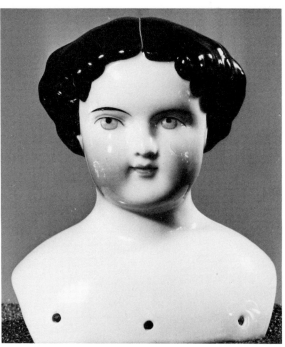

276.

273. "ADELINA PATTI" CHINA DOLL
Period: Third quarter of 19th century.
Body: Cloth with leather arms; or cloth with china
limbs.
Remarks: Extremely well modeled doll with fine detail including brushmarks around face. Ten vertical curls fall low in neck. This particular mold is referred to as *Adelina Patti* after the famous singer.
274. CHINA DOLL WITH BRUSHMARKS AT TEMPLES
Period: Third quarter of 19th century.
Body: Cloth with china limbs.
Remarks: 11" (27.9cm) all original china doll whose hair style exposes ears and is finely brushmarked at temples. Features, including blue eyes, are well painted. *Collection of Mrs. John M. Park, Jr.*

275. FLAT-HEADED BLACK HAIRED CHINA DOLL
Period: Third quarter of 19th century.
Body: Cloth with leather arms; or cloth with china
limbs.
Remarks: Doll with flat hairdo having center part. Well defined curls across back and sides of head. Nicely modeled features. Frequently found.
276. CHINA HEAD - MORE COMMON TYPE
Period: Third quarter of 19th century.
Body: Cloth with leather arms; or cloth with china
limbs.
Remarks: More commonly found black haired china doll of period. It is well modeled; has plain hairdo and blue painted eyes. These dolls may vary in modeling, coloring and size.

125

277. "DOLLY MADISON" CHINA DOLL
Period: Third quarter of 19th century.
Body: Cloth with leather arms; or cloth with china limbs.
Remarks: The name *Dolly Madison* is nomenclature for this type head; comes in various sizes. Molded hairdo has band with bow in center front. This head may be found in parian; with stationary shoulders or swivel neck. May also have molded ribbon and bow in color.

ABOVE RIGHT:
278. BLONDE "DOLLY MADISON" CHINA DOLL
Period: Third quarter of 19th century.
Body: Cloth with leather arms.
Remarks: 22" (55.9cm) china *Dolly Madison* with blonde molded curls; light brown eyebrows; blue painted eyes. This highly glazed blonde doll, with blue painted band and bow, is considered of more value than her black haired counterpart. Blonde china dolls are not as common as black haired ones. *Collection of Mrs. Edgar W. Larson.*

RIGHT:
279. "DOLLY MADISON" CHINA DOLL WITH PIERCED EARS
Period: Third quarter of 19th century.
Body: Cloth with leather arms.
Remarks: 21" (53.3cm) china doll with earrings - unusual in this mold. Highly glazed head has painted blue eyes; rosy cheeks; pierced in ears. Black molded hairdo has black band in back and bow in center front.

280. CHINA DOLL WITH HIGH HAIRDO
Period: Third quarter of 19th century.
Body: Cloth with china limbs.
Remarks: Deeply modeled, 19" (48.3cm) china doll with painted blue eyes and pierced ears. Black banded hair, with center part and four curls on forehead, is brushmarked at sides and drawn to a roll on top. High, vertical curls drop from crown of head to back of neck. *Collection of The Rhode Island Historical Society, Providence, Rhode Island.*

ABOVE RIGHT:
281. "CURLY TOP" CHINA DOLL
Period: Third quarter of 19th century.
Body: Cloth with leather arms; or cloth with china
    limbs.
Remarks: So-called *Curly Top* because of distinctive hair style. Blonde, 14" (35.6cm) in height. This doll has china limbs. *Merrill Collection.*

RIGHT:
282. CHINA DOLL WITH FLOWERS IN HAIR
Period: Last quarter of 19th century.
Body: Cloth with leather arms.
Remarks: 3½" (8.9cm) pink-toned china head with highly detailed modeling. Blue painted eyes have finely drawn brows and lashes. Streaked brown hair is decorated with gold centered, blue molded flowers. A high quality, unmarked, porcelain head.

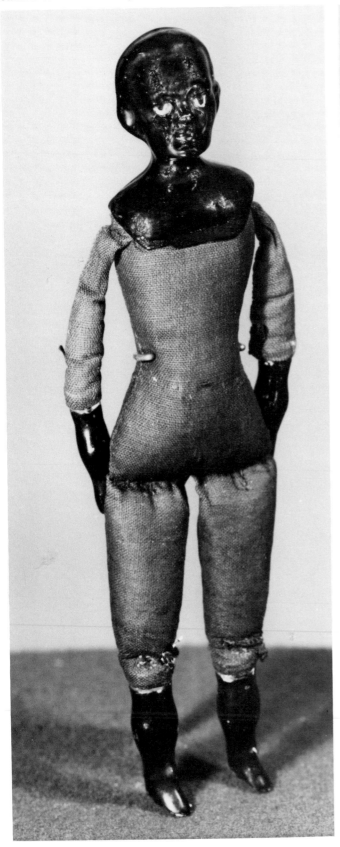

284. BLACK CHINA DOLL
Period: Late 19th century.
Body: All brown cloth.
Remarks: 16" (40.6cm) black doll - rare in china. Well modeled head with ethnic features including tightly curled hair. Whites of eyes are unglazed. Number 3 impressed on back shoulders. For earlier type doll in papier mâché see page 26. *Collection of Mrs. Neil Hobey.*

283. BLACK MAN DOLL IN CHINA
Period: Late 19th century.
Body: Brown cloth with black china limbs.
Remarks: 7" (17.8cm) black china doll with closely molded hair and ethnic features. Black dolls are rarely found in china. *Collection of Mrs. Neil Hobey.*

285. BLACK BOY DOLL IN CHINA
Period: Late 19th century.
Body: Cloth with black china limbs.
Remarks: 8½" (21.6cm) boy doll whose black china head has well modeled ethnic features. *Collection of Shirley F. Sanborn.*

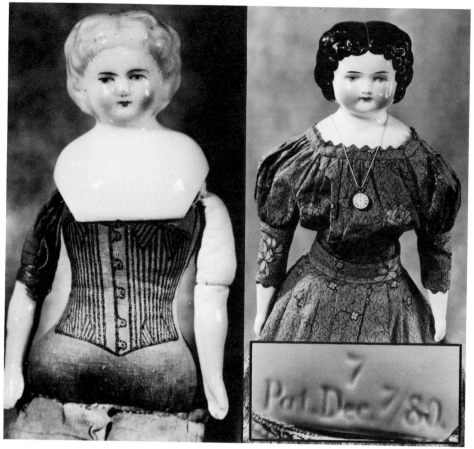

**286. CHINA DOLLS MARKED
WITH THE DOTTER PATENT
OF DEC. 7, 1880**
Period: Last quarter of the 19th
century.
Bodies: Left: cloth with printed corset.
Right: cloth with no printed corset.
Remarks: Two of the few china dolls
bearing identification. Charles T.
Dotter of Brooklyn, New York, obtained a patent in 1880 for a doll body
of cloth with a printed corset. Imported
heads on these bodies are incised on
back of shoulders: "Pat. Dec. 7/80."
Left: 10" (25.4cm) blonde china head
incised: "1//Pat. Dec. 7/80." *Collection of Jessie F. Parsons.*
Right: 21" (53.3cm) black hair china
head incised: "7//Pat. Dec. 7/80."
Because of deterioration of original
body with printed corset, this doll has
a plain cloth body. *Merrill Collection.*

**287. BROTHER AND
SISTER CHINA
DOLLS**
Period: Last quarter of
19th century.
Body: Cloth with
leather arms; or cloth
with china limbs.
Remarks: Brother and
sister china dolls of the
late 1880s. The faces are
identical in size,
modeling and coloring.
Only the hairdos vary -
the girl with hair on
forehead and over ears;
the boy with center part
and ears exposed.

288. CHINA BOY DOLL
Period: Late 19th century.
Body: Cloth with leather arms; or cloth with china limbs.
Remarks: Blonde boy china doll with hair brushed to side, exposing ears. Nicely modeled and well colored. Boy dolls in china are not common.

289. BLONDE CHINA DOLL
Period: Late 19th century.
Body: Cloth with leather arms; or cloth with china limbs.
Remarks: Blonde china head with well defined hair modeling. Similar doll may be found with dark hair.

290. CHINA DOLL IN JESTER COSTUME
Period: Last quarter of 19th century.
Body: Cloth with china limbs.
Remarks: The jester costume of this 6½" (16.5cm) boy doll has bells on cap and at waist. Flesh toned china head has painted features and brushmarked black hair. Doll and costume completely original. *Collection of Mrs. John M. Park, Jr.*

291. CHINA CLOWN WITH MOLDED CAP
Period: Late 19th century.
Body: Cloth with leather arms.
Remarks: 16" (40.6cm) china headed clown with molded-on cap decorated in red and blue. Rosy cheeked face has brown mustache and goatee, blonde hair, blue painted eyes. Silk costume, with white ruff, is belted and braid trimmed. Wears blue leather boots. *Colletion of Mrs. Fidelia Lence.*

290.

291.

292. BLONDE CHINA DOLL WITH BANGS
Period: Late 19th century.
Body: Cloth with leather arms; or cloth with china limbs.
Remarks: Finely modeled 22" (55.9cm) china doll with blonde hair in bangs. May also be found with black hair. Similar dolls were made in parian ware.

294. DOLL WITH DARK HAIR IN BANGS
Period: Late 19th century.
Body: Cloth with leather arms; or cloth with china limbs.

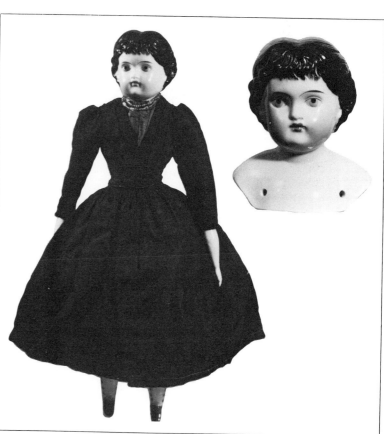

293. CHINA HEAD DOLL WITH BANGS
Period: Last half of 19th century.
Body: Cloth with china forearms and lower legs.
Remarks: 16" (40.6cm) doll with finely molded head with blue painted eyes. Nicely detailed brushmarks on molded bangs. Molded and decorated boots with low heels. *Merrill Collection.*

295. BRUNETTE CHINA DOLL WITH BANGS
Period: Late 19th century.
Body: Cloth with leather arms; or cloth with china limbs.
Remarks: Small, 3½" (8.9cm) china doll head. Short hair style has bangs on forehead, horizontal curls at sides, waves in back. White complexioned head has painted blue eyes, one stroke brows. Incised "Germany" on back shoulders. Late china heads are occasionally found so marked. Dolls with bangs, in both bisque and china, were popular in late 19th and early 20th century. *Collection of Mrs. Gladys Fuller.*

BELOW LEFT:
296. MARKED CHINA HEAD MADE BY KLING
Period: Late 19th century.
Body: Cloth with leather arms; or cloth with china limbs.
Remarks: China doll bearing the mark "Bell with letter K" of the Kling firm of Germany on back of shoulder. May be found with blonde or black molded hair. One of the few china dolls bearing identification marks. *Merrill Collection.*

BELOW RIGHT:
297. BLONDE CHINA DOLL
Period: Late 19th century.
Body: Cloth with leather arms; or cloth with china limbs.
Remarks: Nicely colored blonde head with all over curls. More unusual because it is a blonde. Also comes in black hair.

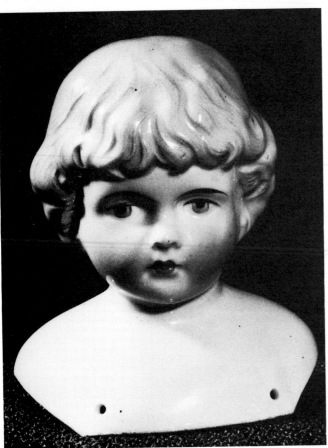

132

298. GROUP OF CHINA "FROZEN CHARLOTTES"
Period: Last half of 19th and early 20th century.
Body: Ceramic; all in one piece.
Remarks: A pillar doll, dubbed *Frozen Charlotte* after heroine of a New England folk ballad. These dolls are found in many sizes; blonde and brunette; dressed and undressed; with great variation as to quality and detail. They were made in china, bisque and parian. Group shown are from 1" (2.5cm) to 4½" (11.5cm) in height. *Merrill Collection.*

299. ALL CHINA DOLL - JOINTED
Period: Last half of 19th century.
Remarks: 8½" (21.6cm) all china doll; elastic strung; jointed at hips and shoulders. An exceptional oddity. Not unlike *Frozen Charlotte* dolls of period except for joints. For shoulder head of identical mold see page 100. *Collection of Rhode Island School of Design.*

300. LARGE PINK-TONED PILLAR OR "FROZEN CHARLOTTE" DOLL
Period: Third quarter of 19th century.
Body: Ceramic; all in one piece.
Remarks: 11½" (29.2cm) *Pillar* or *Frozen Charlotte* china doll with brush-marked hair; brown painted eyes. Molded hair lines on back of head only. Fine detail of modeling extends to ears, fingers and toes. The doll shown is entirely finished in flesh tones. It may also be found with flesh tones on head only. Made in other sizes.

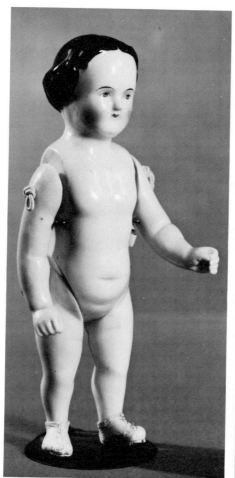

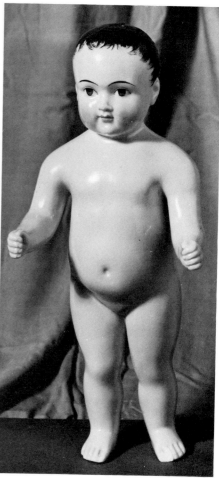

299.

300.

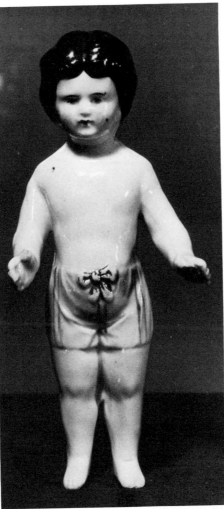

301.   302.

301. "FROZEN CHARLOTTE" WITH MOLDED-ON DRESS

Period: Third quarter of 19th century.
Body: Ceramic; all in one piece.
Remarks: 4" (10.2cm) highly glazed, black doll called *Pillar* or *Frozen Charlotte*. Blackness of head relieved by red-touched eye corners, nostrils and mouth. A well executed doll wearing white molded-on dress banded in orange at neck and sleeves. *Merrill Collection.*

302. "FROZEN CHARLOTTE" WITH MOLDED-ON UNDERPANTS

Period: Late 19th century.
Body: Ceramic; all in one piece.
Remarks: 5" (12.7cm) *Pillar* doll or *Frozen Charlotte* wearing red striped, molded-on underpants decorated with gold bow in front. Molded-on clothing adds interest to this type doll. *Collection of Mrs. Austin P. Cate.*

303. CHINA "FROZEN CHARLOTTE" WITH MOLDED-ON BONNET

Period: Last half of 19th century.
Body: Ceramic; all in one piece.
Remarks: 3½" (8.9cm) highly glazed *Frozen Charlotte* with molded-on ruffled bonnet banded and tied in pink.

304. CHINA BONNET DOLL

Period: Late 19th and early 20th century.
Body: Cloth with china limbs.
Remarks: 7¾" (19.8cm) china headed doll with molded-on poke bonnet tied under chin. Marked "5" on back of shoulder. China bonnetted dolls are unusual - most often found unglazed. *Collection of Mrs. John M. Park, Jr.*

303.   304.

Cloth Dolls - 19th Century _____

Dolls of cloth date from the very early times.

Many of great charm, made at home from this easily available material, may well be called "primitives."

Well known and quite desirable are the manufactured dolls of cloth made in the latter part of the 19th and early 20th century.

Quantities of printed dolls, to be cut out and stuffed, were on the market from the late 19th century. One of the best known being the Arnold Print Company of North Adams, Massachusetts.

305. 1820-1830 CLOTH DOLLS FROM THE AZORES
Period: 1820-1830.
Body: Molded cloth - possibly laminated.
Remarks: Three 9" (22.9cm) antique cloth dolls. Made and costumed in the Azores. Molded cloth heads have delicately embroidered features and period wigs of fine, light brown human hair. Dolls and clothing are all original, authentic and exquisitely detailed. Represented from left to right: *Lady of St. Michaels, Lady of Terceira* and *Lady of High Estate* costumed as a lay sister. Latter holds a book printed in Portuguese. *Merrill Collection.*

306. HOMEMADE CLOTH DOLL
Period: Mid-19th century.
Body: Cloth, stuffed with cotton to waist; attached
  to a sized linen conical skirt cage; no legs; arms
  are rolled cloth.
Remarks: Head is a cotton stuffed cloth form with slightly
stitched modelling to mouth, nose, eyes, and cheeks. Features
painted, the whole then covered with a fine gauze-like fabric
through which the features appear. Human hair strands are
stitched on to pate under the original lace trimmed mob cap.
Lace trimmed dotted swiss dress is also original. 8" (20.3cm) tall.
Merrill Collection.

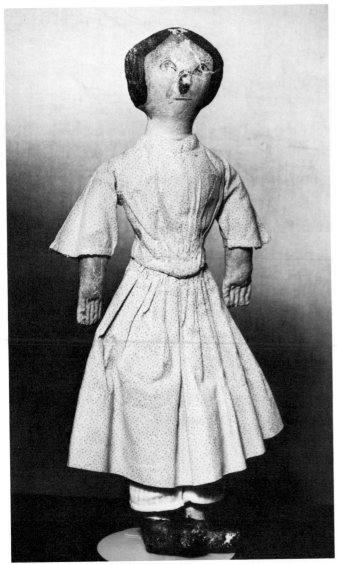

307. EARLY 19th CENTURY CLOTH DOLL
Period: Second quarter of 19th century.
Body: Cloth with fingerless kid arms and stitched-
  on ankle length shoes.
Remarks: An engaging 23" (58.4cm) homemade cloth doll with
stitched-in nose, ink-drawn eyes and mouth, human hair wig.
Wears silk bonnet, off-shoulder print dress, petticoats and ankle
length pantalettes. Early homemade cloth dolls are considered by
some as American folk art. *Collection of The Historical Society
of Old Newbury, Newburyport, Massachusetts.*

LEFT:
308. PRIMITIVE CLOTH DOLL
Period: Mid-19th century.
Body: All cloth.
Remarks: 16½" (41.9cm) early, homemade cloth doll with
simply drawn features and black painted hair. Head, shoulders,
arms and legs are all painted, the latter with black, ankle length
shoes. Wears printed cotton dress and white pantalettes. Homemade cloth dolls are becoming increasingly popular with today's
collectors. *Collection of Mrs. Elmer Morley.*

309. CLOTH DOLLS - PRIMITIVE
Period: Mid-19th century.
Body: All cloth.
Remarks: These 10½" (26.7cm) primitive dolls are homemade; from material at hand. They are crudely made and faceless. From a New Hampshire family and documented as of 1852. Primitive dolls are considered collectible. *Merrill Collection.*

310. PRIMITIVE CLOTH DOLL - GIRL
Period: 19th century.
Body: All cloth.
Remarks: 15" (38.1cm) primitive rag doll from New England. Hands and heads are painted over all. Features embroidered in red and black thread. Hair of tow. Wears original old woolen clothes and hand knit stockings. It is difficult to place the exact age of old homemade dolls. *Merrill Collection.*

311. PRIMITIVE CLOTH DOLL - BOY
Period: 19th century.
Body: Cloth with wooden feet.
Remarks: 16" (40.6cm) homemade rag doll of indeterminate age. The old, hand sewn linen body has hands with stitched fingers and well worn feet of wood. The nose is slightly shaped by stitches. Features are well drawn in black and red ink. Wears original clothing; braid-trimmed trousers; black velvet vest; white shirt; red coat; brown velvet cap. *Merrill Collection.*

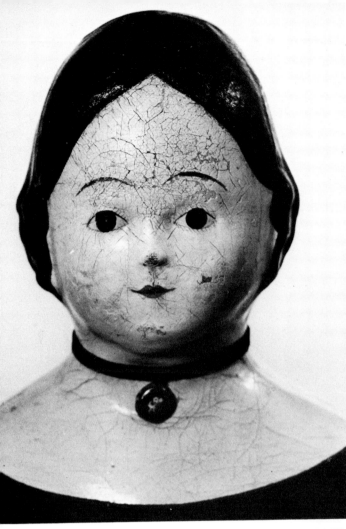

312. "ENIGMA" CLOTH DOLL
Period: Mid-19th century.
Body: Cloth with leather arms.
Remarks: The separate cloth head of this 23" (58.4cm) doll is often referred to as an *enigma* as its origin is unknown. Professionally made with well painted features, it has stiff wire rimming the shoulders to maintain their shape. Contours of the molded head are held in position by firmly packed sawdust. Infrequently found. *Merrill Collection.*

313. "ENIGMA" CLOTH DOLL WITH GLASS EYES
Period: Mid-19th century.
Body: All cloth.
Remarks: 22" (55.9cm) cloth doll often referred to as an *enigma* due to its unknown origin. Note inset glass eyes - a rarity in this particular doll. Usually found with painted eyes. *Collection of The Rhode Island Historical Society, Providence, Rhode Island.*

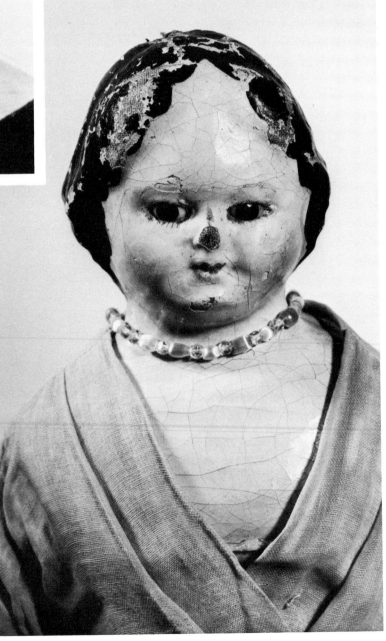

314. PRESSED CLOTH HEAD BY HAWKINS

Period: 1868-1870.

Body: Stuffed cloth with leather hands.

Remarks: The shoulderhead of this 18" (45.7cm) doll is made of sized cloth; die pressed. Painted features include black hair with red band; blue eyes; gilded, molded-on earrings and necklace. Head made and patented by George H. Hawkins of New York - September 8, 1868. It is most unusual to find a Hawkins head on a play doll. They are usually found on toys (see page 250, Illustration 558). *Merrill Collection.*

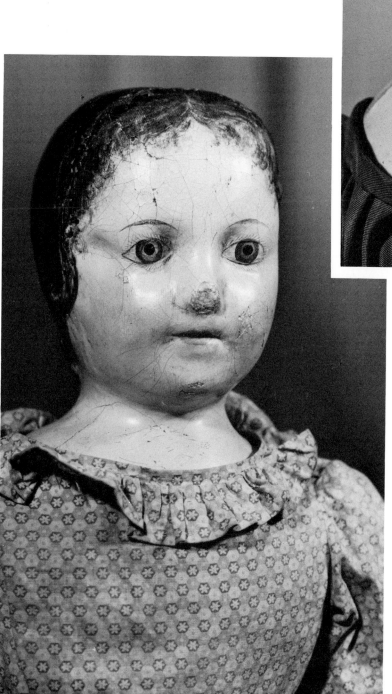

315. CLOTH DOLL - UNMARKED

Period: Last half of 19th century.

Body: All cloth; painted lower limbs.

Remarks: 25" (63.5cm) cloth doll with molded features. Commercially made, it has blue painted eyes with finely drawn lashes; brown painted and molded hair. Lower limbs are of stockinette; painted. Fingers and toes are stitched-in. Unmarked. Believed by many to be an early Izannah Walker. *Merrill Collection.*

139

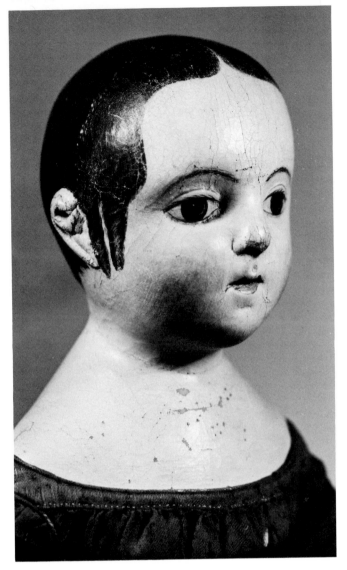

316. IZANNAH WALKER DOLL WITH PAINTED CURLS
Period: Third quarter of 19th century.
Body: All cloth including arms and bare feet.
Remarks: 24" (61cm) cloth doll with painted head, arms and legs. She has large, painted brown eyes with same color eyelashes, brows and hair. Ears are applied. Hair has center part with two vertical curls in front of each ear; brushmarked across back of neck. Not customarily found in this large size and seldom in this fine condition. *Collection of Lorna Lieberman.*

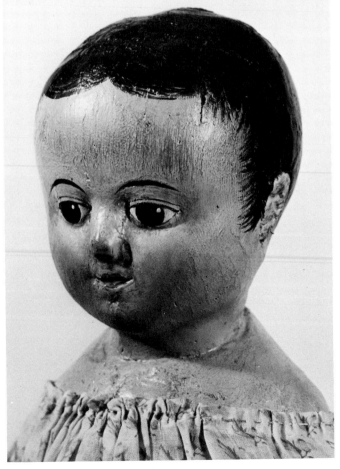

317. IZANNAH WALKER DOLL
Period: Last half of 19th century.
Body: All cloth with flesh painted, stitched-in hands and feet; or stitched-in hands and painted boots.
Remarks: 15" (38.1cm) rag doll with painted features patented by Izannah Walker of Central Falls, Rhode Island, in 1873. Said to have been made as early as 1855. Found with cork-screw curls or brushmarked hairdos. Even in poor condition, they are considered collector's items. *Merrill Collection.*

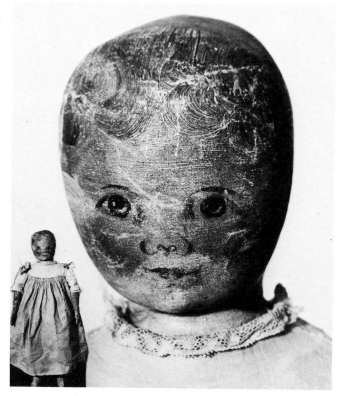

319. COLUMBIA DOLL
Period: Circa 1890.
Body: All cloth with flesh painted hands and feet; stitched fingers and toes.
Remarks: Produced by Miss Emma E. Adams of Oswego, New York. Named *The Columbia Doll*, it was accepted in 1893 by the Commission of the Chicago World's Fair where it received a diploma of merit. Both boy and girl dolls were made with blue and brown eyes; also Black. Came well dressed in sizes from 15 to 29" (38.1 to 73.7cm). Painted by artist and maker, Miss Adams. Dolls not patented, but carry a rubber stamp identification on back of body. *Collection of Mrs. Fidelia Lence.*

318. ARTISTICALLY MADE MAN DOLL
Period: Third quarter of 19th century.
Body: Cloth with oil painted arms.
Remarks: 21" (53.3cm) handmade, all-cloth man doll of great charm. Head, with oil painted features, is extremely well done. Black hair is brushmarked around face. Wears finely made blue wool suit, brocade vest, white shirt, red tie. Carries top hat. *Collection of The Rhode Island Historical Society, Providence, Rhode Island.*

320. HOMEMADE CLOTH DOLL
Period: Last half of 19th century.
Body: All cloth with painted limbs.
Remarks: 20" (50.8cm) homemade cloth doll with painted head, arms and booted legs. Head and torso are of two pieces (front and back) seamed at sides. Legs joined to body at hips. Each homemade cloth doll differs from all others - depending upon the talent and skill of the maker. Thus the delightful and great variety of this type doll. *Merrill Collection.*

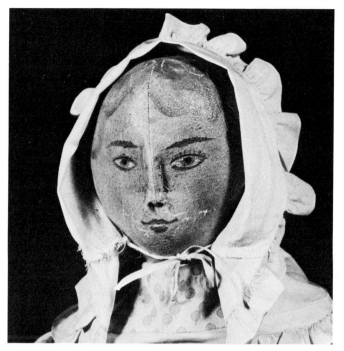

322. HOMEMADE, OIL PAINTED CLOTH DOLL
Period: Third quarter of 19th century.
Body: All cloth with painted arms.
Remarks: Quaint, 26" (66cm) cloth doll whose center seamed head, with well shaped nose, is naively painted. She wears a ruffled bonnet, printed cotton dress over hoopskirt, petticoats and pantalettes. An extremely well made doll — considered highly collectible. *Collection of The Essex Institute, Salem, Massachusetts.*

321. HOMEMADE RAG DOLL WITH NAIVELY DRAWN FEATURES
Period: Last half of 19th century.
Body: All cloth.
Remarks: Prim looking 18" (45.7cm) homemade cloth doll with naively drawn ink features and red touched lips and cheeks. Human hair wig. Wears feather stitched, brown cotton dress with red satin insert in bodice, white apron, hand knitted red stockings and natural colored straw hat. A simply-made but charming doll. *Merrill Collection.*

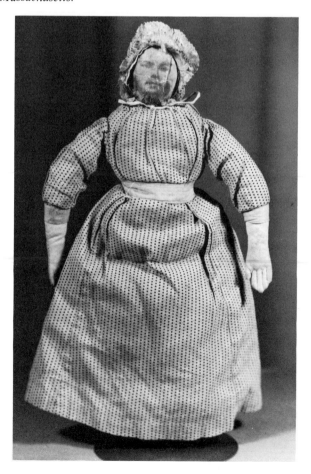

323. PRIMITIVE CLOTH DOLL
Period: Last half of 19th century.
Body: All cloth.
Remarks: Example of an early cloth doll created from materials found in the home. 12" (30.5cm) in height. Gauze covered, lithographed paper face cut from early magazine. Wears original clothes including print dress and net bonnet.

324.

325.

326.

324. HOMEMADE STOCKINETTE CLOTH DOLL
Period: Late 19th century.
Body: Cloth with fingerless cloth arms.
Remarks: A 15" (38.1cm) unsophisticated, homemade rag doll. The stockinette covered head, with embroidered features, has shoe button eyes and braided human hair wig. Hitherto given little regard, the decade of the 1970s saw a great upsurge of interest in the once lowly rag doll. *Merrill Collection.*

325. HOMEMADE BLACK STOCKINETTE DOLL
Period: Last half of 19th century.
Body: Cloth with black stockinette limbs.
Remarks: 18" (45.7cm) homemade Black doll which shows considerable skill in it's making. The stockinette head has stitch molded features; red painted lips, and black shoe buttons as irises against the painted whites of the eyes. The wig, with red ribbon bow, is of black astrakan. Earrings are brass rings.

326. HAND KNITTED DOLL
Period: Made in 1892.
Body: Knitted and stuffed.
Remarks: 16" (40.6cm) hand knitted Black doll with shaped and embroidered facial features. Wig is made of stitched-on worsted ringlets. She is gaily dressed in red, white and blue knitted costume. Instructions for like doll were printed in detail in *Harper's Bazaar* in 1892. *Collection of The Essex Institute, Salem, Massachusetts.*

327. HAND KNITTED DOLL
Period: Circa 1892.
Body: Knitted and stuffed.
Remarks: An interesting example of home knitted doll.

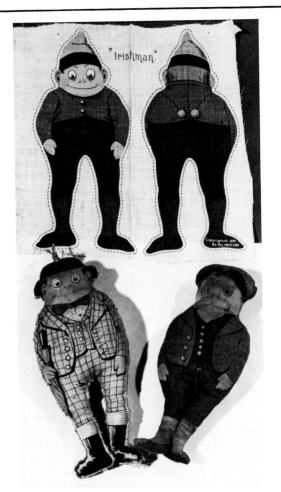

**328. ST. NICHOLAS OR SANTA CLAUS CUT-OUT
CLOTH DOLL**
Period: Patented December 28, 1886.
Body: All cloth.
Remarks: 15" (38.1cm) St. Nicholas or Santa Claus "cut-out"
doll - cut-out; stitched; stuffed at home. Right arm supports
drum and load of miscellaneous toys; left holds American flag.
Patented by E. S. Peck of Brooklyn, New York, on December 28,
1886.

ABOVE RIGHT:
329. CUT-OUT CLOTH "BROWNIE" DOLLS
Period: Copyrighted in 1892.
Remarks: Printed cloth dolls to be cut-out and stuffed.
Top row: Uncut doll.
Bottom row: Two made-up *Brownies*.
Brownie character dolls designed by Palmer Cox, illustrator and
artist, were printed on cloth by the Arnold Print Works and sold
by yard in stores. Twelve different dolls per yard — Canadian,
Chinaman, Dude, German, Highlander, Indian, Irishman, John
Bull, Policeman, Sailor, Soldier, and Uncle Sam. *Brownies* were
also made of other materials.

RIGHT:
330. TERRA COTTA "BROWNIE"
Period: Late 1890s.
Body: Terra cotta; jointed at hips and shoulders.
Remarks: 5½" (14cm) terra cotta *Brownie*, one of the many
sprites designed and copyrighted by Palmer Cox, Canadian born
illustrator, artist and author. Painted features include large,
bulgy blue eyes. Wears cloth cap and painted-on costume. Sits on
copy of *Palmer Cox's Fairy Tales* — one of thirteen Brownie
books. *Merrill Collection.*

331. UNCUT CLOTH "COLUMBIAN SAILOR DOLL"
Period: Patented January 31, 1893.
Remarks: Uncut, brightly printed cloth doll of a Columbian sailor in blue coat, red striped pants, red cap, brown boots. A commemorative doll issued by Arnold Print Works of North Adams, Massachusetts, at time of the Columbian Exposition of 1892. Cloth printed with instructions for completion of doll plus trademark, patent date and doll's name: "Columbian//Sailor Doll//1492."

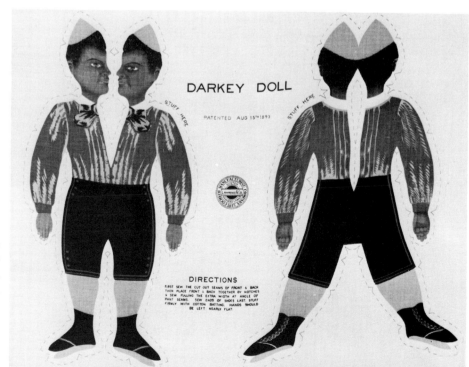

332. "DARKEY DOLL" CUT-OUT
Period: Patented August 15, 1893.
Remarks: Cloth cut-out halves to sew together and stuff with cotton. 16" (40.6cm) figures printed on cotton cloth with tan cap; red jacket; black pants; tan socks; and brown shoes. Manufactured by Cocheco Mfg. Co., and distributed by Lawrence & Co., Boston, Massachusetts. *Merrill Collection.*

ABOVE:
333. ROXANNA COLE DOLLS
Period: Last quarter of 19th century.
Remarks: Right: (white dress and bonnet): 16½" (41.9cm) cloth mask face with drawn (penned) outline of eyes and nose. Hair and shading above eyes is brown pastel pencil. Very dark brown watercolor eyes with pupil and highlight. Mouth is small and very pale pink pastel. Cloth body and original very finely sewn clothing of young child with lace and tucks and frills, etc. (We believe the five Cole dolls in Wenham's collection were *given* to Elizabeth Richards Horton whose International Doll Collection was given to the Historical Association in 1922 and was the nucleus of the Museum's doll collection.) This doll dates from 1901 and is known as *Josie June.* Made by Roxanna Elizabeth McGee Cole of Conway, Arkansas. Museum Accession #519.
Left: (blue dress, carrying broom): same size and construction as #519. Clothing is beautifully sewn and understated. Marvelous hat of pink cotton with pleated brim. Known as *Cinderella.* Museum Accession #518. *Courtesy of the Wenham Museum, Wenham, Massachusetts.*

334. ROXANNA COLE SELF-PORTRAIT
Period: Last quarter of 19th century.
Remarks: 22" (55.9cm) *Grandmother* dressed in black silk taffeta. She holds knitting and attached to her waistband hang three sewing pockets; one holding yarn, one a lace trimmed handkerchief, and one empty to hold the knitting she is holding. She wears metal rimmed glasses and has gray mohair wig. According to Museum records: "Grandma Cole - perhaps a self-portrait in this her 1,000th creation, c.1901, at age 75." Made by Roxanna Elizabeth McGee Cole of Conway, Arkansas. Museum Accession #527.

Note: All the dolls have a bump at the nose, a small shaping created by a hard ball of stuffing inserted under the cloth.
Courtesy of the Wenham Museum, Wenham, Massachusetts.

335. CLOTH DOLL BY BEECHER
Period: 1893 to 1910.
Body: All cloth; handmade.
Remarks: A stuffed rag doll originated by Mrs. Julia Jones Beecher of Elmira, New York, wife of the pastor of the Congregational church. Dolls made by sewing circle of church with all proceeds used for missionary work. Made in several sizes - up to life, in both white and Black. Constructed of old, pink silk jersey underwear with looped wool for hair. Face, hands and feet were shaped by properly placed stitched. Features hand painted.

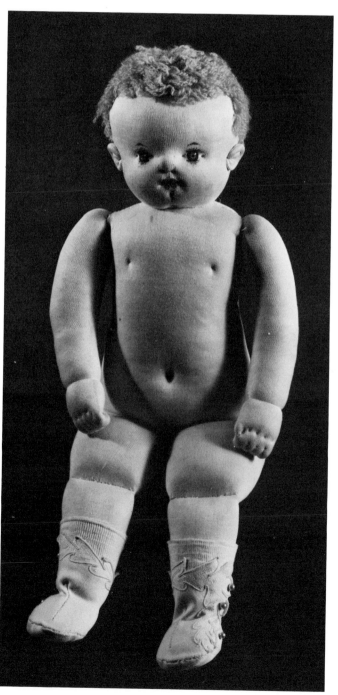

336. CLOTH DOLL BY BEECHER
Period: 1893-1910.
Body: Pink silk jersey.
Remarks: 21"(53.3cm) doll of pink silk jersey. All handmade, it has stitched-in and painted features and looped yarn hair. Shown undressed to illustrate the well made body; shaped entirely by stitches. A missionary doll, originated by Mrs. Julia Jones Beecher of Elmira, New York. *Collection of Mrs. Elmer Morley.*

147

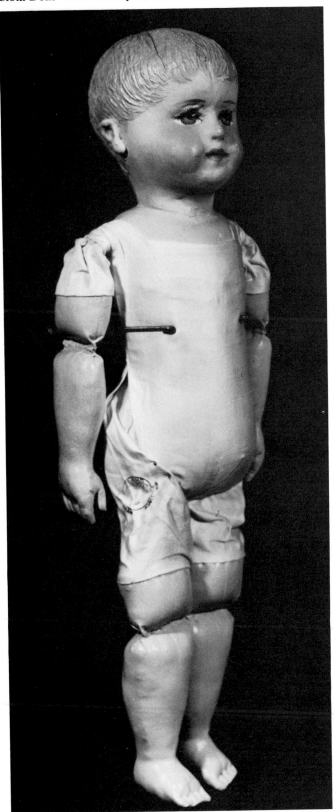

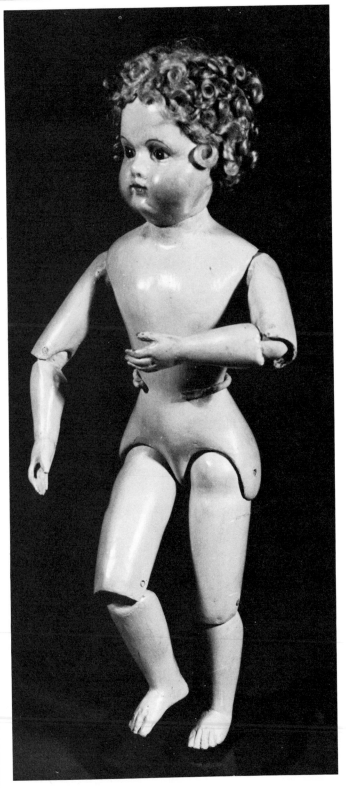

337. CHASE DOLL
Period: Late 19th and early 20th century.
Body: All cloth.
Remarks: First made by Martha Chase of Pawtucket, Rhode Island, in the 1890s. Doll of cloth with raised features, well painted in oils. Torso, covered in sateen, bears trademark on upper leg. Besides regular dolls, several characters were made. Came in various sizes.

338. LAMINATED CLOTH DOLL
Period: Last quarter of 19th century.
Body: Laminated cloth; jointed; wooden pegged.
Remarks: Extremely well modeled 19½" (49.6cm) doll made entirely of laminated cloth. The head has an almost imperceptible wash of wax — as found on the earlier French papier mâché dolls. She has set-in glass eyes; curly mohair wig. This wooden-pegged, hollow bodied doll weighs a scant fourteen ounces. Rare. *French Fashion* dolls, with heads of bisque, may occasionally be found with this type laminated body. *Merrill Collection.*

Leather Dolls - 19th Century

339. PEDLAR DOLL - ENGLISH
Period: Early 19th century.
Body: Cloth stuffed; black, knee-length composition legs.
Remarks: Rare 8" (20.3cm) leather headed pedlar doll with painted features; bead eyes; dark red wig. Wears red wool hooded-cape; painted brown cotton dress; quilted pink chintz petticoat; white neckerchief; black silk bonnet over white lace cap. "Milton Emporium" printed on box in right hand; "C. & H. White, Milton, Portsmouth" labeled on bottom of paper-covered wooden base (see insert). A great variety of pedlar dolls were made to represent the street vendors of London.

340. ALL LEATHER DOLL FROM MARTINIQUE
Period: Mid-19th century.
Body: All leather; brown.
Remarks: Unique brown all leather doll from Martinique. Painted features; black hair wig. Typical costume. Body style similar to French leather bodies of the era.

LEFT:
341. LEATHER DOLL BY DARROW
Period: Third quarter of 19th century.
Body: Cloth with leather arms.
Remarks: 17½" (44.5cm) doll with pressed leather head. Painted features include brown eyes and black molded hair. Comparatively rare. This type doll came in various sizes — mostly brunette in coloring. Made under patent granted to F. E. Darrow of Bristol, Connecticut in 1866. *Merrill Collection.*

342. LEATHER DOLL BY DARROW — BLONDE
Period: Third quarter of 19th century.
Body: Cloth with leather arms.
Remarks: 15" (38.1cm) doll with pressed leather head in blonde coloring. Unusual — most heads came as brunettes. Made by F. E. Darrow of Bristol, Connecticut who, on May 1, 1866, was granted a patent for making doll heads of pressed rawhide. Not too many have survived.

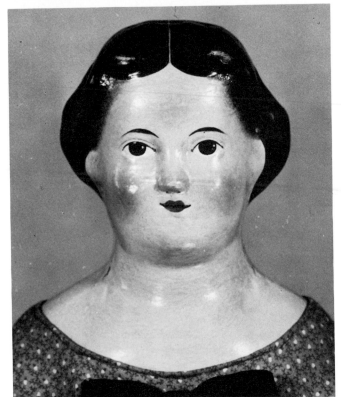

LEFT:
343. DARROW LEATHER DOLL
Period: Third quarter of 19th century.
Body: Cloth with leather arms.
Remarks: Patented head of pressed leather or rawhide. Hand painted. The painted finish is usually in poor condition on these seldom found leather dolls. When marked, the Darrow label is on front of chest. *Merrill Collection.*

344. SIOUX INDIAN DOLL

Period: Circa 1890.

Body: Cloth with wrist length leather hands.

Remarks: 11" (27.9cm) tribal doll representing a Sioux brave. Handmade by American Indians. Brown leather face, with napped finish, is applied to ethnic featured, baked clay head. Wig is of coarse, black hair. Dressed in beaded and fringed buckskin with breast plate of porcupine quills. Early, handmade Indian dolls are of interest. *Collection of Mrs. Eugenia Shorrock.*

345. CORN COB DOLL

Period: 19th century.

Body: Corn cob with attached leather arms.

Remarks: Example of homemade doll using corn cob with cloth covering. The head of this primitive is well painted. The homemade dolls, substitutes for the higher priced commercial ones, come in a great variety and have much charm.

Dolls of Rubber and Gutta Percha - 19th Century

346. DOLL WITH HEAD OF GUTTA PERCHA
Period: Mid-19th century.
Body: Cloth with leather arms.
Remarks: 20" (50.8cm) doll whose gutta percha head has painted features including brown eyes with lower lashes only. Black molded hair, with center part, has twelve vertical curls encircling head. Head is molded of thick, dark brown, gutta percha. Where unpainted, it is resinous, crystalline and brittle in appearance — unlike rubber. Dolls of gutta percha are rare. *Merrill Collection.*

Of great interest, and not often found, are early dolls of gutta percha and rubber — two very similar materials.

By 1850, dolls of soft rubber were made by B. F. Lee of New York under the Charles Goodyear patent for vulcanized rubber. Heads of this material have hardened over the years and, when found, are frequently misshapen.

Doll heads of hard rubber often bear the marks, "Goodyear's Pat. May 6, 1851 Ext. 1865" or "I. R. Comb Co." on the lower back shoulders. They were manufactured by using the hard rubber formula patented in 1851 by Nelson Goodyear, brother of Charles.

Many of the early rubber heads are unmarked.

Molded, colored decorations on these dolls are considered rare.

347. "JENNY LIND" RUBBER DOLL
Period: Mid-19th century.
Body: All rubber.
Remarks: 4" (10.2cm) all rubber doll referred to as *Jenny Lind.* A rare and interesting specimen posed as a singer. Molded costume colored to represent materials.

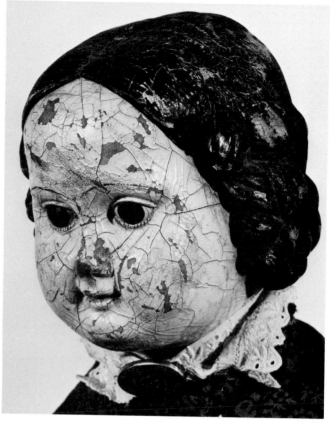

348.

350.

348. GUTTA PERCHA DOLL — WITH FLOWERS IN HAIR
Mid-19th century.
Body: Cloth with cloth or leather arms.
Remarks: Rare 13" (33cm) gutta percha doll head with colorful spray of flowers molded in black hairdo. Only lower lashes are drawn beneath the dark brown painted eyes. *Merrill Collection.*

349. EARLY RUBBER DOLL
Period: Mid-19th century.
Body: Cloth with leather arms.
Remarks: Choice, early, 20½" (52.1cm) doll with head of soft rubber. Features are painted including the typical dark eyes with lower lashes only. Early soft rubber heads, as above, are generally unmarked and were made under the patent granted to Charles Goodyear in 1844 for vulcanized rubber.

350. UNMARKED EARLY RUBBER DOLL
Period: Mid-19th century.
Body: Cloth with cloth or leather arms.
Remarks: Early, unmarked soft rubber doll with deeply sculptured curls evenly ringing her head. Many of the rubber dolls found are of this mold. Well defined features are painted including dark brown eyes with lower lashes.

349.

153

LEFT:
351. EARLY DOLL WITH RUBBER HEAD
Period: Mid-19th century.
Body: Cloth with leather arms.
Remarks: An 18" (45.7cm) well preserved, fine and early rubber headed doll with painted features. Dark eyes have lower lashes only indicated. Molded hair, with long shoulder length curls, has ringlets at sides of face. Unmarked as is usual with this type doll. Soft rubber dolls became brittle with age thus are often found in poor condition. *Collection of The Rhode Island Historical Society, Providence, Rhode Island.*

352. EARLY DOLL WITH HEAD OF RUBBER
Period: Mid-19th century.
Body: Cloth with cloth or leather arms.
Remarks: A 16½" (41.9cm) desirable and seldom seen rubber doll whose painted features include dark brown eyes with lower lashes only. Molded hair has long shoulder curls and single ringlets at temples and cheeks.

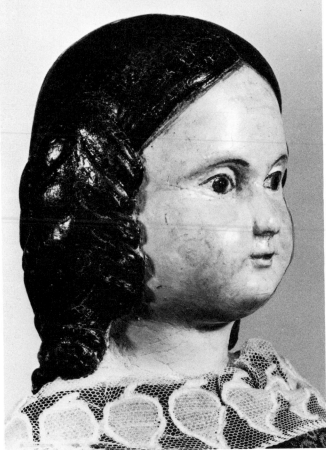

LEFT:
353. RUBBER DOLL — EARLY
Period: Mid-19th century.
Body: Cloth with cloth or leather arms.
Remarks: Early, unmarked soft rubber doll with deeply sculptured curls falling low in back of neck. A finely painted and well modeled doll.

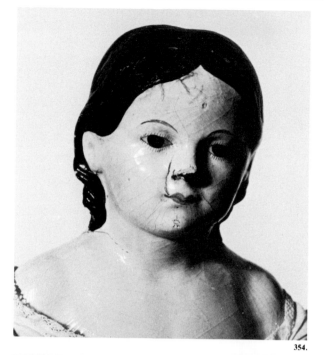

354.

355.

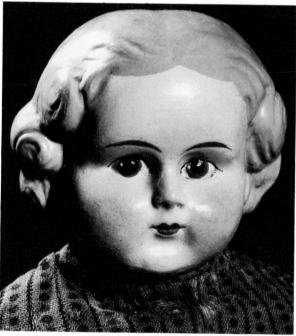

356.

357.

354. EARLY RUBBER DOLL
Period: Mid-19th century.
Body: Cloth with leather arms.
Remarks: Fine and early doll, 18½" (47cm) in height, with unmarked head of soft rubber. The face, with dark brown painted eyes, has a pensive expression. Black, center parted hair, drawn behind exposed ears, ends in back with a row of long, molded curls. *Collection of The Essex Institute, Salem, Massachusetts.*

355. EARLY RUBBER DOLL — UNMARKED
Period: Mid-19th century.
Body: All cloth.
Remarks: The well modeled and expressive face of this 27" (68.6cm) soft rubber doll has a slightly downcast expression. The large, dark, painted eyes have only lower lashes indicated. *Courtesy of The Essex Institute, Salem, Massachusetts.*

356. HARD RUBBER DOLL - MANUFACTURED BY THE INDIA RUBBER COMB COMPANY
Period: Mid-19th century.
Body: Cloth with cloth or leather arms.
Remarks: 15" (38cm) doll head of hard rubber manufactured under the 1851 patent of Nelson Goodyear. The molded hairdo is blonde, the eyes painted blue. Marked on back shoulder, "I. R. Comb. Co." Although comparatively rare, early rubber dolls, when found, are often of this particular mold. *Merrill Collection.*

357. GOODYEAR PATENTED DOLL HEAD
Period: Mid-19th century.
Body: All cloth or cloth with leather arms.
Remarks: 5½" (14cm) rubber doll head with painted blue eyes; exposed ears; swept back, molded blonde hair. Head, in back, is completely covered by large and encircling braids. Impressed on back shoulders: "Goodyear's Pat. May 6, 1851 — Ext. 1865."

155

358. UNUSUAL MOLDED DOLL

Remarks: gutta percha or rubber; head measures 6" (15.2cm) high; molded painted features; many upper and lower straight lashes; dark painted eyes without irises or highlights; band of molded flowers in hair - pinks, blues, and whites with green leaves; hair is molded into long loose curls onto neck. *Unusual feature:* molded rose with two leaves on chest; pink with green leaves. Complete doll stands 20½" (52.1cm) tall. Cloth body whose arms are oil painted. Hands have separate fingers. Leather laced boots are sewn to feet. Doll wears white contemporary dress of muslin. *Collection of Lorna Lieberman.*

359. RUBBER DOLL MADE BY NEW YORK RUBBER COMPANY

Period: 1860s.
Body: Cloth with leather arms.
Remarks: 3½" (8.9cm) rubber doll head in fine, original condition. Painted features include brown eyes. Tucked beneath front ruffle of molded-on blue bonnet is a yellow rose with matching ribbon. Made by New York Rubber Company. Shown in their catalog of 1869. Early rubber dolls are scarce — when bonnetted they are rare. Similar head seen in parian with snood, not bonnet.

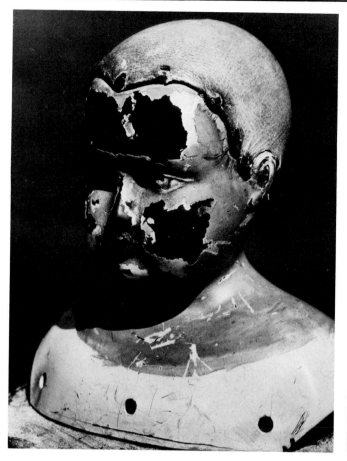

360. HARD RUBBER HEAD — WITH WIG
Period: Mid-19th century.
Body: Cloth with cloth or leather arms.
Remarks: Very thin, brittle, light weight rubber head marked on back shoulder, "Goodyear Pat. May 6, 1851 Ext. 1865." Tacked-on leather is all that remains of original fur wig. Base material is very dark on areas where paint is worn or chipped.

ABOVE RIGHT:
361. HARD RUBBER DOLL — MARKED "BRU"
Period: Circa 1880.
Body: Jointed wood and composition; elastic
   strung.
Remarks: Rare, 16" (40.6cm) doll of typical Bru mold. Well painted socket head, of thin, hard rubber, has inset blue glass eyes and mohair wig. Ears are unpierced. Marked on back of neck (see insert): "Bru/6." Made by Bru firm of Paris. This doll in hard rubber is rare. Generally found in bisque. *Collection of Zelda H. Cushner.*

RIGHT:
362. BONNETTED RUBBER DOLL
Period: Last half of 19th century.
Remarks: 2¼" (5.8cm) rigid, solid rubber doll with molded-on baby bonnet. Part of lower legs and arms missing. Similar in construction to *Frozen Charlottes.*

Parian Dolls - 19th Century

The term "parian" is applied to a smooth, almost soapy feeling bisque, very pale or white in tone, and of high quality. Painted features on doll heads of this material are extremely delicate in coloring.

Most dolls of this material have molded hairdos (with or without decoration); painted or glass eyes; and, occasionally, pierced ears.

Delicate colorings, with touches of gold and lustre, decorate the elaborate moldings sometimes found on the shoulders of parian dolls, i.e., collars, ruffles, guimpes and vests, etc.

Occasionally one is found with a swivel-neck, or one may be found with a bald head and wig.

Parian doll heads are seldom if ever marked.

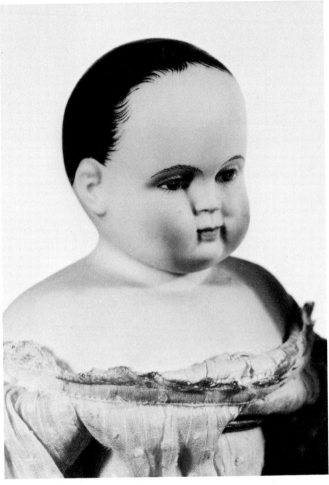

363. BLACK HAIRED PARIAN BABY DOLL
Period: 1855-1860.
Body: Cloth with leather arms.
Remarks: 14" (35.6cm) parian baby with deeply molded shoulders. Delicately tinted head has painted features including blue eyes with finely drawn lashes and brows. Black painted pate is brushmarked in front only.

LEFT:
364. BLONDE PARIAN — UNADORNED
Period: Third quarter of 19th century.
Body: Cloth with leather arms; or cloth with parian limbs.
Remarks: Very well modeled and delicately colored plain parian doll with painted blue eyes and sharply defined blonde curls.

158

365. PARIAN DOLL WITH CURLS LOW ON SHOULDERS

Period: Third quarter of 19th century.
Body: Cloth with leather arms; or cloth with parian limbs.
Remarks: A choice 10½" (26.7cm) blonde parian doll with painted blue eyes and molded curls falling low on broad shoulders. This particular doll has limbs of parian. The booted legs are partially glazed and trimmed with gold lustre. This head was also made with set-in glass eyes. *Courtesy of The Essex Institute, Salem, Massachusetts.*

ABOVE RIGHT:
366. PARIAN BOY DOLL

Period: Third quarter of 19th century.
Body: Cloth with leather arms; or cloth with parian limbs.
Remarks: 16" (40.6cm) plain parian boy doll with deep shoulders. Painted features, including blue eyes. Well defined, blonde molded hair. *Collection of Zelda H. Cushner.*

RIGHT:
367. "JENNY LIND" PARIAN DOLL

Period: Mid-19th century.
Body: Cloth with parian limbs.
Remarks: So-called *Jenny Lind* parian doll; 20" (50.8cm) in height. Delicately tinted features include blue painted eyes. Blonde hair, well detailed, is drawn to braided bun on back of head. For *Jenny Lind* in china which is more commonly found. See page 103.

159

368. BROWN HAIRED PARIAN DOLL
Period: Mid-19th century.
Body: Cloth with leather arms.
Remarks: 15½" (39.4cm) parian doll with blue glass eyes; very delicately painted eyelashes and brows; exposed ears. Brown glazed hair with deep comb marks - unusual. Note similarity in mold to dolls of other materials.

369. PARIAN DOLL WITH MOLDED NECKLACE
Period: Third quarter of 19th century.
Body: Cloth with leather arms; or cloth with parian limbs.
Remarks: Unusual parian doll with dark brown glazed hair and molded-in necklace. Its uniqueness is based on the fact that this particular doll is usually of china with black hair.

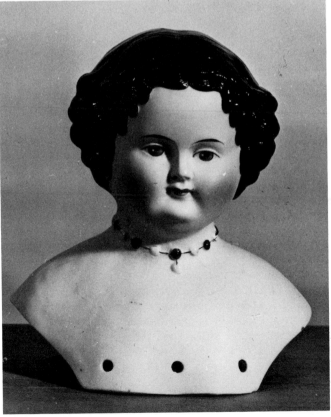

RIGHT:
370. PARIAN "FROZEN CHARLOTTE"
Period: Mid-19th century.
Body: Ceramic; all in one piece.
Remarks: A 6" (15.2cm) pillar doll of high quality called *Frozen Charlotte* after heroine of a New England folk ballad. A white complexioned doll with painted eyes, black band in molded hair. Trim on white glazed stockings matches rose lustre of boots. This type doll was made in other materials. The illustrated doll also came as a shoulderhead on cloth body.

371. PARIAN DOLL WITH "ALICE-IN-WONDERLAND" HAIRDO
Period: Third quarter of 19th century.
Body: Cloth with leather arms; or cloth with parian limbs.
Remarks: High quality parian doll with pale coloring and painted blue eyes. Hair dressed in *Alice-in-Wonderland* fashion with black band. The doll shown is on her original cloth body with parian limbs. Found in various sizes. *Merrill Collection.*

RIGHT:
372. PARIAN DOLL WITH SNOOD
Period: Third quarter of 19th century.
Body: Cloth with leather arms; or cloth with parian limbs.
Remarks: 16" (40.6cm) parian doll with molded blonde hair caught in white dotted blue-green snood. Blue painted bows at side. Painted blue eyes; one stroke light brown brows; dimpled chin. *Courtesy of Mrs. Eleanor C. Garfield.*

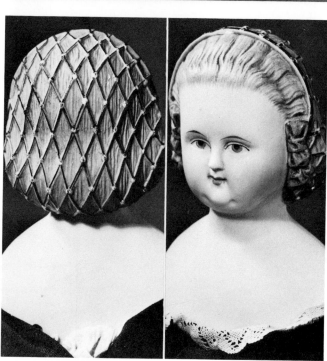

373. PARIAN SHOULDERHEAD — MODEL FOR CLOTH HEAD BY HAWKINS

Period: Third quarter of 19th century.
Body: Cloth with leather arms.
Remarks: 18" (45.7cm) parian headed doll that was obviously used as a model for the cloth head patented by George H. Hawkins of New York in 1868 (see page 250, Illustration 558 and page 139, Illustration 314). Fine parian head has painted features; black band in molded hair; molded earrings and necklace — all faithfully reproduced in Hawkins heads.

BELOW:
374. PARIAN DOLL WITH MOLDED EARRINGS, NECKLACE AND HEAD BAND

Period: Third quarter of 19th century.
Body: Cloth with parian limbs.
Remarks: 13" (33cm) parian doll with painted eyes; finely drawn brows and lashes; rose decorated band in pale molded hair; molded earrings and necklace.

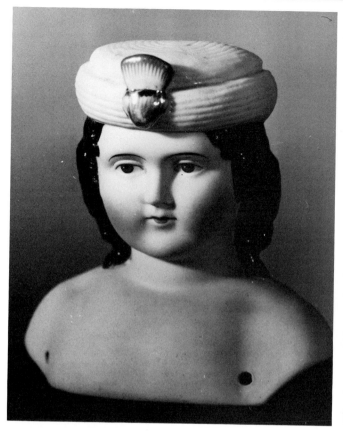

375. HATTED PARIAN DOLL
Period: Third quarter of 19th century.
Body: Cloth with parian limbs.
Remarks: The molded on yellow hat of this parian doll is trimmed with lavender, gold and coral colored lustre plume. Slightly turned and downward looking head has deep blue painted eyes and delicately tinted cheeks. Black hair is glazed, contrasting sharply with the unglazed, starkly white complexion. This head came on original body and complete doll is 23" (58.4cm) in height. *Collection of Zelda H. Cushner.*

376. BONNET DOLL IN PARIAN — LUSTRE TRIMMED
Period: Third quarter of 19th century.
Body: Cloth with parian limbs.
Remarks: 10" (25.4cm) brunette parian doll with finely chiseled features; painted blue eyes. Yellow molded bonnet has rose lustre plume; rose painted ties; multi-colored flowers on facing of brim. *Collection of Mrs. Louise H. Lund.*

377. HATTED DOLL IN PARIAN
Period: Third quarter of 19th century.
Body: Cloth with parian limbs.
Remarks: The molded-on yellow hat of this 10" (25.4cm) parian doll is trimmed with a lavender colored rose and long, lustre plume. Downcast head has painted features and long, brown molded curls falling low on the shoulders. *Courtesy of The Margaret Woodbury Strong Museum, Rochester, New York. Photograph by Barbara W. Jendrick.*

378. PARIAN DOLL WITH MOLDED-ON HAT AND SNOOD
Period: Third quarter of 19th century.
Body: Cloth with parian limbs.
Remarks: The molded-on green hat of this 10½"(26.7cm) parian doll is trimmed in front with a gold and lavender lustre plume. A painted snood holds the molded blonde hair in place. *Courtesy of The Margaret Woodbury Strong Museum, Rochester, New York. Photograph by Barbara W. Jendrick.*

379. MINIATURE, FANCY PARIAN DOLL
Period: Third quarter of 19th century.
Body: Cloth with parian limbs.
Remarks: Finely executed, 4½" (11.5cm) fancy parian doll with delicately painted features. Molded hair, caught in green painted snood, is decorated in front with tassel-trimmed, pink lustre scarf and long, lustre-touched white plume. Could be used as a doll house doll. Miniature dolls of this mold are a rarity. They are generally of larger size. *Merrill Collection.*

380. FANCY PARIAN WITH SWIVEL FLANGE NECK
Period: 1860s.
Body: Cloth with parian limbs.
Remarks: 4" (10.2cm) fancy parian head with flange neck for turning. Pierced ears. Blonde hair, caught in black net, has silver lustre feather at side and rose lustre twisted scarf across front. Rose lustre frill matches head scarf. Blue chemisette has molded forget-me-nots in V of neck. Wears molded beads touched with gold.

382. HIGHLY DECORATED PARIAN DOLL
Period: Third quarter of 19th century.
Body: Cloth with leather arms; or cloth with
parian limbs.
Remarks: A wreath of delicately colored flowers with touches of lustre, encircles the elaborate coiffure of this parian aristocrat. She also wears a molded yellow necklace. Features are painted and the light brown hair, falling low on shoulders, has delicate brushmarks around face. This type doll is sometimes referred to as *Dresden*. The illustrated doll, 14" (35.6cm) tall, has original parian limbs.

**381. PARIAN HEAD WITH SCARF DRAPED, FLOWER
DECORATED HAIR**
Period: Third quarter of 19th century.
Body: Cloth with leather arms; or cloth with
parian limbs.
Remarks: A glazed spray of flowers and white-fringed blue scarf are draped across the blonde molded hair of this 6" (15.2cm) parian doll head. Smooth and delicately tinted, it has pierced ears and highlighted, blue painted eyes. Center parted, swept back molded hair is loosely twisted at back of neck.

RIGHT:
383. PARIAN DOLL WITH SCARF DRAPED HEAD
Period: Circa 1870.
Body: Cloth with parian limbs; or cloth with
leather arms.
Remarks: 6" (15.2cm) delicately colored, blonde parian doll head with painted blue eyes, molded and ornamented hair. Crown of elaborately styled hair is encircled by a twisted scarf of blue and rose secured high on front by a pin with round, flaring white top. Scarf ends, decorated and fringed, fall over doll's left shoulder. Both scarf and pin are glazed and gold touched.
Courtesy of The Margaret Woodbury Strong Museum, Rochester, New York.

384. FANCY PARIAN DOLL WITH BUTTERFLY AND ROSE IN HAIR

Period: 1860s.
Body: Cloth with parian limbs.
Remarks: 14" (35.6cm) doll whose parian head has delicately painted features including carefully detailed eyes. *Unusual feature:* molded and gilded earrings. Elaborate hairdo has a cluster of vertical curls in back and long curling rows of hair in front falling low on shoulders. Gilded comb holds back curls in place. Center front is decorated with a pink rose and blue butterfly.

RIGHT:
385. PARIAN DOLL WITH LONG CURLS IN AN ELEGANT HAIR STYLE

Period: Third quarter of 19th century.
Body: Cloth with parian arms and partially glazed low heeled slippers.
Remarks: A fine 11" (27.9cm) blonde parian doll with painted blue eyes and a molded guimpe with a glazed green bow. The hair style has vertical curls each side of center part brushed over and in back of ear with a glazed black bow on top. Long curls from behind ears fall over sides and back of shoulderplate. Coiled curls in back also create a bun effect. *Merrill Collection.*

386. PARIAN DOLL WITH MOLDED BLOUSE

Period: Third quarter of 19th century.
Body: Leather; not original to this doll.
Remarks: An 18" (45.7cm) finely modelled parian-type shoulder head with a molded pleated blouse pierced by a hole at the center to secure a breast pin ornament. An interesting hair style featuring a glazed blue ribbon at the back of the crown. *Collection of Helen Read.*

RIGHT:
387. BLONDE PARIAN WITH MOLDED BLOUSE
Period: Third quarter of 19th century.
Body: Cloth with leather arms; or cloth with
   parian limbs.
Remarks: This doll, circa 1860, is sometimes dressed as a boy.
The blonde parian head has painted eyes and a molded blouse
with touches of blue and gold on glazed tie and collar. The doll
shown, dressed as a girl, has original parian limbs. Found in
several sizes.

388. PARIAN BOY DOLL
Period: Third quarter of 19th century.
Body: Cloth with leather arms; or cloth with
   parian limbs.
Remarks: Boy doll in parian with light brown hair and blue
painted eyes. A molded, glazed collar and tie, with touches of
blue and gold, tops waist. The same doll may be found with set-in
glass eyes.

RIGHT:
389. GLASS-EYED PARIAN BOY DOLL
Period: Third quarter of 19th century.
Body: Cloth with parian limbs.
Remarks: 15"(38.1cm) parian boy doll with light brown molded
hair; inset glass eyes; finely drawn brows and lashes. Molded and
glazed tie, with touches of blue and gold, tops waist.

390. FANCY PARIAN DOLL
Period: Third quarter of 19th century.
Body: Cloth with leather arms.
Remarks: 16"(40.6cm) parian doll with light brown molded hair banded by blue ribbon and rose lustre bow. Pierced ears; painted blue eyes. Fancy blouse has blue painted band at neck with applied pink flower. Rose lustre forms a V with molded rose at center. *Collection of Zelda H. Cushner.*

392. "DAGMAR" PARIAN DOLL
Period: Third quarter of 19th century.
Body: Cloth with leather arms; or cloth with parian limbs.
Remarks: *Dagmar* parian doll — supposedly named for mother of last Czar of Russia. Note molded guimpe with touches of gold on buttons. Hair dressed in puff at back of neck. This doll was also made in china in both blonde and brunette coloring. *Merrill Collection.*

391. DECORATED PARIAN DOLL
Period: Third quarter of 19th century.
Body: Cloth with leather arms; or cloth with parian limbs.
Remarks: Unusual hairdo with coiled braid in back of head bound by a white glazed scarf striped in rose and blue. Rose colored lapels front the white parian blouse which is topped by a glazed collar. *Collection of Zelda H. Cushner.*

393. SWIVEL-NECK PARIAN DOLL
Period: Third quarter of 19th century.
Body: Cloth with leather arms; or cloth with parian limbs.
Remarks: Exceedingly rare swivel neck parian with glass eyes and pierced ears. Light brown hair is dressed with five large curls on each side of center part; four vertical curls in back.

394. FANCY PARIAN DOLL
Period: Third quarter of 19th century.
Body: Cloth with leather arms; or cloth with
   parian limbs.
Remarks: Fancy parian doll with painted eyes; pierced ears; molded on guimpe decorated in blue, rose and touches of lustre. Round blue earrings with rhinestone centers are original. *Merrill Collection.*

ABOVE RIGHT:
395. FANCY PARIAN DOLL WITH ROSE IN HAIR
Period: Third quarter of 19th century.
Body: Cloth with leather arms; or cloth with
   parian limbs.
Remarks: 5" (15.2cm) elaborately decorated parian head with painted features; pierced ears; molded blonde hair with applied rose. The painted rose colored band of the guimpe, edged in green, is topped by white molded beads and rose lustre ruffle. *Collection of Zelda H. Cushner.*

RIGHT:
**396. FANCY PARIAN HEAD WITH SPRAY OF FLOWERS
IN HAIR**
Period: Third quarter of 19th century.
Body: Cloth with leather arms; or cloth with
   parian limbs.
Remarks: 20½" (52.1cm) blonde parian doll with spray of molded flowers in elaborately styled hair. The delicately tinted head has painted blue eyes; pierced ears. Rose colored bands of the V-necked blouse are topped by a glazed and decorated ruffle. Gold-touched blue bow is at center front. *Collection of Mrs. Louise H. Lund.*

397.

398.

399.

400.

397. PARIAN DOLL WITH FANCY HAIRDO
Period: Third quarter of 19th century.
Body: Cloth with leather arms; or cloth with
  parian limbs.
Remarks: Delicately tinted blonde doll head with pierced ears
and stationary glass eyes. Upswept hair, decorated with blue and
gold lustre bows, has a carefully molded single curl lying low on
each side of the shoulder. *Collection of Mrs. Evelyn Barrows.*

398. PARIAN DOLL WITH BLACK BAND IN HAIR
Period: Third quarter of 19th century.
Body: Cloth with leather arms.
Remarks: 18" (45.7cm) parian doll with set-in glass eyes; pierced
ears; feathered brows. Upswept blonde hair, banded in black,
falls in soft waves to back of neck. *Collection of Zelda H.
Cushner.*

399. PARIAN DOLL WITH BANDED HAIR
Period: Third quarter of 19th century.
Body: Cloth with parian limbs.
Remarks: 17" (43.2cm) parian doll with painted features, includ-
ing blue eyes. Pierced ears. The molded blonde hair with well
defined ringlets and curls, is banded on top in black.

400. PARIAN DOLL WITH NECKLACE
Period: Third quarter of 19th century.
Body: Cloth with leather arms; or cloth with
  parian limbs.
Remarks: Black bands and bows trim the molded blonde
coiffure of this 18" (45.7cm) parian doll. Delicately tinted, it has
set-in glass eyes and pierced ears. The molded guimpe is white,
square necked, and resembles lace in design. The band of the
molded-on necklace is brown. The locket is crimson with gold
center. *Courtesy of The Essex Institute, Salem, Massachusetts.*

**401. "DOLLY MADISON" PARIAN DOLL WITH
SWIVEL-NECK**
Period: Third quarter of 19th century.
Body: Cloth with kid arms.
Remarks: 17" (43.2cm) *Dolly Madison* parian doll with swivel-neck; set-in glass eyes; finely painted features. (May also be found with stationary shoulderhead.) Blonde hairdo, with well modeled waves and curls, has band and bow of blue and gold. This so-called *Dolly Madison*-type head was also made in china. *Merrill Collection.*

ABOVE RIGHT:
402. PARIAN DOLL — ELABORATELY DECORATED
Period: Third quarter of 19th century.
Body: Cloth with leather arms; or cloth with
parian limbs.
Remarks: Elaborately decorated parian doll with set-in glass eyes and pierced ears. Hairdo has pink lustre bows in front, blue lustre trimmed band holding curls in back. Molded pink ruff with touches of lustre on shoulders. Same doll is found in other colorings.

RIGHT:
403. HIGHLY EMBELLISHED PARIAN DOLL
Period: Third quarter of 19th century.
Body: Cloth with leather arms; or cloth with
parian limbs.
Remarks: Rare, elaborately decorated parian doll with set-in glass eyes; pierced ears; delicately drawn brows and lashes. Light brown hair is adorned with glazed bow of blue and gold. White, square-necked guimpe is trimmed with blue painted design, molded gold beads, and pink tinted ruffle. *Merrill Collection.*

171

404. PARIAN DOLL WITH FLOWER BEDECKED HAIR
Period: Third quarter of 19th century.
Body: Cloth with leather arms.
Remarks: Sprays of pink and blue molded flowers, with gold touched leaves, top the massed curls of this fine 19" (48.3cm) parian doll. White complexioned head has blue painted eyes; rosy cheeks; and pierced ears. *Collection of Zelda H. Cushner.*

ABOVE RIGHT:
405. PARIAN DOLL WITH MOLDED EARRINGS AND ROSE LUSTRE CORONET
Period: Third quarter of 19th century.
Body: Cloth with parian limbs.
Remarks: 16½" (41.9cm) aristocratic doll whose smooth parian head has painted blue eyes; finely drawn brows and lashes; delicately tinted cheeks. *Unusual feature:* long, molded earrings. Blonde molded hair, with curls in front, is topped by a coronet of rose lustre. Looped and coiled back hair is held in place by a double band of black molded ribbon. Ends of ribbon fall on left shoulder.

RIGHT:
406. "AUGUSTA VICTORIA" PARIAN DOLL
Period: Third quarter of 19th century.
Body: Cloth with leather arms; or cloth with parian limbs.
Remarks: 18" (45.7cm) parian doll with painted eyes; pierced ears and blue-edged, molded-on guimpe. Beads in hair, neckband and Maltese cross, are glazed in black. Thought to represent Empress Augusta Victoria at the time of her marriage, in 1881, to Wilhelm II, the last German Kaiser. This doll also came without decorated shoulders. *Merrill Collection.*

407. PARIAN DOLLS WITH WIGS

Period: Third quarter of 19th century.
Body: Cloth with leather arms; or cloth with parian limbs.
Remarks: Bald headed parian dolls with hair wigs are considered a rarity.
Right: 17" (43.2cm) bald headed parian doll with painted eyes and mohair wig.
Left: 18½" (47cm) bald headed parian doll with set-in glass eyes; mohair wig; pierced ears. *Merrill Collection.*

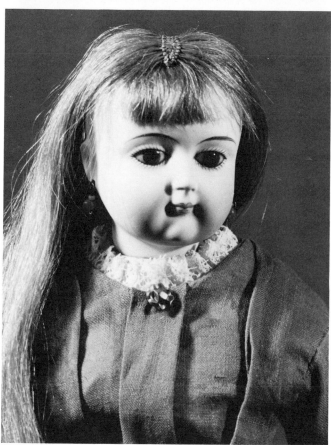

408. SWIVEL-NECK PARIAN

Period: Third quarter of 19th century.
Body: Cloth with leather arms.
Remarks: The head, with swivel-neck, of this 17" (43.2cm) French doll is of pale, fine bisque and has unusual expression. It has set-in glass eyes; closed mouth; pierced-in ears; and an exceptionally long wig of fine, light-brown human hair. Unmarked. Doll is all original, including costume of sheer blue wool with matching hat. *Merrill Collection.*

409. PARIAN DOLL WITH WIG

Period: Last quarter of the 19th century.
Body: Cloth with leather arms; or cloth with parian limbs.
Remarks: Bald headed parian doll with wig. The shoulderhead, fixed in a downward position, is unusual.

RIGHT:
410. PARIAN HATTED DOLL

Period: Third quarter of 19th century.
Body: Cloth with leather arms.
Remarks: 18" (45.7cm) doll wearing a white molded-on hat with blue shaded, double frill and a wide, loosely twisted pink band. Painted features include blue eyes; rosy cheeks. Ears are pierced and neck is encircled by a molded, coral colored ribbon and cross. Molded blonde hair has bangs and, escaping from bonnet in back, is a long, single, softly twisted curl. A rare and beautifully modeled doll. *Collection of Zelda H. Cushner.*

411. TURNED-HEAD PARIAN DOLL

Period: Third quarter of 19th century.
Body: Cloth with leather arms; or cloth with parian limbs.
Remarks: 6" (15.2cm) blonde parian doll head looking slightly downward and to the side. A beautiful head with set-in glass eyes; feathered brows; exposed pierced ears. Molded curls, with three falling low on nape, are topped by braided coronet. *Collection of Zelda H. Cushner.*

RIGHT:
412. PARIAN DOLL WITH CURL ON FOREHEAD

Period: Third quarter of 19th century.
Body: Cloth with parian arms.
Remarks: 24" (61cm) parian doll with turned head on well-rounded deep shoulders. Blue painted eyes; rosy cheeks; exposed ears. Deeply molded blonde hair, with curl on forehead, is banded by blue ribbon and bow.

414. HEAD WITH HAIRDO IN BISQUE — GLASS EYES
Period: Last quarter of 19th century.
Body: Cloth with leather arms; or cloth with
bisque limbs.
Remarks: Excellent quality bisque doll with stationary glass
eyes. The molded blonde hair is fashioned to show the ears.

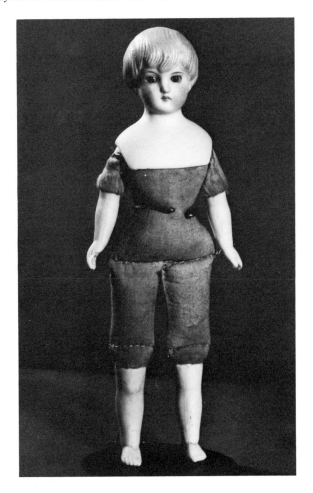

413. PARIAN BOY — DRESSED AS SOCCER PLAYER
Period: Third quarter of 19th century.
Body: Cloth with leather arms.
Remarks: 13" (33cm) boy doll whose parian shoulderhead has
finely drawn features; inset glass eyes; blonde molded hair.
Dressed as a soccer player; wears red jersey and stockings; white
knickers; brown shoes. Initial "H" embroidered on jersey.
Carries soccer ball under left arm. *Collection of Dorothy P.
Burton.*

RIGHT:
415. PARIAN CHILD DOLL
Period: Third quarter of 19th century.
Body: Cloth with parian limbs.
Remarks: 8" (20.3cm) all original parian doll with set-in glass
eyes; painted features; short, simply styled blonde molded hair.
Unusual feature: molded bare feet rather than the usual slippers
or boots. Numbers "131-4" are incised on back shoulders. *Merrill
Collection.*

175

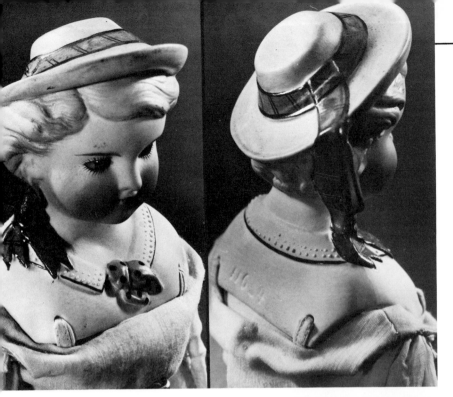

416. PARIAN DOLL WITH MOLDED HAT AND BLOUSE

Period: Third quarter of 19th century.
Body: Cloth with leather arms.
Remarks: 14½" (36.9cm) parian doll with molded blouse and hat; set-in glass eyes; blonde hair. Gray molded-on hat trimmed with rose colored band and streamers; accented in gold. White collar of blouse outlined in gold. Tie in center front is blue with dots in darker shade. Doll shown in front and rear views. Marked on back of shoulders with numbers "116-4."
Collection of Mrs. Mildred B. Fink.

417. HATTED BOY DOLL IN BISQUE

Period: Third quarter of 19th century.
Body: Cloth with china hands.
Remarks: 16½" (41.9cm) boy doll with bisque, hatted shoulderhead. Head turned slightly to right. Blonde hair; set brown eyes; and closed mouth. Applied bisque ruffle around neck. Shoulders outlined in blue trim. Gray bisque hat with black trim. Back of shoulders incised "160-5." Head believed to have been made by Kling & Co., Ohrdruf, Thüringia, Germany.
Merrill Collection.

RIGHT:
418. BLUE SCARF PARIAN DOLL
Period: Third quarter of 19th century.
Body: Cloth with leather arms; or cloth with parian limbs.
Remarks: Rare and beautiful 19½" (49.6cm) blonde parian doll with glass eyes and molded blue scarf. Sometimes referred to as *Blue Scarf* or *Queen Louise*. Caution should be used in purchasing this doll as it has been reproduced. Most reproductions are marked as such. Original dolls are unmarked. *Merrill Collection.*

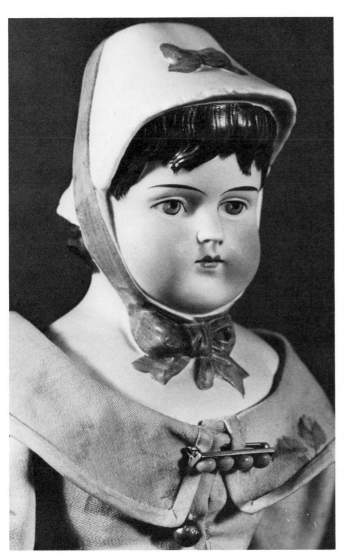

419. BONNET DOLL IN PARIAN
Period: Last quarter of 19th century.
Body: Cloth with leather arms.
Remarks: 18" (45.7cm) parian doll with molded-on yellow bonnet tied and bowed in purple. A delicately tinted doll with painted features including blue eyes. Brown molded hair worn in bangs.

420. HATTED PARIAN DOLL WITH BRAID AT SIDE
Period: Last quarter of 19th century.
Body: Cloth with leather arms.
Remarks: 19" (48.3cm) blonde parian doll with molded-on hat. Folds of the blue banded white hat are lightly shadowed in blue. Delicately tinted head has painted features including blue eyes. Blonde molded hair has heavy braid along left side of face. *Collection of Mrs. Louise H. Lund.*

421. BISQUE DOLL WITH COLORFUL, MOLDED-ON BLOUSE

Period: Last quarter of 19th century.
Body: Cloth with bisque arms.
Remarks: 16" (40.6cm) doll whose pink toned bisque head has stationary glass eyes; closed mouth; pierced-in ears. Molded blonde hair, gently waved, has bangs and center part. *Unusual feature:* Molded-on blue blouse with rose-striped white collar tied with dark blue, tasseled cord.

422. PARIAN DOLL WITH BLACK BOW IN HAIR

Period: Third quarter of 19th century.
Body: Cloth with parian limbs.
Remarks: Elaborate hairdo of a fine 18" (45.7cm) parian doll shown front and back. The upswept blonde hair, with excellent detail in modeling, has black bow in front. Delicately tinted head has painted blue eyes; pierced ears.

BELOW:
423. PARIAN HEAD WITH ROSES IN HAIR

Period: Third quarter of 19th century.
Body: Cloth with parian limbs.
Remarks: A 6" (15.2cm) parian doll head whose brightly colored cheeks contrast sharply with the stark whiteness of the molded blouse. Simulated embroidery decorates the pink-edged neck ruffle. The side-turned, downward looking head has glass eyes, pierced ears, and three roses tucked in the blonde hair. Back shoulders incised with numbers "135-10." This same head came with undecorated hair. *Collection of Marie Lynch.*

424. A PARIAN TURNED HEAD DOLL
Period: Last quarter of 19th century.
Body: Cloth with leather arms.
Remarks: A 16" (40.6cm) doll with a parian shoulderhead noticeably turned to the left. It has a rather plain hair style, but has nicely threaded set, blue glass eyes. The body, not original to this head, is of cloth with leather arms. The legs have printed red striped stockings to the knee joints and sewed on red leather boots with tassels. *Merrill Collection.*

ABOVE RIGHT:
425. HEAD WITH HAIRDO IN BISQUE - PAINTED EYES
Period: Last quarter of 19th century.
Body: Cloth with leather arms; or cloth with bisque limbs.
Remarks: 11" (27.9cm) doll whose finely modeled, pale bisque head has blonde, molded hairdo. Features, including eyes, are well painted.

RIGHT:
426. PLAIN PARIAN DOLLS
Period: Last quarter of 19th century.
Body: Cloth with leather arms.
Remarks: 24" (61cm) and 19½" (49.6cm) excellent quality parian dolls with molded blonde hairdo; exposed ears; set-in blue glass eyes, and finely drawn features. Both dolls from the same original modelling, but made from molds of different sizes. The 24" (61cm) doll is large for this type. They are found in several sizes. *Merrill Collection.*

427.

428.

429.

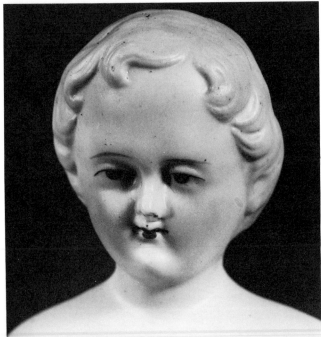

430.

427. PARIAN DOLL WITH BOW IN HAIR
Period: Third quarter of 19th century.
Body: Cloth with leather arms; or cloth with parian limbs.
Remarks: Pale colored parian doll with deep blue painted eyes; pierced ears; dark blue ribbon in hair.

428. FULL CHEEKED PARIAN DOLL
Period: Third quarter of 19th century.
Body: Cloth with parian limbs.
Remarks: Short necked, 14" (35.6cm) plain parian doll. Turned head has unusually full cheeks; painted blue eyes. Molded blonde hair has bunched curls on each side of center part. Parian legs have mauve boots trimmed in black. *Collection of Mrs. Elmer Morley.*

429. UNADORNED PARIAN DOLL WITH PIERCED EARS
Period: Third quarter of 19th century.
Body: Cloth with parian limbs.
Remarks: Finely modeled 10" (25.4cm) parian doll with painted eyes; reddish blonde molded hair; pierced ears.
Note: pierced ears are only occasionally found on plain parian dolls.

430. PARIAN DOLL WITH BOYISH HAIR STYLE
Period: Third quarter of 19th century.
Body: Cloth with parian limbs.
Remarks: 12" (30.5cm) plain parian headed doll whose molded yellow hair is short and boyish in style. Shoulders are deeply modeled, and the finely featured face has ochre colored eyebrows and blue painted eyes. Numeral "11" is incised on back shoulders. *Collection of The Children's Museum, Boston, Massachusetts.*

431. UNTINTED BISQUE MOLDED HAIR STYLE
Period: Last quarter of 19th century.
Body: Cloth with leather arms.
Remarks: 12" (30.5cm) doll with elaborately molded hair style. Dressed in a striped blue and red wool skirt, a figured blouse covered by a fur trimmed leather jacket. *Collection of Jane W. Alton.*

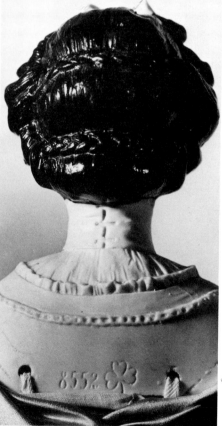

432. "IRISH QUEEN" IN PARIAN
Period: Late 19th and early 20th century.
Body: Cloth with leather arms; or cloth with ceramic limbs.
Remarks: 18" (45.7cm) parian doll referred to as *Irish Queen* by some collectors. Elaborately dressed black hair trimmed with blue bow. Painted intaglio eyes; open-closed mouth with molded teeth. Molded blouse has high collar of period. Gold trim at neck. Incised (on back shoulders); "8552" (with trefoil - see illustration). *Merrill Collection.*

Bisque Dolls - 19th Century

The term "bisque" derives from biscuit ware — an *unglazed* ceramic product which is fired before coloring and once again after color application.

The bisque category includes the following:

1. All bisque dolls — made entirely of bisque (head, body and limbs).
2. Heads only of bisque — mounted on bodies of other materials.
3. Heads with arms and/or legs of bisque — mounted on bodies of other materials.

Three types of bisque heads are commonly found:

1. Stationary Shoulderhead. A head and shoulder molded in one piece.
2. Socket Head. A head alone — without shoulders. This head turns freely when mounted on a jointed composition body.
3. Swivel-Neck Head. A socket head joined to a *separate* shoulder piece by a spring, allowing the head to pivot.

The majority of marks found on bisque dolls are those of French or German makers and aid in determining age and origin.

The workmanship of French dolls is generally better than the German although some of the latter so closely resemble the French that it is difficult to distinguish between them, especially if unmarked.

It is usual for bisque dolls to have either stationary or sleeping eyes — the former extensively used in the French.

Their mouths may be closed or open — the former used almost entirely by the French, although fine German closed mouth dolls were made.

A distinguishing feature of the French doll is the cork crown used in the head opening under the wig. The German doll has a disc of plaster or cardboard instead.

Shoulderheads of bisque may have molded hair instead of wigs, and come with glass or painted eyes.

Details to look for are:

1. Quality of bisque — fine or coarse.
2. Coloring — good or poor.
3. Expression.
4. Open or closed mouth — the closed mouth thought to be better especially in those of German make.

Body types are important. Some of the more common are pictured on the following pages.

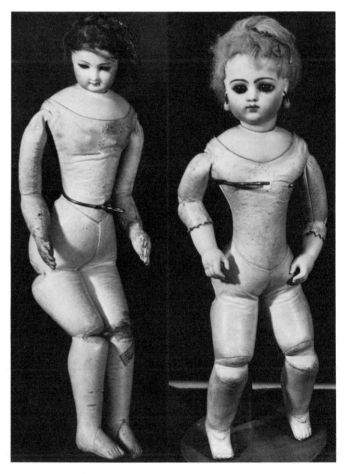

433. TYPICAL LEATHER BODIES — FRENCH
Left: small waisted, shapely leather body most commonly found on so-called *French Fashion* dolls. Gussets at joints, stitched toes, all leather arms. Unmarked as are most of these early French bisques.
Right: 14½" (36.9cm) leather body of this French child doll has characteristics of doll at right with the exception of bisque forearms as opposed to all leather. This doll is marked "F. G."

(Continued on page 199).

15" (38.1cm) cloth
Izannah Walker. See
Page 140, Illustration
317.

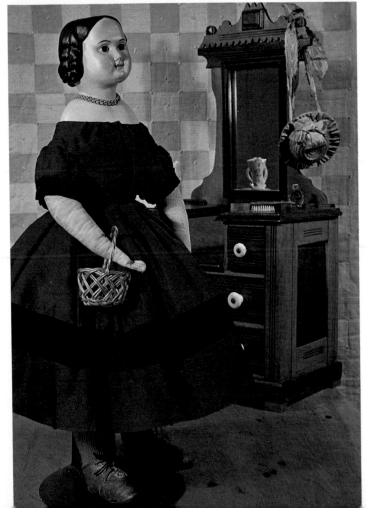

TOP LEFT:
Pair of primitive cloth dolls 15" (38.1cm) and 16" (40.6cm) tall respectively and nicely dressed. See Page 137, Illustrations 310 and 311.

TOP:
23" (58.4cm) "Enigma" cloth doll. See Page 138, Illustration 312.

LEFT:
Large hard rubber doll with cloth body standing in front of fine Victorian doll-sized bureau.

OPPOSITE PAGE:
Rare 13" (33.0cm) gutta percha doll with flowers molded in hair. See Page 153, Illustration 348.

13" (33cm) light brown-haired parian doll with interesting molded hairstyle. See Page 168, Illustration 392.

BELOW LEFT:
Fancy 17" (43.2cm) parian doll with glass eyes and swivel neck, lustre trim in hair. See Page 171, Illustration 401.

BELOW:
Fancy parian doll with pierced ears and lustre trimmed molding on shoulders. See Page 169, Illustration 394.

OPPOSITE PAGE:
Fancy parian shoulderhead - an example of the fine quality and delicate modelling in this material. See Page 165, Illustration 381.

ABOVE:
16½" (41.9cm) boy doll with parian-quality molded shoulderhead with hat, glass eyes and collar. See Page 176, Illustration 417.

6" (15.2cm) fancy parian shoulderhead with set in glass eyes, pierced ears, molded flowers and ruffled color. See Page 178, Illustration 423.

ABOVE:
Pair of parian dolls with wigs; doll
on left with glass eyes, doll on right
with painted eyes. See Page 173,
Illustration 407.

18½" (47cm) bald-headed parian
doll with mohair wig, glass eyes,
pierced-in ears. See Page 173,
Illustration 407.

ABOVE:
18" (45.7cm) unmarked French china lady doll with set in glass eyes, beautiful long china arms. See Page 120, Illustration 261.

17" (43.2cm) parian doll with long human hair wig, glass eyes, pierced in ears, swivel neck. See Page 173, Illustration 408.

TOP LEFT:
17" (43.2cm) unmarked French
bisque lady doll with all kid body.
See Page 203, Illustration 443.

TOP:
13½" (34.3cm) French lady doll. See
Page 201, Illustration 440.

Another view of the fine white
bisque and delicacy of this early type
of French lady doll.

TOP LEFT:
14" (35.6cm) French bisque lady doll with kid body, unusually full mohair wig and lovely comb. See Page 203, Illustration 442.

TOP:
26" (66cm) French bisque lady doll with kid body, especially fine bisque and execution of features. See Page 203, Illustration 441.

19" (48.3cm) French bisque lady doll with kid body, another particularly beautiful head.

18" (45.7cm) marked Simonne lady
doll. See Page 204, Illustration 444.

BELOW:
Simonne lady doll with trunk
containing a number of costumes
and accessories.

193

This type of bisque head is frequently found on the twill-over-papier-mâché body and is usually considered a French lady doll. However, it bears strong resemblance to the heads found with a Simon & Halbig incised mark.

OPPOSITE PAGE:
17" (43.2cm) French bisque doll with Bébé Breveté stamped on kid body and H incised on left shoulder. See Page 217, Illustration 478.

BELOW:
17" (43.2cm) marked Bébé Breveté with incised H on left shoulder with original trunk and wardrobe.

ABOVE:
    19" (48.3cm) marked Bru Jne/6
French bisque doll. See Page 213,
Illustration 465.

    21" (53.3cm) marked R. 2. D.
French bisque doll. See Page 224,
Illustration 493.

ABOVE:
14½" (36.9cm) French bisque doll on marked Jumeau body. See Page 214, Illustration 470.

18" (45.7cm) German closed mouth bisque doll marked 302/8. See Page 227, Illustration 503.

Two small French-type all bisque dolls. See Page 264, Illustration 589.

BELOW:
Large group of small all bisque and doll house dolls.

198

(Continued from page 182).

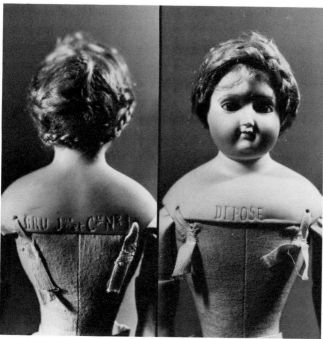

434. BISQUE DOLL MARKED "BRU J^{ne}"
Period: 1885-1890.
Body: Cloth with long, well proportioned parian arms.
Remarks: 14" (35.6cm) bisque doll with stationary blue glass eyes; delicately drawn features; mohair wig. Shoulderhead marked:
(front) "DEPOSE."
(back) "BRU J^{ne} et Cie No. 1."
Bru markings most unusual on this type doll head. Made by Bru firm of Paris.

435. FRENCH BISQUE DOLL — MARKED "B 3 S"
Period: Third quarter of 19th century.
Body: All leather.
Remarks: 17" (43.2cm) bisque doll of the *French Fashion* type. The stationary shoulderhead, very pale in tone, has set-in blue glass eyes; closed mouth; human hair wig. Marked: "B 3 S." Maker uncertain. *Collection of Mrs. Elmer Morley.*

LEFT:
436. BISQUE DOLL — MARKED "E. B."
Period: Third quarter of 19th century.
Body: Cloth with leather arms.
Remarks: 20½" (52.1cm) doll whose smooth, white complexioned shoulderhead has inset blue glass eyes; delicately drawn features; highly colored cheeks; mohair wig. Marked on front shoulders: "E 8 Depose B." Possibly made by E. Barrois of Paris. *Collection of Lorna S. Lieberman.*

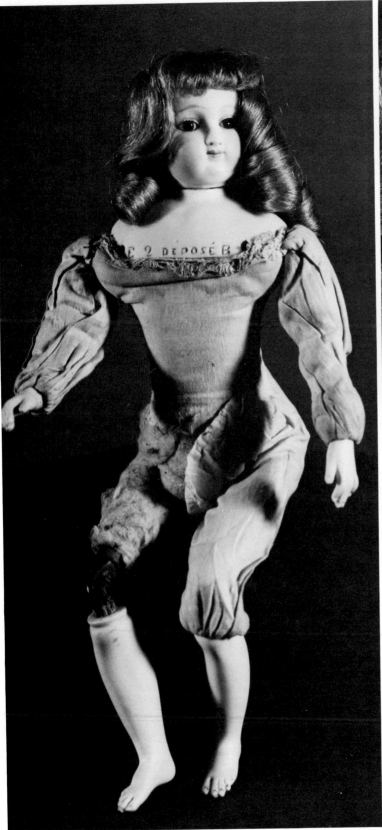

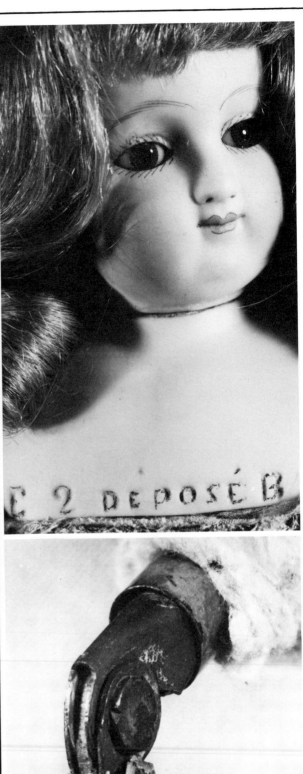

437. FRENCH BISQUE DOLL MARKED "E B"

Period: Third quarter of 19th century.

Body: Wooden with metal jointed limbs (see insert); hands and lower legs of bisque.

Remarks: Fine and early 14½" (36.9cm) French doll whose pale bisque head, with flanged neck, has stationary glass eyes; rosy cheeks; closed mouth; human hair wig. Body type unusual — see above description. Front shoulders incised: "E 2 Depose B" (see insert). Possibly made for the Paris Shop of E. Barrois. For another doll marked "E B," see page 199, Illustration 436. *Collection of Miss Zelda Cushner.*

200

438. BISQUE DOLL — MARKED ROHMER
Period: Third quarter of 19th century.
Body: Leather with bisque arms; leather covered
    wooden joints in shoulders and knees.
Remarks: 15½" (39.4cm) Mme. Rohmer doll. The swivel-
necked head has painted features including blue eyes; light
colored lambs wool wig. Body carries the oval blue stamp of the
Mme. Rohmer dolls. Wears original costume. *Collection of
Yesteryear's Museum, Sandwich, Massachusetts.*

ABOVE RIGHT:
**439. "FRENCH FASHION" BISQUE DOLL OF
        EXCEPTIONAL MOLD**
Period: Third quarter of 19th century.
Body: All leather.
Remarks: 21" (53.3cm) fashionable French lady doll. Swivel-
necked head; tinted pink above eyes is very pale, almost parian in
tone and quality. Of unusual expression, she has wide, deep blue
stationary glass eyes; pierced ears; feathered brows; light mohair
wig. *Collection of Mr. and Mrs. Raymond Knapp.*

RIGHT:
440. 13½" (34.3cm) FASHIONABLE LADY DOLL
Period: Third quarter of 19th century.
Body: Cloth with leather arms.
Remarks: 13½" (34.3cm) so-called *French fashionable lady* doll.
Fine, swivel-neck shoulderhead with glass set eyes; closed mouth;
pierced-in ears; and human hair wig. Unmarked, as is common
with this type of doll. *Merrill Collection.*

OPPOSITE PAGE:
441. TYPICAL SO-CALLED "FRENCH FASHION" DOLL — UNMARKED
Period: Circa 1870.
Body: All leather.
Remarks: 26" (66cm) unmarked so-called *French Fashion* doll showing characteristic detail and expression of these much sought after dolls. This fashionably dressed lady doll is correctly referred to as a *Parisienne*. Her fine quality swivel-necked bisque head has stationary glass eyes; closed mouth; pierced ears and mohair wig. *Merrill Collection.*

ABOVE:
442. FRENCH FASHION-TYPE BISQUE DOLL
Period: Third quarter of 19th century.
Body: All leather.
Remarks: A 14" (35.6cm) swivel-neck shoulderhead of finest quality bisque. Has stationary blue glass eyes; closed mouth; and was made from a mold forming an unusually life-like profile. The wig is original and is coiffed in a most fascinating styling. Head is unmarked except for a "2" incised at base of neck. *Merrill Collection.*

443. FRENCH FASHION BISQUE DOLL
Period: Third quarter of 19th century.
Body: All leather.
Remarks: Fine example of the so-called *French Fashion* doll — an erroneous term applied to a luxury *play* doll never intended to be a fashion mannequin. The pale bisque swivel-neck head has stationary glass eyes; closed mouth; mohair wig. The doll is 17" (43.2cm) in height and is unmarked. Wears original white organdy and blue taffeta costume. *Merrill Collection.*

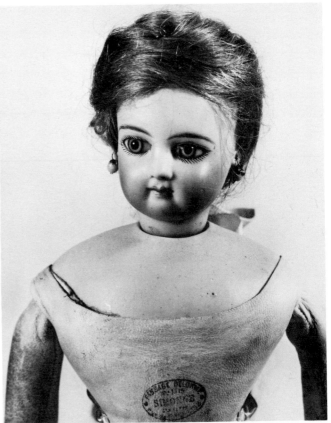

444. "FRENCH FASHION" DOLL BY SIMONNE — WITH WARDROBE AND ACCESSORIES
Period: Circa 1870.
Body: All leather.
Remarks: 18" (45.7cm) swivel-necked bisque doll with stationary glass eyes; closed mouth; pierced ears; mohair wig. Body stamped: "Passage Delorme//No. la 13//Simonne//Paris//Rue de Rivoli 188." Bought for little Carrie Elizabeth Day of Boston, Massachusetts, who was born in 1866 and whose initials are on side of trunk. The trunk is labeled: "Nathan Neat//London, Paris and Vienna//Leather Goods.//336 Washington Street //Boston." *Merrill Collection.*

445. "FRENCH FASHION" DOLL BY SIMONNE
Period: Third quarter of 19th century.
Body: All leather.
Remarks: 18" (45.7cm) swivel-necked pale bisque doll with pierced ears; set-in glass eyes; finely drawn features; human hair wig. Stamped (in oval) on front of body: "Passage Delorme//No. la 13//SIMMONE//Paris//Rue de Rivoli 188." *Merrill Collection.*

RIGHT:
446. "FRENCH FASHION" DOLL — WITH PAINTED EYES
Period: Third quarter of 19th century.
Body: Leather with bisque arms.
Remarks: Fine unmarked French bisque similar to dolls made by Mme. Rohmer of Paris. The bisque arms are joined to the gusseted kid body by wooden joints. She has swivel-neck; painted eyes; pierced ears; closed mouth and mohair wig. Bought in Paris in 1870 with wardrobe. *Collection of Miss Ruth Whittier.*

447 and 448. FRENCH BISQUE DOLL WITH KINTZBACH PATENTED HANDS

Period: 1870s.
Body: Cloth with china hands and sewed-on
   leather boots.
Remarks: The swivel-necked French bisque head of this 27"
(68.7cm) doll is mounted on a cloth body with hands patented by
Martin Kintzbach of Philadelphia (Patent #95489, dated October
5, 1869). Although seldom found, this combination of French
bisque head on a commercially made body with Kintzbach china
hands is correct. Doll is all original and wears a white satin gown
with 24" (61cm) train. *Merrill Collection.*

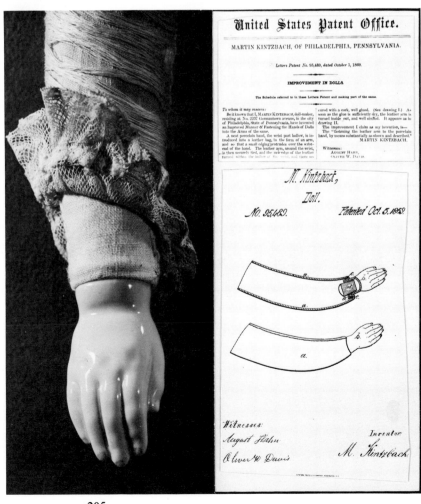

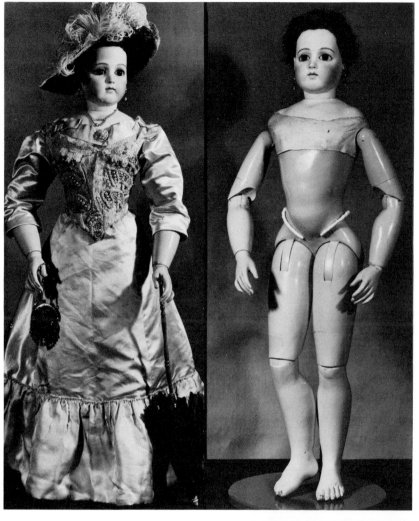

ABOVE:
449. 34" (86.4cm) "FRENCH FASHION" DOLL WITH WOODEN BODY
Period: Third quarter of 19th century.
Body: All wooden; fully jointed.
Remarks: Left: size, plus characteristics of the finest French dolls, classifies this specimen as unique. The delicately tinted bisque head has swivel-neck; pierced, applied ears; stationary brown glass eyes; closed mouth; brown human hair wig. Wears original satin gown. Unmarked except for size number (12) incised on right shoulder.
Right: undressed doll, showing fully articulated all wooden body.

450. "FRENCH FASHION" DOLL BY JUMEAU
Period: Third quarter of 19th century.
Body: Cloth with leather arms and sewn-on boots of red leather.
Remarks: 22" (55.9cm) *French Fashion* doll. The bisque head, with swivel neck, has blue stationary glass eyes; pierced ears; closed mouth and mohair wig. Wears original costume of purple silk with matching hat. Marked: "E 7 J." Made by Jumeau of Paris. *Collection of Mrs. Elmer Morley.*

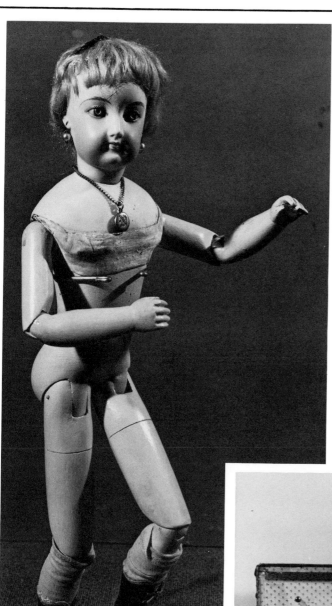

451. ALL WOODEN FRENCH DOLL BODY
Remarks: 18" (45.7cm) French bisque doll with rare all wooden body; articulated in joints; wooden pegged; enameled. Head, with swivel-neck, of fine, pale bisque; closed mouth; pierced ears; stationary glass eyes. Unmarked. Doll dressed in Illustration 452.

BELOW:
452. FRENCH DOLL WITH TRUNK OF CLOTHES AND ACCESSORIES
Period: Bought in Paris in 1865.
Body: All wooden; fully jointed.
Remarks: 19" (48.3cm) *French Fashion* doll with original domed trunk partitioned to hold doll, dresses, hat box, hats, gloves, fan, pocket book, underwear, corsets, etc. Occasionally dolls were purchased in this manner - in trunk with wardrobe. Trunk marked: "Aux Enfants Sages//Benon & Cie//Passage Jouffroy//Paris//Commission Exportation."

453. "FRENCH FASHION" DOLL WITH PAINTED EYES — MARKED "F.G."
Period: Third quarter of 19th century.
Body: All leather.
Remarks: 19" (48.3cm) *French Fashion* doll with stationary shoulderhead of fine bisque. Unusual for type with painted eyes and maker's mark. Pierced-in ears; blonde mohair wig. Incised across back of shoulders: "F. 3 G." Probably made by firm of F. Gaultier of Paris. *Collection of Mrs. Elmer Morley.*

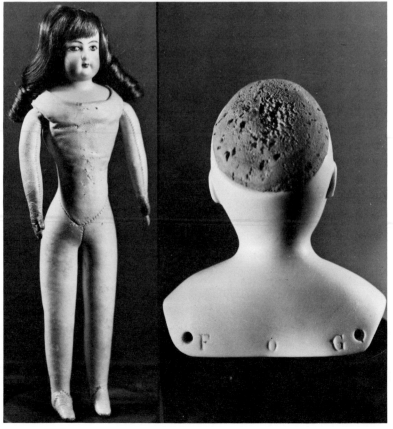

RIGHT:
455. "FRENCH FASHION" DOLL MARKED "F.G."
Period: Third quarter of 19th century.
Body: All leather; unjointed.
Remarks: Small, desirable 12½" (31.8cm) French doll. *Unusual features:* painted rather than the usual glass eyes and an unjointed leather body with stitched mitten type hands. Back shoulders marked: "F O G." Made by F. Gaultier of Paris.

LEFT:
454. "FRENCH FASHION" DOLL WITH PAINTED EYES — MARKED "F.G."

Period: Third quarter of 19th century.

Body: All leather.

Remarks: The bisque shoulderhead of this 16" (40.6cm) French doll has large, dark blue painted eyes; closed mouth; pierced ears; finely drawn brows and lashes; mohair wig. Marked: "F.G." Made by F. Gaultier of Paris. *Collection of Shirley F. Sanborn.*

RIGHT:
456. "FRENCH FASHION" BISQUE DOLL — MARKED "F.G."

Period: Third quarter of 19th century.

Body: Jointed wooden; leather covered; bisque arms.

Remarks: 15" (38.1cm) *French Fashion* bisque doll with swivel neck; pierced ears; set-in blue glass eyes; light mohair wig. Marked (within scroll) on left shoulder: "F.G." On right shoulder "#2." Made by F. Gaultier of Paris. *Collection of Mrs. Elmer Morley.*

BELOW:
457. "F.G." HEAD ON GESLAND TYPE BODY

Period: Third quarter of 19th century.

Body: Stockinette-covered metal frame; jointed at knees, shoulders, elbows, wrists; hands and lower legs of bisque.

Remarks: 23" (58.4cm) French fashionable lady with Gesland type body. Shown with and without original costume. Pale swivel-necked head has stationary blue glass eyes; closed mouth; pierced-in ears; finely drawn brows and lashes; mohair wig. Shoulder of bisque head marked: "F.G." plus number "6." Head made by firm of F. Gaultier of Paris.

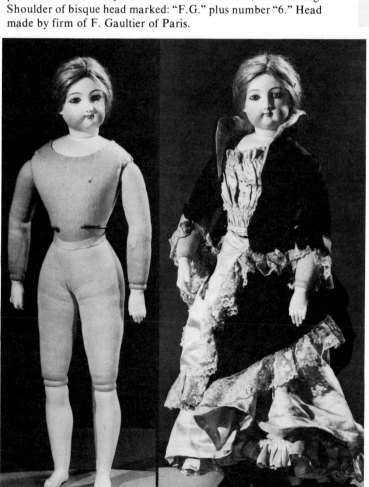

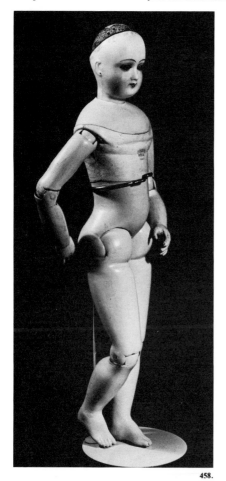

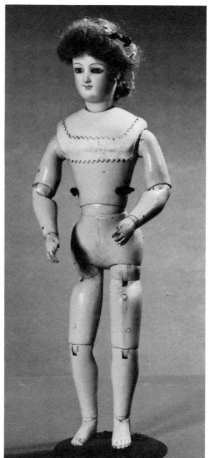

458.   459.   460.

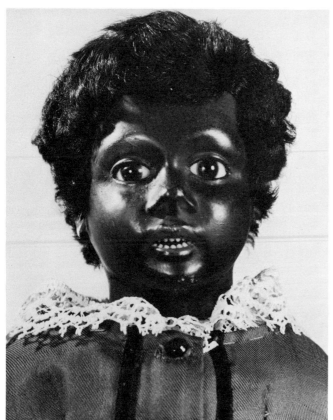

458. FRENCH DOLL WITH PRESSED LEATHER BODY

The hollow, unstuffed body of this 17" (43.2cm) French bisque doll is of cloth-lined pressed leather. Note unusual, well designed wooden-pegged joints. Rarely found.

Swivel-necked head, of pale bisque, has stationary blue glass eyes; closed mouth; pierced ears; cork crown. Wig missing.

Stamped on chest: "Poupee//Brevete//S.G.D.G." *Collection of Mrs. Ralph H. Lein.*

459. ALL WOODEN FRENCH DOLL BODY WITH BALL JOINTED SWIVEL AT WAIST

16½" (41.9cm) French bisque doll with rare all wooden body — enameled; wooden pegged; fully articulated in joints including a ball jointed swivel at waist.

Bisque head, with swivel-neck, has blue stationary glass eyes; pierced ears; closed mouth.

460. BLACK "FRENCH FASHION" DOLL

Period: Third quarter of 19th century.
Body: All leather; black.
Remarks: 15" (38.1cm) Black *French Fashion* doll whose swivel-necked bisque head has black stationary glass eyes; closed mouth; pierced-in ears; black mohair wig. Unmarked. Black dolls, in this category, are rare. *Collection of Mrs. Fidelia Lence.*

461. BLACK BISQUE DOLL — FRENCH TYPE

Period: Last quarter of 19th century.
Body: Cloth with bisque arms and legs.
Remarks: 16" (40.6cm) Black bisque doll with swivel-neck; stationary glass eyes; black fur wig. *Unusual feature:* open mouth showing two rows of tiny, set-in teeth. Doll has all the appearance of the French. Unmarked.

461.

462. BISQUE DOLL WITH TWILL COVERED WOODEN BODY

Period: Third quarter of 19th century.
Body: Jointed wooden with bisque limbs.
Remarks: 10" (25.4cm) unmarked French doll with swivel neck. The solid cranium head is mounted on a shoulder piece by elastic held in place by wooden pin. Closed mouth; pierced ears; blue set-in glass eyes; feathered brows; curly mohair wig. Note the bisque legs with bare feet and the very shapely twill covered wooden body. *Collection of Zelda H. Cushner.*

BELOW:

463. BISQUE DOLL WITH TWILL COVERED BODY

Period: Third quarter of 19th century.
Body: Molded papier mâché with wooden joints; twill covered; upper arms of wood; lower of bisque.
Remarks: Exceptional 14" (35.6cm) French bisque doll whose adult shaped body is molded of papier mache; twill covered. This type body is sometimes mistakenly called wooden - twill covered. Fine bisque head has closed mouth; pierced ears; stationary glass eyes; blonde mohair wig. Unmarked.

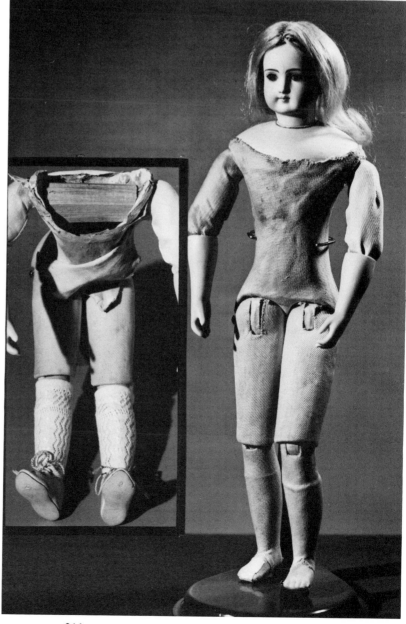

211

464. FRENCH BISQUE DOLLS — BY BRU

Examples of French bisque dolls by Bru of Paris, one of the leading makers of dolls from 1866-1899.

Note the expressive faces; well proportioned bodies; and distinctive arms — typical of these luxury dolls. *Collection of Mrs. Louise H. Lund.*

212

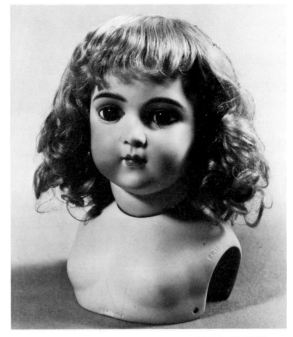

465. FRENCH BISQUE DOLL BY BRU

Period: Circa 1880.

Body: Leather with lower arms of bisque; upper arms of leather covered wood.

Remarks: 19" (48.3cm) bisque headed doll by Bru of Paris. Swivel-necked head has stationary glass eyes; closed mouth; pierced ears and blonde mohair wig. Wears finely detailed costume and Bru marked shoes. Marked: "Bru Jne/6." *Merrill Collection.*

466. FRENCH BISQUE HEAD — MARKED "BRU"

Period: Circa 1880.

Body: Leather with bisque arms.

Remarks: A striking example of the much sought after bisque dolls by the eminent Bru firm of Paris. Note the expressive face and well modeled bust characteristic of these dolls. The swivel-neck head is of finest French bisque; stationary glass eyes (brown); closed mouth; pierced ears.

467. NURSING BRU — "BEBE TETEUR"

Period: Patented 1879.

Body: Kid with wooden legs; bisque arms.

Remarks: 16" (40.6cm) nursing doll by Bru of Paris. The fine swivel-necked bisque head has set-in glass eyes; pierced ears and mohair wig. Open mouth is pursed to receive a feeding bottle. Key in back of head operates the sucking mechanism. Marked: "Bru Jne #4." *Bebe Teteur* originally came with lambskin wig; dressed as an infant. *Collection of Mrs. Louise H. Lund.*

468. BLACK BISQUE DOLL — MARKED "BRU"

Period: Circa 1880.

Body: Brown leather covers stuffed torso and upper wooden limbs; forearms of bisque, lower legs of wood.

Remarks: A rare 17" (43.2cm) black bisque doll by Bru of Paris. The swivel-necked head has large, stationary glass eyes; closed mouth; pierced ears. Black human hair wig is replacement for original one of lambs wool. Marked on back of head: Dot within circle plus "Bru Jne." Marked on shoulder: "Bru Jne" plus size number "5." *Collection of Mr. and Mrs. Raymond Knapp.*

467.

468.

469. FRENCH COMPOSITION JOINTED BODIES

Remarks: Left: 13½" (34.3cm) ball and socket composition body; elastic strung, excepting head which is spring mounted. Marked: "Jumeau//Medaille d'Or Paris." Made by Jumeau after 1873. This French firm made complete dolls. Note one-piece hand and forearm — typical of French dolls although this rigid wrist may be found on some German dolls.

Right: 16½" (41.9cm) ball and socket composition body; completely elastic strung. Made by the French firm of Jumeau. Marked "Depose//Tete Jumeau//Bte•SGDG//7" and three red marks fired in. Body unmarked.

470. JUMEAU DOLL — MARKED "Medaille d'Or"

Period: Circa 1880.

Body: Ball jointed composition; elastic strung.

Remarks: 14½" (36.9cm) doll with delicately tinted head of pale, smooth bisque. It has large inset glass eyes; closed mouth and lambskin wig. Wears original clothes. Body marked: "Jumeau//Medaille d'Or//Paris." "3/o" incised in bisque at lower edge of neck. This doll is sometimes referred to as the *Portrait Jumeau. Merrill Collection.*

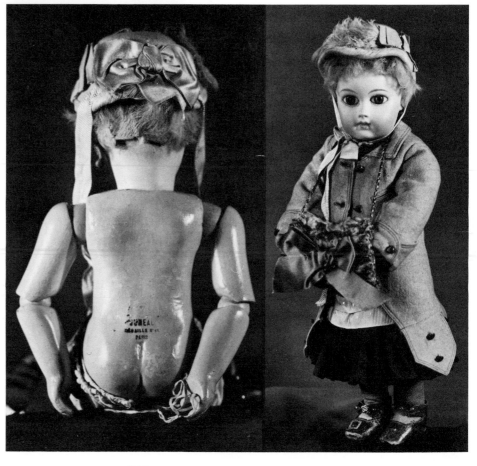

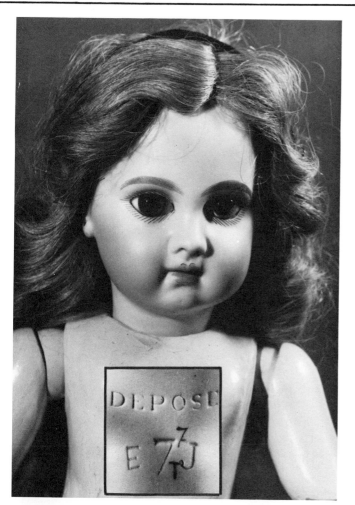

LEFT:
471. FRENCH JUMEAU DOLL — MARKED "E.J."
Period: Circa 1880.
Body: Jointed composition; elastic strung.
Remarks: 16" (40.6cm) French bisque doll with brown stationary glass eyes; pierced ears; closed mouth; blonde human hair wig. Marked on back of head (see insert): "Depose//E 7 J." Body stamped: "Jumeau//Medaille D'or//Paris." *Collection of Zelda H. Cushner.*

ABOVE:
472. FRENCH DOLLS BY JUMEAU
Period: Circa 1880.
Body: Ball jointed composition; elastic strung.
Remarks: A pair of 12" (30.5cm) blue and brown eyed French bisque dolls by Jumeau. Closed mouths; pierced ears; lambs-wool wigs. Wear original clothes including heeled boots. Marked: "Jumeau//Medaille d'Or//Paris."

473. BÉBÉ JUMEAU — MARKED "E.J."
Period: Circa 1880.
Body: Jointed composition; elastic strung.
Remarks: 24" (61cm) French bisque doll with blue stationary glass eyes; pierced ears; closed mouth. Human hair wig. Marked on back of head: "E.J." plus size number "9." Body marked: "Jumeau//Medaille d'Or//Paris." Made by Jumeau, one of the finest of French doll makers. *Merrill Collection.*

ABOVE:
474. BÉBÉ JUMEAU
Period: Circa 1884.
Body: Jointed composition; elastic strung.
Remarks: 17" (43.2cm) Bébé Jumeau — one of a line of fine dolls made by the Jumeau firm of Paris. The delicately tinted bisque socket head has stationary glass eyes; closed mouth; finely executed brows and lashes; and mohair wig. Head marked: "Depose//Tête Jumeau//B^{te} SGDG." The illustrated doll was a Christmas present to a little girl in Boston, Massachusetts, in 1884. *Merrill Collection.*

ABOVE RIGHT:
475. FRENCH BISQUE DOLL — UNMARKED
Period: Circa 1880.
Body: All leather with large, well proportioned bisque arms.
Remarks: Unmarked French bisque doll strongly resembling those made by the Bru firm of Paris. The head, with swivel neck, is of pale, smooth bisque with expressive set-in glass eyes and lambs wool wig. *Collection of Shirley F. Sanborn.*

476. FRENCH BISQUE DOLL — MARKED "A.T."
Period: Last quarter of 19th century.
Body: Jointed composition; elastic strung.
Remarks: 18" (45.7cm) French doll whose delicately tinted, pale bisque head has stationary blue glass eyes; pierced ears; light mohair wig. Marked on back of head: "A 7 T." Although unproven, dolls bearing this mark are thought to have been made by A. Thuillier of Paris. Comparatively rare, they are highly prized by collectors.

477. FRENCH BISQUE HEAD — MARKED "H"
Period: Last quarter of 19th century.
Body: Jointed composition; elastic strung.
Remarks: 18" (45.7cm) French doll whose socket head has stationary blue glass eyes; closed mouth; pierced ears; mohair wig. Head marked "2 ● H." Maker unknown. Dolls bearing the H mark are extremely rare and desirable.

RIGHT AND BELOW:
478. and 479. FRENCH BISQUE DOLL - MARKED "H"
Period: 1870s.
Body: Leather with bisque arms.
Remarks: 17" (43.2cm) French bisque doll with typical features. Documented as purchased for child born in 1870. Wears original costume. Note large hands; characteristic of dolls by Bru and those stamped "Bébé Brevete." Incised "H" on left shoulder. Maker uncertain. *Merrill Collection.*

My name is Flossie Plaisted. I belonged to Daisy (Emily) Plaisted. Daisy was born in 1870. I lived with Daisy on Appleton Street in Waterville until 1904 when Daisy married Dr. L.G. Bunker when I came to 44 Silver Street in Waterville to live.

OPPOSITE PAGE:
480. FRENCH BISQUE DOLL - MARKED "H"
Period: 1870s.
Body: Leather with bisque arms.
Remarks: 17" (43.2cm) French bisque doll with typical features. Documented as purchased for child born in 1870. Wears original costume. Note large hands; characteristic of dolls by Bru and those stamped "Bébé Brevete." Incised "H" on left shoulder. Maker uncertain. *Merrill Collection.*

ABOVE:
481. FRENCH "BÉBÉ SCHMITT" ON A WOODEN BODY
Period: Third quarter of 19th century.
Body: All wooden.
Remarks: An 18" (45.7cm) swivel-neck bisque shoulderhead doll with fully molded bosom. Shoulder plate is attached to a fully articulated wooden body with a kid skin band. The finely made body has well carved hands and feet with a swivel turning in the upper arms and legs. The head has set, blue paperweight eyes and well modelled pierced ears. Back of head is incised: "B^{te} o SGDG." The mark of Schmitt & Fils, Paris. *Merrill Collection.*

482. FRENCH CHILD DOLL ON JOINTED COMPOSITION BODY
Period: Last quarter of 19th century.
Body: Jointed composition; elastic strung.
Remarks: Typical of the French child doll of the 1880s. The fine bisque socket head has stationary glass eyes; closed mouth; lambskin wig. This particular doll bears the mark of the Schmitt firm of Paris. Costume is original.

483. FRENCH CHILD DOLL — MARKED "F.G."
Period: Last quarter of 19th century.
Body: Leather with bisque forearms.
Remarks: The swivel-necked shoulderhead of this 14" (35.6cm)
French child doll is of pale, smooth bisque. It has stationary glass
eyes; closed mouth; pierced ears and lambskin wig. Shoulder
piece marked "4" on right and "F.G." on left. Head marked: "F.
5/0 G." Made by F. Gaultier of Paris. *Merrill Collection.*

ABOVE RIGHT:
484. FRENCH CHILD DOLL — MARKED "F.G."
Period: Last quarter of 19th century.
Body: Jointed composition; elastic strung.
Remarks: 17½" (44.5cm) French doll with bisque socket head.
Set-in brown glass eyes; pierced ears; closed mouth. Marked:
"F.G." on back of neck. Made by F. Gaultier of Paris. *Collection
of Mrs. Elmer Morley.*

RIGHT:
485. FRENCH CHILD DOLL — MARKED "F. G."
Period: Last quarter of 19th century.
Body: Jointed composition; elastic strung.
Remarks: The bisque socket head of this 16" (40.6cm) French
child doll has stationary glass eyes; closed mouth; mohair wig.
Bears incised mark "F.G." in scroll (see insert). Made by firm of
F. Gaultier of Paris who won a silver medal at the Paris
Exposition of 1878 for fine quality dolls.

486. HATTED MAN DOLL IN BISQUE
Period: Third quarter of 19th century.
Body: Gesland type (see page 209, Illustration 457). Stockinette covered metal frame; jointed at knees, shoulders, elbows, wrists; bisque hands and shoes.
Remarks: The bisque shoulderhead of this 18½" (47cm) man doll has molded-on black hat; brown molded hair; moustache and sideburns; painted features. Unmarked. Costume copied from the original, using old fabrics. *Courtesy of The Margaret Woodbury Strong Museum, Rochester, New York. Photograph by Barbara W. Jendrick.*

488. FRENCH CHILD DOLL BY STEINER
Period: Last quarter of 19th century.
Body: Jointed composition; elastic strung.
Remarks: Fine 18" (45.7cm) French bisque doll with stationary glass eyes; feathered brows; pierced ears; closed mouth and human hair wig. Marked: "J. STEINER//B:T^e SGDG//Paris //FI^{re} A 11."

487. WIRE-EYED FRENCH DOLL BY STEINER
Period: Circa 1880.
Body: Jointed composition; elastic strung.
Remarks: 15" (38.1cm) French child doll in original costume. Delicately tinted bisque; lambskin wig; pierced ears; eyes that operate by lever protruding from behind ear. Marked on head in red script, "Steiner Bourgoin Suc — sgdg." Made by Jules Nicholas Steiner of Paris. *Merrill Collection.*

RIGHT:
489. FRENCH DOLL WITH "AU NAIN BLEU" SHOP LABEL
Period: Last quarter of 19th century.
Body: Jointed composition; elastic strung.
Remarks: 16" (40.6cm) doll with pale bisque head. Delicately tinted, it has blue stationary glass eyes; pierced ears; closed mouth; light mohair wig. Head unmarked. Excepting mouth, it strongly resembles the crying doll head by Jules Steiner. Body bears label of famous Paris toy shop: "Au Nain Bleu//E. Chauviere//Bould des Capucines, 27//Paris." *Collection of Mr. and Mrs. Raymond Knapp.*

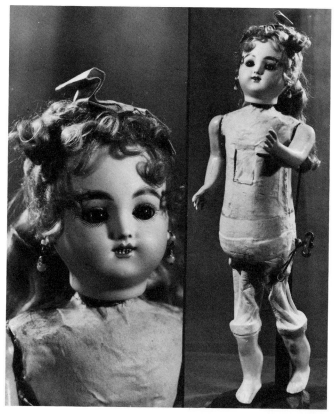

BELOW:
491. MECHANISM AND DIRECTIONS FOR OPERATION OF JULES STEINER'S CRYING BABY

Period: Last quarter of 19th century.

Remarks: Left: cloth covering, limbs and key-wound mechanism of an 18" (45.7cm) baby which, when wound, kicks, cries and moves its head. Made by Jules Steiner of Paris. Bisque head has stationary glass eyes; open mouth with teeth; lambskin wig. **Right:** reassembled doll.

Directions for operating Jules Steiner's Crying Babies were printed in French, English, German and Spanish. Following is the English.

"To make the mecanism (sic) work it is sufficient to wind up with the brass key attached to the baby, turning to the right, just as one winds up a watch or clock.

"When the movement is wound up, one must, to obtain the work, push behind the iron-wire which is near the key; one can stop the movement, as one whises (sic) in pulling to one's self the iron wire.

"When the baby is wound up, not to forget to lift up the arms like those of a child who calls, holding out his arms.

"Even children can wind up themselves this mecanism (sic) without danger."

J. St., brevete's. g. d. g., Paris.

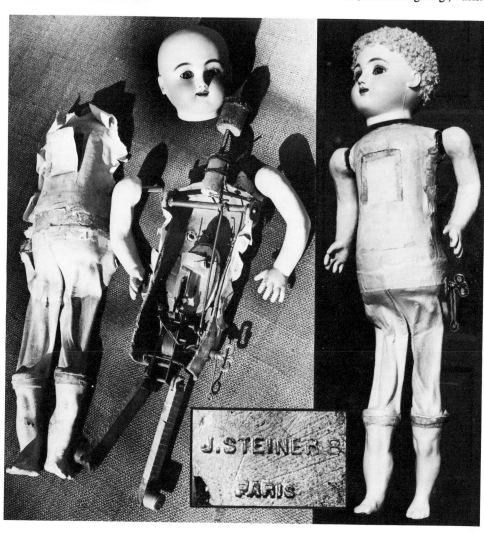

ABOVE:
490. CRYING DOLL BY JULES STEINER

Period: Last quarter of 19th century.

Body: Mechanism in cloth covered torso; composition limbs; thinly coated with wax.

Remarks: 18" (45.7cm) key-wound mechanical doll that cries "mama" and "papa" while moving head, arms and legs. Bisque head has set-in glass eyes; pierced ears; open mouth with two rows of tiny teeth; mohair wig. Bears mark of Jules Steiner of Paris on mechanism within body — not marked elsewhere. Shop label on back of body. *Collection of Mrs. Ralph Flather.*

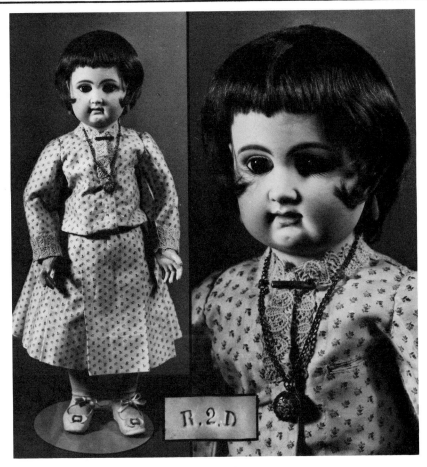

ABOVE LEFT:
492. FRENCH CHILD DOLL — MARKED "R.D."
Period: Last quarter of 19th century.
Body: Composition; elastic strung.
Remarks: 15" (38.1cm) French child doll with brown stationary glass eyes; pierced ears; closed mouth; blonde mohair wig. A fine quality bisque doll made by Rabery & Delphieu of Paris. Marked: "R. 2/0 D."

ABOVE RIGHT:
493. FRENCH CHILD DOLL MARKED "R.2.D"
Period: 1875-1898.
Body: Light weight composition; elastic strung.
Remarks: 21" (53.3cm) French bisque bébé with stationary almond shaped eyes and a blush of lavender shadow above the eyes. Original wig with brown mohair (illustration shows a replacement human hair wig). A fine quality French bisque doll made by Rabery & Delpieu of Paris. Marked: "R.2.D." *Merrill Collection.*

494. FRENCH BISQUE DOLL — MARKED "E D"
Period: Last quarter of 19th century.
Body: Composition; elastic strung.
Remarks: 24" (61cm) French child doll resembling those made by Jumeau. The delicately tinted head has large blue set-in glass eyes; pierced ears; human hair wig. *Unusual feature:* molded tongue and teeth within open-closed mouth. Marked: "10 E D Depose." It is difficult to ascribe dolls marked "E D." Several French doll makers had these initials.

495. FRENCH BISQUE DOLL BY JULLIEN
Period: Last quarter of 19th century.
Body: Jointed composition; elastic strung; jointed
at shoulders and hips only.
Remarks: 19½" (49.6cm) French doll typical of fine French
bébés. Large, stationary glass eyes; heavily painted brows; closed
mouth; pierced ears; human hair wig. Marked: "J. 6 J." Probably
made by Jullien of Paris.

ABOVE RIGHT:
496. FRENCH CHILD DOLL — MARKED "PARIS-BÉBÉ"
Period: Last quarter of 19th century.
Body: Composition; elastic strung.
Remarks: 13" (33cm) French child doll with stationary brown
glass eyes; pierced ears; closed mouth; mohair wig. Stamped (in
red) on head: "Paris-Bebe//Tete Depose 4." Stamped on body:
Eiffel Tower trademark plus "Paris Bebe Depose" (see insert).
Made in France by Danel & Cie.

RIGHT:
497. FRENCH BISQUE DOLL — MARKED "P. G."
Period: Last quarter of 19th century.
Body: Composition; elastic strung; jointed at hips
and shoulders only.
Remarks: 16" (40.6cm) French doll with fine bisque socket head.
Stationary brown glass eyes; pierced ears; closed mouth; mohair
wig. Bears strong resemblance to Jumeau dolls. Marked: "P.G."
(see insert). Maker uncertain. *Merrill Collection.*

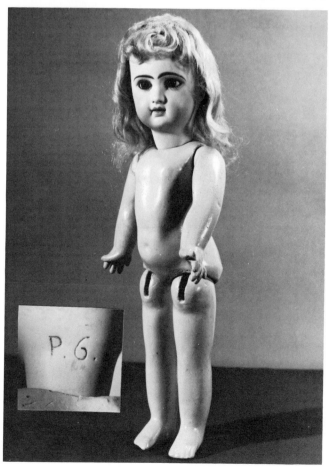

225

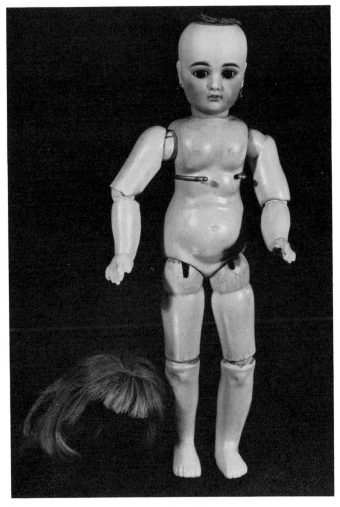

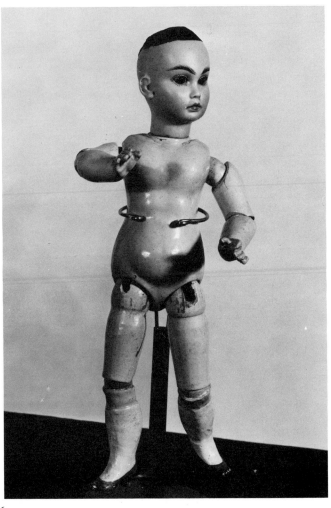

498. SO-CALLED "BELTON" DOLL HEAD

Belton — a name attached to a socket head, wholly of bisque, including cranium. When twine is threaded through two holes in top of skull, the head may be securely tied to the elastic-strung composition body.

This type head is usually of fine bisque with stationary glass eyes; pierced ears; closed mouth; and hair wig. Unmarked.

Although the doll has some French characteristics, it is probably of German origin.

ABOVE RIGHT:
499. SWIVEL-NECKED BISQUE HEAD ON PAPIER MÂCHÉ SHOULDER PLATE

Period: Last quarater of 19th century.
Body: All leather.
Remarks: 18" (45.7cm) doll with unique feature — bisque socket head, of Belton type, mounted on shoulder plate of papier mâché. Delicately tinted bisque head has closed mouth; stationary glass eyes; finely drawn brows; pierced-in ears; human hair wig. Unmarked.

RIGHT:
500. ORIENTAL DOLL IN BISQUE

Period: Late 19th century.
Body: Composition; elastic strung.
Remarks: 9½" (24.2cm) fine quality bisque doll with oriental features. Yellow tinted bisque; glass eyes and closed mouth. Head closed on top. So-called *Belton* type. Note interesting up-turned toes on molded slippers. Doll is unmarked probably made in Germany.

501. FRENCH CHILD DOLL ON LEATHER BODY
Period: Last quarter of 19th century.
Body: Leather with bisque arms.
Remarks: Example of a 15" (38.1cm) French child doll with swivel-neck bisque head; stationary glass eyes; closed mouth; pierced ears; lambskin wig. The 15" (38.1cm) doll is unmarked. Wears original blue and red satin costume. *Merrill Collection.*

502. BISQUE DOLL MARKED "W. D."
Period: Late 19th and early 20th century.
Body: Jointed composition; elastic strung.
Remarks: 16" (40.6cm) German doll whose bisque socket head has stationary glass eyes; heavily painted brows; closed mouth; pierced ears; light mohair wig. Marked on back of head (see insert): "W.D./7." Maker uncertain. *Collection of Nancy Shurtleff.*

RIGHT:
503. EARLY GERMAN BISQUE DOLL
Period: Last quarter of 19th century.
Body: Leather with bisque arms.
Remarks: 18" (45.7cm) German doll comparable to French in quality. Swivel-necked bisque head has blue stationary glass eyes; pierced ears; closed mouth; blonde mohair wig. Marked: "302//8." *Merrill Collection.*

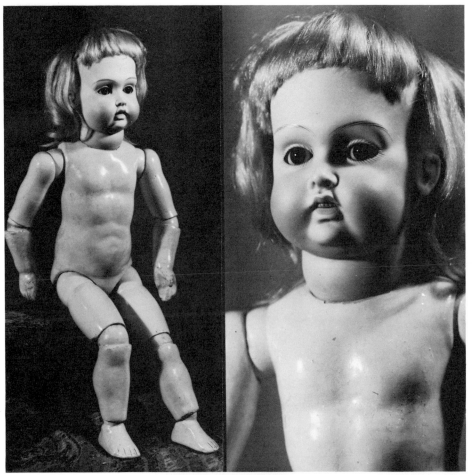

504. BISQUE DOLL OF UNCOMMON MOLD AND BODY
Period: Late 19th century.
Body: Jointed wood and composition; elastic strung.
Remarks: 16" (40.6cm) doll whose fine socket head, full at cheeks and neck, has sleeping eyes; open-closed mouth with molded-in upper teeth; light mohair wig. Body differs from usual; legs are jointed at ankles. Illustrated doll is unmarked. Uncertain whether made in France or Germany.

BELOW:
505. BISQUE HEAD DOLL
Period: Last quarter of 19th century before 1890.
Body: Ball jointed strung composition.
Remarks: A 25½" (64.8cm) fine quality bisque, nicely molded head with open-closed mouth and molded upper teeth. Blue paperweight eyes and feathered eyebrows. Head has a rather thick, straight sided neck, and a roll of "fat" on back of neck below the incised "15." These characteristics are common to heads made by the German firm of J. D. Kestner Co., and this head is attributed to this Company. Note the composition dome is incised "B.5." Body marked GERMANY with red rubber stamp. *Merrill Collection.*

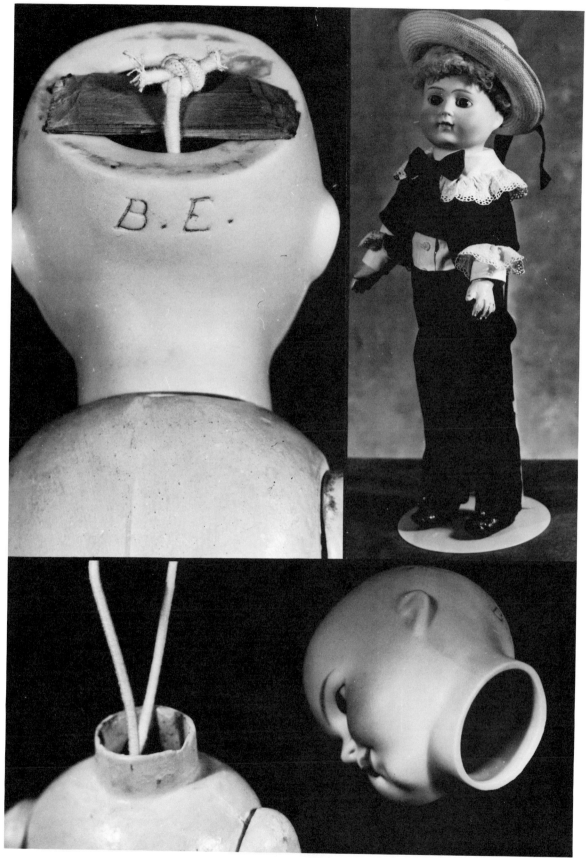

506. BOY BISQUE DOLL — INCISED "B. E."
Period: Last quarter of 19th century.
Body: Composition; elastic strung.
Remarks: 18" (45.7cm) boy doll in bisque - rare. The flange-necked head has set-in brown glass eyes; feathered brows; closed mouth; lambskin wig. Incised on back of neck: "B. E." Maker unknown. *Merrill Collection.*

LEFT:
507. CHILD DOLL OF LATE 19th CENTURY
Period: Late 19th century.
Body: Jointed composition; elastic strung.
Remarks: All original 12" (30.5cm) child doll - shown dressed and undressed. Typical of late 19th century French dolls. Fine bisquet socket head has stationary glass eyes; pierced ears; closed mouth; mohair wig over cork crown. Maker uncertain. Marks on back of head poorly impressed. One impression seems to read: "1 : 6." Similar to 136 mold. *Merrill Collection.*

509. EARLY GERMAN DOLL — MARKED #911
Period: Last quarter of 19th century.
Body: All leather.
Remarks: A 17" (43.2cm) German made doll equal to the finest French in quality. Swivel-necked head has stationary glass eyes; closed mouth; pierced-in ears; mohair wig. Completely original. Rim of head is marked: "911/7" plus a crosshatch (see insert). Maker uncertain.

LEFT:
508. FRENCH-TYPE BISQUE DOLL — MARKED #136
Period: Last quarter of 19th century.
Body: Composition strung body with closed wrists and ball jointed hips.
Remarks: 15" (38.1cm) bisque doll with set blue paperweight eyes; closed mouth; French cut pate; cork dome; and human hair wig. Back of head incised: "136//10." Maker unknown but thought to be a fine quality German doll. *Merrill Collection.*

230

510. GERMAN BISQUE DOLLS OF SUPERIOR QUALITY

Period: Late 19th century.
Body: Jointed composition; elastic strung.
Remarks: Left: 24" (61cm) German doll — a successful rival of the French made dolls of the period. Bisque socket head has sleeping glass eyes; closed mouth; mohair wig. As with the French dolls, wrists are unjointed — a characteristic not generally found in German made dolls. Dressed in finely made, original costume. Doll is incised: "15."
Right: 19" (48.3cm) ball and socket composition body; elastic strung. Note unjointed wrists. Fine quality bisque head — generally found on this type body. *Merrill Collection.*

BELOW:
512. CLOSED MOUTH BISQUE DOLL ON LEATHER BODY

Period: Late 19th century.
Body: Leather with bisque arms.
Remarks: 28" (71.1cm) closed mouth; sleeping eyed bisque doll with head slightly turned to side. Marked: "Made in Germany/N." Made in Germany by the J. D. Kestner Company who produced dolls of the highest quality. *Merrill Collection.*

511. CLOSED-MOUTH BISQUE DOLL ON JOINTED COMPOSITION BODY

Period: Late 19th century.
Body: Jointed composition; elastic strung.
Remarks: 18" (45.7cm) closed wrists; closed mouth; sleeping eyed bisque doll of high quality. Incised: "3." Although it has many characteristics of the French doll of the period, it is probably of German manufacture — possibly by the firm of J. D. Kestner. *Merrill Collection.*

544. BLACK BISQUE DOLL
Period: Late 19th and early 20th century.
Body: Black leather body with lower legs of cloth;
lower arms of black bisque.
Remarks: Black bisque shoulderhead with open mouth; glass
eyes; and black mohair wig. Doll made in Germany.

545. GERMAN BISQUE BOY DOLL
Period: Early 20th century.
Body: Leather with bisque arms.
Remarks: 12" (30.5cm) German bisque boy doll with typical hair
style; glass eyes; closed mouth. Unmarked. Known as *The
American Schoolboy. Merrill Collection.*

**546. GERMAN BISQUE DOLL BY
ERNST HEUBACH**
Period: Late 19th and early 20th
century.
Body: Leather with lower arms of
bisque.
Remarks: 20" (50.8cm) doll with smooth,
pale bisque head. Stationary glass eyes,
of type found in fine French dolls, have
long, finely drawn lashes and heavily
painted brows. Open mouth has four
upper teeth and wig is of human hair.
Marked: "Made in Germany//ᴲK
(within horse shoe)//Hch.2.H." Made by
German firm of Ernst Heubach.

245

547.

548.

550.

549.

547. "UNCLE SAM" BISQUE CHARACTER DOLL
Period: Late 19th century.
Body: Composition; elastic strung.
Remarks: *Uncle Sam* bisque character doll in original costume. Extremely well done. Dark brown glass eyes; mohair wig and beard; stands 16" (40.6cm) in height. Wears red and white striped trousers; blue vest with white stars; blue coat with tails; gray hat. Made in Germany. Marked: "S 5." *Merrill Collection.*

548. BICYCLIST CHARACTER DOLL
Period: Late 19th century.
Body: Composition; elastic strung.
Remarks: 14" (35.6cm) boy character doll in original blue wool costume of a bicyclist. Dark brown stationary glass eyes; mohair wig; open mouth with teeth; prominent nose. Marked: "M 1." on back of head. Bought at Hanke's store, Cincinnati, Ohio, in 1897. *Collection of Mrs. G. B. Walker.*

LEFT:
549. AMERICAN INDIAN DOLLS
Period: Late 19th and early 20th century.
Bodies: Composition; elastic strung; jointed at hips and shoulders.
Remarks: Identical pair of 8½" (21.6cm) dolls representing American Indians. Red-toned bisque heads, streaked with green war paint; have brown painted eyes; closed mouths; blue bead earrings; coarse hair wigs. Fringed flannel costumes have brown shirts and colored pants; one blue, the other red. Neck bands of gilt paper. Pierced right hands carry feathered spears. Marked: "115/15." *Collection of Mrs. Eleanor C. Wehrly.*

550. BLACK ALL BISQUE DOLL
Period: Late 19th and early 20th century.
Remarks: Ethnic featured, 5" (12.7cm) well modelled, all bisque Black doll. Has stationary glass eyes; closed mouth; mohair wig; bare feet. All original including cotton costume and slat bonnet. Unmarked. *Merrill Collection.*

551. BISQUE DOLLS IN ORIGINAL FOREIGN COSTUMES
Period: Late 19th and early 20th century.
Body: Jointed composition; elastic strung.
Remarks: Group of bisque foreign dolls in original costumes. From left to right: 14" (35.6cm) gaily costumed bisque doll; unmarked. 15" (38.1cm) bisque doll in Scottish costume; marked: "S.F.B.J." 11in (27.9cm) bisque doll in Alsatian costume; marked: "S.F.B.J. Paris." 12" (30.5cm) bisque doll in costume of Lorraine; marked: "S.F.B.J. Paris." 10½in (26.7cm) dark bisque character doll of an American Indian warrior; marked: "Germany." All of these dolls have glass eyes; open mouths with teeth; and mohair wigs.

552. BISQUE DOLLS IN ORIGINAL FOREIGN DRESS
Period: Late 19th century.
Bodies: Cloth with bisque limbs.
Left: 9" (22.9cm) bisque doll with closed mouth; stationary glass eyes; mohair wig. Black Forest costume (German) is complete and original.
Right: 7" (17.8cm) bisque doll with closed mouth; stationary glass eyes; mohair wig. Original costume.
   Both dolls, of fine bisque, are unmarked. Probably of German manufacture.

553. BOULOGNE FISHERMAN — MARKED "F.G."
Period: Circa 1890-1900.
Body: Cloth with terra cotta boots; wooden arms.
Remarks: 10" (25.4cm) Boulogne fisherman. Pink bisque head has painted features and hair; pierced ears. Costume original with exception of replaced scarf and cap. Marked: "F * G" on back shoulders. Probably made by F. Gaultier of Paris. One of a pair. Came with a like doll dressed as a fisherwoman. *Collection of Mrs. John M. Park, Jr.*

Mechanical and Novelty Dolls
of Various Materials - 19th Century

554. AUTOPERIPATETIKOS OR WALKING DOLL
Period: Patented July 15, 1862.
Body: Mechanism contained in cardboard housing beneath skirt; leather arms attached to padded torso.
Remarks: 9½" (24.2cm) walking doll with original box. The reinforced cloth head has painted features and hair. The key wound clockworks, hidden beneath skirt, operates the metal feet which cause the doll to walk. Printed on base is: "Patented July 15th, 1862; also, in England." *Merrill Collection.*

555. WALKING DOLL WITH CHINA HEAD
Period: Third quarter of 19th century.
Body: Torso, with leather arms; top key-wound
  mechanism.
Remarks: 10" (25.4cm) key-wound mechanical doll with decorated china head. When wound, the metal feet are set in motion
and doll walks. The molded snood is tinted in blue-green tones,
has a pale gray ruffle, and is decorated on top center with a small
cluster of grapes or berries. This same head, mounted on a cloth
body with china limbs, was also made as a play doll. *Courtesy of
The Essex Institute, Salem, Massachusetts.*

556. WALKING ZOUAVE DOLL
Period: Third quarter of 19th century.
Body: Mechanism contained in cardboard housing
  of torso; leather arms.
Remarks: 10" (25.4cm) autoperipatetikos or walking doll with
original box. Molded and painted fabric head. Painted features
include dark brown eyes; black mustache, beard and hair.
Original blue and red Zouave costume.

557. DOLL PLAYING SPINET
Period: Third quarter of 19th century.
Body: All wooden with pegged joints at knees;
arms mounted by stiff wires.
Remarks: Mechanical doll playing spinet whose papier-mâché head has painted blue eyes and black hair caught in gilded snood. A 6½" (20.3cm) x 8" (16.5cm) string-drawn toy. Mechanism which causes doll to move and music to tinkle is housed in yellow-painted wooden base. When set in motion, doll appears to play spinet as music sounds. *Collection of Miss Zelda Cushner.*

BELOW:
558.
LEFT: DOLL RIDING TRICYCLE
Period: 1868-1870.
Body: Wood with metal limbs.
Remarks: Doll with molded, painted head of stiffened cloth riding spring-wound tricycle. She has molded-on earrings touched with gilt. A label tacked to shoulders reads: "X.L.C.R. DOLL HEAD Sept. 8, 1868." Made by George H. Hawkins of New York. 11" (27.9cm) metal tricycle marked: "Pat. Feb. 1st, 1870, January 25, 1870." *Merrill Collection.*
RIGHT: WALKING DOLL WITH CARRIAGE
Period: 1868.
Body: Wood with metal limbs.
Remarks: A 10½" (26.7cm) mechanical walking doll pushing three-wheeled carriage. Pressed cloth head is by Hawkins; labeled: "X.L.C.R. DOLL HEAD, Patented Sept. 8, 1868." Painted features; blonde hair with black band; molded-on gilt-painted earrings. Wears original clothes; dress of white gauze with pink ribbon sash. Red wooden carriage, with metal wheels, has gold decorations on sides. Toy is spring operated — set in motion by winding of rear left wheel.

559. BOY RIDING VELOCIPEDE

Period: Last quarter of 19th century.

Remarks: All original toy of boy riding velocipede — overall measurement 10" (25.4cm) x 11½" (29.2cm). Fine quality head, of smooth, pale bisque; has black molded hair; blue painted eyes; closed mouth. Wooden hands grasp ivory tipped handle bars. Braid trimmed, brass buttoned suit is of blue, buff and rose colored satin. Blue cap of like material. Boy pedals across floor when key-wound mechanism is set in motion. *Collection of Mrs. Fidelia Lence.*

560. MAN RIDING VELOCIPEDE

Period: Last quarter of 19th century.

Remarks: Man riding velocipede — overall measurement 12" (30.5cm) by 11" (27.9cm). Rider's papier mâché head has painted features including brown eyes and black mustache. Hands of wood; high boots of papier mâché. Doll pedals across surface when key-wound velocipede is set in motion.

562. BISQUE WALKING DOLL

Period: Last quarter of 19th century.

Body: Cloth torso, with leather arms, top key-wound clockworks housed in cone-shaped container.

Remarks: 13" (33cm) mechanical doll with bald type bisque head; painted features; mohair wig. When wound, doll glides across floor. By turning the rear wheel on the base (see illustration) doll travels in circles. Bought at the Philadelphia Centennial (World's Fair) in 1876. *Merrill Collection.*

563. PAIR OF WALTZING FRENCH DOLLS

Period: Third quarter of 19th century.

Bodies: Mechanized. Lady's arms of bisque; gentleman's hands of metal.

Remarks: A pair of 13½" (34.3cm) French musical and waltzing dolls. When key-wound, music sounds while dolls glide across floor, turn in circles, then reverse their movements. Plays two tunes. The swivel-necked French bisque heads have gray-blue stationary glass eyes; closed mouth; pierced ears; white mohair wigs. Wear original costumes. Unmarked. *Courtesy of The Margaret Woodbury Strong Museum, Rochester, New York. Photograph by Barbara W. Jendrick.*

OPPOSITE PAGE: LEFT:
561. FRENCH BISQUE DOLL BEARING IZZARD OF LONDON LABEL

Period: Third quarter of 19th century.

Body: Carton moule upper torso, with bisque arms, is mounted on three-wheeled cone shaped housing which contains key-wound mechanism.

Remarks: 14½" (36.9cm) mechanical doll whose French bisque shoulderhead has glass eyes; feathered brows; open mouth with upper and lower molded-in teeth; blonde mohair wig. When set in motion, doll glides forward while raising and lowering long bisque arms. By turning rear wheel on wooden base, doll travels in circles. Imported from France by Izzard of 136 Regent Street, London, whose shop label appears on base of doll. Unmarked, but this type known to have been made by Jules Steiner.

564. FRENCH DOLL PLAYING THE PIANO

Period: Third quarter of 19th century.

Body: Mechanized. Composition arms.

Remarks: French musical and mechanical toy. Doll 19½" (49.6cm); piano 14½" (36.9cm) high. As music plays, the doll's hands glide across keyboard while head moves back and forth, up and down. Plays four tunes. The swivel-necked bisque head has brown stataionary glass eyes; closed mouth; pierced ears; human hair wig. Costume copied from original. Head, made by Jumeau of Paris, is marked: "Depose//E 6 J." *Courtesy of The Margaret Woodbury Strong Museum, Rochester, New York. Photograph by Barbara W. Jendrick.*

565. SEATED FRENCH DOLL PLAYING THE PIANO

Period: Third quarter of 19th century.

Body: Mechanized. Metal hands.

Remarks: French musical and mechanical toy — 13½" (34.3cm) high. Wooden piano has handles at sides, ivory keyboard, metal candle sconces. As music plays, doll's hands move across the keyboard while head moves up and down, back and forth. The French bisque head has blue-gray stationary glass eyes; closed mouth; pierced ears; human hair wig. Wears original costume. Unmarked. *Courtesy of The Margaret Woodbury Strong Museum, Rochester, New York. Photograph by Barbara W. Jendrick.*

566. FRENCH MECHANICAL SHEPHERDESS MARKED "JUMEAU"

Period: Third quarter of 19th century.
Body: Wooden legs; bisque arms; key-wound mechanism in torso.
Remarks: Fine bisque head of this 22" (55.9cm) mechanical shepherdess has large stationary glass eyes; closed mouth; pierced ears; white mohair wig. Marked: "Depose//Tete Jumeau//Bte SGDG//7." When set in motion, doll moves head from side to side, then looks downward while raising and lowering lid of basket which contains a bleating lamb. *Collection of Mrs. Fidelia Lence.*

BELOW:
567. FRENCH MECHANICAL DOLL BY JUMEAU
Period: Third quarter of 19th century.
Body: Mechanized with bisque arms.
Remarks: 14" (35.6cm) bisque headed doll marked "Depose Tete Jumeau." Brown stationary glass eyes; closed mouth; blonde mohair wig. Original costume. When wound by key, doll strums mandolin and turns head. Plays two tunes. *Collection of Miss Zelda H. Cushner.*

254

570. FRENCH DOLL EATING CHOCOLATE AND READING BOOK

Period: Third quarter of 19th century.

Body: Mechanized. Arms of bisque.

Remarks: A French musical and mechanical toy — 17" (43.2cm) in height. The bisque headed doll, seated on basket, moves her head up and down, to and fro, while eating chocolate and reading her book. "Tête Jumeau" marked head has blue stationary glass eyes; closed mouth; human hair wig. Wears original costume. *Courtesy of The Margaret Woodbury Strong Museum, Rochester, New York. Photograph by Barbara W. Jendrick.*

568.

568. FRENCH DOLL PLAYING VIOLIN

Period: Last quarter of 19th century.

Body: Mechanized. Wooden legs; bisque arms.

Remarks: Mechanical doll mounted on music box — overall height 19" (48.3cm). Bisque head has stationary glass eyes; closed mouth; pierced ears; mohair wig. Marked: "Depose//Tete Jumeau." When key-wound mechanism is set in motion, doll plays violin. Initials "L.B." cast in box key. Made by Leopold Lambert of Paris, maker of mechanical toys.

569. FRENCH MECHANICAL DOLL — BY JUMEAU

Period: Third quarter of 19th century.

Body: Mechanized with bisque arms.

Remarks: Overall 19" (48.3cm) fine, French mechanical doll, marked "Jumeau." When wound, turns and bows head; raises and lowers arms; and looks in mirror through lorgnette. A rare item — one of the best of bisque dolls given life-like motion.

569.

570.

BELOW:
572. FRENCH MECHANICAL MAGICIAN
French bisque head figure raises top of die-painted box to reveal head. Original clothing.

571. FRENCH MECHANICAL DOLL — POURS TEA
Period: Last quarter of 19th century.
Body: Mechanized. Bisque arms.
Remarks: Mechanical doll, in provincial costume, mounted on music box, overall height 21" (53.3cm). Bisque head marked "Tete Jumeau//4." Holds wooden tea set. Music box plays as doll turns head, pours tea, extends and retracts tea tray. Initials "L.B." cast in box key. Bottom of box labeled: "L.B.//Modele Depose//Carmen." Made by Leopold Lambert of Paris, maker of mechanical toys.

573. FRENCH MECHANICAL DOLL WITH BIRD AND FLOWERS

Period: Third quarter of 19th century.
Body: Mechanized with arms of bisque.
Remarks: 17" (43.2cm) French mechanical doll mounted on three wheeled metal platform. Bisque head has stationary glass eyes; closed mouth; pierced ears. Wears original costume of rose and brown satin. Unmarked. Doll holds bouquet of flowers in right hand while brightly feathered bird perches on left. When key-wound mechanism on under side of platform is set in motion, doll turns head, raises and lowers flowers, and chirping bird rotates on his perch. *Collection of Mrs. Raymond Knapp.*

574. MILKMAID AND COW — FRENCH

Period: Last quarter of 19th century.
Remarks: Fine, unmarked French doll mounted on platform with chamois covered, glass eyed cow. Doll has stationary brown glass eyes; mohair wig over cork crown; bisque arms; wooden legs. When key-wound mechanism is set in motion, doll turns head first right, then left, while tapping back of cow as though to start her along. Meanwhile cow turns head from side to side as toy moves across surface. *Collection of Perelman Antique Toy Museum, Philadelphia, Pennsylvania.*

LEFT:
575. BISQUE HEAD MECHANICAL DOLL
Period: Last quarter of 19th century.
Body: Papier mâché shell containing rods and
  levers producing the action.
Remarks: Bisque head doll 10½" (26.7cm), including platform 12½" (31.8cm) tall. Finely modelled head with moustache and goatee. Set in brown glass eyes. Raspberry and lavendar wool costume trimmed with cream colored leather. D'Artagnan cavalier style. Action includes arms movement and head turning, while travelling ahead or in circles. Brass mechanical movement marked: "G. Vichy//Paris." *Collection of Jane W. Alton.*

BELOW:
576. BARE BACK CIRCUS RIDER
Period: Late 19th century.
Remarks: Intriguing 24" (61cm) x 17" (43.2cm) (overall) pull toy of bisque headed doll riding four dappled gray horses. Horses are felt covered and glass eyed. Bisque head of doll has stationary glass eyes; open mouth with teeth; mohair wig. Marked: "9//5/0." When toy is pulled, bells ring while wheel-mounted horses gallop.

LEFT:
577. MECHANICAL WAX-OVER-COMPOSITION DOLL WHO TOSSES ARMS UPWARD

Period: Third quarter of 19th century.

Body: Wooden limbs wired to box like torso which houses mechanism and voice box (see illustration).

Remarks: 10½" (26.7cm) simple mechanical doll with wax-over-composition head. Molded blonde hair; pupilless glass eyes; painted features. When mechanism in torso is pressed, doll tosses arms upward, squeaks and turns head. *Collection of Mrs. Frank Maitland.*

578. MECHANICAL LADY MAGICIAN

Period: Circa 1890.

Body: Mechanized. Arms and slippered legs of composition.

Remarks: Lady magician mounted on box containing key-wound mechanism — 17½" (44.5cm) overall. Composition head has brown glass eyes with lashes; human hair wig. Doll sits before table with inverted cone in each hand. When set in motion, she turns head, blinks eyes, raises and lowers arms to disclose four changes of various colored marbles — the familiar shell game. *Collection of Toy Cupboard Museum, South Lancaster, Massachusetts.*

LEFT:
579. DANCING DOLL ON MUSIC BOX — FRENCH

Period: Last quarter of 19th century.

Body: Padded torso over wooden core. Wooden arms; loosely hung, slender wooden legs.

Remarks: Dancing doll mounted on inlaid wooden music box — 11" (27.9cm) x 5¾" (14cm) overall. Bisque head of spindle mounted figure has set-in blue glass eyes; closed mouth; light mohair wig. Circular sticker on box has trademark "A (harp symbol) M" plus "Marque de Fabrique — Paris." Also labeled as playing "Carmen Polka." Doll pirouettes as music plays. *Collection of Miss Zelda Cushner.*

580. MECHANICAL DOLLS — PULL TOYS
Period: Late 19th and early 20th century.
Remarks: Uncomplicated mechanical dolls — pull toys set in motion by pushing or pulling of conveyance. **From left to right:** Clown with bisque head; wooden limbs. Twirls wooden propeller. Marked: "Made in Germany." 14" (35.6cm) in height overall; c.1910. Wax-over-composition baby in wicker basket - 11" (27.9cm) overall. Doll moves, cries, kicks limbs. Unmarked. Made in last quarter of 19th century. 12" (30.5cm) clown with bisque head and wooden limbs. Moves head from side to side while clashing cymbals. Marked: "Made in Germany." c.1910. 12" (30.5cm) clown with bisque head and wooden limbs. Doll plays wooden violin while turning head from side to side. Marked: "Made in Germany." c.1910. *Merrill Collection.*

FAR LEFT:
581. MECHANICAL BALANCING CLOWNS
Period: Late 19th and early 20th century.
Remarks: 27" (68.6cm) crank operated mechanical toy of large clown balancing smaller one on head. Head of larger doll, with set-in glass eyes, appears to be of a clay-like substance. Smaller one has head of bisque. When cranked, music box plays, small clown revolves and large clown moves head while strumming mandolin. Unmarked. *Collection of Perelman Antique Toy Museum, Philadelphia, Pennsylvania.*

582. CLOWN PLAYING HARP
Period: Late 19th century.
Remarks: Mechanical clown playing harp — overall measurement 12" (30.5cm) x 8" (20.3cm). Papier mâché head has painted features including blue eyes and smiling mouth with five painted teeth. Sits on decorated metal drum which houses key-wound mechanism. When set in motion, music of plucked strings sounds while clown moves head and strums harp. Dressed in lace-trimmed white satin costume.

583. RATTLES AND MAROTTE
Period: Late 19th and early 20th century.
Body: Bellows or music box mounted on wooden handle.
Left: 14½" (36.9cm) rattle with German bisque head. Whistle in tip of wooden handle. Squeaks when shaken.
Center: 13½" (34.3cm) rattle with German bisque clown head. Squeaks and clashes cymbals when shaken.
Right: 10" (25.4cm) marotte with French type bisque head on stick mounted music box. When twirled, music plays. *Merrill Collection.*

584. MAROTTE
Period: Late 19th and early 20th century.
Body: Padded music box mounted on stick.
Left: 12½" (31.8cm) musical doll, stick mounted. Dressed to represent rabbit. Gloved hands hold drum sticks over small, velvet covered drum. Bisque head has blue glass eyes; closed mouth. When stick is twirled, figure revolves while music plays. These dolls may be found in a variety of dress. Several names are given to this type doll — *Musical Doll, Folly Head, Poupart* and *Musical Rattle.*
Right: 11" (27.9cm) Marotte with bisque head dressed as court jester with rabbit ears; kid-covered wood arms with drumsticks over small matching drum of ivory velvet and blue satin; when twirled, plays "Auld Lang Syne" and "Bluebells of Scotland."

585. CREEPING BABY BY IVES
Period: Last quarter of 19th century.
Body: Key-wound brass clockworks within cardboard torso; composition arms and legs.
Remarks: 11" (27.9cm) mechanical doll in original condition and costume. Wax-over-composition head has painted features including blue eyes and smiling mouth with five painted teeth. Invented by Robert J. Clay. Advertised in catalog of Ives, Blakeslee & Williams Company as "A doll that creeps around in good imitation of a live baby." Price (in 1893) $48.00 per dozen.

587. THREE FACED DOLL IN BISQUE MARKED "C.B."
Period: Late 19th and early 20th century.
Body: Cloth with composition limbs; arms elastic
strung.
Remarks: Three faced doll — sleeps, smiles, cries. Crying face with molded tears. Bisque faces appear by turning brass ring on top of head. Head, beneath hood of papier mâché, revolves on papier mâché shoulder piece. Voice box within body operated by pull strings. Marked on back shoulders: "C.B." (within oval). Probably made by Carl Bergner of Sonneburg who also made a similar two-faced doll in wax. *Collection of Mrs. Louise H. Lund.*

BELOW:
588. THREE FACED DOLL IN BISQUE MARKED "D.R.P."
Period: Late 19th and early 20th century.
Body: Cloth with composition limbs; arms elastic
strung.
Remarks: 13" (33cm) three-faced doll — sleeps, smiles, cries. Crying face without tears. Bisque faces appear by turning brass ring on top of head. Head, beneath hood of papier mâché, revolves on deep papier mâché shoulder piece. Stamped (in rectangle) on back of shoulders: "D.R.P." *Collection of Mrs. Louise H. Lund.*

OPPOSITE PAGE:
586. THREE FACED DOLL IN BISQUE RED RIDING HOOD, GRANDMOTHER, WOLF
Period: Late 19th and early 20th century.
Body: Jointed composition; elastic strung.
Remarks: 14" (35.6cm) three-faced doll of Red Riding Hood. Bisque faces alternately appear from within papier mâché hood by turning brass ring atop head. A well detailed doll. *Grandmother* and *Red Riding Hood* have brown glass eyes; closed mouths; mohair wigs. Dark face of wolf has painted eyes; red molded tongue. Doll wears print dress; red hooded-cape and carries wicker basket.

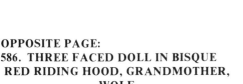

All Bisque Dolls - 19th Century

The types of all bisque dolls shown are ones most often found. They range in size from three to eight inches (7.6 to 20.3cm), although larger and smaller ones do appear. The rigid all bisque limbs are strung with either elastic or fine wire.

They vary in quality from coarse stone to fine French bisque, and were produced during the late 19th and early 20th centuries.

Although some fine and rare French all bisque dolls do appear, the majority of these dolls were made in Germany.

Prices are determined by the quality of the bisque, detail in modeling, condition and size.

589. FRENCH-TYPE DOLLS IN ORIGINAL COSTUMES
Period: Late 19th and early 20th century.
Remarks: A group of 3¼" (8.3cm) to 5" (12.7cm) dolls all in original costumes. The three larger dolls are considered earlier and have kid-lined, wooden pegged joints. All five have stationary glass eyes; closed mouths; mohair wigs. Fine condition and original clothes give these dolls added value. *Merrill Collection.*

590. FRENCH-TYPE ALL BISQUE DOLL
Period: Late 19th century.
Remarks: A pert, 6" (15.6cm) all bisque doll of the French type. It has sleeping eyes; closed mouth and mohair wig over cork pate. Joints are kid lined. Unmarked. Costume, of lace-trimmed red satin, is original. Dress has bustle back. *Merrill Collection.*

591. SMALL SIZED ALL BISQUE DOLLS
Period: Late 19th and early 20th century.
Remarks: Left: 3½" (8.9cm) fine quality doll with swivel neck; glass eyes; closed mouth; mohair wig. Has molded knee-length socks and blue-bowed black slippers.
Right: 5" (12.7cm) doll of French quality. Swivel-necked head has stationary glass eyes; open-closed mouth with molded-in teeth; mohair wig. Wears molded-on, long black stockings and brown one-strap slippers. Clothing is original. *Merrill Collection.*

592. ALL BISQUE DOLL OF FRENCH QUALITY
Period: Late 19th century.
Remarks: 7" (17.8cm) all bisque doll with set-in glass eyes; closed mouth; light blonde mohair wig; kid lined joints. Note unusually high black strapped boots.

593. DOLLS OF FRENCH QUALITY
Period: Late 19th century.
Remarks: Left: 8" (20.3cm) all bisque doll with appearance and quality of the French. Joints lined with kidskin; closed mouth; set-in glass eyes; molded on stockings and boots.
Right: 6" (15.2cm) all bisque doll with fine modeling; set-in glass eyes; molded on stockings and boots. Quality of French dolls.

594. SHOULDER JOINTED ALL BISQUE DOLL
Period: Late 19th century.
Remarks: 5" (12.7cm) all bisque doll of fine quality. Jointed at shoulders only. Painted blue eyes; closed mouth; mohair wig. Wears molded-on white stockings and tan colored, heeled boots. Unmarked.

595. ALL BISQUE DOLLS IN FOREIGN DRESS
Period: Circa 1890.
Remarks: Documented pair of fine all bisque dolls bought in Germany in 1892. 7½" (19.1cm) tall; open and shut eyes; finely painted and modeled boots; ribbed stockings; wearing foreign costumes.

596. GROUP OF ALL BISQUE DOLLS
Period: Late 19th and early 20th century.
Remarks: All bisque dolls in original costumes. Approximately
4" (10.2cm) to 5" (12.7cm) in height. **Left to right:** Jointed boy
doll with molded hair; painted eyes; molded shoes and socks.
Jointed girl doll with set-in glass eyes; mohair wig; molded yellow
boots. Unmarked, but has appearance and quality of the French
dolls. Unjointed all bisque doll of the *Frozen Charlotte* type.
Painted features; molded light brown hair.

598. "FROZEN CHARLOTTE" IN BISQUE
Period: Last half of 19th century.
Remarks: 5" (12.7cm) pillar doll. Called *Frozen Charlotte* after
heroine of a New England folk ballad. The untinted bisque head
has painted blue eyes and blonde molded hair. This type doll was
made in other materials including china and parian.

597. WELL PROPORTIONED ALL BISQUE DOLL
Period: Late 19th century.
Remarks: 8" (20.3cm) doll of fine bisque. Blonde molded
hairdo; blue painted eyes; early type tasseled boots in blue.

599. BISQUE DOLL WITH MOLDED RUFFLE
Period: Late 19th century.
Body: Cloth with bisque limbs.
Remarks: Small bisque doll head with molded ruffle at shoulder
edge. Pink-toned head has painted blue eyes; one-stroke brows;
molded blonde hair with bangs.

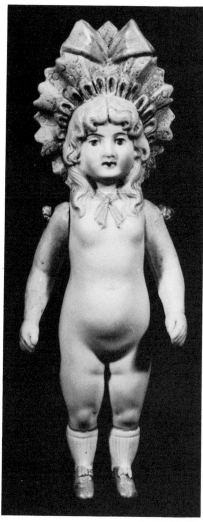

602.

600.

601.

603.

600. ALL BISQUE BONNET DOLL
Period: Late 19th century.
Body: All bisque with movable arms.
Remarks: 6" (15.2cm) all bisque bonnetted doll with painted features; blonde hair. Unusual. Dolls of this type generally have shoulder heads mounted on cloth bodies. Blue off-the-face bonnet has pink ties and bow. Molded on white socks and blue slippers. Marked on back with number "6."

601. SMALL, UNJOINTED BISQUE BONNET DOLL
Period: Early 20th century.
Body: All stone bisque. Construction same as
pillar or *Frozen Charlotte* doll.
Remarks: 2¾" (7.1cm) unjointed, inexpensive stone bisque doll. Molded-on white ruffled bonnet has bow of pink. Shoes match bow in color. Doll originally sold for pennies.

602. BISQUE BONNET DOLL
Period: Late 19th and early 20th century.
Body: Cloth with stone bisque limbs.
Remarks: 8½" (21.6cm) stone bisque doll with painted features; blonde hair. Molded-on bonnet has turned back brim decorated with pink flowers. Tied under chin with blue bow. Marked on back shoulder with size number "4." *Collection of Mrs. Neil Hobey.*

603. BISQUE BONNET DOLL
Period: Late 19th and early 20th century.
Body: Cloth with coarse, stone bisque limbs.
Remarks: Larger 12" (30.5cm) bisque doll with painted features; blonde hair and molded pink bonnet. Center of rosette and bow under chin are trimmed with gold. Back shoulders are incised with numbers: "94//2."

604. BISQUE BONNET DOLLS
Period: Late 19th and early 20th century.
Body: Cloth with stone bisque limbs.
Remarks: Additional examples of coarse stone bisque hatted dolls. These German made dolls came on cloth bodies with bisque limbs.
Left: Reddish brown band on bonnet matches ribbon tie. Molded blouse on shoulders.
Right: Doll wears white molded bonnet with blue facing and blue bows. Doll on right: *Merrill Collection.*

605. BISQUE BONNET DOLLS
Period: Late 19th and early 20th century.
Body: Cloth with stone bisque limbs.
Remarks: Two examples of coarse stone bisque bonnet dolls. They are found in various sizes — the smaller seemingly more plentiful. Made in Germany.
Left: Stone bisque doll with yellow-brown bonnet.
Right: Stone bisque bonnet doll wears white hat decorated with pink flowered band and blue bow.

606. HATTED DOLLS OF BISQUE
Period: Late 19th and early 20th century.
Body: Cloth with coarse stone bisque limbs.
Remarks: This illustration shows two, approximately 8" (20.3cm) to 10" (25.4cm), bonnet dolls with their original bodies. Dolls of this type were made with many different style hats.
Left: Doll with turn-back blue bonnet. Wears a molded gold necklace.
Right: Yellow off-the-face bonnet trimmed with red bow.

607. BISQUE HATTED DOLL
Period: Late 19th and early 20th century.
Body: Cloth with stone bisque limbs.
Remarks: 10" (25.4cm) stone bisque doll with molded-on hat and necklace. Pink plume decorates green upturned hat brim. Painted features include blue eyes. Slightly parted lips show tiny molded-in teeth. Bisque legs have knee-length ribbed socks and brown one-strap slippers.

609. BISQUE DOLL WITH MOLDED-ON TAM AND BLOUSE
Period: Late 19th and early 20th century.
Body: Cloth with bisque limbs.
Remarks: 15" (38.1cm) stone bisque doll with painted blue eyes; blonde hair. Wears pink molded-on tam-o-shanter and white molded-on blouse with gilt trim.

608. TWIN HATTED DOLLS
Period: Late 19th and early 20th century.
Body: Cloth with stone bisque limbs.
Remarks: Pair of small, identical 10" (25.4cm) bisque dolls with white molded-on hats and blouses. Differ only in coloring of hat bands and blouse bows; one pink, the other blue. Both have painted blue eyes; blonde hair.

610. BISQUE HATTED DOLL
Period: Late 19th and early 20th century.
Body: Cloth with bisque limbs.
Remarks: Pale bisque hatted doll somewhat finer in quality than those of stone bisque. Head, 3¾" (9.6cm) in height, has painted features; blonde hair. Wears pink molded-on hat with rosette in front, bow in back. White molded-on blouse has buttons and bow in front, beads at collar edge. Remains of gold trim still show on hat and blouse. *Collection of Bertha Hanscom.*

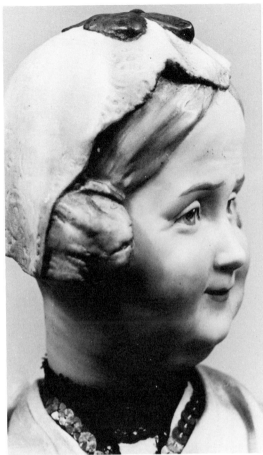
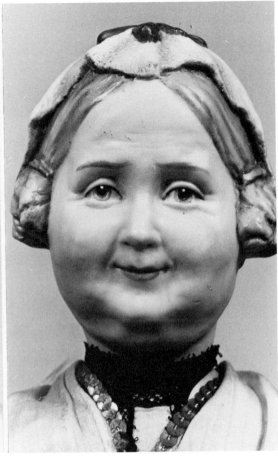

ABOVE:

611. BISQUE HATTED DOLL OF ELDERLY WOMAN
Period: Early 20th century.
Body: Jointed composition; elastic strung.
Remarks: The bisque socket head of this 15½" (39.4cm) doll has a lace embossed, scarf type, molded-on white bonnet with blue bow on top. Gray molded hair is tied at sides with blue ribbon. The wrinkled, double chinned face has painted eyes and a smiling, closed mouth. Unmarked. Molding of face and color of bisque resembles the character type dolls made by Gebrüder Heubach of Germany. *Courtesy of The Margaret Woodbury Strong Museum, Rochester, New York. Photograph by Barbara W. Jendrick.*

612. HATTED DOLL IN BISQUE
Period: Early 20th century.
Body: Cloth with bisque limbs.
Remarks: Smiling faced bisque hatted doll. Gray hat with white plume tops hairdo of gray curls. Stamped in ink under shoulder: "Made in Germany." Impressed on outer shoulder: "9557." Suggestive of figurine type or pincushion dolls.

Doll House Dolls - Bisque - 19th Century

The term "doll house" is used to describe the small character dolls made almost entirely for this purpose.

These German-made dolls have wire-stiffened cloth bodies; bisque heads and limbs.

They are found, individually or collectively, as members of a fully staffed household of the period —1890-1920. Most interesting are the characters such as grandma, grandpa, chauffeur and maid.

613. FAMILY MEMBERS AND SERVANTS OF THE DOLL HOUSE
Period: Early 20th century.
Bodies: Cloth with bisque limbs.
Remarks: German made doll house dolls — 3½" (8.9cm) to 5½" (14cm) in height. From left to right: *Grandpa, Mother, Maid, Father, Butler, Chef* with molded-on cap, and *little girl*. Fine condition and original clothing gives added interest and value to these dolls. *Merrill Collection.*

614. DOLL HOUSE FAMILY IN BISQUE
Period: Late 19th and early 20th century.
Bodies: Cloth with bisque limbs.
Remarks: Assembled family of bisque doll house dolls ranging in size from 3½" (8.9cm) to 6½" (16.5cm). Included in group are *parents, bald headed grandfather, little boy* and the *baby* in a cradle. *Merrill Collection.*

ABOVE:
615. GERMAN DOLL HOUSE DOLLS
Period: Late 19th and early 20th century.
Bodies: Cloth with bisque limbs.
Left: 6" (15.2cm) bald-headed bisque *Grandpa* with finely painated features.
Right: Small glass-eyed bisque lady with original, highly-styled mohair wig. Overall height 5½" (14.3cm).

617. DOLL HOUSE DOLL — LADY
Period: Late 19th and early 20th century.
Body: Cloth with bisque limbs.
Remarks: Exceptionally fine 7" (17.8cm) bisque doll house doll with glass eyes and mohair wig. All original. *Unusual feature:* all bisque arms strung through pierced bisque shoulders. *Merrill Collection.*

LEFT:
616. DOLL HOUSE DOLL WITH PERIOD WIG
Period: Late 19th and early 20th century.
Body: Cloth with bisque limbs.
Remarks: 8" (20.3cm) bisque doll with period style hairdo. Bisque shoulderhead with set-in glass eyes; painted features. This particular doll has white mohair wig. Marked: "S & H 1160 6/0." Head made by the German firm of Simon & Halbig.

618. GERMAN DOLL HOUSE DOLLS
Period: Late 19th and early 20th century.
Body: Cloth with bisque limbs.
Remarks: Left: Mustached man doll house doll about 7"
(17.9cm) in height.
Right: 7" (17.9cm) bisque doll well modeled in the likeness of the
Kaiser. Brought to the United States in 1892.

LEFT:
619. DOLL HOUSE DOLL DRESSED AS SOLDIER
Period: Early 20th century.
Body: Cloth with bisque limbs.
Remarks: 7¼" (18.5cm) doll house doll representing World War
I soldier. Wears khaki uniform and molded-on visored cap.
Carries tin rifle on shoulder. Painted features include blue eyes
and light brown mustache. This doll house doll may also be
found dressed as a chauffeur.

Bisque Dolls - 20th Century

620.

621.

622. PORTRAIT DOLL OF WILLIAM THOMAS SAMPSON
Period: 1902.
Body: Composition; elastic strung.
Remarks: 15" (38.1cm) portrait doll of Spanish-American War Commander William T. Sampson. Bisque head has molded brown hair; eyebrows and beard. Eyes incised. Head of Belton-type. Belted blue uniform has gilt buttons, gold fringed epaulets. Black molded boots. Papier mâché hat has gold-striped red, white and blue rosette. Unmarked. *Courtesy of the Margaret Woodbury Strong Museum, Rochester, New York. Photography by Barbara W. Jendrick.*

620. PRESIDENT McKINLEY PORTRAIT DOLL
Period: Circa 1901.
Body: Composition; elastic strung.
Remarks: 15" (38.1cm) overall, all original bisque headed portrait doll of U.S. President McKinley. Molded brown hair and brows; incised blue eyes. The head is of the Belton-type. Belted, blue felt uniform has gilt buttons, gold fringed epaulets. Black, molded boots. Glued-on black papier mâché hat has red, white and blue rosette with gold striping. Unmarked. *Courtesy of Miss Lois J. Meredith.*

621. ADMIRAL DEWEY PORTRAIT DOLL
Period: Circa 1898.
Body: Composition; elastic strung.
Remarks: 9" (22.9cm) bisque headed portrait doll of Admiral George Dewey. Molded gray hair and mustache; brown glass stationary eyes. The head, with partial mohair wig, is of the Belton-type. Blue felt uniform is gold braid trimmed and has metal buttons and epaulets. Hat missing. Wears molded black boots. Unmarked. Made in other sizes.

622.

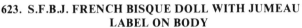

623.

624.

625.

623. S.F.B.J. FRENCH BISQUE DOLL WITH JUMEAU LABEL ON BODY

Period: First quarter of 20th century.
Body: Composition and wood; elastic strung.
Remarks: 15" (38.1cm) fine quality bisque doll with sleeping eyes; hair lashes; pierced ears; open mouth with teeth. Head marked "S.F.B.J." — initials of firm organized in 1899 by merger of French doll makers Société Francaise de Fabrication de Bébés et Jouets. Body bears paper label as shown in insert. Translation: "Faithful (or exact) Copy — Jumeau Made." *Courtesy of Mrs. John Cockcroft.*

624. #301 S.F.B.J. FRENCH BISQUE DOLL

Period: First quarter of 20th century.
Body: Composition and wood; elastic strung.
Remarks: Fine quality, 21" (53.3cm) doll whose head of extremely thin bisque has sleeping eyes with hair lashes; molded and painted brows; open mouth with teeth; human hair wig. Head marked: "R//S.F.B.J.//301//Paris//8." Circular label on body reads "Fabrication Francaise//Paris//S.F.B.J." *Merrill Collection.*

625. FRENCH PROVINCIAL DOLLS BY S.F.B.J.

Period: First quarter of 20th century.
Body: Composition; elastic strung.
Remarks: Pair of 8" (20.3cm) dolls in French Provincial costumes. Identical bisque heads have glass eyes; open mouths; mohair wigs. Marked: *Left:* "23//SFBJ//60//Paris." *Right:* "22//France//SFBJ//60//Paris." Made by Société Francaise de Fabrication de Bébés et Jouets.

626. A FRENCH KISS-THROWING DOLL MARKED S.F.B.J.

Period: Early 20th century.
Body: Jointed composition; elastic strung.
Remarks: 22½" (57.2cm) French bisque doll marked "Depose SFBJ." A mechanical doll, in original costume, who walks, turns head from side to side, flirts eyes, and throws kisses. *Merrill Collection.*

RIGHT:
627. FRENCH WALKING DOLL BY S.F.B.J.

Period: Early 20th century.
Body: Composition; arms elastic strung; legs attached to mechanism within torso.
Remarks: When hand propelled, this 16" (40.6cm) French doll walks as head turns from side to side. The bisque socket head has stationary glass eyes; open mouth with molded-in upper teeth; human hair wig. Marked: "S.F.B.J." *Collection of Shirley F. Sanborn.*

RIGHT:
628. BOY CHARACTER DOLL — BY S.F.B.J.

Period: First quarter of 20th century.
Body: Jointed composition; elastic strung.
Remarks: 20" (50.8cm) laughing boy character doll. Attractive, well modeled head has stationary glass eyes; open mouth with six molded-in upper teeth; light brown painted hair. Marked: "S.F.B.J.//227//Paris//8." This doll also made as a Black with skin wig.

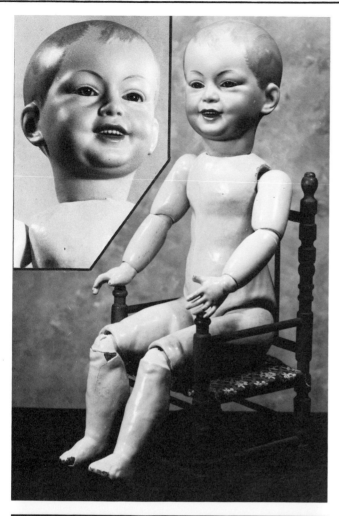

630. FLOCKED HAIR BOY DOLL — MARKED "S.F.B.J."
Period: Early 20th century.
Body: Jointed composition; elastic strung.
Remarks: The fine bisque head of this 14" (35.6cm) boy doll has set-in glass eyes; open-closed mouth with molded-in upper teeth; light brown flocked hair. Marked: "S.F.B.J.//237//Paris." *Collection of Mrs. Fidelia Lence.*

LEFT:
629. CHARACTER DOLL — MARKED "S.F.B.J."
Period: First quarter of 20th century.
Body: Composition; elastic strung.
Remarks: 22" (55.9cm) French character doll with sleeping eyes; smiling open-closed mouth with molded teeth and tongue; brown mohair wig. Marked: "S.F.B.J. 236 Paris." *Collection of Mrs. Mildred B. Fink.*

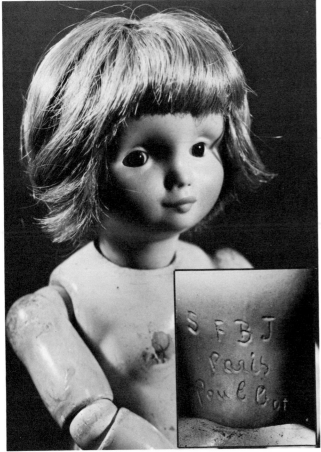

631. SMILING DOLL BY S.F.B.J.
Period: First quarter of 20th century.
Body: Jointed composition; elastic strung.
Remarks: The bisque socket head of this 13½" (34.3cm) doll has open-closed smiling mouth showing two molded-in teeth; sleeping glass eyes with hair lashes; mohair wig. Marked on back of head: "S.F.B.J.//236//Paris." *Collection of Shirley F. Sanborn.*

632. BISQUE DOLL BY S.F.B.J.
Period: Early 20th century.
Body: Composition; elastic strung; jointed at hips and shoulders.
Remarks: A beguiling little bisque headed doll with huge side-set glass eyes; closed smiling mouth; mohair wig. Marked: "S.F.B.J.//245//Paris//0." *Collection of Mrs. Fidelia Lence.*

633. POULBOT DOLL BY S.F.B.J.
Period: Early 20th century.
Body: Jointed composition; elastic strung.
Remarks: A wistful 13" (33cm) character doll whose bisque head has broad forehead with widely-spaced stationary glass eyes; closed mouth. Human hair wig is replacement for earlier one of mohair. Marked (see insert): "SFBJ//Paris//Poulbot."

634.

635.

634. FRENCH BISQUE DOLL MADE IN LIMOGES

Period: Circa 1900.
Body: Cloth with bisque arms; bisque legs with bare feet.
Remarks: French bisque doll with molded teeth; sleeping eyes; pierced-in ears; mohair wig. Marked on back of shoulders: "Cherie O// Fabrication Francaise//ALC E//Limoges." Made by A. Lanternier & Co. of Limoges. Although French, these dolls generally lack the quality of earlier French dolls. *Collection of Mrs. John M. Park, Jr.*

635. JAPANESE LADY DOLL MADE IN FRANCE

Period: 1930s.
Body: Jointed composition; elastic strung.
Remarks: 12" (30.5cm) bisque doll with sleeping eyes; open mouth with teeth; black mohair wig. All original. Marked (see insert): "Unis France// 71-110//301." Dolls made by Société Francaise de Fabrication de Bébés et Jouets sometimes bore this mark. "Made in France" is impressed on lower torso. This doll was purchased new in 1935.

636. "PETITE FRANCAIS" BY J. VERLINGUE

Period: 1915-1921.
Body: Jointed composition; elastic strung.
Remarks: 13" (33cm) French bisque doll with blue glass eyes; molded-in teeth in open mouth; brown mohair wig. Marked with anchor trademark plus incised: "Petite Francaise//France// JV//3" (see insert). The name "Liane" is often found below the anchor on this trademark. Made by J. Verlingue.

637. WORLD WAR I RED CROSS NURSES MADE IN PARIS

Period: World War I.
Body: Composition; elastic strung; jointed at shoulders and hips.
Remarks: Pair of 8" (20.3cm) dolls dressed as World War I Red Cross nurses. All original. Bisque socket heads have painted features including blue eyes. Wigs of mohair. Molded boots are painted brown. Both dolls are marked: "60//Paris."

279

OPPOSITE PAGE:

638. FRENCH BISQUE DOLL — MARKED "A. MARQUE"
Period: Early 20th century.
Body: Jointed composition with bisque forearms;
elastic strung.
Remarks: Slender-necked bisque head of this 22" (55.9cm)
French doll has broad forehead; prominent pierced ears; pointed
chin; wide-spaced stationary glass eyes; closed mouth; blonde
human hair wig. Marked: "A. Marque" in impressed script on
back of head (see insert). An appealing, seldom seen doll.
Collection of Mr. and Mrs. Raymond Knapp.

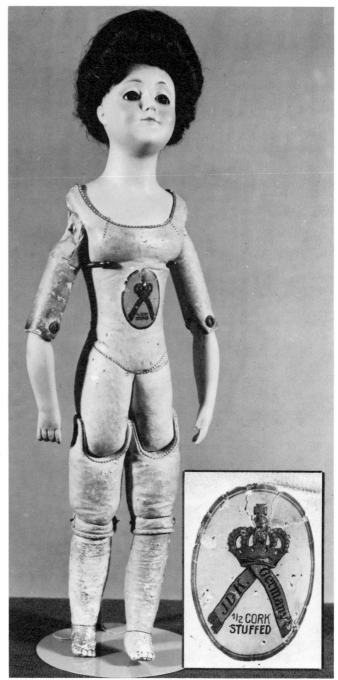

RIGHT:

639. "GIBSON GIRL" BISQUE DOLL
Period: Circa 1910.
Body: Leather with bisque arms.
Remarks: 16" (40.6cm) *Gibson Girl* showing well marked, adult
shaped body. Paper sticker on chest printed: "JDK//Germany//
1/2 Cork Stuffed." Smaller versions of this doll usually have
thicker waists and the trademark is stamped in blue. Fine bisque
head of illustrated doll is incised: "163/3." Made by the J. D.
Kestner Company of Germany. *Collection of Mrs. Elmer E.
Morley.*

LEFT:

640. "GIBSON GIRL" BISQUE DOLL
Period: Circa 1910.
Body: Leather with bisque arms.
Remarks: A 12" (30.5cm) glass-eyed, bisque headed character-
costume doll referred to as *Gibson Girl.* Resembles the drawings
of American artist, Charles Dana Gibson. Made by the J. D.
Kestner Company of Germany, mold #172. The leather body is
stamped with the mark of this firm. Made in several sizes, blonde
and brunette, for the George Borgfeldt Corporation, exclusive
agent for the Kestner Company in the United States. *Merrill
Collection.*

641. TYPICAL GERMAN BISQUE DOLL CLOSED MOUTH
Period: Early 20th century.
Body: Composition fully jointed, including wrists.
Remarks: Large size (29" [73.7cm]) good quality bisque doll with closed mouth; human hair wig; sleeping eyes. Marked: "M// Made in Germany."

ABOVE RIGHT:
642. TYPICAL GERMAN BISQUE DOLL OPEN MOUTH
Period: Early 20th century.
Body: Composition fully jointed, including wrists;
  elastic strung.
Remarks: Large size (32" [81.3cm]) good quality bisque doll with open mouth; sleeping eyes; human hair wig. Marked: "M//Made in Germany."

RIGHT:
643. #143 GERMAN BISQUE DOLLS BY KESTNER
Period: Early 20th century.
Body: Jointed composition; elastic strung.
Remarks: Two good quality bisque dolls with sleeping blue eyes; open mouths with teeth; heavily drawn brows.
Left: 13½" (34.3cm) doll with human hair wig.
Right: 13in (33cm) doll with blonde mohair wig.
  Both dolls bear identical marks: "B.//Made in Germany// 6//143." Made by the J. D. Kestner firm of Germany.

645. LETTIE LANE'S "DAISY" — LADIES HOME JOURNAL'S PREMIUM DOLL

Period: 1911.

Body: Jointed composition; elastic strung.

Remarks: 18" (45.7cm) bisque headed premium dolls with sleeping eyes; open mouths with teeth; mohair wigs. One doll given for three subscriptions to the *Ladies Home Journal.* Named *Daisy.*

Left: Doll marked: "C½//Made in Germany//171//7." Made by Kestner.

Right: Doll marked: "Germany//Heinrich Handwerck//Simon & Halbig//1." Made by Handwerck. Home Patterns were sold to costume *Daisy* as per full color pages in the *Ladies Home Journal. Collection of Mr. and Mrs. Thomas J. Kiley.*

ABOVE:

644. GERMAN BISQUE DOLL BY KESTNER MOLD #154

Period: Early 20th century.

Body: Leather with bisque arms.

Remarks: 18" (45.7cm) doll, all original, made in Kestner's often found mold #154. Of good quality, the pretty bisque head has blue sleeping eyes; open mouth with teeth; blonde mohair wig. Body stamped with famous Kestner trademark — crown with streamers (see insert). Head marked: "7½//154//DEP//C½//Made in Germany." Made by the J. D. Kestner Company of Germany.

RIGHT:

646. BISQUE DOLL WITH FUR EYEBROWS

Period: Circa 1910.

Body: Jointed composition; elastic strung.

Remarks: An 18½" (49.6cm) doll whose bisque socket head has sleeping eyes with hair lashes; open mouth with teeth; human hair wig. Realism in eyebrows was achieved by inserting fur through arched slits above eyes. Head marked: "C½.//Made in Germany//7½.//J.D.K.//215." Made in Germany by J. D. Kestner Company who patented fur eyebrows in 1910. This type doll may also be found with shoulderhead on leather body. *Merrill Collection.*

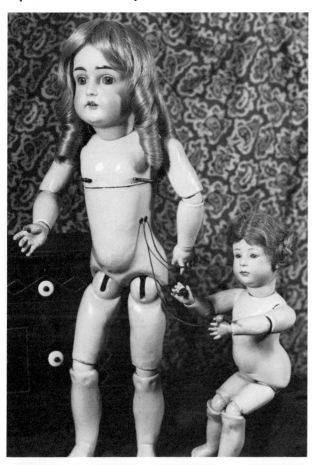

LEFT:
647. KESTNER DOLL WITH VOICE BOX.
Period: Early 20th century.
Body: Jointed composition; elastic strung.
Left: 19" (48.3cm) bisque doll with voice box operated by pull strings. Cries "mama," "papa." Bisque head has open mouth with teeth; sleeping eyes; human hair wig. Head marked: "D//Made in Germany//8//174." Body stamped: "Germany//2" in red. Made by the J. D. Kestner Co. of Germany.
Right: 12" (30.5cm) character doll with #6969 head by Heubach. See page 296, Illustration 682 for description.

BELOW:
648. COMPONENTS OF A KESTNER DOLL WITH VOICE BOX
Remarks: Unassembled 19" (48.3cm) doll showing interesting body construction. Voice box, inserted in mid-section of torso (third left, bottom row) is operated by pull string. Made by the J. D. Kestner Company of Germany.

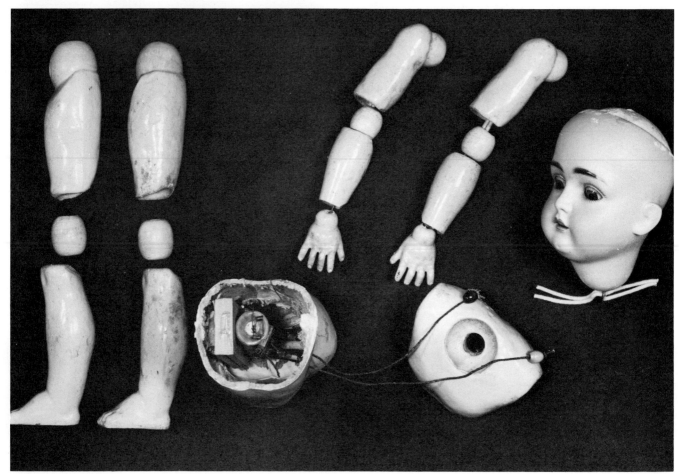

649. BISQUE DOLL — BY J. D. KESTNER

Period: First quarter of 20th century.

Body: Jointed composition; elastic strung.

Remarks: 12½"(31.8cm) bisque character doll with thoughtful expression. She has closed mouth; sleeping eyes; brown mohair wig. Marked: "b. 3. Made in Germany 208."

651. BOY DOLL WITH HEAD BY J. D. KESTNER

Period: First quarter of 20th century.

Body: Kid body with bisque hands.

Remarks: A 15" (38.1cm) character boy doll with finely molded head. Hair painted on slightly modelled pate. Head is incised: "H. 401.3/0 S." Mark of a head made by J. D. Kestner Co. for Herm Steiner Co. *Merrill Collection.*

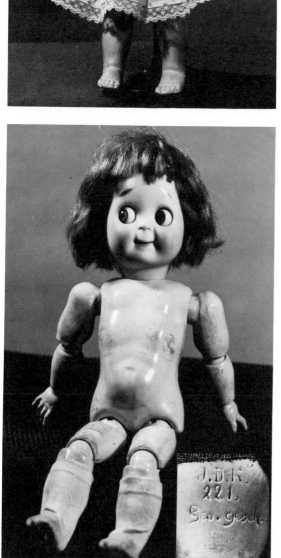

650. BISQUE DOLL BY KESTNER

Period: Early 20th century.

Body: Jointed composition; elastic strung.

Remarks: Roguish face of this 11½" (29.2cm) bisque headed doll has side-set blue glass eyes; raised eyebrows; upturned smiling mouth. Wears brown mohair wig. Marked on back of head (see insert): "J.D.K.//221// Ges.gesch." Made by German firm of J. D. Kestner.

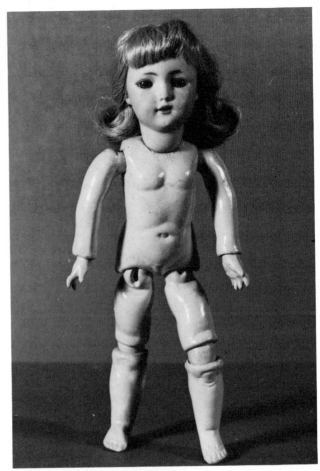

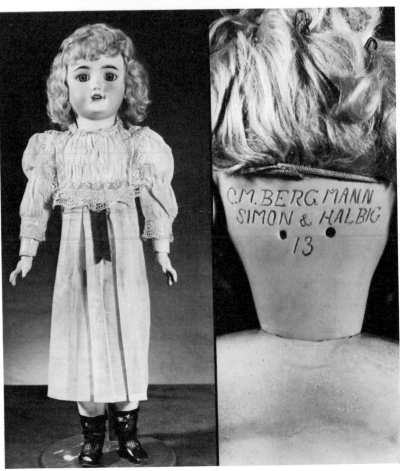

CLOCKWISE:

652. BISQUE DOLL WITH PURSED LIPS AND DIMPLES

Period: Early 20th century.
Body: Jointed composition; elastic strung.
Remarks: 12" (30.5cm) bisque headed doll with dimples; open mouth with teeth; sleeping eyes; human hair wig; pierced ears. *Unusual feature:* pursed lips. Marked: "S & H//1279//Dep.// Germany 5." Made by Simon & Halbig.

653. UNIQUE ARM CONSTRUCTION ON JOINTED COMPOSITION BODY

Period: Early 20th century.
Body: Jointed composition; elastic strung.
Remarks: 11" (27.9cm) bisque headed doll with stationary glass eyes; open mouth with teeth; blonde mohair wig. Marked: "1279//Germany// Simon & Halbig//S&H." The unique feature of the ball-jointed, elastic strung composition body of this doll is the one piece arm from shoulder to wrist. It is minus the elbow joint usually found in this type body.

654. "COLUMBIA BABY" GERMAN BISQUE DOLL/C.M. BERGMANN

Period: Early 20th century.
Body: Jointed composition; elastic strung.
Remarks: 28" (71.1cm) bisque doll with sleeping eyes; open mouth; pierced ears and mohair wig. Dressed as originally purchased from store. Ribbon on dress printed: "Columbia Baby." Head marked: "C.M.Bergmann//Simon & Halbig//13." Head made to order by Simon & Halbig for doll maker, C. M. Bergmann. Distributed in the United States by Louis Wolf & Co. of New York, New York and Boston, Massachusetts. *Merrill Collection.*

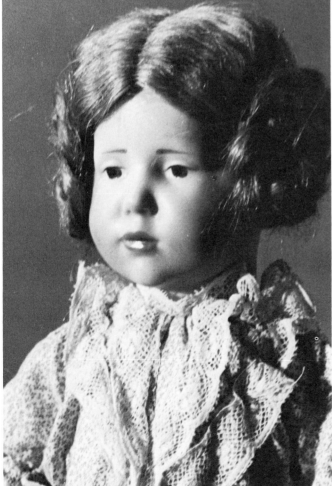

LEFT:

655. GERMAN BISQUE DOLL/C.M. BERGMANN

Period: Early 20th century.

Body: Jointed composition; elastic strung.

Remarks: 22" (55.9cm) bisque doll with sleeping brown eyes; open mouth with teeth; pierced ears; light mohair wig. Marked: "S & H//C.M.B.//9." A C. M. Bergmann *Fine Jointed Doll* with head by Simon and Halbig. See insert for illustrated box label. Called a *Columbia* doll. Distributed in United States by Louis Wolf & Co.

656. FLIRTY-EYED BISQUE DOLL

Period: Early 20th century.

Body: Jointed composition; elastic strung.

Remarks: Flirty-eyed German bisque doll bearing the mark "K & R with star" (Kämmer & Reinhardt). Eyes sleep in addition to rolling from side to side. Advertised in 1908 as "Flirt." Distributed by Strobel & Wilken of New York. This type flirty-eyed doll was also made by other German doll makers.

LEFT:

657. "MARIE" — CHILD DOLL BY K & R

Period: Early 20th century.

Body: Composition; elastic strung.

Remarks: A 15½" (39.4cm) "pouty" character doll in bisque by Kämmer & Reinhardt of Germany. Marked: "K & R" (with star) and "#114." Called *Marie*. This firm made many character dolls following the introduction of *Baby*. They are said to have been named for the children who posed for them: *Annie, Hans, Gretchen, Marie, Peter, Elsa, Carl* and *Walter*. Introduced in America by Strobel & Wilken, of New York, in 1910. *Collection of Shirley F. Sanborn.*

658. POUTY DOLLS BY K & R — #114
Period: Early 20th century.
Body: Jointed composition; elastic strung.
Left: 17½" (44.5cm) boy with pouty expression. Bisque socket head has brown painted eyes; closed mouth; mohair wig.
Right: 20" (50.8cm) girl with pouty expression. Bisque socket head has blue painted eyes; closed mouth; light mohair wig. Marked: "K (star) R//114." Made by Kämmer & Reinhardt of Germany. Came with both blue and brown painted and molded eyes. *Collection of Mrs. Elmer Morley.*

659. BISQUE DOLL #117 BY K & R
Period: Early 20th century.
Body: Jointed composition; elastic strung.
Remarks: 19" (48.3cm) bisque socket head with brown set eyes and blonde human hair wig. Fine quality bisque. Original dress. Head marked: "K ★ R//Simon & Halbig//117//46." Head made by German firm, Simon & Halbig for Kämmer & Reinhardt Co. *Merrill Collection.*

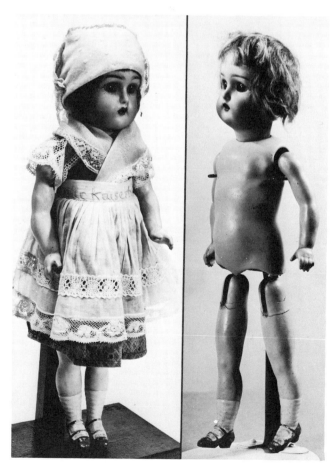

CLOCKWISE:

660. FLIRTY—EYED BISQUE DOLL #117n BY K & R
Period: Early 20th century.
Body: Jointed composition; elastic strung.
Remarks: The bisque socket head of this 19" (48.3cm) doll has flirting eyes with hair lashes; open mouth with teeth; mohair wig. In addition to rolling from side to side, eyes sleep. *Unusual feature:* rubber rather than the usual composition hands. Marked: K (star) R//Simon & Halbig//117n//Germany." Made by German firm of Kämmer & Reinhardt. *Collection of Shirley F. Sanborn.*

661. BISQUE DOLL BY KÄMMER & REINHARDT
Period: Early 20th century.
Body: Composition; elastic strung.
Remarks: 20" (50.8cm) bisque character doll with flirty eyes; closed smiling mouth; painted upper lashes; human hair wig. Marked: "K (star) R//Simon Halbig//124." A *Brother* doll, marked: "123," was also made to pair with the illustrated doll. Made by the German firm of Kämmer & Reinhardt, with head produced by the fine factory of Simon & Halbig. *Collection of Mrs. Fidelia Lence.*

662. BISQUE WALKING DOLL IN FOREIGN COSTUME
Period: Early 20th century.
Body: Composition, with elastic strung arms; mechanism within body allows doll to walk and turn head; hand propelled.
Remarks: 12" (30.5cm) bisque walking doll with sleeping eyes; open mouth with teeth; mohair wig. Original (German) costume. Embroidered on apron band is "Atlantic Kaiserhof Berlin." Marked: "Simon & Halbig//K & R with star//Made in Germany." Doll is shown dressed and undressed.

663. BISQUE DOLL BY HEUBACH KÖPPELSDORF
Period: First quarter of 20th century.
Body: Jointed composition; elastic strung.
Remarks: The bisque socket head of this 24" (61cm) doll has sleeping eyes with hair lashes; open mouth with teeth; brown mohair wig. Marked: "Heubach//250.4//Koppelsdorf//Germany." Old dolls are occasionally found in bridal ensemble. Made by the German firm of Heubach Köppelsdorf, it was a present to a child in the early 20th century. *Merrill Collection.*

BELOW LEFT:
664. PAINTED BISQUE DOLL
Period: 1920-1930.
Body: Jointed composition; elastic strung.
Remarks: 9" (22.9cm) foreign dressed doll. The painted bisque socket head has sleeping eyes; open mouth with teeth and mohair wig. Wears molded black slippers and knee length white socks. Marked: "Heubach Koppelsdorf//251.17/109//Germany." This cheaper and lower cost bisque head was achieved by a special painting process which eliminated the necessity of a second firing.

665. CHILD DOLL BY HEUBACH KÖPPELSDORF
Period: 1930.
Body: Jointed composition; elastic strung.
Remarks: 11½" (29.2cm) late bisque headed doll with sleeping eyes; open mouth with teeth; blonde mohair wig. Padded cloth at bust is tacked to body as is petticoat. Marked with name and trademark of Heubach Köppelsdorf plus "312//10/0//Germany" (see insert). Illustrated doll is all original. Came in story book costume.

666. HEUBACH DOLL WITH MOLDED AND PAINTED EYES
Period: Early 20th century.
Body: Composition; elastic strung; jointed at hips and shoulders.
Remarks: 8" (20.3cm) doll whose bisque socket head has open-closed mouth with teeth and mohair wig. Note the molded and painted eyes that closely resemble those of glass. Made by Gebrüder Heubach of Germany. A unique specimen. Differs from and lacks quality of most dolls from this firm. Marked with sunburst trademark plus "8178//Germany//Gebruder Heubach//DRG//486986." *Collection of Germaine L. Bachand.*

667. BISQUE DOLL BY HEUBACH KÖPPELSDORF
Period: First quarter of 20th century.
Body: Composition; elastic strung; jointed at hips and shoulders only.
Remarks: 14" (35.6cm) doll of great appeal. Dimpled face has open mouth with teeth; sleeping brown eyes; mohair wig. Wears original costume. Marked: "Heubach Koppelsdorf//300//2/0//Germany."

LEFT:
668. SMALL DOLL BY GEBRÜDER HEUBACH
Period: Early 20th century.
Body: Cloth with bisque arms.
Remarks: Small, 7" (17.8cm) doll with pouty expression. Bisque head has stationary glass eyes; closed mouth; mohair wig. Bears square trademark of Gebrüder Heubach plus "7345//14/0//Germany." Unusual to find so small a doll with this firm's mark. Could be used as a doll house doll. *Collection of Mrs. G. B. Walker.*

291

LEFT:
669. LAUGHING GIRL BISQUE DOLL BY HEUBACH
Period: Early 20th century.
Body: Jointed composition; elastic strung.
Remarks: 15½" (39.4cm) laughing bisque doll whose open-closed mouth shows two rows of tiny teeth. Painted features include blue intaglio eyes. Light molded hair has crossed braids in back, blue glazed band in front. Bears mark of Gebrüder Heubach Company of Germany plus the numbers "80" and "50." *Collection of Mrs. Louise H. Lund.*

BELOW LEFT:
670. GIRL DOLL BY HEUBACH
Period: Early 20th century.
Body: Leather with bisque arms.
Remarks: 11" (27.9cm) coquette doll with smiling open-closed mouth; intaglio eyes cast to side. Hair banded with glazed blue ribbon and bow. Bears square Heubach mark plus number "4" and "Germany." Also comes in socket head with composition body.

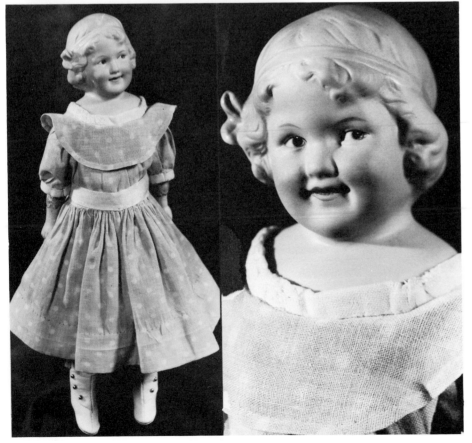

OPPOSITE PAGE, LEFT:
672. LAUGHING BOY BY HEUBACH
Period: Early 20th century.
Body: Composition; elastic strung.
Remarks: 12" (27.9cm) laughing character doll with light molded hair; side-glancing intaglio eyes; open-closed mouth with two molded-in lower teeth. Note molded bisque loop at end of socket head for passage of elastic for stringing — unusual. Marked with small green "17" plus incised "2// 6897//Germany." Probably made by Gebrüder Heubach who often stamped their doll heads with small green numbers. *Collection of Mrs. Harold Bauer.*

RIGHT:
674. LAUGHING BOY DOLL
Period: Early 20th century.
Body: Leather with elastic strung composition arms.
Remarks: 13" (33cm) dimpled and laughing boy whose bisque head has blue intaglio eyes; open-closed mouth with painted-in teeth; molded blonde hair. Marked on back shoulders: "Made in Germany//GES.9.41//16// OA GESCH." Patented in Germany. Maker uncertain. *Collection of Virginia C. Murray.*

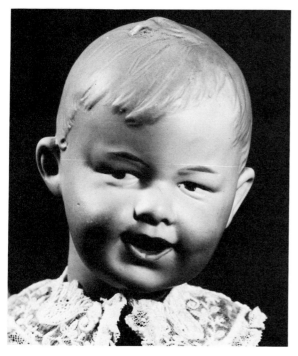

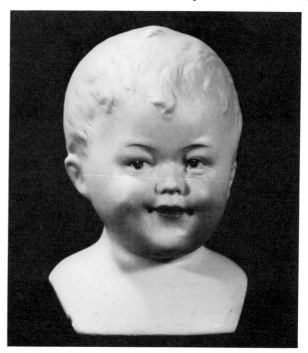

671. LAUGHING BOY DOLL BY HEUBACH
Period: Early 20th century.
Body: Jointed composition; elastic strung.
Remarks: A 19" (48.3cm) laughing boy bisque doll with open-closed mouth; painted intaglio eyes and painted hair. Bears the mark of the Gebrüder Heubach Company of Germany and the number "7911." One of the many character dolls made by this firm. *Merrill Collection.*

673. SMILING DOLL BY HEUBACH
Period: Early 20th century.
Body: Leather with bisque arms.
Remarks: Pink-toned bisque doll head with blue intaglio eyes and light molded hair. Smiling open-closed mouth shows two small molded-in teeth. Bears square Heubach trademark plus "8724 2/0 D//Germany." Made by Gebrüder Heubach Company of Germany.

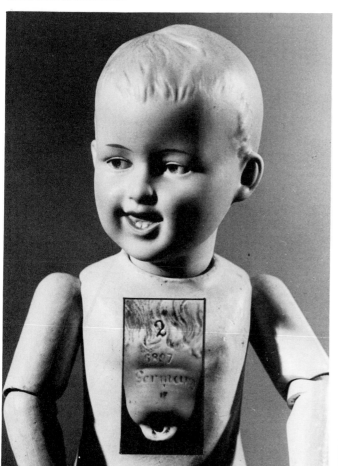

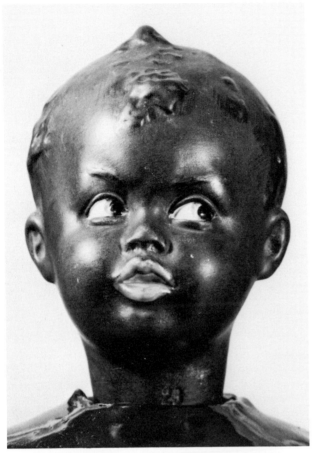

675. BLACK DOLL BY HEUBACH
Period: Early 20th century.
Body: Jointed composition; elastic strung.
Remarks: 14" (35.6cm) Black character doll whose deep brown bisque head has painted features including light brown intaglio eyes; open-closed mouth; molded black hair and brows. Bears Heubach mark, plus word "Germany" on back of neck. #23 incised on neck front. Made by Gebrüder Heubach firm. *Collection of Zelda H. Cushner.*

BELOW LEFT:
676. "WHISTLING JIM" BY HEUBACH
Period: Circa 1914.
Body: Pink twill torso; felt legs; elbow length composition arms; jointed at shoulders and hips.
Remarks: *Whistling Jim,* a 13" (33cm) character doll with bellows inserted in back of torso. When squeezed, doll whistles. The flange-necked bisque head has painted features; intaglio eyes; pierced hole in pursed lips. Bears the mark of the Gebrüder Heubach Company of Germany plus the numbers "5," "37," and "74." *Collection of Zelda H. Cushner.*

BELOW RIGHT:
677. SMILING BOY BY HEUBACH
Period: Early 20th century.
Body: Jointed composition; elastic strung.
Remarks: Large 17½" (44.5cm) doll whose bisque head has a crookedly smiling open-closed mouth; blue painted eyes; light brown painted hair. Bears square Heubach trademark plus number "5." Made by German firm of Gebrüder Heubach. *Collection of Shirley F. Sanborn.*

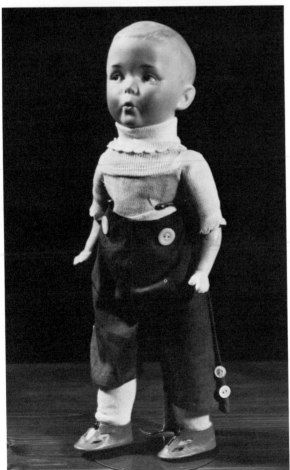

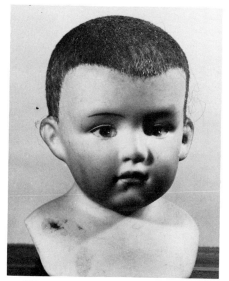

678. BISQUE BOY DOLL — BY HEUBACH
Period: Early 20th century.
Body: Leather with bisque arms.
Remarks: Pink-toned bisque boy doll with unusual flocked hair; intaglio eyes; painted features. One of the many child dolls made by the German firm of Gebrüder Heubach, and so marked. Flocked hair may also be found on bisque dolls made by Kämmer & Reinhardt of Germany. *Merrill Collection.*

679.

679. DOLL BY ERNST HEUBACH
Period: Early 20th century.
Body: Composition; elastic strung.
Remarks: 10" (25.4cm) bisque doll manufactured by Ernst Heubach of Köppelsdorf, Germany. A boy doll with molded and painted features including eyes glancing to side. The smiling and dimpled face has lower lip drawn under two tiny painted teeth. Marked: "E. H. 262 DRGM Germany." Also made with side-cast sleeping eyes and hair wig. *Merrill Collection.*

680. BOY DOLL
Period: Early 20th century.
Body: Jointed composition; elastic strung.
Remarks: 19" (48.3cm) boy with characteristics of dolls by Gebrüder Heubach. The bisque socket head has painted features; intaglio eyes; open-closed mouth; light brown painted hair. Some collectors refer to this doll as *Tommy Tucker*. Marked: "8//Germany." *Collection of Mrs. Louise H. Lund.*

681. DOLL BY HEUBACH
Period: Early 20th century.
Body: Jointed composition; elastic strung.
Remarks: 9½" (24.2cm) doll whose pink-toned bisque head has painted features; intaglio eyes; molded light brown hair. Marked with square trademark of Gebrüder Heubach plus "5/0 D// 87//93//Germany." Has the usual highlight at top of eye. Could be dressed as boy or girl. Made by Gebrüder Heubach firm of Germany.

680.

681.

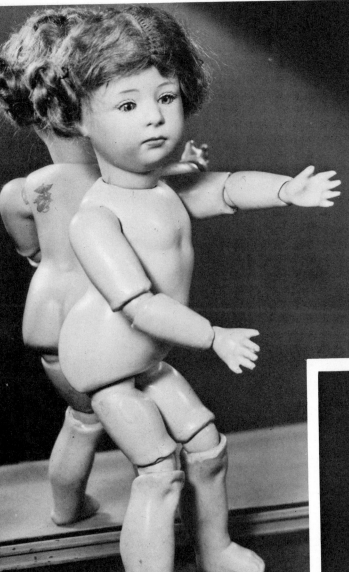

682. CUNO AND OTTO DRESSEL DOLL WITH HEAD BY HEUBACH

Period: Early 20th century.
Body: Jointed composition; elastic strung.
Remarks: 12" (30.5cm) Cuno and Otto Dressel doll with bisque character head by Gebrüder Heubach. Head marked: "6969// Germany//3" plus number "17" in green. Body stamped with Dressel's "Holtz Masse" trademark. The Dressels used heads by others for their dolls.

683. SOLEMN FACED DOLL BY HEUBACH

Period: Early 20th century.
Body: Jointed composition and wood; elastic strung.
Remarks: 18" (45.7cm) all original little girl doll of solemn mien. Sometimes called a *pouty*. Deep pink-toned socket head has sleeping eyes; downturned closed mouth; mohair wig. Bears sunburst trademark of Gebrüder Heubach plus "7246//7//Germany" (see insert). This head, minus Heubach trademark, was also supplied to Cuno & Otto Dressel for use on some of their dolls.

684. AMERICAN INDIAN DOLL BY HEUBACH
Period: Early 20th century.
Body: Cloth with dull red composition arms.
Remarks: 14" (35.6cm) all original character doll of aged American Indian woman. Deeply wrinkled bisque head has painted blue eyes; down turned closed mouth; white mohair wig. Dressed in two-piece fringed leather costume. Bears Heubach mark plus "894//1//87//Germany" on back shoulders (see insert). Body stamped: "Hair Stuffed — Germany." Most unusual doll. *Collection of Miss Zelda Cushner.*

685. BISQUE CHILD DOLL
Period: First quarter of 20th century.
Body: Jointed composition; elastic strung.
Remarks: 14½" (36.9cm) bisque doll of little girl. Bisque socket head has painted blue eyes cast to side; closed mouth with parted lips; molded light brown hair styled in Dutch cut. Mark on back of head appears to be: "H (?) J 1." *Collection of Shirley F. Sanborn.*

686. BISQUE — HUNGARIAN DOLL

Period: First quarter of 20th century.

Body: Cloth with molded composition limbs.

Remarks: 17" (43.2cm) (20" [50.8cm] overall) all original doll in foreign dress — shown dressed and undressed. The bisque head has glass eyes; open mouth with teeth; human hair wig. Dressed in conventional version of Hungarian costume. The headdress, called párta, is completely covered with vividly colored sequin and ribbon flowers. Bisque head, by Armand Marseille, is marked: "Germany// 370//A.O.M." *Merrill Collection.*

687. BISQUE DOLL WITH SHOULDERHEAD #370 BY ARMAND MARSEILLE

Period: Early 20th century.

Body: Leather with bisque forearms.

Remarks: Commonly found bisque headed doll with sleeping eyes; open mouth with teeth; mohair wig. Made by the Armand Marseille Company of Germany. Marked: "370//A.M.//0½// D.E.P." The most frequently found bisque dolls have heads marked "#370" (shoulderhead) or "#390" (socket head).

688. "FLORODORA" BISQUE DOLL

Period: Early 20th century.

Body: Leather with bisque arms.

Remarks: 16½" (41.9cm) doll whose bisque shoulderhead has sleeping eyes; open mouth with teeth; mohair wig. Head marked: "370//A 4/0 M//Germany." Body has oval paper sticker printed: "Florodora//Made in Germany." The *Florodora* trademark was registered in Germany by United States distributor, George Borgfeldt & Co. Made by the German firm of Armand Marseille. *Florodora* dolls were also made with bisque socket heads mounted on elastic strung, composition bodies.

298

RIGHT:

689. "FLORODORA" BISQUE DOLL

Period: Early 20th century.

Body: Jointed wood and composition; elastic strung.

Remarks: 17" (43.2cm) bisque doll with sleeping eyes; hair lashes; open mouth with teeth; brown human hair wig. Marked: "Made in Germany//Florodora//A.1.M." The *Florodora* trademark was registered in Germany by United States distributor, George Borgfeldt & Company. Made by the German firm of Armand Marseille. *Florodora* dolls were also made with bisque shoulderheads mounted on leather bodies.

690. "MY PLAYMATE" BOXED DOLL WITH WARDROBE

Period: Early 20th century.

Body: Jointed composition; elastic strung.

Remarks: A boxed, 12" (30.5cm) doll with wardrobe — all in original and unused condition. Bisque socket head has sleeping eyes; open mouth with teeth; mohair wig. Doll marked: "Made in Germany//Armand Marseille//DRMR//24011//Florodora// A 3/0 M." Box labelled: "My Playmate//Dressed Doll" plus the trademark (Celebrate) of the George Borgfeldt & Company of New York.

RIGHT:

691. LARGE GERMAN BISQUE DOLL BY ARMAND MARSEILLE

Period: Early 20th century.

Body: Jointed composition; elastic strung.

Remarks: 36" (91.4cm) doll whose bisque socket head has brown sleeping eyes; open mouth with teeth and human hair wig. Wears original lace dress over blue silk; white stockings and slippers. Head marked: "A. 15 M." Made by the German firm of Armand Marseille. *Merrill Collection.*

692. SMILING BISQUE DOLL BY ARMAND MARSEILLE
Period: Early 20th century.
Body: Jointed composition; elastic strung.
Remarks: 10" (25.4cm) dimpled and smiling bisque doll. Closed mouth; sleeping blue eyes; mohair wig. Marked: "Germany// 550//A 4/0 M//DRGM." Made by Armand Marseilles firm of Germany. *Collection of Mrs. G. B. Walker.*

693. "DUCHESS" — A GERMAN BISQUE DOLL
Period: First quarter of 20th century.
Body: Strung body with closed wrists; not original body.
Remarks: A 7" (17.8cm) doll with head incised: "Duchess// 1914//A.M." Head produced by Armand Marseille Co., Germany. Doll distributed by Geo. Borgfeldt & Co., New York City, New York. *Merrill Collection.*

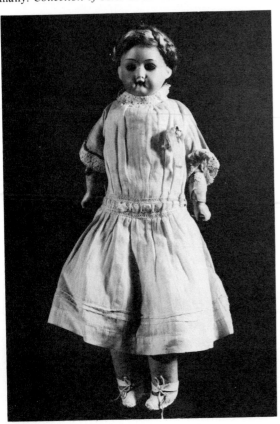

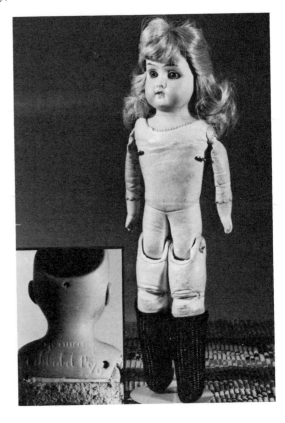

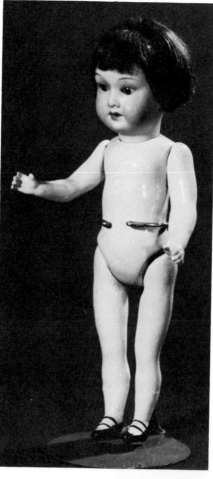

FAR LEFT:
696: "JUST ME" CHILD DOLL
Period: Circa 1925.
Body: Composition; elastic strung.
Remarks: 7½" (19.1cm) child doll with
painted bisque head. Sleeping eyes; closed
mouth; mohair wig. Eyes slightly cast to
side. Marked: "JUST ME.//Registered//
Germany//A 310/7/0. M." Made by the
German firm of Armand Marseille.

697. SMALL DOLL WITH "390"
HEAD BY ARMAND MARSEILLE
Period: 1920-1930.
Body: Composition; elastic strung;
   jointed at shoulders and hips.
Remarks: 8" (20.3cm) bisque headed
child doll. Glass eyes; open mouth with
teeth; mohair wig. Wears painted two-
strap black slippers and white socks.
Unusual to find this head in so small a
size. Body is of late type. Marked:
"Armand Marseille//Germany//390//A
11/0 M."

OPPOSITE PAGE, LOWER LEFT:
694. DOLL WITH PIERCED HOLE IN LIPS
Period: Early 20th century.
Body: Leather with bisque arms.
Remarks: 11½" (29.2cm) doll whose bisque shoulderhead has
blue stationary glass eyes; blonde mohair wig and pierced hole
between slightly parted lips. Marked: "570//AM 2/0 DEP//
Armand Marseille." Made in Germany by Armand Marseille.

OPPOSITE PAGE, LEFT:
695. "MABEL" — GERMAN BISQUE DOLL
Period: Early 20th century.
Body: Leather with patented metal joints at hips;
   cloth lower legs; bisque lower arms.
Remarks: 12" (30.5cm) bisque doll with stationary glass eyes;
open mouth with teeth; mohair wig. Marked on back shoulders:
"Germany//Mabel//14/0." Made by German firm of Armand
Marseille. It was not uncommon in this period of German doll
makers to use other names on their bisque doll heads such as
Ruth, Pansy, Viola, Daisy and *Marguerite*.

RIGHT:
698. "KIDDIEJOY" CHILD DOLL
Period: Circa 1925.
Body: Cloth or kid with bisque or composition
   arms strung through shoulders.
Remarks: Large, 6" (15.2cm) head of pink tinted bisque. Very
light molded hair; set-in glass eyes; open mouth with teeth.
Marked (see insert): "Germany//Kiddiejoy//372//A 2 M."
Made by Armand Marseille for Hitz, Jacobs and Kassler, New
York agents and importers. See page 353, Illustration 800, for
baby doll marked "Kiddiejoy."

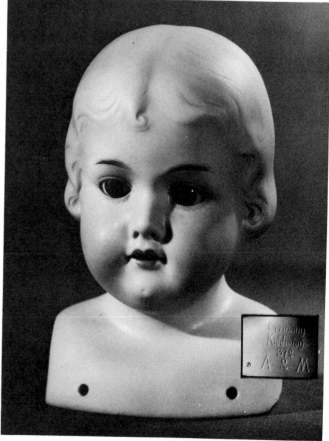

699. BISQUE BOY DOLL
Period: Early 20th century.
Body: Composition; elastic strung.
Remarks: 6½" (16.5cm) goggle-eyed doll with roguish expression. Bisque head has intaglio eyes; closed mouth; painted light brown hair. Round cheeked smiling face has double chin. Marked: "320//A. 11/0 M.//Germany." Made by Armand Marseille firm of Germany.

700. BISQUE DOLL BY ARMAND MARSEILLE
Period: Early 20th century.
Body: Composition; elastic strung.
Remarks: 7½" (19.1cm) smiling bisque doll with sleeping eyes turned to side. An appealing specimen with roguish expression. Wears dark brown mohair wig. Rather heavy composition legs have molded socks and slippers. Dressed in original crocheted costume; a method of dressing often found on small dolls of this era. Marked: "323 Germany A. 11/0 M." Made by German firm of Armand Marseille.

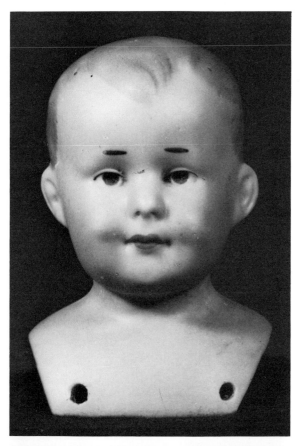

701. BISQUE HEAD BY ARMAND MARSEILLE

Period: Early 20th century.

Body: Leather with bisque arms.

Remarks: 3" (7.6cm) pink bisque shoulderhead with smiling, dimpled expression. Blue intaglio eyes; closed mouth; light brown molded hair. Marked: "600//A. 5/0 M.//Germany//DRGM." Made by Armand Marseille of Germany. Similar to child dolls made by Gebrüder Heubach. *Collection of Mrs. Neil Hobey.*

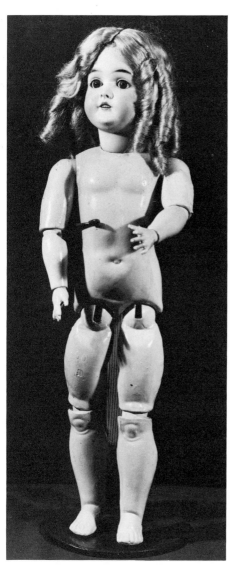

703. "QUEEN LOUISE" — GERMAN BISQUE DOLL

Period: Circa 1910.

Body: Composition; elastic strung.

Remarks: 24" (61cm) doll with bisque socket head and fully jointed composition body. She has sleeping eyes with hair lashes; open mouth with teeth; mohair wig. Marked: "29 Queen Louise 100//Germany." The trademark *Queen Louise* was registered in the United States by distributor, Louis Wolf & Co. of Boston and New York.

702. BISQUE DOLL BY LOUIS WOLF & CO.

Period: Early 20th century.

Body: Leather with bisque forearms.

Remarks: German made 16" (40.6cm) doll whose bisque head has stationary glass eyes; open mouth with teeth; human hair wig. Marked: "LW&C.//5/0" (see insert). Made for Louis Wolf & Company of Boston and New York, an importer who handled dolls from Germany, France and England.

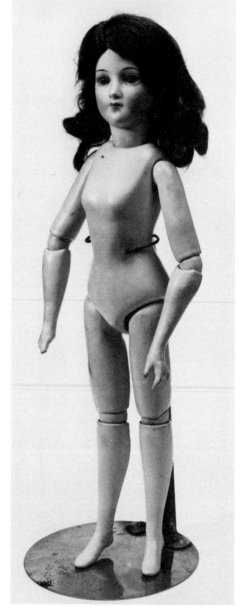

704. CUNO & OTTO DRESSEL DOLL WITH HEAD BY ARMAND MARSEILLE

Period: Early 20th century.

Body: Leather with bisque arms.

Remarks: 24" (61cm) doll whose smooth bisque shoulderhead has sleeping eyes; open mouth with four molded-in upper teeth; human hair wig. Back shoulders marked: "A 1776 M//COD 7 DEP//Made in Germany" (see insert). Chest stamped with "Holz-Masse" mark of Cuno & Otto Dressel. Doll was produced by the German firm of Cuno & Otto Dressel with head made to their order by Armand Marseille.

RIGHT:

705. YOUNG LADY BISQUE DOLL

Period: 1920-1930 era.

Body: Jointed composition; elastic strung.

Remarks: 14" (35.6cm) bisque headed young lady doll. Feet modeled in rasied position, enabling doll to wear high heeled shoes. The slim-faced socket head has sleeping eyes; closed mouth; mohair wig. Smoothly enameled composition body is adult in form. Bisque head is marked: "C. & O.D.//Germany//2." Distributed by Cuno and Otto Dressel of Germany.

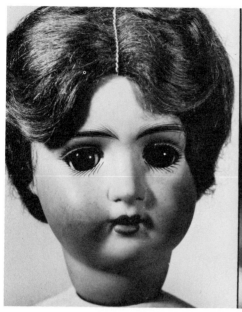

706. GERMAN BISQUE DOLL BY ALT, BECK & GOTTSCHALCK
Period: Early 20th century.
Body: Jointed composition; elastic strung.
Remarks: 18" (45.7cm) bisque headed doll with sleeping eyes; open mouth with teeth; mohair wig. Marked (see insert): "ABG (entwined)//1362//Made in Germany." Made by Alt, Beck & Gottschalck who also made a bisque headed baby with moveable porcelain tongue.

707. BOY DOLL BY C. M. BERGMANN
Period: Early 20th century.
Body: Stuffed stockinette with rubber hands; jointed at neck only.
Remarks: 13" (33cm) boy doll, in original costume. Dimpled and laughing face has open mouth with two upper teeth; sleeping eyes; human hair wig. Bisque socket head is mounted on soft, flesh-colored stockinette body with rubber hands of matching color. Marked (see insert): "B//4/1//C.M.Bergmann//0//Germany." *Collection of Mrs. Eleanor C. Wehrly.*

708. GERMAN BISQUE DOLL MARKED "L.H.B."
Period: Early 20th century.
Body: Leather with bisque forearms.
Remarks: 14½" (36.9cm) German made doll whose bisque shoulderhead has sleeping eyes; open mouth with teeth and blonde mohair wig. Marked: "Made in Germany//L.H.B. 3/0."

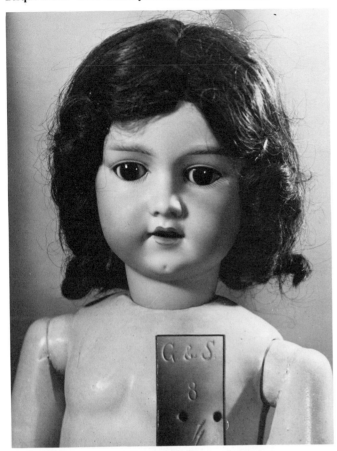

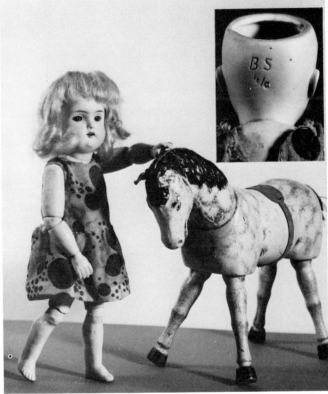

LEFT:

709. GERMAN BISQUE DOLL — MARKED "G & S"

Period: First quarter of 20th century.

Body: Jointed composition; elastic strung.

Remarks: 26" (66cm) doll whose bisque socket head has brown sleeping eyes with hair lashes; open mouth with teeth; human hair wig. Marked on back of head (see insert): "G & S//8." Made by German firm of Guttmann & Schiffnie.

710. BISQUE DOLL — MARKED "B.S."

Period: Early 20th century.

Body: Jointed composition; elastic strung.

Remarks: Small, good quality 9" (22.9cm) fully jointed child doll. Bisque socket head has sleeping eyes; open mouth with teeth; mohair wig. Marked: "B S//4/0." Maker unknown.

LEFT:

711. GERMAN BISQUE DOLL IN 1908 BRIDAL ENSEMBLE

Period: 1908.

Body: Jointed composition; elastic strung.

Remarks: 24" (61cm) bisque headed doll with sleeping eyes; open mouth with teeth; mohair wig. Head incised: "G. & S.6//Germany" (see insert). Probably made by Guttmann & Schiffnie. Dressed in finely made crepe de chine wedding gown; lace trimmed veil; elbow length silk gloves. Doll and entire outfit, a Christmas gift in 1908, is in excellent state of preservation.

RIGHT:

712. "VIOLA" — GERMAN BISQUE DOLL

Period: Early 20th century.

Body: Composition; elastic strung.

Remarks: 24" (61cm) bisque doll with sleeping eyes; hair lashes; open mouth with teeth; mohair wig. Marked: "Viola//H & Co//Germany." Made by Hamburg & Company who registered trademark "Viola" in 1903. This firm also made dolls marked *Santa, Dolly Dimple* and *Marguerite.*

713. "DOLLY DIMPLE" BY HAMBURGER & CO.

Period: 1907.

Body: Composition; elastic strung.

Remarks: 14" (35.6cm) smiling and dimpled bisque doll. Sleeping eyes; open mouth with molded upper teeth; blonde wig. Unusual expression. Marked: "Dolly Dimple H Germany 5." Made by Hamburger & Company of Germany who made other name dolls. *Courtesy of Mrs. Roger Clapp.*

RIGHT:

714. HEINRICH HANDWERCK DOLL WITH PATENT STAMP ON FOREHEAD

Period: Early 20th century.

Body: Jointed composition; elastic strung.

Remarks: Round eyed, 18" (45.7cm) doll with "Gesetzl. Geschutzt" stamped in purple on upper forehead (see insert). An unusually placed mark meaning "registered" or "patented" in German. Bisque socket head has sleeping eyes with hair lashes; open mouth with teeth; mohair wig. Back of head marked: "79.//10//H//2." Body stamped: "Handwerck." Made in Germany by the firm of Heinrich Handwerck. *Merrill Collection.*

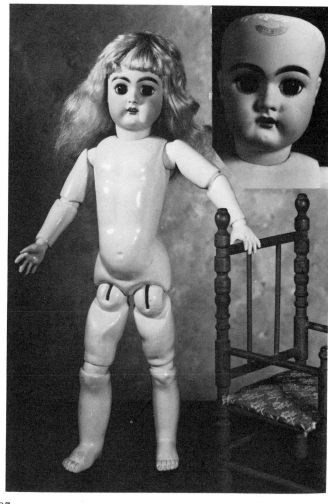

715. GERMAN BISQUE DOLL — MARKED "WALKURE"
Period: Circa 1910.
Body: Jointed composition; elastic strung.
Remarks: 24" (61cm) German bisque doll with sleeping glass eyes; pierced ears; open mouth with teeth; human hair wig. All original including costume. Marked: "Walkure//Germany//12." Made by the Kley & Hahn firm of Germany. *Merrill Collection.*

718. GERMAN BISQUE DOLL BY GEBRÜDER KRAUSS

Period: Early 20th century.
Body: Jointed composition, elastic strung.
Remarks: Good quality, 21" (53.3cm) doll whose bisque head has sleeping eyes; open mouth with teeth; mohair wig. Head marked within sunburst: "G^br K." Made by the German firm of Gebrüder Krauss.

OPPOSITE PAGE, TOP RIGHT:
716. CHARACTER DOLL BY GEBRÜDER KNOCH

Period: Early 20th century.
Body: Leather with bisque arms.
Remarks: 12" (30.5cm) bisque headed character doll with intaglio eyes; open-closed laughing mouth with two lower molded-in teeth; painted hair. Marked: "G.K./N." (within crossed bars). Also "Made in Germany//Ges. No. 216 Gesch//16/o A" (see insert). Made by Gebrüder Knoch of Germany. Illustrated head replacd an earlier one. It is mounted on a commercially made 19th century body. Correct body is listed above. *Collection of Rev. John Upton.*

OPPOSITE PAGE, BOTTOM:
717. BISQUE DOLL — MARKED "S & C"

Period: First quarter of 20th century.
Body: Composition; elastic strung.
Remarks: 12" (30.5cm) bisque headed doll with sleeping eyes; hair lashes; open mouth with teeth; mohair wig. *Unusual feature:* pierced nostrils. Head marked: "S & C//Made in Germany//30." Dolls with pierced nostrils were made by other German firms. *Courtesy of Mrs. John Cockcroft.*

RIGHT:
719. GERMAN BISQUE HEAD ON "KIDLYNE" IMITATION LEATHER BODY

Period: Early 20th century.
Body: Imitation leather with gussets at knees; patented metal joints at hips; bisque lower arms.
Remarks: Bisque shoulderhead, with glass eyes and open mouth with teeth, is marked: "G^br 170 K//9/0//Germany." Maker uncertain. More than one German maker had initials G.K. Body of imitation leather, a cheaper substitute for the genuine, has oval sticker on chest (see insert) printed "Kidlyne//Germany."

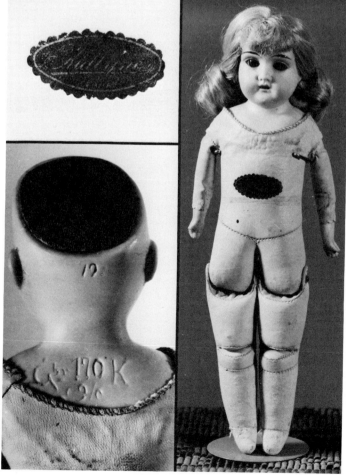

721. "HANNA" — POLYNESIAN BISQUE DOLL

Period: First quarter of 20th century.

Body: Composition; elastic strung; jointed at hips and shoulders.

Remarks: 6¾" (17.2cm) brown bisque doll with sleeping glass eyes; open mouth with teeth; black mohair wig. Wears original Polynesian costume. Marked: "S H//Hanna//12/0" plus "P B" within star. Made by German firm of Schoenau & Hoffmeister.

Note: The letters "S H" in above markings should not be confused with those found on dolls by Simon & Halbig. *Merrill Collection.*

720. BISQUE HEADED DOLL BY PAUL SCHMIDT

Period: 1921-1925.

Body: Leather with bisque lower arms; knee-length cloth legs.

Remarks: Comparatively late, 15" (38.1cm) bisque headed doll with sleeping eyes; open mouth with teeth; one stroke eyebrows; brown mohair wig. Marked: "Germany//P. Sch.//4/0." Made by the German firm of Paul Schmidt of Sonneburg.

RIGHT:

722. GERMAN BISQUE DOLL — MARKED "A.W."

Period: Early 20th century.

Body: Jointed composition; elastic strung.

Remarks: 24" (61cm) German bisque doll with sleeping eyes; open mouth with teeth; mohair wig. Marked (in script): "A.W.//Special//Germany" (see insert). Made by the German firm of Adolf Wislizenus.

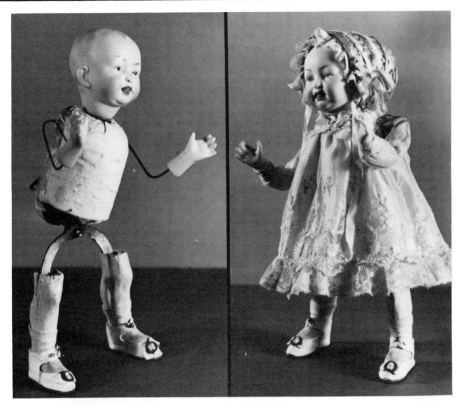

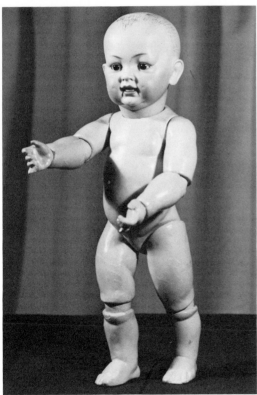

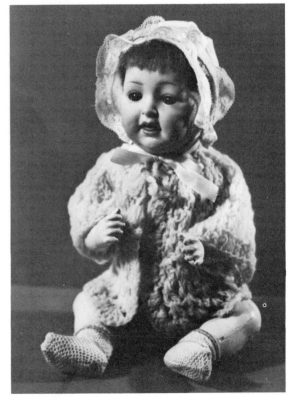

734. GERMAN BISQUE MECHANICAL TODDLER

Period: Early 20th century.

Body: Mechanism housed in body; bisque hands; composition lead-weighted feet.

Remarks: 11" (27.9cm) toddling baby with key-wound clockworks in torso. Bisque head has painted eyes; smiling open-closed mouth with molded-in teeth; light painted hair. When set in motion, doll toddles swaying from side to side. Marked: "151//2/0." *Merrill Collection.*

735. COMPOSITION TODDLER BODY — FULLY JOINTED

Period: Early 20th century.

Body: Fully jointed composition; elastic strung.

Remarks: 22" (55.9cm) dimpled and smiling toddler with sleeping eyes; open-closed mouth with molded-in teeth; light painted hair. Note fully jointed arms and legs of this thick set toddler. Dolls with this type baby head usually come on bent limb bodies. Head marked: "151//13."

736. LAUGHING BISQUE BABY — MOLD #152

Period: Early 20th century.

Body: Composition; elastic strung.

Remarks: 13" (33cm) dimpled and laughing baby. Bisque socket head has brown sleeping eyes; open mouth with two upper teeth; brown mohair wig. Bisque tongue and lower lip are molded in one piece. Marked: "Made in Germany//152./5." Made by the eminent firm of J. D. Kestner.

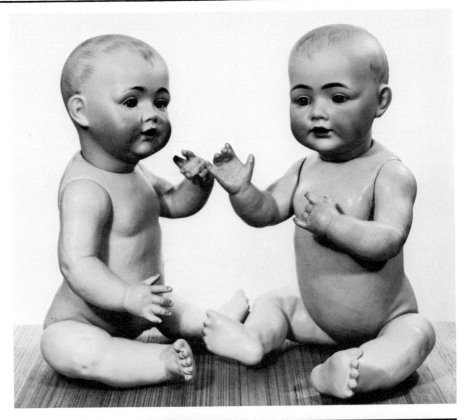

737. LARGE BISQUE BABIES BY KESTNER

Period: First quarter of 20th century.
Bodies: Composition; elastic strung; jointed at shoulders and hips.
Remarks: 22" (55.9cm) life-size bisque babies. Socket heads have sleeping eyes; open mouths with teeth; movable tongues; painted hair. One doll has blue eyes, the other brown. Marked: "J.D.K.//17// Made in Germany." Made by J. D. Kestner Company of Germany.

BELOW:
738. BISQUE BABY DOLL — BY KESTNER

Period: First quarter of 20th century.
Body: Composition; elastic strung.
Remarks: 11" (27.9cm) bisque baby doll of high quality. Socket head, on bent limb body, has sleeping eyes; open-closed mouth; delicately painted light brown hair. Marked on back of neck: "J.D.K. Made in Germany 7." This same doll may be found with shoulder type head mounted on a kid body with composition limbs.

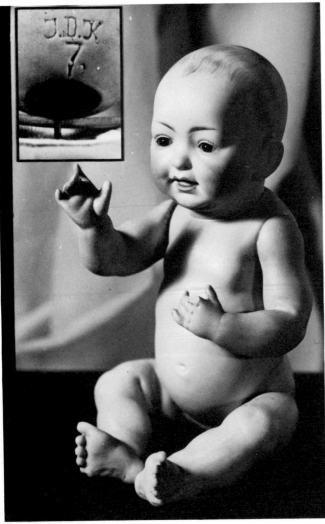

739. BABY DOLL WITH ROGUISH EYES

Period: First quarter of 20th century.
Body: Composition; elastic strung.
Remarks: 13" (33cm) bisque headed character doll with sleeping eyes looking sidewise. Open-closed mouth with up-turned corners. Mohair wig. Unmarked except for incised numbers "165/4" at base of neck.

740. SIMON & HALBIG SLEEPING EYE DOLL WITH MECHANICAL FLIRTY EYE FEATURE
Period: First quarter of 20th century.
Body: Ball-jointed composition.
Remarks: 28" (71.1cm) Simon & Halbig doll. In addition to usual sleep eyes, it has a clockwork which operates the flirty eye motion. Head is marked: "1294//Made in Germany//9//55." *Collection of Phyllis Hilton.*

741. "KAISER BABY"

Period: Early 20th century.

Body: Jointed composition; elastic strung.

Remarks: Baby #100 — first in a line of realistic character dolls by the German firm of Kämmer & Reinhardt. Referred to as *Kaiser Baby* by many collectors. A rather homely baby with painted features; painted (blue) intaglio eyes; large ears. Marked: "K & R" with star. Distributed in the United States by Strobel & Wilken in 1910.

BELOW:

742. BLACK "KAISER BABY"

Period: Early 20th century.

Body: Brown composition; jointed at hips and shoulders; elastic strung.

Remarks: 10" (25.4cm) Black *Kaiser Baby*. Bisque head has brown intaglio eyes and finely painted black hair. First in a line of character dolls by Kämmer & Reinhardt — model #100. Marked: "28//K (star) R//100." Black dolls are scarce — considered highly collectible. *Collection of Nancy Shurtleff.*

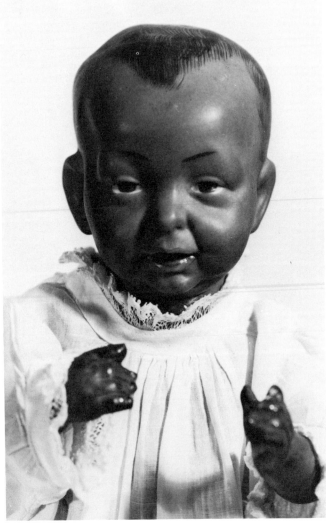

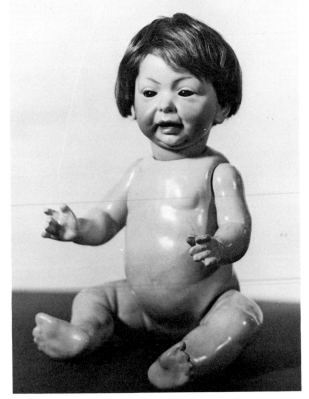

743. "KAISER" MOLD BABY DOLL WITH WIG AND SLEEPING EYES

Period: Early 20th century.

Body: Jointed composition; elastic strung.

Remarks: 14" (35.6cm) bisque *Kaiser Baby* from the same mold as Baby #100 by Kämmer & Reinhardt. Extremely rare with applied wig and sleeping glass eyes. Unmarked except for the number "36" which also appears on fully marked Kaiser babies. *Collection of Mrs. Louise H. Lund.*

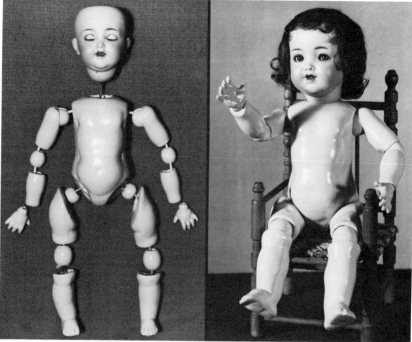

745. FLIRTY-EYED, BALL-JOINTED TODDLER BY K & R
Period: First quarter of 20th century.
Body: Fully jointed composition; elastic strung.
Remarks: 15" (38.1cm) toddler whose bisque socket head has open mouth with two upper teeth; mohair wig. Glass eyes move sidewise, independent of sleeping metal lids. Marked: "K (star) R//32." Made by German firm of Kämmer & Reinhardt. *Unusual feature:* Ball-joints at hips. Not generally found on toddler bodies. *Courtesy of Mrs. Irving J. Duffy.*

744. BOY TODDLER CHARACTER DOLL
BY K & R
Period: Circa 1910.
Body: Jointed composition; elastic strung.
Remarks: 15" (38.1cm) toddler with molded light brown hair; sleeping brown glass eyes; closed mouth. Unusual boy doll. Marked: "K & R (with star)//S & H//115/38." Head made by Simon & Halbig for the firm of Kämmer & Reinhardt. *Collection of Mrs. Eugenia S. Shorrock.*

RIGHT:
746. #116A BABY DOLL BY K & R
Period: First quarter of 20th century.
Body: Jointed composition; elastic strung.
Remarks: 17" (43.2cm) bisque headed baby by German firm of Kämmer & Reinhardt. One of a variety of character dolls by this company. Has dimpled, laughing face with open-closed mouth showing two tiny painted-in teeth; blue sleeping eyes; mohair wig. Marked: "K (star) R//Simon & Halbig//116A." Distributed in the United States by Strobel & Wilkin of New York. *Merrill Collection.*

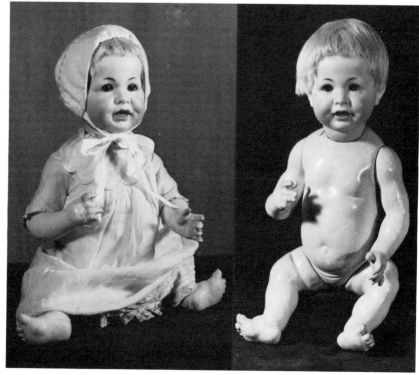

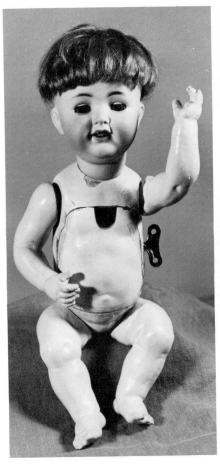

FAR LEFT:
747. MECHANICAL BABY BY K & R — #126

Period: First quarter of 20th century.

Body: Jointed composition; elastic strung; mechanism within torso.

Remarks: 15½" (39.4cm) mechanical baby. Bisque head has open mouth showing tongue; moving eyes with hair lashes; mohair wig. When key-wound mechanism is set in motion, doll cries, blinks eyes, moves tongue, raises and lowers arms. Marked: "K (star) R//Simon & Halbig//126." Made by Kämmer & Reinhardt of Germany. This model (#126) is generally found minus mechanism. *Collection of Virginia C. Murray.*

748. K & R #126 TODDLER

Period: Circa 1927.

Body: Composition; elastic strung; jointed at hips and shoulders only.

Remarks: 8½" (21.6cm) doll whose bisque socket head has blue sleeping eyes; one stroke brows; open mouth with teeth; blonde mohair wig. The well rounded composition body, with extended arms and fingers, is remindful of the Kewpie doll. Marked: "K (star) R//Simon & Halbig//Germany//126.21." This same numbered head (126) may be found on bent limb baby dolls as well as child dolls dressed as both boys and girls.

749. BISQUE CHARACTER BABY

Period: Early 20th century.

Body: Composition; elastic strung; jointed at shoulders and hips.

Remarks: 14½" (36.9cm) well modeled, smiling character baby with blue glass eyes; open-closed mouth; light mohair wig. Marked: "1428/9." *Collection of Mrs. Elmer Morley.*

750. GERMAN BISQUE DOLL — TODDLER

Period: Circa 1923.

Body: Composition; elastic strung.

Remarks: 12" (30.5cm) bisque headed toddler of fine quality. Sleeping eyes with hair lashes; open mouth with teeth; light brown mohair wig. The good quality composition body has unusual and well designed joints at hips. Bisque head is incised: "Walterhaus//TPI//Germany//1," the mark of the Thüringer Puppen-Industrie, Inc., Walterhausen. *Courtesy of Mrs. John Cockcroft.*

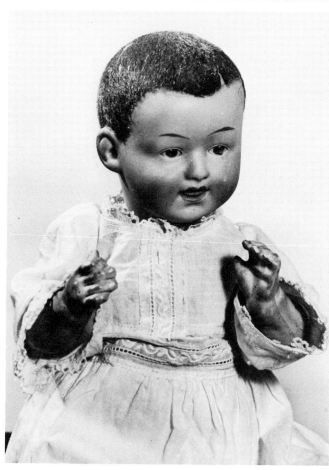

LEFT:
751. SMILING HEUBACH BABY WITH FLOCKED HAIR
Period: Early 20th century.
Body: Jointed composition; elastic strung.
Remarks: Smiling, 9½" (24.2cm) baby doll whose open-closed mouth shows molded tongue and teeth. Painted features include intaglio eyes. Hair is flocked. Bears mark of the Gebrüder Heubach Company of Germany plus numbers "0," "35," and "13." *Collection of Mrs. Elmer Morley.*

BELOW LEFT:
752. FLOCKED HAIR BABY DOLL BY HEUBACH
Period: Early 20th century.
Body: Composition; elastic strung.
Remarks: 6" (15.2cm) baby doll whose bisque head has painted features; intaglio eyes and flocked hair. Same baby was made with painted hair. One of many character dolls made by the Gebrüder Heubach Company of Germany. Bears the square mark of this firm plus the word "Germany" on back of head. *Merrill Collection.*

BELOW:
753. CHARACTER BABY BY HEUBACH
Period: Early 20th century.
Body: Jointed composition; elastic strung.
Remarks: 15½" (39.4cm) character baby whose expressive bisque head has painted eyes; squinted lids; yawning open-closed mouth; lightly molded and painted hair. Bears sunburst trademark of Gebrüder Heubach firm of Germany plus numbers "77" and "81." Also printed in green is a small number "33." *Collection of Mrs. Fidelia Lence.*

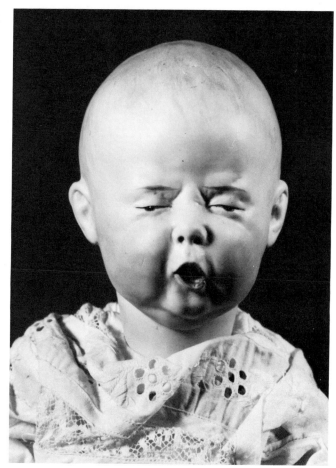

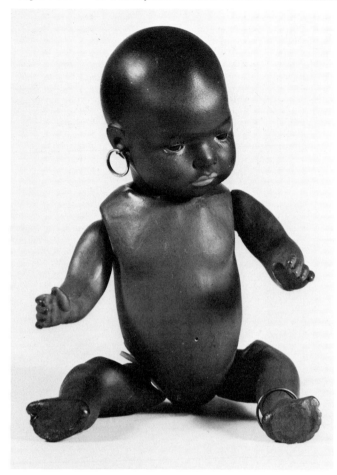

**754. BLACK BISQUE BABY BY HEUBACH
KÖPPELSDORF**
Period: First quarter of 20th century.
Body: Composition; elastic strung.
Remarks: 7" (17.8cm) Black bisque baby with set-in glass eyes; painted features. Wears original brass earrings and ankle bracelet. Marked: "Heubach Köppelsdorf//399 • 16/0//Germany." *Collection of Miss Ruth Whittier.*

OPPOSITE PAGE, TOP:
756. "BABY STUART" BISQUE DOLL BY HEUBACH
Period: Early 20th century.
Body: Leather with bisque arms.
Remarks: Holes for attaching ribbon ties are in the upturned corners of the molded bisque bonnet of this so-called *Baby Stuart*. It is white in color and decorated with small pink roses. The solemn pink bisque face, with closed mouth and blue intaglio eyes, contrasts sharply with the white of the bonnet. This 9½" (24.2cm) doll was also produced with bisque socket head on composition body. Bears square mark of the Gebrüder Heubach firm of Germany and the number "8228" under kid on shoulders. *Merrill Collection.*

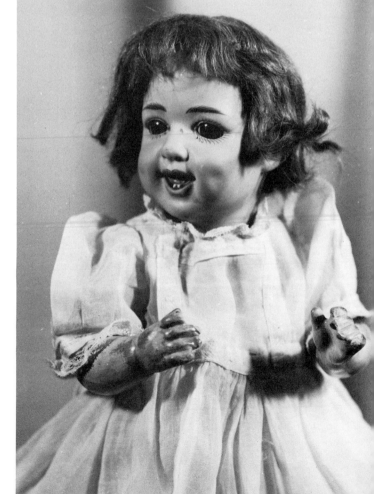

755. LAUGHING BABY BY HEUBACH
Period: Early 20th century.
Body: Composition; elastic strung.
Remarks: 12" (30.5cm) dimpled and laughing baby with open-closed mouth showing molded tongue and two lower teeth; glass eyes; mohair wig. Bears trademark of the Gebrüder Heubach Company of Germany plus number "6."

BELOW LEFT:
757. BONNETTED BISQUE BABIES
Period: Early 20th century.
Body: Bent limb composition; elastic strung.
Remarks: With the exception of bonnets, two quite similar smiling babies. Both have intaglio eyes; open-closed mouths showing two molded-in upper teeth.
Left: 8" (20.3cm) baby wearing molded-on white bonnet tied in blue. Marked: "RA//29-19."
Right: 8½" (21.6cm) baby wearing molded-on cap with blue pompon. Marked: plus "28-12." ◇ *Collection of Shirley F. Sanborn.*

BELOW:
758. BONNETTED BISQUE BABY
Period: Early 20th century.
Body: Bent limb composition; elastic strung.
Remarks: White molded bonnet, tied in blue, is worn by this 8½" (21.6cm) character baby. Pink toned bisque head has light brown hair at bonnet edge; blue intaglio eyes; laughing open-closed mouth showing molded tongue and two small upper teeth. Marked on back of head: "22 - 9/0." *Collection of Bertha Hanscom.*

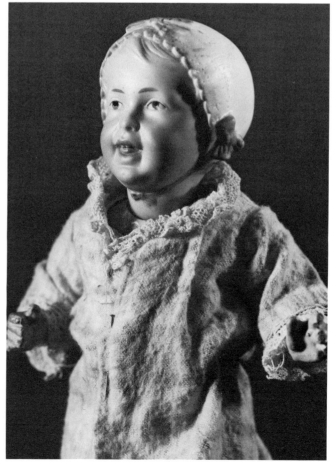

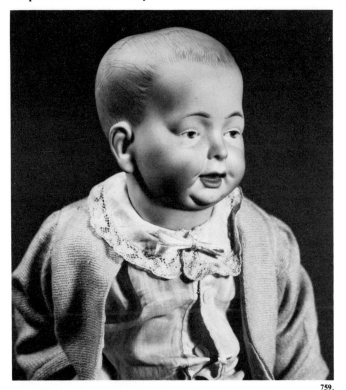

759.

761.

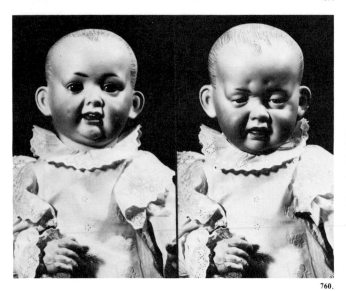

760.

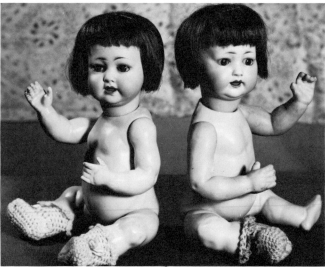

762.

759. BISQUE BABY MARKED "F 1 B"
Period: First quarter of 20th century.
Body: Composition; elastic strung; jointed at
  shoulders and hips.
Remarks: 15" (38.1cm) bisque headed baby with molded light
brown hair; blue painted eyes; smiling open-closed mouth
showing molded-in tongue. Marked: "F 1 B//Germany." Possibly
made by Fleischaker & Baum of New York whose trademark was
EFFanBEE. *Collection of Celia Ann Havender.*

760. TWO-FACED BISQUE BABY
Period: Early 20th century.
Body: Composition; elastic strung.
Remarks: Rare 16" (40.6cm) two-faced baby in bisque —
probably made in Germany. Head swivels, revealing on one side
a smiling sleeping eyed baby; on the other a crying one with
painted eyes. Head swivels on elastic used for stringing body.
Crying face marked "567," smiling marked "9." *Merrill Collection.*

761. CHARACTER BABY BY KLEY & HAHN
Period: First quarter of 20th century.
Body: Composition; elastic strung; jointed at
  shoulders and hips.
Remarks: Large, 22" (55.9cm) character baby whose bisque
socket head has intaglio blue eyes; open-closed mouth with
molded-in tongue; light brown painted hair. Marked: "K &
H//548//15//Germany." Made by the German firm of Kley &
Hahn. *Collection of Virginia C. Murray.*

762. BISQUE BABY DOLLS BY KLEY & HAHN
Period: First quarter of 20th century.
Bodies: Composition; elastic strung.
Remarks: 14" (35.6cm) twin babies whose bisque socket heads
have sleeping eyes with hair lashes; brown human hair wigs.
Unusual feature: The inset roof and tongue of each open mouth is
of bisque, molded in one piece, and painted to match the lips in
color. Two upper teeth are of white porcelain. Marked: "K & H"
over numerals "167-6." Made by Kley & Hahn of Germany.

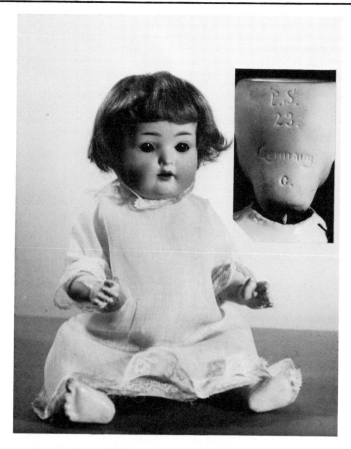

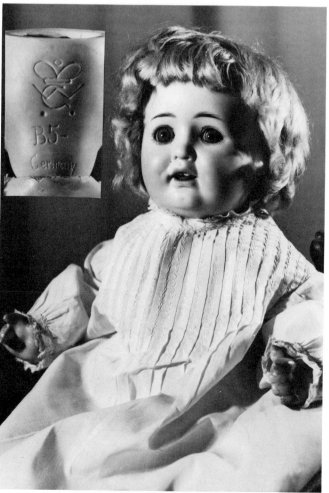

ABOVE LEFT:

763. BISQUE BABY MARKED "P.S."
Period: Early 20th century.
Body: Composition; elastic strung.
Remarks: The bisque socket of this 11" (27.9cm) baby has sleeping eyes; open mouth with teeth and brown mohair wig. Dressed in cheaply made, original manufacturer's clothes. A typical German bisque baby marked: "P.S.//23.//Germany//0." Possibly made by the German firm of Paul Schmidt of Sonneburg.

ABOVE:

764. BISQUE BABY — MARKED "P.M."
Period: First quarter of 20th century.
Body: Composition; elastic strung.
Remarks: 10" (25.4cm) baby doll. Bisque socket head has blue sleeping eyes; open mouth with teeth; brown mohair wig. Marked: "P.M.//23//Germany//3/0." Probably made by German firm of Otto Reinecke.

765. GERMAN BISQUE BABY BY WILLIAM GOEBEL
Period: First quarter of 20th century.
Body: Composition; elastic strung.
Remarks: 14" (35.6cm) baby doll whose bisque socket head has sleeping eyes; open mouth with two upper teeth; light mohair wig. Head bears the mark of the William Goebel firm of Germany plus "B5//Germany" (see insert).

LEFT:

766. GERMAN BABY BY BÄHR & PRÖSCHILD

Period: Early 20th century.

Body: Jointed composition; elastic strung.

Remarks: Appealing, 11" (27.9cm) baby doll. Bisque socket head has sleeping eyes; open-closed mouth with molded-in teeth; mohair wig. Wears original clothing including hooded cape. Marked: "585//0//B&PO (within X)//Germany." Made by the German firm of Bähr & Pröschild. *Collection of Frieda P. Marion.*

BELOW LEFT:

767. GERMAN BISQUE TODDLER BY BÄHR & PRÖSCHILD

Period: Early 20th century.

Body: Jointed composition; elastic strung.

Remarks: 13" (33cm) toddler. Bisque socket head has sleeping eyes; open mouth with two upper teeth; mohair wig. Head marked with letters "B & P/O" within X, plus "Germany" (see insert). Made by Bähr & Pröschild. Note jointed, straight limbed, thick-set toddler body as opposed to the bent limbed generally found with this type head.

BELOW:

768. SMILING BISQUE BABY BY FRANZ SCHMIDT & COMPANY

Period: Early 20th century.

Body: Jointed composition; elastic strung.

Remarks: 18" (45.7cm) dimpled and smiling baby whose bisque socket head has sleeping eyes; pierced nostrils; open mouth with two upper teeth and mohair wig. *Unique feature:* retractable tongue activated by the motion of the sleeping eyes. This type tongue may also be found in heads by Alt, Beck & Gottschalck. Marked: "F. S. & Co.//1272/45//Deponiert." Made by the German firm of Franz Schmidt. This head also came with painted hair as well as on a toddler body. *Merrill Collection.*

OPPOSITE PAGE

21" (53.3cm) bisque lady doll marked 7925/2 39, an especially fine German turned head. See Page 204, Illustration 513.

(Continued on page 343.)

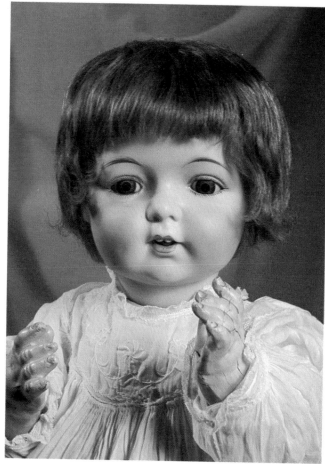

OPPOSITE PAGE:
Top: 18½" (49.6cm) marked Kestner doll with inset fur eyebrows and full wardrobe. See Page 283, Illustration 646.

Bottom: 8" (20.3cm) Kestner 192 doll pushing a pair of celluloid twins in an interesting metal carriage. *Merrill Collection.*

TOP LEFT:
9½" (24.2cm) Heubach "Baby Stuart" bisque baby doll. See Pages 322 and 323, Illustration 756.

TOP:
20" (50.8cm) marked Fulper American bisque baby doll. See Page 352, Illustration 796.

6¾" (17.2cm) all bisque "Baby Bud" doll. See Page 359, Illustration 817.

19" (48.3cm) marked K★R/Simon & Halbig/117/46 bisque doll. See Page 288, Illustration 659.

BELOW:
20" (50.8cm) marked K★R/114 bisque doll. See Page 288, Illustration 658 right.

OPPOSITE PAGE:
10" (25.4cm) German bisque doll marked 104, bisque pate with three holes. Dressed as Red Riding Hood.
Merrill Collection.

331

10½" (26.7cm) marked Simon & Halbig 1078 bisque doll. *Merrill Collection.*

BELOW:
Miscellaneous group of bisque doll house dolls photographed in an interesting butcher's shop. *Merrill Collection.*

OPPOSITE PAGE:
Pair of attractive brown bisque marked Simon & Halbig dolls dressed in regional costumes of India-European version. *Merrill Collection.*

Beautiful china shoulderhead made by Dressel & Kister. This company is known for its china half-figures and this unusual head exhibits their high quality. See Page 367, Illustration 847.

BELOW:
Very beautiful example of a china half-figure, from the painting used by Baker's Chocolate, "La Belle Chocolatiere." *Shirley Sanborn Collection.*

OPPOSITE PAGE:
Top Left: 13" (33cm) stockinette head clown with wool embroidered features and hair. Photographed with the 1914 Butler Bros. Catalog advertising this type of doll. See Page 419, Illustration 1011. *Merrill Collection.*

Top Right: Group of "Skookum" Indian dolls designed by Mary McAboy. See Page 374, Illustration 872.

Group of Door of Hope dolls. See Page 375, Illustration 876.

335

OPPOSITE PAGE:

Top: 8" (20.3cm) wooden "Dutch" doll standing by a wonderful old toy kitchen. See Page 377, Illustration 881. *Merrill Collection.*

Bottom: Group of Schoenhut dolls of different styles. See Pages 378-379.

18" (45.7cm) *Gladdie* designed by Helen K. Jensen and made in Germany. See Page 390, Illustration 926.

TOP RIGHT:
16" (40.6cm) composition shoulderhead boy with interesting signature or tradename on back of shoulders. See Page 385, Illustration 912.

RIGHT:
Composition *Shirley Temple.* See Page 394, Illustration 938. *Merrill Collection.*

12" (30.5cm) composition *Campbell Kid,* an advertising doll made by E. I. Horsman for the Campbell Soup Company. See Page 381, Illustration 897.

BELOW LEFT:
26" (66cm) nodding papier mâché mechanical clown whose clockwork mechanism also causes tongue to go in and out; glass eyes; body reinforced with strips of German newsprint circa 1920. *Merrill Collection.*

BELOW:
14" (35.6cm) K★R celluloid baby with flirty eyes. See Page 404, Illustration 969.

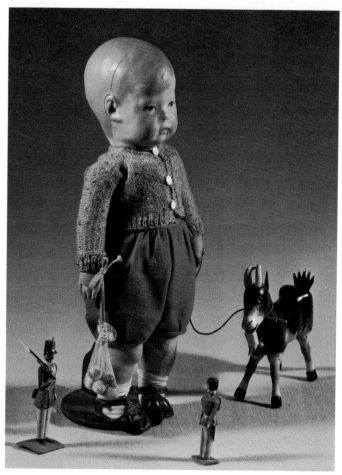

ABOVE:
14" (35.6cm) Brückner-patented black cloth doll. See Page 420, Illustration 1013.

ABOVE RIGHT:
22" (55.9cm) stockinette molded *Philadelphia Baby* made by J. B. Sheppard & Co. See Page 427, Illustration 1030.

17" (43.2cm) Käthe Kruse cloth doll. See Page 424, Illustration 1024.

ABOVE:
22" (55.9cm) and 12½in (31.8cm)
Martha Chase babies. See Page 422,
Illustration 1017.

17" (43.2cm) Lenci girl with felt head
and limbs, muslin torso, all original
organdy and felt clothing, molded
and painted brown eyes; marks of a
fine Lenci doll include applied felt
ears and separate first and fourth
fingers. See Page 426 for other Lenci
dolls. *Clara Hobey Collection.*

ABOVE:
Group of Norah Wellings dolls. See
Page 430, Illustration 1038.

King George VI cloth doll made by
the J. K. Farnell Co., Ltd. of
England. See Page 431, Illustration
1040.

FOLLOWING PAGE:
16" (40.6cm) *Uncle Sam*, a bisque character doll of German make
in the late 19th - early 20th century. See Page 246, Illustration
547.

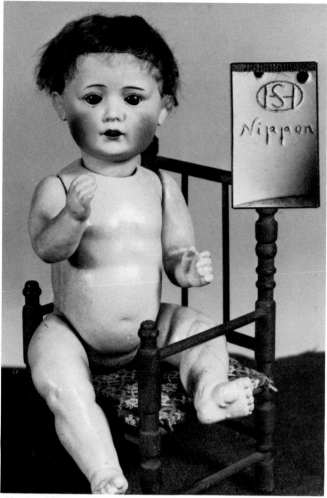

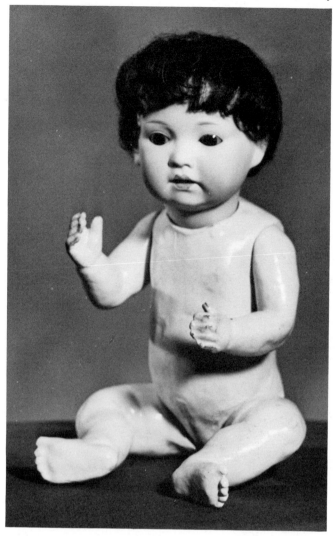

(Continued from page 326.)

CLOCKWISE:

769. BISQUE BABY DOLL MARKED "NIPPON"
Period: World War I era.
Body: Jointed composition; elastic strung.
Remarks: 14" (35.6cm) Japanese made baby doll of good quality. The bisque socket head has blue sleeping eyes; open mouth with teeth; mohair wig. Marked: "SH (superimposed within oval)//Nippon" (see insert).

770. BISQUE BABY DOLL — MADE IN JAPAN
Period: World War I era.
Body: Composition; elastic strung.
Remarks: 14" (35.6cm) baby doll made in Japan when World War I caused an end to importation of German dolls. The highly colored bisque socket head has sleeping eyes; open mouth with teeth; brown mohair wig. Although the quality and workmanship is inferior to the German-made dolls, there is a certain charm to the oriental cast of the face. Marked: "F.Y.//Nippon//203."

**771. JAPANESE BABY DOLL BY MORIMURA
BROTHERS**
Period: Circa 1918-1922.
Body: Jointed composition; elastic strung.
Remarks: 14" (35.6cm) good quality Japanese made baby doll. Bisque head has sleeping eyes; open mouth with teeth; mohair wig. Marked: "2//M B//Japan//4." Made in Japan for the large Japanese importing firm of Morimura Brothers of New York. Small celluloid baby doll is 3½" (8.9cm) tall. Strung arms and legs. "Made in Japan" and an unreadable mark on the back.
Merrill Collection.

LEFT:
772. BISQUE BABY DOLL — MADE IN JAPAN
Period: World War I
Body: Composition; elastic strung.
Remarks: 12½" (31.8cm) baby whose bisque head has stationary glass eyes; open mouth with teeth; painted hair. Marked: "M13//RE (within diamond)//Nippon." Made during World War I when importation of German dolls ceased. This same firm made child dolls—see page 312, illustration 727. Japanese made bisque dolls were not equal to German in quality and workmanship.

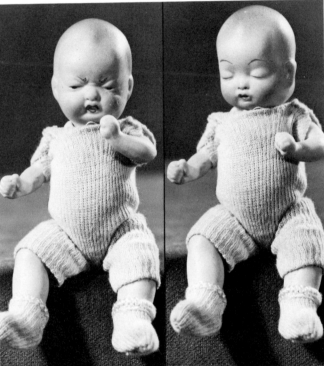

773. TWO-FACED ALL BISQUE BABY MADE IN JAPAN
Period: First quarter of 20th century.
Remarks: 5" (12.7cm) all bisque two-faced baby jointed at neck, shoulders and hips. When turned, the elastic-strung socket head shows either a sleeping or crying face. Marked: "Made in Japan."

LEFT:
774. BLACK BISQUE BABY MADE IN JAPAN
Period: First quarter of 20th century.
Remarks: 4" (10.2cm) Black bisque baby with painted eyes; closed mouth. Three holes provided in head for insertion of three tufts of black mohair. An inexpensive doll. Marked on back: "Japan."

RIGHT:

775. "NEW BORN BABE" BY AMBERG

Period: Copyrighted in 1914.

Body: Cloth with composition hands; squeak box in torso.

Remarks: 10½" (26.7cm) baby whose bisque head, with flange neck, has sleeping eyes; closed mouth; light brown painted hair. Head marked: "Germany//A-R//LA&S 886.2," was designed by artist Jeno Jusko and made in Germany for Louis Amberg & Son of New York. This baby also came with open mouth with teeth as well as on a strung, composition body. *Merrill Collection.*

776. "NEW BORN BABE" BY AMBERG

Period: Copyrighted in 1914.

Body: Composition; elastic strung. Jointed at shoulders and hips.

Remarks: 8" (20.3cm) baby whose bisque socket head has sleeping eyes; closed mouth; light brown painted hair. Modeled from a three day old infant. Marked: "© L. Amberg & Son// Germany//886//5/0 K." Made in Germany for Louis Amberg of New York. This baby also came with flange-necked bisque head mounted on cloth body. *Collection of Shirley F. Sanborn.*

RIGHT:

777. SCOWLING ALL BISQUE BABY

Period: Early 20th century.

Remarks: 6" (15.2cm) all bisque baby whose head, with scowling expression, has brown painted eyes; slightly parted open-closed mouth showing painted-in teeth; light brown painted hair. An appealing infant who seems about to cry. Unmarked. Made in Germany.

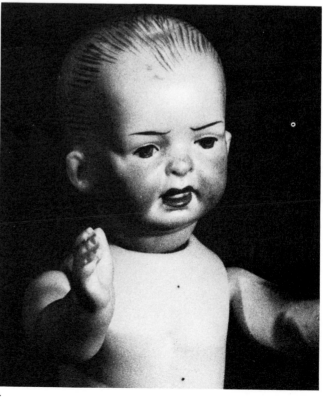

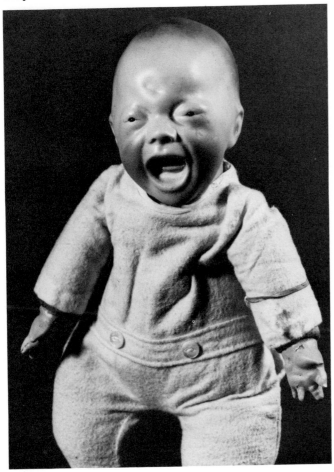

778. BAWLING BABY IN BISQUE
Period: 1920s.
Body: Cloth with composition hands.
Remarks: Squint-eyed 12" (30.5cm) doll representing a bawling baby. Toothless and almost bald, the expressive bisque head has tiny blue glass eyes and wide open mouth with molded-in tongue and gums. Incised on back of head: "225//2/O.1.C.//Made in Germany." *Collection of Mrs. Fidelia Lence.*

779. BISQUE BABY DOLL BY GEORGENE AVERILL
Period: Circa 1918.
Body: Cloth with celluloid hands.
Remarks: 11" (27.9cm) bisque headed baby with molded light brown hair; sleeping eyes; open laughing mouth with set-in tongue and two lower teeth. Marked: "Copr. by Georgene Averill//Germany." Made in Germany for the American creator of dolls Georgene Averill, known as "Madame Hendren."

780. "BONNIE BABE" BY GEORGENE AVERILL
Period: Copyrighted in 1926.
Remarks: 5½" (14cm) and 4½" (11.5cm) all bisque jointed *Bonnie Babe* dolls designed by Georgene Averill. Molded light brown hair; open-closed mouth with two lower teeth. May be found with blue or brown glass eyes; blue or pink slippers. Manufactured in Germany for George Borgfeldt & Company of New York. *Collection of Mrs. Louise H. Lund.*

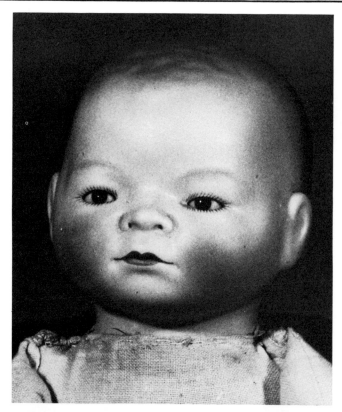

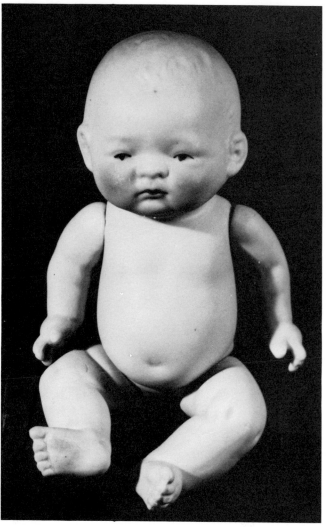

ABOVE LEFT:

781. BYE-LO BABY

Period: Copyrighted in 1923.

Body: Cloth with celluloid hands.

Remarks: *Bye-Lo* bisque baby doll created by Grace Storey Putnam. Marked on head: "Copr. by Grace S. Putnam — Made in Germany." Later models were made in composition by Cameo Doll Co. This much sought after doll has painted features and sleeping glass eyes. Several German firms manufactured the bisque *Bye-Lo* heads for George Borgfeldt & Co. of New York who advertised in 1925 that it was for sale in all leading department stores in seven sizes from 9 to 20" (22.9 to 50.8cm). *Merrill Collection.*

ABOVE RIGHT:

782. ALL BISQUE "BYE-LO" BABY

Period: Circa 1925.

Remarks: Rare 6" (15.2cm) all bisque *Bye-Lo* baby doll with swivel-neck; sleeping glass eyes; molded pink shoes and white socks. Created by Grace Storey Putnam. Printed label on front of body reads: "Bye-lo Baby© Germany G. S. Putnam." Incised on back: "4 15 Corp. by Grace S. Putnam Germany." *Merrill Collection.*

783. IMITATION "BYE-LO" BABY MADE IN JAPAN

Period: Late 1920s.

Remarks: 5½" (14cm) stone bisque version of the popular *Bye-Lo* baby. A cheaper doll with painted blue eyes and light brown painted hair. Jointed at shoulders and hips. Bears Y in circle trademark plus incised "Made in Japan." An imitation of the German made *Bye-Lo.*

347

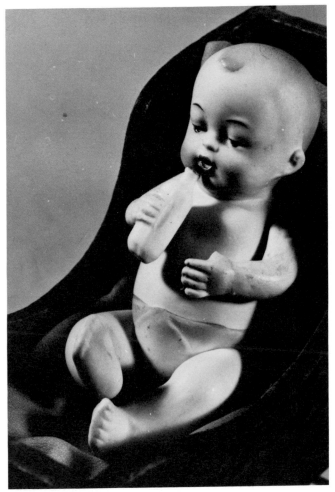

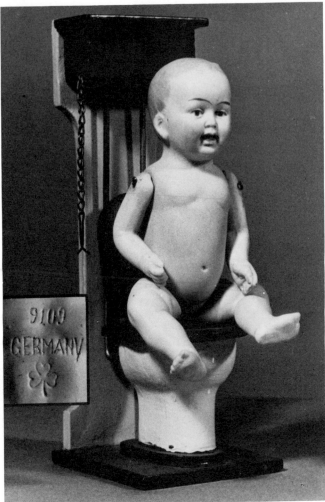

ABOVE LEFT:
784. "BABYKINS" BY GRACE S. PUTNAM
Period: 1931.
Body: Cloth with composition limbs.
Remarks: Approximately 20" (50.8cm) baby doll created by Grace S. Putnam. Bisque head has blue glass eyes; open-closed mouth; light painted hair. Marked on head: "Babykins//Cop. by Grace S. Putnam//Made in Germany//143. 5/50." Made in Germany for Borgfeldt & Co. of New York. Grace S. Putnam is better known for her earlier (1923) and more often found *Bye-Lo* baby. *Collection of Mrs. Fidelia Lence.*

LEFT:
785. BISQUE BABY WITH TREFOIL MARK
Period: 1920s.
Remarks: 5½" (14cm) stone bisque baby with light brown molded hair; blue painted eyes; open-closed mouth with parted lips. Back of torso marked: "9109//Germany" plus a well incised trefoil. *Collection of Mrs. Austin P. Cate.*

ABOVE RIGHT:
786. BABY HOLDING NURSING BOTTLE
Period: First quarter 20th century.
Remarks: 5" (12.7cm) all bisque baby holding red-tipped nursing bottle in right hand. Wears blue molded-on diapers. Painted features include down-cast blue eyes; open-closed mouth pursed as though to receive the bottle and light brown hair. Unmarked. Probably German made.

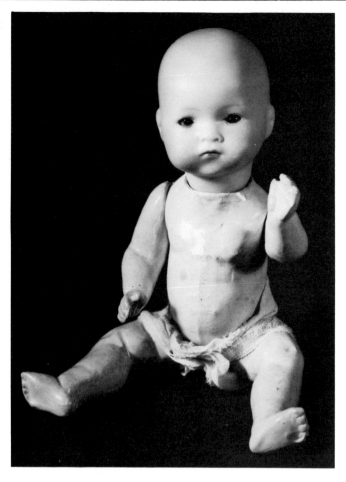

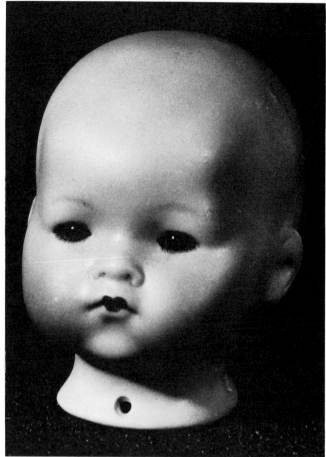

CLOCKWISE:
787. DREAM BABY
Period: 1924.
Body: Composition; elastic strung; jointed at
shoulders and hips.
Remarks: 8½" (21.6cm) *Dream Baby* whose bisque socket head
has blue sleeping eyes; closed mouth; light painted hair. This doll
is generally found with flange neck head on stuffed cloth body.
Marked: "AM//Germany//341//4/0//K." Made by the German
firm of Armand Marseille. *Merrill Collection.*

788. DREAM BABY
Period: 1924.
Body: Cloth with composition or celluloid hands.
Remarks: So-called *Dream Baby.* Made by Armand Marseille
in Germany in 1924, shortly after the marketing of the popular
Bye-Lo baby doll. The bisque head has light brown painted hair
and sleeping glass eyes. Marked: "AM//Made in Germany."

789. ORIENTAL BABY BY ARMAND MARSEILLE
Period: First quarter of 20th century.
Body: Composition; elastic strung; jointed at hips
and shoulders.
Remarks: 8" (20.3cm) bisque baby with oriental features. The
olive complexioned head has black painted hair; stationary black
glass eyes; closed mouth. Unusual — most babies are of
Caucasian mold. Illustrated doll redressed. Marked: "AM//
Germany//353//5/0//K." Made by German firm of Armand
Marseille. *Collection of Virginia C. Murray.*

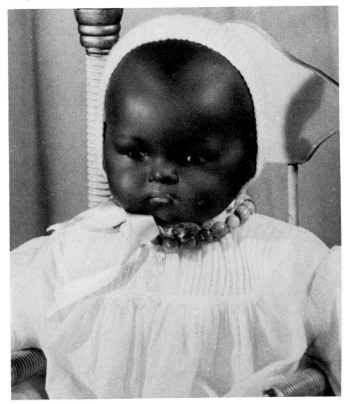

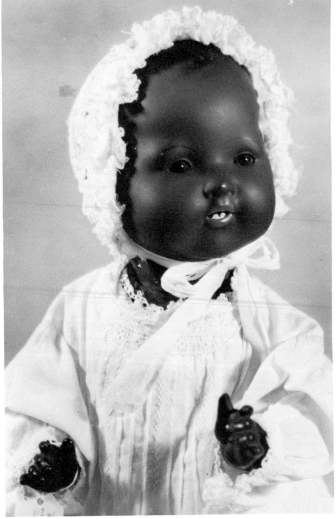

LEFT:
790. DREAM BABY IN BROWN BISQUE
Period: Circa 1924.
Body: Brown cloth with brown composition hands.
Remarks: Seldom found brown bisque *Dream Baby* in large size, 20" (50.8cm). Made by Armand Marseille Co. of Germany. Head marked: "AM//Germany." Head of smooth, dark brown bisque with black painted hair and sleeping eyes. Except for color, it is identical with the white *Dream Baby* more commonly found. *Merrill Collection.*

791. LIGHT BROWN "DREAM BABY" REPRESENTING A POLYNESIAN
Period: 1924.
Body: Composition; elastic strung; jointed at shoulders and hips.
Remarks: All original 8" (20.3cm) *Dream Baby* with light brown sprayed-on finish. The bisque socket head has black painted hair; sleeping eyes; closed mouth. Marked: "AM//Germany//341 2/0 K." Mold is same as that used for white baby. Wears lace-edged diaper under grass skirt. Made by Armand Marseille. *Collection of Jimmy and Fay Rodolfos.*

LEFT:
792. DREAM BABY IN BROWN BISQUE — VARIANT
Period: Circa 1924.
Body: Jointed composition; elastic strung; jointed at shoulder and hips.
Remarks: 18" (45.7cm) brown bisque *Dream Baby* with two unusual features — socket head on strung body; open mouth with teeth. Generally found with flange necked head on cloth body; closed mouth. The illustrated baby has the usual sleeping eyes and painted hair. Marked: "A.M.//Germany.//351./5.K." Made by Armand Marseille. *Collection of Virginia C. Murray.*

793. BISQUE BABY DOLL BY ARMAND MARSEILLE

Period: First quarter of 20th century.
Body: Composition; elastic strung.
Remarks: An appealing, good quality, 18" (45.7cm) baby doll with bisque socket head on bent limb body. She has sleeping eyes; open mouth with teeth; light brown mohair wig. Typical of the popular baby doll of era. Marked: "A. 6 M.//DRGM//267/1." Made by the German firm of Armand Marseille.

794. MECHANICAL BABY MARKED "A.M."

Period: First quarter of 20th century.
Body: Jointed composition; elastic strung.
Remarks: 20" (50.8cm) baby with key-wound mechanism in torso. When activated, it allows doll to cry while moving it's arms up and down. Bisque socket head has sleeping eyes; open mouth with teeth; mohair wig. Head made by Armand Marseille of Germany and is marked: "A.M."

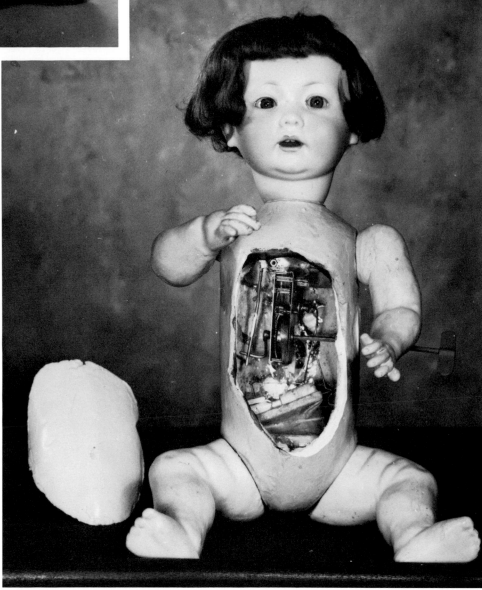

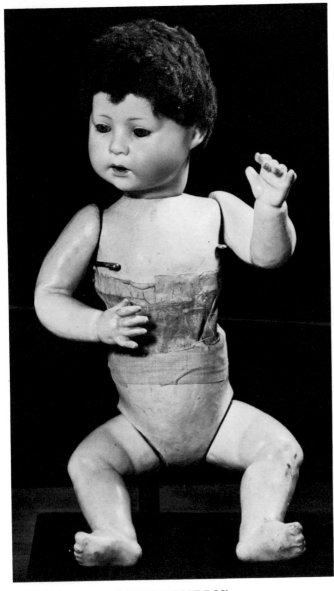

OPPOSITE PAGE:
797. "TYNIE BABY" BY HORSMAN
Period: 1924.
Remarks: 9" (22.9cm) all bisque baby whose slightly frowning face has light brown painted hair; sleeping eyes. Made to compete with the popular *Bye-Lo* baby. Marked on head: "© 1924 by//E. I. Horsman Co., Inc.//Made in Germany//38." Wears original *Tynie Baby* pin. Also came with heads of bisque or composition mounted on cloth stuffed bodies. *Collection of Shirley F. Sanborn.*

798. "TYNIE BABY" BY HORSMAN
Period: 1924.
Body: Cloth with composition arms.
Remarks: 12" (30.5cm) bisque headed baby whose slightly scowling face has sleeping eyes; closed mouth; painted hair. Marked: © 1924 by//E.I.Horsman Co., Inc.//Made in Germany." Wears original tagged clothing. Made to compete with the popular *Bye-Lo* baby. The illustrated *Tynie Baby* was also made in composition as well as all bisque. *Collection of Shirley F. Sanborn.*

799. BISQUE BABY DOLL BY GERLING
Period: Circa 1925.
Body: Cloth with composition hands.
Remarks: 15" (38.1cm) baby doll somewhat resembling the *Dream Baby* by Armand Marseille. The bisque head has sleeping eyes; light brown painted hair; pierced nostrils. Voice box in body. Head marked: "3//Arthur A. Gerling//Made in Germany." *Collection of Mrs. Samuel R. Conde.*

800. "BABY PHYLLIS" AND "KIDDIEJOY"
Period: Circa 1925.
Body: Cloth with composition arms.
Remarks: Two German bisque babies.
Left: 10" (25.4cm) closed-mouth baby with sleeping eyes. Marked: "Baby Phyllis//Made in Germany//2//401//10." Made for the Baby Phyllis Doll Co. of New York.
Right: 10" (25.4cm) closed-mouth baby with sleeping eyes. Marked: "Germany//Kiddiejoy//1/0." Made for Hitz, Jacobs and Kassler who handled *Kiddiejoy* dolls. *Courtesy of Mrs. William Hilton.*

795. BISQUE BABY WITH VOICE BOX
Period: First quarter of 20th century.
Body: Composition; elastic strung.
Remarks: 16" (40.6cm) bisque character baby with stationary blue glass eyes; open mouth with two teeth; brown fur wig. *Unusual feature:* voice box in midriff — when squeezed, baby cries. Marked: "Germany//233 A 4½ M." Made by Armand Marseille. *Collection of Mrs. Elmer Morley.*

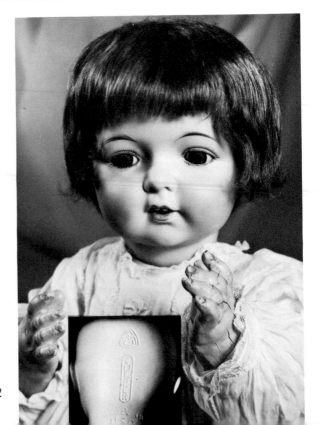

RIGHT:
796. FULPER BABY DOLL — AMERICAN MADE
Period: Circa 1920.
Body: Jointed composition; elastic strung.
Remarks: 20" (50.8cm) all original baby doll. Bisque socket head has mohair wig; open mouth with two upper teeth; celluloid and metal sleeping eyes bearing 1918 patent of Samuel Marcus. Marked: "Fulper//Made in U.S.A.//8." Made by Fulper Pottery Co. of New Jersey who also made dolls of all bisque. *Merrill Collection.*

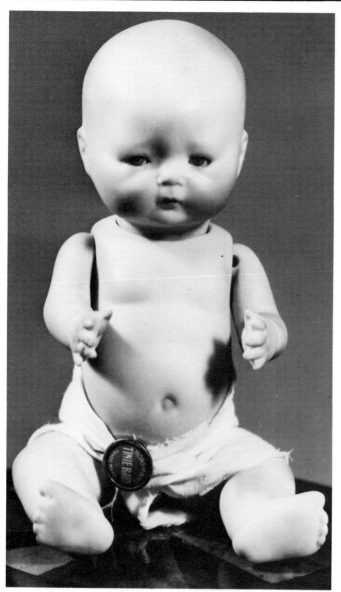

797.

798.

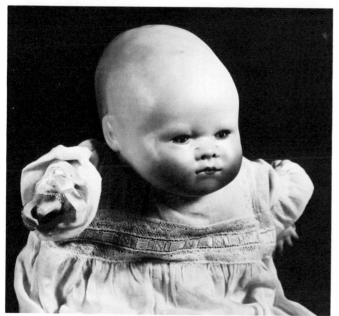

799.

800.

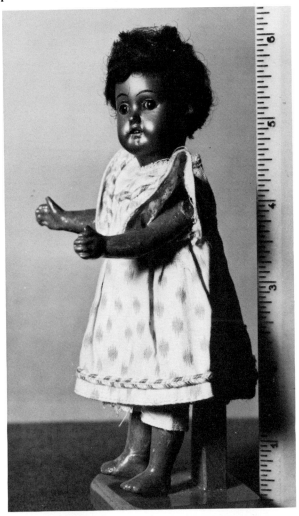

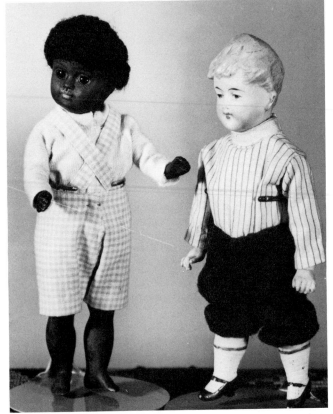

LEFT:
801. BLACK BISQUE DOLL — MARKED "R"
Period: Early 20th century.
Body: Composition; elastic strung; jointed at hips and shoulders.
Remarks: 6" (15.2cm) Black bisque headed doll with stationary glass eyes; open mouth with teeth; curly mohair wig. Marked on head: "50//18/0//R. Dep." Maker uncertain. *Merrill Collection.*

802. BLACK BISQUE DOLL — FLANGE NECKED
Period: Early 20th century.
Body: Composition; elastic strung; jointed at hips and shoulders.
Remarks: 8" (20.3cm) Black bisque doll whose flange necked head has stationary glass eyes and open mouth with teeth. Wig is a replacement. Marked on back of neck: "3/0."

LEFT:
803. ALL BISQUE BOY DOLLS
Period: Early 20th century.
Left: 6½" (16.5cm) Black boy doll with well modelled ethnic features. Socket head has glass eyes; closed mouth; mohair wig and bare feet. Wears old cotton costume. Unmarked.
Right: 6" (15.2cm) white boy doll with painted features; molded blonde hair and molded-on socks and slippers. Wears old costume. Marked: "5174//15½." Boy dolls, being scarcer than girl dolls, are considered highly collectible. *Merrill Collection.*

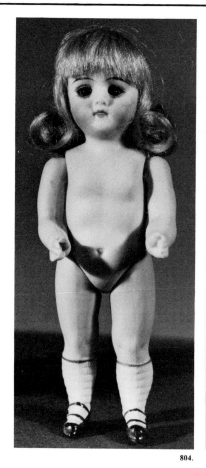

804.

805.

806.

804. ALL BISQUE DOLL BY KESTNER

Period: Early 20th century.

Remarks: 5½" (14cm) all bisque doll; jointed at shoulders and hips. Sleeping brown eyes; closed mouth; blonde mohair wig. Wears white ribbed socks with blue bands and brown two-strap slippers. Back of head marked with numbers "130 over 4." Probably made by German firm of J. D. Kestner.

805. GERMAN MADE ALL BISQUE DOLL

Period: Early 20th century.

Remarks: 5½" (14cm) all bisque doll with sleeping eyes; open-closed mouth with molded-in teeth; blonde mohair wig. Marked on back of head with numbers "150 over 3½." Probably made by German firm of J. D. Kestner. *Collection of Mrs. John M. Park, Jr.*

806. ALL BISQUE CHILD

Period: Early 20th century.

Remarks: 7" (17.8cm) all bisque doll of fine quality. Open and shut eyes; brown mohair wig; open mouth with tiny teeth. Very expressive. *Unusual feature:* long black molded stockings and brown strap slippers.

807. ALL BISQUE DOLL IN LABELLED BOX

Period: Early 20th century.

Remarks: 5½" (14cm) all bisque doll with sleeping eyes; open mouth with teeth; mohair wig; molded socks and slippers. Marked on head and limbs: "83//100" only. Came in original box labeled: "Our Darling//1/12 Doz. No. 83/100//Baby// Made in Germany." Note that the country of origin is on box only — not on doll. *Merrill Collection.*

807.

LEFT:

808. ALL BISQUE CRAWLING BABY

Period: Early 20th century.

Remarks: 4½" (11.5cm) all bisque baby with swivel neck; glass eyes; human hair wig. Note jointed limbs bent in crawling position. Appears to be French in quality. Unmarked. *Collection of Mrs. John M. Park, Jr.*

809. LETTIE LANE'S DOLL HOUSE DOLL

Period: 1908-1915.

Remarks: Bisque copy of the doll house doll from the popular *Lettie Lane* paper doll series published by the *Ladies Home Journal.* 3½" (8.9cm) high, she has stationary glass eyes; closed mouth; mohair wig. Original costume duplicates that of her prototype. Marked: "36/8/Germany." *Lettie Lane*'s play doll *Daisy* was also brought out in bisque (see page 283, Illustration 645). *Collection of Rhode Island School of Design. On permanent loan to the Toy Cupboard Museum, South Lancaster, Massachusetts.*

LEFT:

810. ALL BISQUE DOLL IN CROCHETED COSTUME

Period: Early 20th century.

Remarks: 5½" (14cm) all bisque doll with brown sleeping eyes; mohair wig; molded socks and slippers. Marked on head: "160/4½/0." Wears hand crocheted two-piece dress, bonnet, ruffled petticoat and under pants. Countless dolls of this type were dressed at home in this manner. *Merrill Collection.*

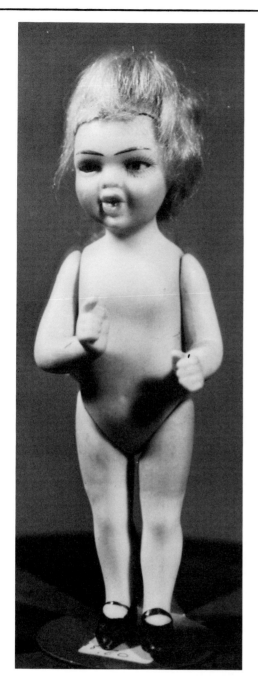

811. ALL BISQUE DOLL BY ORSINI
Period: Copyrighted in 1920.
Remarks: 5" (12.7cm) doll with sleeping eyes; pursed open mouth with teeth; mohair wig. Note pointing index finger on right hand. Marked: "J.I.O. © 1920//44." One of several dolls designed by Jeanne I. Orsini of New York. *Collection of Shirley F. Sanborn.*

812. ALL BISQUE DOLL BY ORSINI
Period: Copyrighted in 1920.
Remarks: 5" (12.7cm) doll with open-closed mouth showing molded teeth and tongue; set-in glass eyes; mohair wig. Note pointing index finger on right hand. Marked: "J.I.O. © 1919//47." Sticker on chest printed: "Vivi//Reg. U.S. Patent Office//Copr. 1920 J. I. Orsini.//Patent Applied For.//Germany." Doll shown with original box. *Collection of Miss Ruth Whittier.*

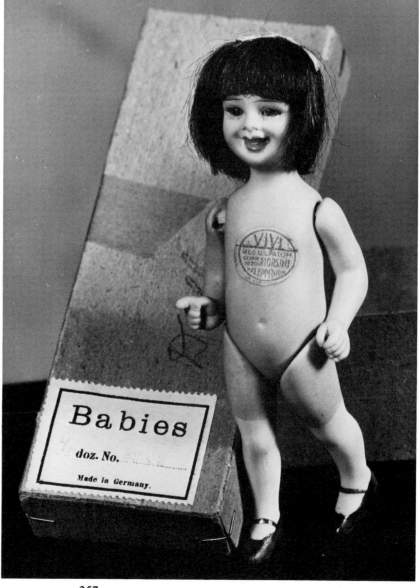

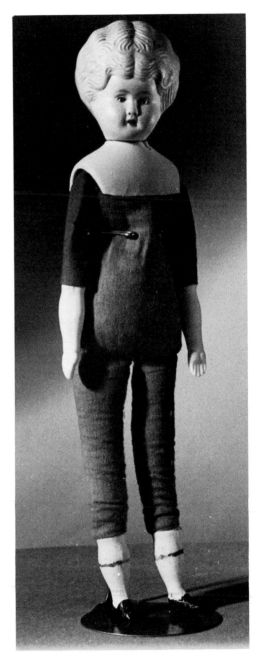

LEFT:
813. UNDRESSED ALL BISQUE DOLLS
Period: Early 20th century.
Left: 6½" (16.5cm) stone bisque doll with painted eyes; hairdo and underwear molded in material. Unusual. Made in Germany.
Right: 7½" (19.1cm) all bisque doll with boyish hairdo; painted eyes; wearing molded-on socks and slippers. Made in Germany.
Merrill Collection.

814. UNDRESSED ALL BISQUE DOLLS
Period: Early 20th century.
Left: 7" (17.8cm) stone bisque sister to doll shown on right of page 358, Illustration 813. She has blue painted eyes and bow in hair.
Right: 6¾" (17.2cm) stone bisque doll with painted eyes; blonde hair. Molded-on underwear.

815. JAPAN MADE DOLL WITH FLANGE NECKED HEAD
Period: Early 20th century.
Body: Red cloth with stone bisque limbs.
Remarks: 12" (30.5cm) doll whose head, of white stone bisque, has pale painted features. Note two-piece head with flange neck — unique in this type doll. An unglazed and cheaper version of the more commonly found German made dolls of the period. Marked on back shoulders: "Patented//Japan."

358

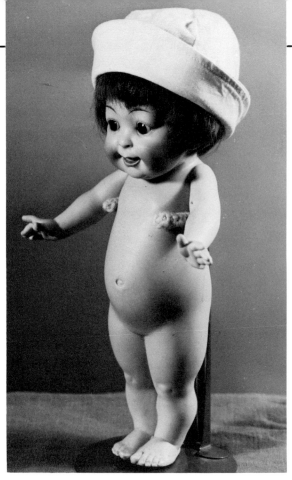

816. "OUR FAIRY" ALL BISQUE DOLL
Period: 1914.
Remarks: 12" (30.5cm) all bisque doll with side-set glass eyes; open-closed mouth with two molded-in upper teeth; mohair wig. Jointed at shoulders. Doll originally carried "Our Fairy// Germany" sticker on chest. Made in Germany for the firm of Louis Wolf & Company. Competed with the *Kewpie* dolls, see page 360. *Collection of Virginia C. Murray.*

817. "BABY BUD"
Period: 1916.
Remarks: 6¾" (17.2cm) all bisque novelty doll with sleeping glass eyes cast to side; tongue showing between parted lips; light brown mohair wig. Jointed at shoulders only. Unusual. This doll is generally found with painted eyes and molded hair. Wears white molded-on shirt tinted and edged in blue. Marked on back (see insert): "Baby Bud//Germany." *Baby Bud* trademark was registered in Germany by Butler Brothers of New York in 1915. *Merrill Collection.*

FAR LEFT:
818. BOY DOLL WITH EYES TO SIDE
Period: Early 20th century.
Body: Composition; elastic strung.
Remarks: Whimsical bisque boy doll whose sleeping eyes gaze permanently to one side. Differs from the "flirty-eyed" doll whose gaze rolls from side to side.

819. ALL BISQUE DOLL WITH SIDE-SET EYES
Period: Early 20th century.
Remarks: Large, side-set sleeping eyes and smiling open-closed mouth give this 7½" (19.1cm) all bisque doll a winsome expression. She has feathered brows; painted upper and lower lashes and wears light mohair wig. Bisque legs have molded on light blue socks and black slippers. Marked on back of head are numbers "401 over 18." German made, possibly by the firm of W. Goebel.

LEFT:
820. KEWPIE DOLLS — BY ROSE O'NEILL

Period: Copyrighted in 1913.
Body: All bisque; elastic strung arms.
Remarks: A group of bisque *Kewpies* ranging in size from 5" (12.7cm) to 9" (22.9cm). Designed by Rose O'Neill, made in Germany by J. D. Kestner and other firms. Originals marked "O'Neill" on sole of foot. A similar doll *Scootles* was also designed by Rose O'Neill but is not commonly found. Although sometimes made of rubber, celluloid and composition, it is the bisque *Kewpie* that is most desirable. American made composition *Kewpies* produced by the Cameo Doll Company in the 1920s are frequently found. These winsome dolls, with blue bud wings and painted features, have lightly indicated hair with topknot. Eyes glance to left as well as right. *Merrill Collection.*

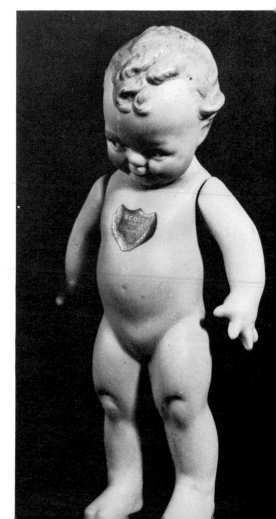

821. KEWPIES IN ACTION — VARIANTS

Period: Copyrighted in 1913.
Bodies: All bisque.
Remarks: Examples of the many all bisque *Kewpies* in action. Made in Germany. Marked: "O'Neill." **From left to right:** 4¼" (10.9cm) (overall) *Kewpie* seated in green wicker chair. 6½" (16.5cm) helmeted *Kewpie* soldier with sword. 4½" (10.9cm) helmeted *Kewpie* soldier with bugle and dagger at sides. 3½" (8.5cm) *Kewpie* soldier with visored cap, sword and gun. Action *Kewpies* are prized by many collectors.

RIGHT:
822. "SCOOTLES" DOLL — BY ROSE O'NEILL

Period: Copyrighted in 1925.
Body: All bisque; elastic strung arms.
Remarks: German made, 7" (17.8cm) all bisque *Scootles* with yellow molded hair; painted blue eyes. Designed by American artist Rose O'Neill. Resembles somewhat her more commonly found *Kewpie* doll. Bears paper label on chest. Marked: "Scootles" on foot. *Scootles* was also made in all composition by the Cameo Doll Company in the 1930s. *Collection of Mrs. Louise H. Lund.*

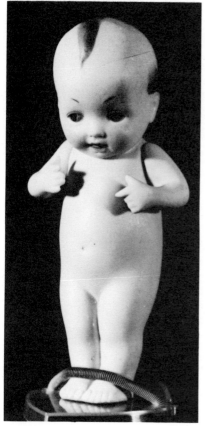

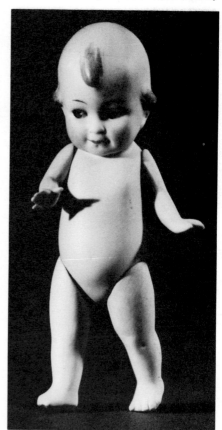

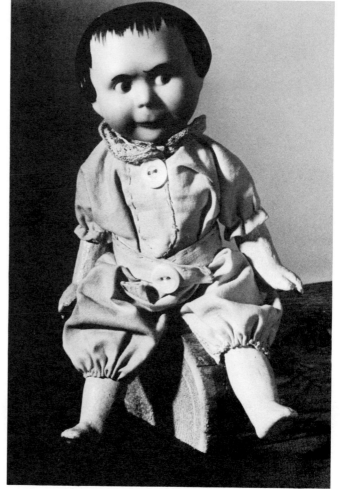

ABOVE, LEFT TO RIGHT:

823. "CUPID" TYPE ALL BISQUE DOLL

Period: Pre World War I.

Remarks: 5½" (14cm) boy doll of pink tinted bisque — jointed at shoulders only. Slightly turned and downcast head has painted sideward looking eyes and open-closed mouth with molded upper teeth. Hair on bald head consists of painted rim in back, forelock in front. Doll is unmarked. One of several similar type dolls made in competition to Rose O'Neill's popular *Kewpie*. *Merrill Collection.*

824. "GOGGLE EYED" BISQUE DOLL WITH MOLDED HAIR

Period: First quarter of 20th century.

Body: Composition; elastic strung.

Remarks: 6½" (16.5cm) smiling character doll with expression resembling the *Kewpie* dolls. Painted black eyes look to side; blonde molded hair wears blue bow and band. Molded blue shoes with gilt buckles; white socks. Marked (with crown): "P G 12/0 Germany." *Collection of Mrs. Goodrich L. Johnson.*

825. ALL BISQUE "CUPID" DOLL

Period: Early 20th century.

Remarks: 5½" (14cm) all bisque doll called *Cupid*. Made in competition to the popular *Kewpie* of the day (see page 360, Illustration 820). Features are painted including eyes and light brown forelock. Limbs are elastic strung. Marked: "Germany// 10954." Not as commonly found is a sister doll, in same size, but with painted blue hair bows. Both dolls distributed by Butler Brothers. *Merrill Collection.*

RIGHT:

826. BOY CHARACTER DOLL

Period: First quarter of 20th century.

Body: Composition; elastic strung; jointed at hips and shoulders.

Remarks: Most unusual character doll with quizzical expression. 6½" (16.5cm) in height. The pink-toned bisque head has intaglio brown eyes cast to side; upturned smiling mouth; black painted brows and hair. Marked: "31 - 12/0."

361

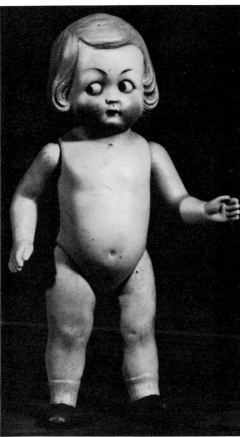

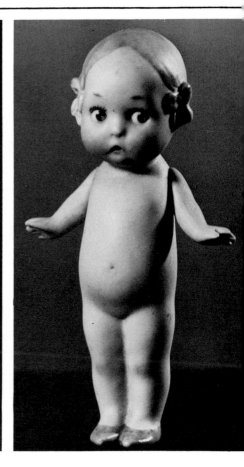

ABOVE, LEFT TO RIGHT:

827.
Period: Early 20th century.
Remarks: 5" (12.7cm) all bisque boy with side-cast intaglio eyes; blonde, side parted hair. Molded on rompers are tinted blue. Came in other sizes and with clothing in various color combinations. Made in Germany before World War I. Unmarked. *Merrill Collection.*

828. BISQUE DOLL WITH ROGUISH EXPRESSION
Period: Early 20th century.
Remarks: 7" (17.8cm) coarse quality bisque doll with gaze cast to side. Eyes with this expression are referred to as "rougish," "goggle" or "goo-goo." Blonde hair is bobbed. Wears ribbed socks and slippers. Made in Germany.

829. ALL BISQUE DOLL — BY HEUBACH
Period: Second decade of 20th century.
Remarks: 4½" (11.5cm) all bisque girl doll who, along with a brother, was made in competition to the popular *Kewpie.* She has side cast, intaglio eyes and small, triangular shaped mouth. Molded hair bows and pointed slippers are of a matching light blue. Made by Gebrüder Heubach firm of Germany. *Collection of Mrs. George O. Vosburgh.*

830. ALL BISQUE JAPANESE DOLLS
Period: Circa 1925.
Remarks: Three dolls of coarse quality stone bisque. Designed in imitation of the popular *Kewpie.* Inferior in quality to the German made dolls. All have painted features, are highly colored, and stand 6½" (16.5cm), 6" (15.2cm) and 4½" (11.5cm) respectively. Marked: "Made in Japan."

831. STONE BISQUE DOLL WITH MOLDED COLLAR
Period: First quarter of 20th century.
Body: Cloth with stone bisque limbs.
Remarks: 6" (15.2cm) all original doll whose stone bisque head has molded on white collar; painted features; mohair wig. Bisque legs have brown painted boots with blue lacings. Marked on back shoulders: "Germany//8."

832. DOLL OF STONE BISQUE
Period: Early 20th century.
Remarks: Later type 7" (17.8cm) all bisque doll of coarser quality. Painted blue eyes; mohair wig; slippers and stockings molded in material.

833. HALF-BISQUE DOLL
Period: Circa 1910.
Body: Cloth with stone bisque torso, hands and feet.
Remarks: Uncommon 6½" (16.5cm) doll with bisque head and torso in one piece. Molded blouse has yellow collar with pink ruffle and blue bow. Pink bow in hair. Painted features. Half bisque dolls were also made in other forms — children and adults. Mold for this doll, minus torso section, was used in making shoulderheads. Marked: "Germany" on lower back edge of torso. _Collection of The Children's Museum, Boston, Massachusetts._

FAR RIGHT:
834. STONE BISQUE DOLL
Period: First quarter of 20th century.
Body: Cloth with stone bisque limbs; typical for this type.
Remarks: 12½" (31.8cm) complete and original stone bisque doll with pale, blue trimmed collar and pink hair ribbon. Contemporary with the stone bisque bonnet dolls. Made in Germany.

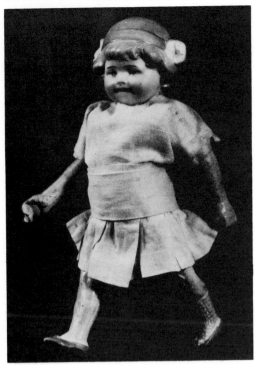

835. CHARACTER DOLL BY WILLIAM GOEBEL
Period: First quarter of 20th century.
Body: Composition; elastic strung; jointed at
shoulders and hips.
Remarks: 6" (15.2cm) character doll whose molded brown hair
has a blue band with pink rosettes. Eyes are painted blue and
open-closed smiling mouth shows two tiny teeth. Bears trademark
over super-imposed letters "W G" plus "S//13/0//Germany."
Made by German firm of William Goebel. *Collection of Mrs.
George Vosburgh.*

836. CHARACTER DOLL — BY REVALO
Period: First quarter of 20th century.
Body: Elastic strung composition; jointed at
shoulders and hips.
Remarks: 9" (22.9cm) bisque headed character doll with pink
ribbon in molded brown hair; highlighted, gray, intaglio eyes;
open-closed smiling mouth; molded-in teeth. Marked: "REVALO
//1//DEP." Made by the Gebrüder Ohlaver firm of Germany.
Collection of Mrs. G. B. Walker.

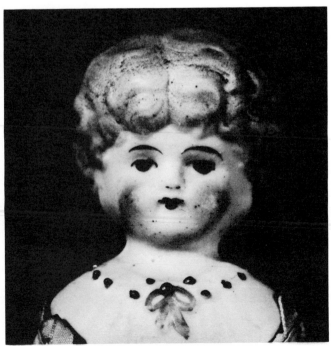

837. DOLL OF STONE BISQUE
Period: Early 20th century.
Remarks: 7" (17.8cm) doll of stone bisque. Nicely molded
hairdo tied with two blue ribbon bows; painted blue eyes and
molded stockings and slippers.

838. STONE BISQUE DOLL WITH MOLDED BLOUSE
Period: Early 20th century.
Body: Cloth with stone bisque limbs.
Remarks: 10" (25.4cm) stone bisque doll whose molded-on
blouse has pink bow and gilt touched buttons.

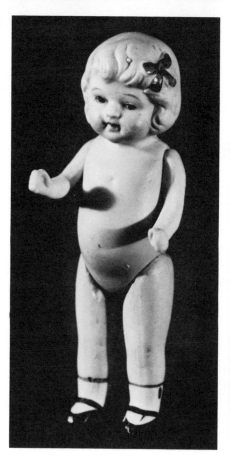

839. "SNOW BABIES"
Period: Early 20th century.
Remarks: A group of popular *Snow Babies* — 1¼" (3.2cm) to 2" (5.1cm) in height. Little hooded bisque figures in white, grout finished suits. Pink tinted faces have painted features and light brown forelocks. Dolls shown with grout finished polar bears; one seated on yellow sled, one walking. Sled and bottom of feet marked "Germany." *Merrill Collection.*

LEFT:
840. SMALL CHARACTER DOLL
Period: First quarter of 20th century.
Remarks: 3¼" (8.3cm) pink bisque toddler with molded green bow in yellow painted hair. Jointed only at shoulders. Stands quite well on molded, toed-in feet. Wears original brown net costume. Marked on back: "Made in Germany."
RIGHT:
841. ALL BISQUE DOLL — MADE IN JAPAN
Period: Pre World War I
Remarks: 6½" (16.5cm) stone bisque doll, elastic strung at hips and shoulders. Painted features include sideward looking eyes and hair with molded red bow. Brown slippers and white socks are painted on. A cheaply made and priced little doll brought out to compete with the popular, better quality, all bisque German made dolls. Marked on back shoulders: "Made in Japan."

842. "HAPPIFAT"
Period: Circa 1914.
Remarks: 3½" (8.9cm) *Happifat* boy — all bisque with elastic strung arms. A corpulent little fellow with painted features and molded-on light brown pants; green jacket and shoes. An equally rotund sister was made to pair with this doll. *Happifats* were also made in composition. Based on illustrations by Kate Jordan which appeared in John Martin's Book. *Happifat* trademark registered in U.S. and Germany by Borgfeldt.

843.

844.

845.

846.

843. SMALL ALL BISQUE DOLLS WITH MOLDED-ON CLOTHING

Period: Circa 1920-1930.

Remarks: 2½" (6.4cm) to 3" (7.6cm) all bisque dolls with molded-on clothing and elastic strung, moveable heads. Two at left known as Irish couple. Each has a pierced hand to allow for holding flower with the girl at right still clutching a fabric rose. This type doll was made in a great variety including comic strip characters. These dolls are unmarked. *Merrill Collection.*

844. HEbee-SHEbee ALL BISQUE CHARACTER DOLL

Period: 1920s.

Remarks: In the 1920s, E. I. Horsman of New York made droll little composition dolls in likeness of the then popular magazine cover characters created by Charles H. Twelvetrees. Called *HEbee-SHEbees,* they also came in German bisque. The illustrated doll is 6½" (16.5cm) *HEbee-SHEbee,* with painted molded-on clothing and dog in tow, is a copy of the German made all bisque. It is marked on back: "Made in Japan." *Merrill Collection.*

845. COMIC STRIP CHARACTERS FROM "MOON MULLINS"

Period: 1920s.

Remarks: Group of small, German made, all bisque dolls representing characters portrayed in Frank Willard's comic strip, *Moon Mullins.* All have moveable necks and are colored as those in the strip. From left to right: *Kayo, Moon Mullins, Emmy,* and *Lord Plushbottom.* Many characters from other comic strips were so made. *Merrill Collection.*

846. SNOW WHITE AND THE SEVEN DWARFS

Period: 1938.

Remarks: *Snow White and the Seven Dwarfs,* 2½" (6.4cm) to 3¼" (8.3cm) in height, in original box. Each little unjointed, painted bisque figure carries it's name, Walt Disney copyright, and is stamped "Japan." They are colorful but of inferior quality. "© 1938 Walt Disney Enterprises" is printed on box cover, plus "Distributors//Geo. Borgfeldt Corporation//New York//Japan."

China Dolls - 20th Century

847. CHINA DOLL BY DRESSEL, KISTER AND COMPANY

Period: Late 19th and early 20th century.
Body: Cloth with porcelain limbs.
Remarks: The flesh toned porcelain head of this 20" (50.8cm) doll is slightly turned, beautifully modeled and finely detailed. The streaked, molded hair is done in the "teapot handle" coiffure which was popular around 1890. Underside of shoulders (see insert) bears the ultramarine mark of Dressel, Kister & Company of Bavaria. Play dolls by this firm are rare — they are better known for their high quality half dolls. *Merrill Collection.*

848. CHINA PINCUSHION DOLLS

Period: Early 20th century.
Body: Stuffed cloth; foundation for skirt.
Remarks: China figure at left is wire stiffened and mounted on original lace and satin box. An ornamental china doll, finely executed. Has elastic strung arms and china legs. Suggestive of pincushion dolls. Group of china pincushion dolls — from 2" (5.1cm) to 5" (12.7cm) in height. Interest is now being shown by collectors for these colorful German made figures. *Merrill Collection.*

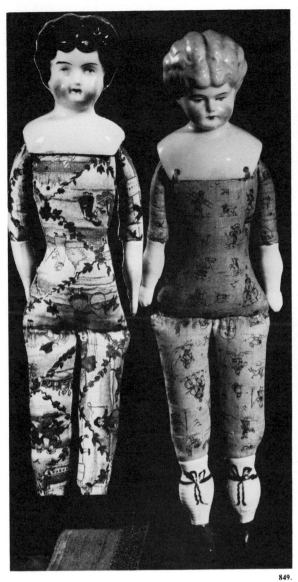

850.

851.

852.

853.

849.

849. CHINA LIMBED DOLLS WITH COLORFULLY PRINTED BODIES

Period: Late 19th and early 20th century.
Bodies: Cloth with china limbs.
Remarks: Children at play wearing Kate Greenaway sytled dresses are printed in bright colors on the cloth bodies of these china headed dolls. These colorful bodies also came in other designs such as Flags of All Nations and A.B.C.'s Butler Brothers of New York advertised in their 1895 catalog that their china limbed dolls had cloth bodies "figured in pleasing subjects for children." *Merrill Collection.*

850. LATE CHINA DOLL WITH PIERCED EARS

Period: Early 20th century.
Body: Printed cloth with china limbs.
Remarks: 8" (20.3cm) *Low Brow*, late china doll with china limbs. Cloth body of colorful scenic print. Typical of the late china dolls with the exception of pierced ears, almost never found in these dolls. A unique specimen.

851. "AGNES" — A PET-NAME CHINA DOLL

Period: Early 20th century.
Body: Cloth with china limbs.
Remarks: Pet-name china doll, molded collar and name, outlined in gold, on front. This German made china doll may be found with many different names, i.e., *Agnes, Bertha, Daisy, Dorothy, Edith, Ethel, Florence, Helen, Mabel, Marion,* and *Pauline.*

852. "HELEN" — A BLONDE PET-NAME CHINA DOLL

Period: Early 20th century.
Body: Cloth with china limbs.
Remarks: *Helen,* a 13" (33cm) pet-name china doll with painted blue eyes; blonde hair. Collar of molded blouse and name in center front, outlined in gold. Molded hair of this type doll finished in both blonde and brunette coloring.

853. CHINA DOLL WITH JEWELED NECKLACE

Period: Early 20th century.
Body: Cloth with china limbs.
Remarks: 16" (40.6cm) china doll with blue painted eyes; black molded hair. *Unusual feature:* gilded necklace whose pendant is set with green and rose stones. Gilded chain appears on front of neck only.

368

Novelty Dolls - 20th Century

854. HEUBACH DOLLS ON SLED — CANDY BOX
Period: Early 20th century.
Bodies: Cloth stuffed; cardboard candy boxes
within torsos.
Remarks: An unusual, all original, candy container consisting of four fleece clad dolls seated on an 11½" (29.2cm) wooden sled. Identical bisque heads have painted features; closed mouths and bear the trademark of the Gebrüder Heubach firm of Germany. A candy box is concealed within the torso of each individual doll. *Collection of Mr. and Mrs. Richard E. Hale.*

855. GENERAL GEORGE WASHINGTON ON A HORSE —
CANDY BOX
Period: Early 20th century.
Body: Wooden limbs attached by wires to wooden
torso.
Remarks: A 9" (22.9cm) x 11" (27.9cm) all original candy container sold in the early part of the 20th century to commemorate the February 22nd birthday of George Washington. The bisque head, an excellent likeness of the General, has painted eyes; white mohair wig and is marked: "16/921." The glass eyed, felt covered horse has lambskin mane and mohair tail. The interior of the candy box is exposed by removing the head of the horse. *Merrill Collection.*

LEFT:
856. ANIMATED, VOCALIZED DOLL AND ANIMALS ON MUSIC BOX

Period: Circa 1905.
Body: Composition; jointed at arms only.
Remarks: Crank operated music box with animated doll, pony, sheep, and birds in trees. Each figure has a separate pull string which allows for it's movement and sound. The 7" (17.8cm) bisque headed doll cries "mama" and "papa" upon pulling it's string. It is marked on head within sunburst "G. br K." plus numbers "44 -15." Made by Gebrüder Kraus of Germany. Entire toy of Swiss or German origin.

857. WALKING DOLL WITH CHILD IN TOW
Period: Early 20th century.
Body: Upper body, with wooden arms, mounted on cone shaped container housing a wheeled key-wound clock works.
Remarks: With wooden hands attached, the illustrated walking doll has child firmly in tow. Bisque heads of both dolls have glass eyes; open mouths with teeth; mohair wigs. When set in motion, larger doll walks across floor with child along side. Head of walking doll marked: "Made in Germany//A. 10/0 M." Made by German firm of Armand Marseilles.

858. HEUBACH WALKING DOLL
Period: Early 20th century.
Body: Key-wound mechanism within cone shaped housing, mounted on wheeled wooden base; composition arms.
Remarks: 9" (22.9cm) walking doll. Bisque head has open-closed smiling mouth showing two lower teeth; intaglio eyes; molded hair. When set in motion, doll cries and walks in circles. Marked with sunburst trademark of Gebrüder Heubach plus number "7604." Made in Germany. *Collection of Shirley F. Sanborn.*

859. FRENCH DOLL DRIVING EARLY AUTO
Period: Early 20th century.
Remarks: 9" (22.9cm) x 9½" (24.2cm) intriguing toy — a French doll driving an early car with attached poodle running alongside. Doll, marked: "F.G.," has stationary glass eyes; open mouth with teeth; mohair wig. Car is light blue with gilt trim. Spring wound.

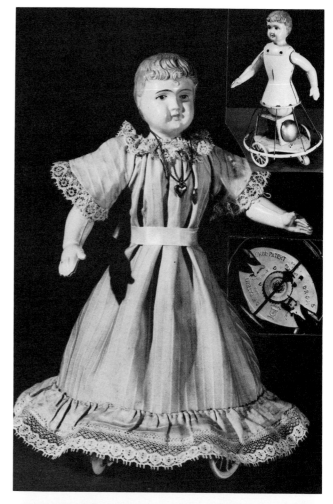

860. GERMAN MECHANICAL DOLL BY LEHMAN
Period: Early 20th century.
Body: All metal with spring-strung arms; wheel mounted and mechanized.
Remarks: All original, 9¼" (23.6cm) doll with celluloid head on mechanized, metal body. When in motion, bell rings. Directional wheels on base determine whether doll circles or travels in a straight line. Wears original cotton dress. Base carries patent information and trademark of the Lehman Company of Germany, maker of tin wind-up toys. *Merrill Collection.*

861. CELLULOID SWIMMING DOLL
Period: Early 20th century.
Body: Cork torso; wooden jointed legs; wooden arms with metal cupped hands.
Remarks: A key-wound, 10" (25.4cm) celluloid headed bathing doll whose arms and legs move in swimming motions when mechanism is released. She has molded blonde hair; painted features. Wears original pink-trimmed, blue cotton bathing suit. Shop name on ribbon band of suit: "Au Nain Bleu//406, 408, 410 Rue St. Honare//Paris." Swimming dolls were also made with bisque heads.

371

FAR LEFT:

862. COMPOSITION MECHANICAL TODDLER

Period: Early 20th century.

Body: Mechanism housed in body; composition arms; wooden legs with lead feet.

Remarks: 7½" (19.1cm) key-wound goggle-eyed mechanical toddler. Composition head has smiling closed mouth; brown painted side-cast eyes; molded blonde hair. Dress appears to be original. When set in motion, doll toddles, swaying from side to side. Illustrated doll unmarked. *Collection of Lorna S. Lieberman.*

LEFT:

863. BALL THROWING CLOWN

Period: Early 20th century.

Body: Wooden limbs (on wires) attached to wooden torso.

Remarks: 11" (27.9cm) doll mounted on wooden platform. White painted composition head has molded blue tufted hair and clown features. Two drawstrings operate action of wooden ball which is thrown overhead from hand to hand.

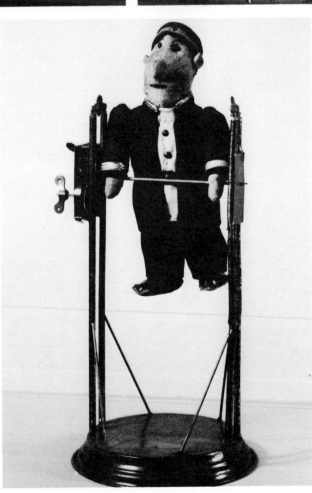

864. STEIFF DOLL ON TRAPEZE

Period: Early 20th century.

Body: Felt.

Remarks: 8" (20.3cm) Steiff doll on mechanical, key-wound trapeze. Performs somersaults when activated. Dressed as a University student. His molded felt face, with typical center seam, has black button eyes and painted features. Made by the Steiff firm of Germany. *Merrill Collection.*

865. JAPANESE MADE MECHANICAL DOLL

Period: First quarter of 20th century.

Body: Celluloid; elastic strung.

Remarks: 6" (15.2cm) celluloid doll attached to a mechanical swing in wire frame. Doll performs acrobatically when key-wound spring is activated. It has molded-on clothing, painted features, molded blonde hair and is marked: "Bokuno Tomodachi." Frame marked: "Jitsuyo Shinan//Tokyo//No. 107.566." *Merrill Collection.*

866. THE SIBYL FORTUNE TELLING DOLL
Period: 1925-30.
Body: Cloth stuffed torso attached to cardboard
  base by spindle; composition hands.
Remarks: 10" (25.4cm) fortune telling doll, with composition head, made and costumed to represent an old witch. Cardboard base has days of week, months of year, signs of the zodiac. Questions and answers printed on multi-colored leaves forming skirt of doll. A complete and novel working doll in labeled box containing full instructions. Made by The Sibyl Fortune Telling Doll Co., 1738 South Oxford Avenue, Los Angeles, California. *Collection of Mrs. Eugenia Shorrock.*

868. SURPRISE DOLL IN BOX
Period: Early 20th century.
Body: Coil spring within torso; wooden hands.
Remarks: 6" (15.2cm) x 8" (20.3cm) small, blue painted trunk containing spring mounted German bisque doll. Head has stationary glass eyes; open mouth with teeth; mohair wig. When trunk is opened by releasing clasp, doll jumps up as in popular jack-in-the-box toy. Unusual. *Collection of Toy Cupboard Museum, South Lancaster, Massachusetts.*

867. COMPOSITION DOLLS COVERED WITH RABBIT SKIN BUNTINGS
Period: Early 20th century.
Body: Composition; elastic strung; jointed at hips
  and shoulders only.
Remarks: Composition dolls, 12" (30.5cm) and 8" (20.3cm) respectively, wearing glued-on rabbit fur buntings. Face, hands and bare feet are finished in a pale flesh tone. Features, including blue eyes, are well painted. These dolls, possibly holiday gifts, may also be found with heads of bisque.

869. BISQUE BATHING GIRL
Period: 1920s.
Remarks: 5" (12.7cm) molded bisque figure, wearing a mohair wig, is dressed in a silk bathing suit. The same material is used for the head covering. Differs from the usual porcelain figurine with molded costume. Probably German made. *Merrill Collection.*

Ethnic & Portrait Dolls - 20th Century

LEFT:

870. SEMINOLE INDIAN DOLL

Period: Circa 1915.

Body: Cloth stuffed with wire stiffened limbs.

Remarks: 25" (63.5cm) squaw made by the Seminole Indians of Florida. Leather head has shaped nose and mouth; painted features; black horse hair wig. Colorfully costumed in a multi-patterned calico dress and apron; fringed shawl; bandanna head scarf and beaded moccasions. A desirable item for those who collect dolls, primitives or Indian artifacts. *Merrill Collection.*

871. HOPI INDIAN SQUAW

Period: 1914.

Body: All cloth.

Remarks: 9" (22.9cm) tribal doll handmade by American Indians. All cloth with beaded features and black yarn hair. Dressed in beaded buckskin. Documented as a Hopi Indian doll bought in 1914 at the Grand Canyon of the Colorado. There is much interest today in Indian artifacts including dolls. *Merrill Collection.*

LEFT:

872. AMERICAN INDIAN DOLLS BY MARY McABOY

Period: Circa 1915.

Body: Padded cloth; stiff wooden legs.

Remarks: Family group of American Indian dolls — 6½" (16.5cm) to 14" (35.6cm) high. Composition heads have painted features; black mohair wigs. Feet marked with paper label reading "Skookum (Bully Good) Indian//Trademark registered//USA//Patented." These blanket wrapped dolls came in various tribal costumes. Designed by Mary McAboy of Missoula, Montana. They were sold through the second quarter of the 20th century and could be purchased in tobacco stores in addition to other retailers. *Merrill Collection.*

LEFT:
873. MOROCCAN LEATHER DOLLS
Period: Indeterminate.
Bodies: All leather; unjointed.
Remarks: The side-turned, leather heads of these 16" (40.6cm) Moroccan dolls have well shaped and painted features; horse hair wigs and beard. They are lavishly dressed in colorful silks and brocades. The lady wears long pearl earrings; flowing veil and gold and rose colored slippers. The man's slippers are of purple leather with gold tooling. A handsome pair of leather dolls with finely detailed, native costumes. *Collection of Norma Rodenbaugh.*

875. WOODEN DOLLS BY MARY WHITTIER
Period: First half of 20th century.
Bodies: All wooden; head, torso, legs in one piece; wrist length hands attached to shoulders by wires.
Remarks: Two pairs of wooden figures (6" [15.2cm] to 6½" [16.5cm]) whittled by Mary Whittier of New Hampshire.
Left: *George* and *Martha Washington.*
Right: *New Hampshire Grandpa* and *Grandma.* Copied from old photograph of typical New Hampshire folks.
 Dolls were carved with a jack knife and painted with water colors.

876. "DOOR OF HOPE" MISSION DOLLS
Period: 1901-1946.
Bodies: All cloth or cloth with lower arms of wood.
Remarks: Group of character dolls, 9" (22.9cm) to 12" (30.5cm) high, with hand carved wooden heads and finely made, minutely detailed Chinese costumes. Assembled and dressed at the Methodist founded Door of Hope Mission in Shanghai, China, to not only instruct homeless girls but to help fund their work. Over twenty types were made. **Left to right:** *Amah and child, girl, gentleman, mourner, lady* and *farmer.* Mission was closed by Communists take over of China. No dolls available after 1946. *Merrill Collection.*

874. CHICKEN VENDOR IN WAX BY VARGAS
Period: Second quarter of 20th century.
Remarks: 6½" (16.5cm) character doll in wax; mounted on wooden base. Realistically modeled figure representing Black street vendor of New Orleans. Clothing dipped in wax and applied to figure. Carries chickens by hand and in basket. One of the many street vendors made by the Vargas family of New Orleans. They are no longer being made. *Merrill Collection.*

877. "LIBERTY BOY" COMPOSITION DOLL
Period: World War I (1917-1918).
Body: Composition; jointed at shoulders and hips by metal springs.
Remarks: 12" (30.5cm) all composition character doll made by Ideal Novelty and Toy Company of Brooklyn, New York. Molded khaki uniform of World War I (felt hat missing). Molded composition head has painted features and turns.

878. MAN DOLL — MADE IN CANADA
Period: Circa 1925.
Body: Cloth with composition arms.
Remarks: 20" (50.8cm) man doll whose composition head is finished in soft matt tones. A rather well modeled young man whose painted features include brown eyes and light hair. Wears hand tailored suit and straw hat. Made and dressed in Canada. Marked: "Reliable//Made in Canada" (see insert).

879. KING ALBERT I OF BELGIUM
Period: Circa 1918.
Body: Stuffed cloth with molded hands and high, black laced boots.
Remarks: A 19½" (49.6cm) portrait doll of King Albert I of Belgium, hero of World War I. The finely executed plaster of Paris head has brown molded hair and mustache; blue painted eyes. The original dark blue uniform is ribbon belted in national colors — black, gold, red. Decoration is formed by a pierced Belgium coin. Unmarked. *Merrill Collection.*

880. CHARLES II AND NELL GWYNNE
Period: Mid 20th century.
Bodies: Cloth with wax limbs.
Remarks: 26" (66cm) poured wax portrait dolls of Charles II and mistress Nell Gwynne. Made by Gems (Wax Models) Ltd. for Josephine Tussaud's London Wax Museum. Produced only during slack periods, they are done exactly as the life-sized museum figures with inset glass eyes and inserted hair. Dolls in likeness of Anne Boleyn, Nathan Hale and a Tudor lady and gentleman were also made. Josephine Tussaud is a great, great granddaughter of Madame Tussaud who founded the famous London wax works which bears her name. *Collection of Mrs. Elmer Morley.*

Wooden Dolls - 20th Century

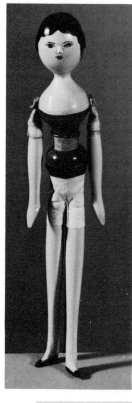

881. WOODEN "DUTCH" DOLLS — 20th CENTURY
Period: 20th century.
Bodies: (left & right) Pegged wooden; **(center)** wooden head made to go on cloth stuffed body.
Remarks: Late, poorly made *Dutch* dolls —crude joints allow little movement. The wooden head, in center, has scooped out shoulders. The dolls pictured are still available — they were purchased for very little in Pollack's toy store in London in 1966. *Merrill Collection.*

882. 20th CENTURY WOODEN DOLL WITH RED PAINTED TORSO
Period: Early 20th century.
Body: All wooden with kidskin hung wooden limbs.
Remarks: 13½" (34.3cm) wooden doll with painted features and red painted torso. Bears paper sticker of a Cambridge, Massachussets, gift shop of the 1920s. Small, 6½" (16.5cm) dolls of this type were also sold in the gift shop of the House of Seven Gables in Salem, Massachussets, in the same decade. These dolls are late, cheaper versions of carved wooden dolls made in Bohemia in the mid-19th century. *Merrill Collection.*

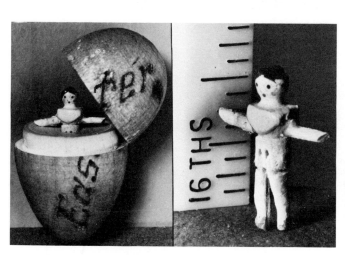

883. TINY WOODEN DOLL IN EGG
Period: Early 20th century.
Body: All wood; jointed at hips and shoulders.
Remarks: Pegged-wooden doll, scarcely more than 1/2" (1.3cm) in height, encased in a 1¼" (3.2cm) wooden egg. "Easter" is burned across side of egg. Doll's head and features are painted as are the red slippered feet. An Easter present to a child in England during the early years of the 20th century. *Courtesy of Ellen T. Fite.*

884. "HOUSE OF SEVEN GABLES" DOLLS
Period: 20th century.
Bodies: Jointed wooden; wooden pegged.
Remarks: 20th century copies of an early wooden doll. Both about 9" (22.9cm) in height. Doll on right purchased in 1940. Made expressly for the gift shop of the "House of Seven Gables" in Salem, Massachusetts, by a succession of individual craftsmen. Sold dressed or undressed. Still available in 1973 in three sizes. *Merrill Collection.*

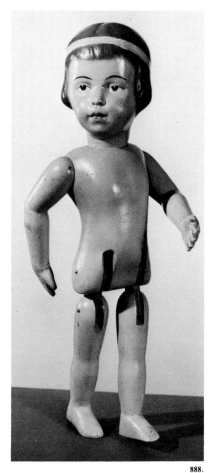

885.

886.

888.

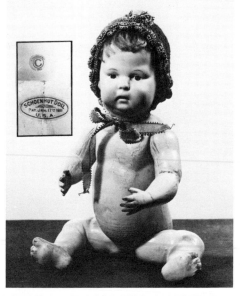

885. "ROLLY-DOLLY" BY SCHOENHUT
Period: 1908.
Body: Molded and painted papier mâché; head
elastic strung.
Remarks: 14" (35.6cm) roly-poly type doll with movable head;
painted features. Wears pleated cloth ruff. Costume is painted
orange with yellow trim. This doll came in various sizes and
designs. Patented in 1908 by A. Schoenhut & Company of
Philadelphia, famous for their wooden dolls. The doll shown,
made prior to the wooden dolls, bears circular paper sticker on
bottom which reads: "Schoenhut Rolly Dolly."

886. SCHOENHUT WOODEN DOLL — ALL ORIGINAL
Period: Early 20th century.
Body: All wood; fully jointed with metal springs.
Remarks: 16½" (41.9cm) all wooden Schoenhut doll with
pensive expression. Found in pristine condition. She has blue
painted intaglio eyes; fine mohair wig. Clothing all original
including underwear and shoes with eyelets on soles. Made by A.
Schoenhut & Co. of Philadelphia, Pennsylvania.

888. ALL WOOD SCHOENHUT WALKABLE DOLL
Period: Patented 1911, 1913, 1920.
Body: All wood; jointed at neck, shoulders and
hips.
Remarks: 14" (35.6cm) Schoenhut all wooden doll — shown
undressed to illustrate non-mechanical, free swinging joints at
hips. Catalog claimed it could be "led by the hand and will walk
like a real little tot (not mechanical)." Rare to find painted hair
on a walkable doll; usually came with mohair wigs. Illustrated
doll marked: "Schoenhut Walkable Doll//Patents U.S.A.//Jan.
17, 1911//Dec. 31, 1913//Mar. 2, 1920." Made by A. Schoenhut
& Co. of Philadelphia, Pennsylvania. *Merrill Collection.*

887. WOODEN BABY DOLL BY SCHOENHUT
Period: 1913.
Body: All wooden; spring jointed at neck;
shoulders and hips.
Remarks: 15" (38.1cm) all wooden baby with painted features;
mohair wig. Printed paper label on back of head reads: "H. E.
Schoenhut © 1913." Oval paper label on back shoulders reads:
"Schoenhut Doll Pat. Jan. 17th 1911 U.S.A." Made in various
sizes. The Schoenhut Company of Philadelphia, Pennsylvania,
also made child dolls — both boys and girls. *Courtesy of Mrs.
Ross Blasingame.*

LEFT:
889. SCHOENHUT WOODEN DOLL
RUBBER ELASTIC STRUNG
Period: 1924.
Body: All wooden; elastic strung.
Remarks: 16" (40.6cm) all wooden jointed doll strung with rubber elastic rather than the more expensive metal springs used in earlier dolls by this firm. She has painted blue eyes; blonde mohair wig. One of a long line of dolls made by A. Schoenhut & Company of Philadelphia, Pennsylvania.

RIGHT:
891. PORTRAIT DOLL "TEDDY"
ROOSEVELT BY SCHOENHUT
Period: Early 20th century.
Body: All wooden; elastic strung.
Remarks: 9" (22.9cm) all wooden Schoenhut doll — an excellent likeness of Theodore Roosevelt in hunting garb. Wears khaki uniform with pistol, dagger and ammunition box at belt. Rifle slung across shoulder. Wooden hat attached to head. Body is typical of the many characters made by the A. Schoenhut Co. of Philadelphia, Pennsylvania. *Merrill Collection.*

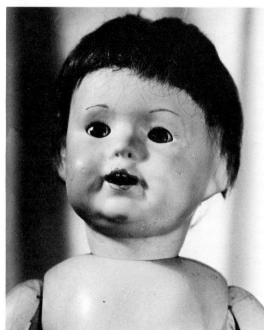

890. SCHOENHUT DOLL WITH SLEEPING EYES
Period: 1921.
Body: All wood; fully jointed with metal springs.
Remarks: 17" (43.2cm) all wooden doll with sleeping decal eyes; open mouth with inserted metal teeth, mohair wig. Marked on shoulders: "Schoenhut Doll//Pat. Jan. 17th 1911//U.S.A.." Made by A. Schoenhut & Co. of Philadelphia, Pennsylvania, who patented moving eyes for their dolls in 1921. *Collection of Mrs. John W. Lorentzen.*

892. SCHOENHUT CIRCUS FIGURES RINGMASTER,
CLOWN AND LION
Period: Early 20th century.
Body: All wooden; elastic strung.
Remarks: 9" (22.9cm) all wooden circus dolls representing a ringmaster and clown. Part of an elaborate circus containing animals and circus personalities. Performers may also be found with heads of bisque. Made by the A. Schoenhut Company of Philadelphia, Pennsylvania. *Merrill Collection.*

379

LEFT:

893. ALL WOODEN JOINTED BABY DOLL BÉBÉ TOUT en BOIS

Period: 1914.

Body: All wooden; elastic strung.

Remarks: 11" (27.9cm) Bébé Tout en Bois (Baby in Wood). Trademark registered in Germany, for a fully jointed doll, by Rudolf Schneider. Doll has set-in blue glass eyes; painted hair and features. Right hand is clenched with pierced opening from front to back.

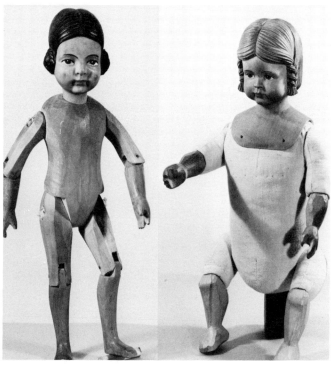

895. SWISS ALL WOODEN JOINTED DOLL

Period: Early 20th century.

Body: All wooden; joints of articulated body are wooden pegged at neck, elbows and knees; elastic strung at hips and shoulders.

Remarks: 9¾" (24.9cm) carved wooden doll made in Switzerland. Painted features on natural wood finish. Deeply carved hair, with center part from front to back, is drawn into braided buns covering ears.

SWISS WOODEN DOLLS WITH CLOTH OR WOOD BODIES

Period: Early 20th century.

Body: Cloth with wooden limbs; elastic strung at hips and shoulders, or all wood jointed at shoulders, elbows, hips and knees.

Remarks: 14" (35.6cm) carved wooden dolls made in Switzerland. Painted features, on natural wood finish, include blue eyes. Straight bobbed hair, deeply carved, has center part and braids at sides. *Collection of Nancy Shurtleff.*

LEFT:

894. WOODEN MANNEQUIN DRESSED AND UNDRESSED

Period: Early 20th century.

Body: All wooden; jointed.

Remarks: Although dressed as a doll, and used as a plaything, this 19½" (49.6cm) figure was originally produced as an artist's model. As such, it is not truly a play doll. Body stamped in purple ink: "F. Weber & Co., Philadelphia." Original price of $4.20 is penciled on back. Sticker of art store reads: "B. L. Makepeace, Inc., Boston, Mass." Company still in business in 1983.

Various Compositions - 20th Century
including celluloid, rubber, vinyl

LEFT:
896. "BECASSINE" — FRENCH COMPOSITION DOLL
Period: Circa 1910.
Body: Jointed composition; elastic strung.
Remarks: Most unusual, 16" (40.6cm) doll in original French costume. Apron labelled: "Becassine//Depose." Thin composition head has round, painted eyes and dot for mouth. Cap is tacked to unwigged head. *Becassine* is pictured on cover and listed within a catalog on French dolls and their accessories by M. Henri Gauthier of Paris in 1910. *Collection of Miss Elma B. Fuller.*

897. "CAMPBELL KIDS" BY HORSMAN
Period: Copyright 1910.
Body: Flesh-colored stuffed cloth with composition hands; jointed at shoulders and hips.
Remarks: Pair of *Campbell Kid* dolls made by E. I. Horsman Co. in likeness of drawings used by the Campbell Soup Company. Heads of composition with painted features; molded hair; eyes cast to side. Clothing appears to be original. 11" (27.9cm) boy in blue and white seersucker rompers; 12" (30.5cm) girl in red and white printed pinafore. Both dolls marked on back of neck: "E.I.H. © 1910."

LEFT:
898. "UNEEDA BISCUIT KID"
Period: Patented December 8, 1914.
Body: Cloth with arms and high black boots of composition.
Remarks: 15½" (39.4cm) composition doll made to represent boy pictured on Uneeda biscuit package. Wears original yellow cloth rain coat. Missing is rain hat and miniature box of Uneeda crackers. Unmarked except for label on sleeve which reads: "Uneeda Kid//Patented Dec. 8, 1914//Ideal Novelty and Toy Co.//Brooklyn, N.Y." Patented by Morris Michton of the above firm.

381

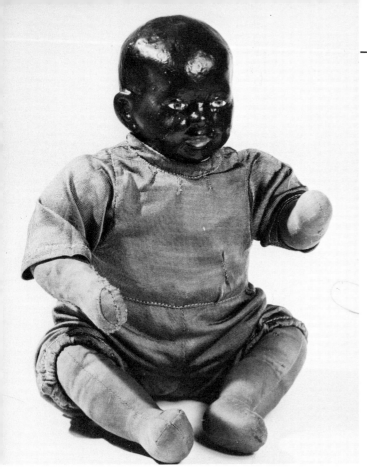

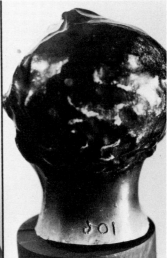

899. BLACK "BABY BUMPS" BY HORSMAN

Period: 1912.

Body: Brown cloth; stuffed.

Remarks: A Black version of a character doll by E. I. Horsman Company of New York. Approximately 12" (30.5cm) high with open-closed smiling mouth and painted features. The mold of this *Can't Break 'Em* composition doll strongly resembles the bisque baby doll (#100) by the German firm of Kämmer & Reinhardt. Wears original blue silk jersey rompers.

900. BLACK COMPOSITION DOLL OF EARLY 20th CENTURY

Period: Circa 1914.

Body: Cloth with black composition forearms; gaily striped cloth legs; black cloth feet.

Remarks: 14½" (36.9cm) Black composition doll with painted features including incised eyes and parted lips showing two painted-in teeth. Material of head plus the molding of hair and forearms are identical to *Baby Grumpy*. Head marked: "J O I." *Collection of Mrs. Elmer Morley.*

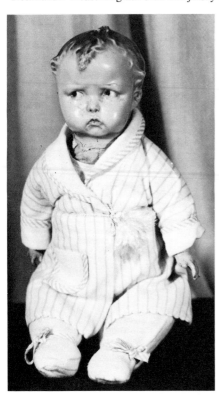 

FAR LEFT:
901. "BABY GRUMPY" CHARACTER DOLL

Period: 1914.

Body: Cloth with composition limbs.

Remarks: Scowling, 14" (35.6cm) character baby whose composition head has incised eyes cast to side, down-turned closed mouth; and molded hair. Made over a period of years with variations in body style. Marked: "174." Made by Fleischaker & Baum (EFFanBEE) of New York, a company that is well known for their character dolls. *Collection of Mrs. Elmer Morley.*

LEFT:
902. COMPOSITION DOLL MARKED "METRO"

Period: Early 20th century.

Body: Cloth with composition arms.

Remarks: 12" (30.5cm) smiling composition doll with painted features. Marked, within diamond, on back shoulders (see insert): "Metro Doll." Question unanswered as to maker. Mr. Joseph L. Kallus, who headed the Metro Doll Co. for the short time it existed in 1921, states (1973) that this doll was not made by his concern.

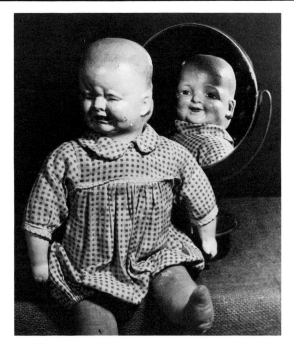

903. TWO-FACED COMPOSITION BABY
Period: First quarter of 20th century.
Body: Cloth with composition arms and legs.
Remarks: 16" (40.6cm) two-faced doll in unbreakable composition. A crying or smiling face is exposed by rotating the flange-necked head. Both faces have painted hair and features. Doll is unmarked. A "mama" and "papa" voice box is imbedded in cloth body. Wears original red and white checked rompers. Multi-faced dolls are always of interest.

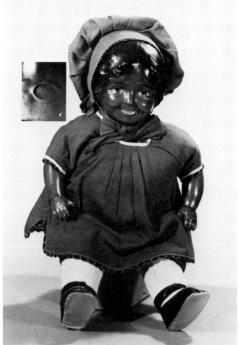

905. SMILING BLACK CHARACTER DOLL
Period: First quarter of 20th century.
Body: Cloth with composition arms.
Remarks: 16" (40.6cm) Black character doll with composition head of excellent quality. Smiling face has painted features including open-closed mouth showing tongue and two rows of teeth and brown eyes with upper lashes only. Wears original red cotton costume with white socks and black shoes. Crying voice box in body. Marked on back of head with capital "C" only (see insert).

904. COQUETTE DOLL IN COMPOSITION
Period: Circa 1912.
Body: Cloth with composition forearms; jointed at shoulders and hips.
Remarks: 15" (38.1cm) well modeled coquette doll whose composition head has smiling open-closed mouth with painted teeth; blue painted eyes cast to side. Brown hair has molded band in like color. Unmarked. Coquette dolls were made in other materials.

906. "DOLLY WALKER" BY HARRY H. COLEMAN
Period: 1917-1923.
Body: Torso wire mesh covered wooden frame; jointed arms and legs.
Remarks: 28" (71.1cm) mechanical doll who walks when hand propelled. Composition head has painted features; blonde mohair wig. Patented in Britain and United States by Harry H. Coleman. Called *Dolly Walker*. First made in 28" (71.1cm) size, later in 18" (45.7cm) and 24" (61cm) sizes. Also came with painted hair and sleeping eyes.

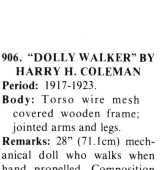

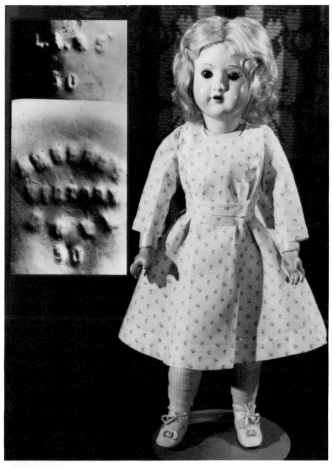

907. FRENCH COMPOSITION DOLL MARKED SFBJ
Period: Early 20th century.
Body: Composition; elastic strung.
Remarks: 9" (22.9cm) composition doll with stationary glass eyes; light mohair wig; closed mouth. Marked: number "16" in blue on neck front; "35//SFBJ//Paris//6/0" on back of head. This type doll uncommon in composition, generally found with bisque head.

FAR LEFT:
909. RALEIGH COMPOSITION DOLL
Period: 1918.
Body: Jointed composition; wire spring strung.
Remarks: 13½" (34.3cm), light weight, hand painted, all composition doll. Painted features include eyes; smiling open-closed mouth showing four upper teeth; brown hair with blue barrett. Came in sizes 11½" (29.2cm), 13½" (34.3cm), and 18½" (47cm). One of a variety of artistic, well made dolls by Jessie McCutcheon Raleigh of Chicago, Illinois. Distributed by Butler Bros. of New York.
Collection of Mrs. Elmer Morley.

910. AMERICAN MADE COMPOSITION DOLL WITH CELLULOID EYES AND METAL HANDS
Period: Circa 1920.
Body: Jointed composition with metal hands.
Remarks: Interesting 25" (63.5cm) doll thought to have been made in Springfield, Massachusetts. Head, of thin, light weight composition, has open-closed mouth with molded-in teeth; sleeping celluloid eyes marked: "S.M. 1918" on mechanism; mohair wig. Celluloid eyes so marked were patented in 1918 by Samuel Marcus.
Collection of Nancy Shurtleff.

OPPOSITE PAGE: TOP RIGHT:
908. AMBERG'S VICTORY DOLL
Period: 1919.
Body: Jointed composition; elastic strung.
Remarks: 22" (55.9cm) Amberg's *Victory Doll* whose composition head, in "Ambisc" finish, has metal sleeping eyes; open mouth with teeth; and blonde mohair wig over unpainted, molded hair. Doll in fine and original condition. Marked on shoulders: "Amberg's Victory Doll." On head: "L.A. & S.//50." Made by Louis Amberg & Son of New York. *Merrill Collection.*

RIGHT:
911. CHILD DOLL BY DORA PETZOLD
Period: 1920.
Body: Muslin and stockinette torso; stockinette limbs.
Remarks: 25" (63.5cm) doll with flange necked head mounted on cloth body. Painted features include blue eyes and closed mouth. Wig of auburn mohair. Lower torso and sole of foot marked: "DORA PETZOLD//Registered//Trade Mark//DOLL//Germany." Made and distributed by Dora Petzold of Berlin who also made baby dolls. *Collection of Mrs. George O. Vosburgh.*

BELOW:
912. 17" (43.2cm) COMPOSITION HEAD DOLL
Period: First quarter of 20th century.
Body: Cloth with many similarities to those made by Käthe Kruse.
Remarks: A 16" (40.6cm) signed composition shoulderhead of unusual boyish appeal. Painted features and hair. The signature incised on back of shoulders has not been identified at time of publication. *Merrill Collection.*

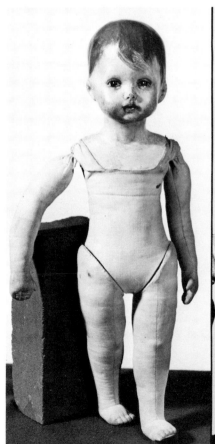

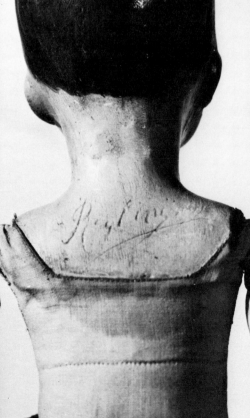

RIGHT AND BELOW:
913. & 914. THE "FAMLEE DOLL" IN
ORIGINAL BOX
Period: Patented April 12, 1921
Body: Cloth with composition limbs;
voice box within torso.
Remarks: A boxed set of the *Famlee Doll*.
Consists of one doll body with five inter-
changeable heads — each with own costume.
Came with complete and detailed instruc-
tions for assembling this 16" (40.6cm) doll.
Heads differed as to race and nationality and
extras could be purchased along with cos-
tumes from a list of 18. Made by the Berwick
Doll Company, 478-480-482 Broadway, New
York. Marked on voice box: "Patented May
25, 1915//Mfd. in U.S.A.//by//The Art
Metal Works//Newark, N.J.//Other
Patents Pending."

Dollie's Clothes

Of course you want dollie's dress to always look nice and neat. So always put the extra dresses back on these cards. If you throw the dresses around topsey-turvey they'll get all wrinkly and won't look nice at all.

While you are fixing the heads to change Ruth into Mary or into Sam, your playmate can take the dress off the card and put the other one back on.

It's great fun changing round the dollies and dressing them up. And it will be heaps and heaps more fun as you keep adding to the family—the Chinese boy, the Clown, the Indian, the Colored Boy, and so many others. If you get another head and dress every now and then, it won't be long before your happy Famlee Set will be just as big as any other girl's.

Here are the Famlee characters that make up the full set. You can get those that you haven't already at the same place where the dollie came from. If every so often you get one or two heads with costumes to match, soon you will have the whole set complete.

Pierrette	No. 102	Dutch Girl	No. 110
The Clown	No. 103	Susie Bumps	No. 111
Chinese Boy	No. 104	Soldier Boy	No. 112
Colored Boy	No. 105	Dolly Dimple	No. 114
Indian Girl	No. 106	Baby	No. 115
Dutch Boy	No. 107	Sailor Girl	No. 116
French Girl	No. 108	Nurse	No. 118
Sailor Boy	No. 109	Commander	No. 120

BERWICK DOLL COMPANY
Makers of
Famlee Doll
A whole family of dolls in one
478-480-482 Broadway,
New York.

915. JACKIE COOGAN BY HORSMAN
Period: 1921.
Body: Cloth with composition lower arms.
Remarks: 14" (35.6cm) boy doll in likeness of film star Jackie Coogan as he appeared in *The Kid*. Composition head, with molded Dutch cut hair, has painted features including side-cast eyes. Shoulderhead marked: "E.I.H. Co.//19©21." Dressed in original green checked overalls and green jersey. Clothing tagged: "Jackie Coogan Kid//Licensed by Jackie Coogan// Patent Pending." Doll made by E. I. Horsman Company of New York. *Collection of Mrs. Elmer Morley.*

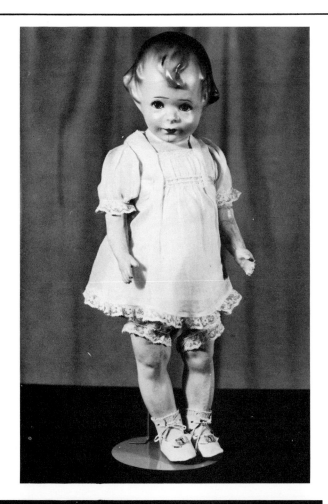

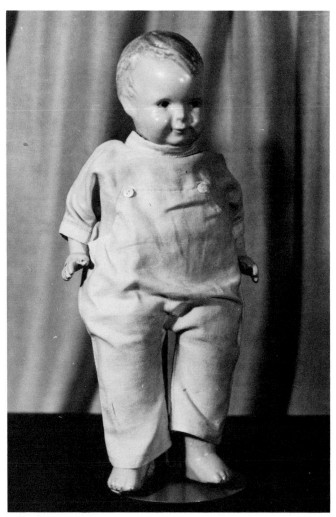

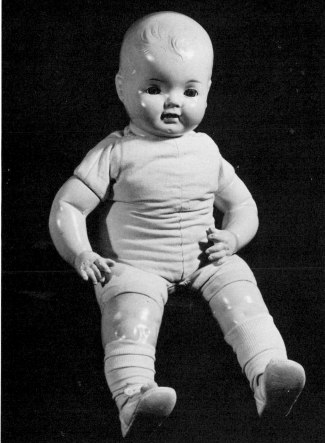

LEFT:
916. "MIBS" CHARACTER DOLL
Period: 1921.
Body: Cloth with composition limbs.
Remarks: An appealing 16" (40.6cm) character doll with composition head; painted features. All original, it was shown in the Smithsonian Institution Traveling Exhibition Series 1975-1976. Still retains ribbon sash which is printed: "Please love me, I'm Mibs." Created by Hazel Drukker and manufactured by Louis Amberg & Son of New York. *Collection of Mrs. Elmer Morley.*

917. "ROMPER BOY" BY GRACE (COREY) ROCKWELL
Period: 1921.
Body: Cloth with composition limbs.
Remarks: 13" (33cm) *Romper Boy* by Grace (Corey) Rockwell — one of a variety of dolls by this American designer with heads of either bisque or composition. The composition head of this doll has painted features and is marked: "Century Doll Co.//1921 Made//© by Grace Corey." *Collection of Mrs. Elmer Morley.*

LEFT:
918: "BABY HENDREN" COMPOSITION DOLL
Period: 1920s.
Body: Cloth with composition baby limbs.
Remarks: 22" (55.9cm) composition baby doll with voice box in body. She has open and shut eyes; molded light brown hair and open mouth. This good quality life-size doll wears infant clothes. Made by Georgene Hendren Averill (Madame Hendren). Marked: "Baby Hendren." American made.

LEFT:
919. "TYNIE BABY" BY HORSMAN
Period: 1924.
Body: Cloth with composition limbs.
Remarks: 15" (38.1cm) composition baby whose smooth finish resembles celluloid in appearance. All original doll with sleeping eyes; painted features; light brown molded hair. Marked on back of head: "© 1924//E.I. Horsman Co., Inc." Also came in all bisque as well as bisque head on cloth body.

920. "BUBBLES" — COMPOSITION DOLL BY EFFANBEE
Period: 1924.
Body: Cloth with composition arms and legs.
Remarks: Large, 24" (61cm) baby doll with composition head and deep shoulders molded in one piece. A well finished doll with sleeping eyes; open mouth with two upper teeth; molded light brown hair. Voice box in body. Arms, strung with metal springs, are modeled so doll may put left index finger in mouth. Marked: "Effanbee//Bubbles//Copr. 1924 — Made in U.S.A." Label in dress: "Effanbee//Bubbles//Reg. U.S. Pat. Office."

LEFT:
921. "MY DREAM BABY" IN COMPOSITION
Period: Circa 1925.
Body: Cloth with composition hands.
Remarks: 13" (33cm) composition *My Dream Baby* with open mouth showing teeth (mold #351). Flanged-neck head has sleeping eyes; painted hair. Marked: "A.M.//Germany." Made by Armand Marseilles of Germany. *My Dream Baby* is most often found with closed mouth (mold #341) and of bisque. *Courtesy of Helen M. Deschene.*

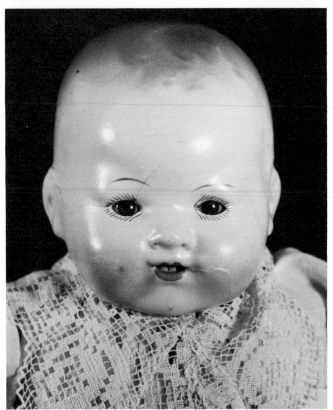

RIGHT:
922. "PETITE SALLY" COMPOSITION DOLL
Period: Circa 1925.
Body: Cloth with composition arms and legs.
Remarks: 14" (35.6cm) composition doll with sleeping eyes; hair lashes; painted features; mohair wig. Voice box in body. Marked on back of head: "Petite Sally."

923. "PATSYETTE" AND "PATRICIA" BY EFFanBEE
Period: 1927.
Body: Jointed composition.
Remarks: Two of a line of *Patsy* dolls made by Fleischaker & Baum of New York whose trademark was EFFanBEE. Claimed to have been the first all composition doll modeled after an American child, with tiltable head and movable limbs. *Collection of Betty Thacher.*
Left: 9" (22.9cm) Effanbee *Patsyette* #117.
Right: 14½" (36.9cm) Effanbee *Patricia* #103.

RIGHT:
924. COMPOSITION DOLLS BY LOUIS AMBERG
Period: 1928.
Body: All composition.
Remarks: Pair of 8½" (21.6cm) composition boy and girl dolls by Louis Amberg & Son of New York City. Ball joints at mid-riff allows dolls to swivel. Arms are elastic strung at shoulders. Molded shoes and socks. Painted features; molded and painted hair. Marked at back of shoulders (see insert): "Pat. Appl'd for//LA.&S. © 1928."

CLOCKWISE:

925. "MARGIE" BY JOSEPH L. KALLUS

Period: 1929.

Body: Wooden; jointed.

Remarks: 10" (25.4cm) composition headed character doll with molded hair and painted features including large side-glancing eyes. Jointed wooden body allows doll to stand and assume various postures. Designed by Joseph L. Kallus. Made by the Cameo Doll Company. *Collection of Miss Ruth E. Whittier.*

926. "GLADDIE"

Period: 1929.

Body: Cloth with composition limbs.

Remarks: 18" (45.7cm) doll whose head of clay, finished in "bisculoid," has laughing mouth showing tongue and teeth; sleeping eyes; light molded hair. Wears original costume. Marked: "Gladdie//Copyriht, By//Helen K. Jensen//Germany" (note word "Copyright" is misspelled in markings). This doll sculptured by American artist Helen K. Jensen. Made in Germany for George Borgfeldt & Co. of New York. *Collection of Mrs. Elmer Morley.*

927. MAE STARR PHONOGRAPH DOLL

Period: Circa 1930.

Body: Cloth with composition limbs.

Remarks: The spring wound phonograph embedded in the body of this 29½" (75cm) doll has metal cone for sound emission, crank, starting lever and opening for records. Came with six cylindrical records of various nursery rhymes. Composition head has sleeping eyes; open mouth with teeth; human hair wig. Marked: "Mae Starr Doll" on back shoulders (see insert).

928. SMILING COMPOSITION DOLL
Period: Second quarter of 20th century.
Body: Cloth with composition arms.
Remarks: 18" (45.7cm) doll whose smiling composition head has molded blonde hair; open-closed mouth with painted teeth; metal eyes that open, wink and shut independently of each other. Marked on back of shoulders: "Ideal" (within a diamond) plus the letters "U.S. of A." Made by the Ideal Novelty and Toy Company of New York. *Collection of Miss Ruth E. Whittier.*

930. "STEPPIN BABY" BY EUGENE GOLDBERGER
Period: 1930s.
Body: Metal with composition arms.
Remarks: The painted composition head of this 10" (25.4cm) walking doll is mounted on a metal body with overly large feet. Doll walks when key-wound mechanism within body is set in motion. Made by E. Goldberger Corporation of New York. Tag attached to arm reads: "EEGEE STEPPIN BABY Doll//Pat. Pending."

929. COMPOSITION DOLL BY ARRANBEE DOLL COMPANY
Period: 1930s.
Body: Composition; elastic strung.
Remarks: 12" (30.5cm) all composition doll with painted features including eyes and blonde, molded hair. Made by the Arranbee Doll Company of New York. Marked on body: "R. & B.//Doll Co."

931. "GENUINE HORSMAN ART DOLL"
Period: Second quarter of 20th century.
Body: Cloth with composition arms and legs.
Remarks: 14" (35.6cm) toddler doll in original box — dressed in original clothes. Painted features and sleeping eyes; molded hair. Label reads: "A Genuine Horsman Art Doll." Made by E. I. Horsman Company of New York. Doll unmarked except for tag on clothing. *Collection of Mrs. Donald J. Marion.*

932. "PATSY BABY" BY EFFanBEE
Period: Purchased in 1933.
Body: Jointed composition; elastic strung.
Remarks: 10" (25.4cm) composition baby doll with painted features; molded light brown hair; sleeping eyes. Marked: "EFFanBEE//PATSY BABY" on back shoulders. One of a line of *Patsy* dolls by Fleischaker & Baum of New York whose trademark was EFFanBEE.

933. "DY-DEE" RUBBER DOLL BY EFFANBEE
Period: 1935.
Body: Rubber; jointed at hips and shoulders.
Remarks: The hard rubber head of this 10½" (26.7cm) baby doll has set-in soft rubber ears; molded light brown hair; sleeping eyes. Mouth has opening to receive nursing bottle. Following "feeding" doll wets diapers. Very popular doll of the day. Marked on back: "Effanbee Dy-Dee Doll" plus a list of United States and foreign patents. *Collection of Mrs. Elmer Morley.*

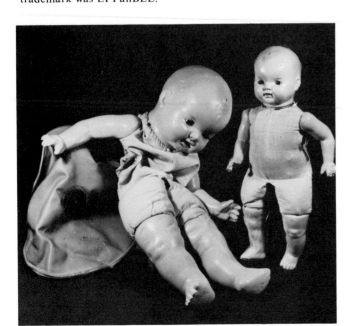

934. COMPOSITION BABY DOLL WITH INFLATABLE BODY
Period: 1935.
Body: Cloth with inflated rubber insert. Cloth and composition legs; composition arms.
Remarks: 21" (53.3cm) baby whose composition head has painted hair; open mouth with teeth. Eyes sleep by swinging of counterweight or manipulation of lever at back of neck. Realistically soft body is achieved by inserting an inflatable rubber bladder through opening in cloth body (see illustration). Mark on back of neck is indistinct: "(?) Toy Co."

935. THE "MAGIC SKIN" BABY DOLL
Period: Circa 1940.
Body: Flexible plastic; jointed at head and
shoulders.
Remarks: 19" (48.3cm) baby doll whose plastic head has sleeping
eyes with lashes; molded light brown hair. The body, of flexible
plastic, wrinkles and feels like real flesh. Advertised as "The
Magic Skin Baby." The one piece body can be bathed without
damage. Marked on back of head: "Ideal Doll//Made in
U.S.A.//Pat. No. 2252077." Made by Ideal Novelty & Toy Co.
of New York. First doll to be made of a new material — plastic.

936. UNEEDA DOLLS
Period: Second quarter of 20th century.
Body: All composition; jointed arms and legs.
Remarks: Pair of 12" (30.5cm) composition dolls with painted
features; sleeping eyes; molded hair. In original condition. Label
on box in which pair were sold reads: "Uneeda Doll Co.//Made
in the U.S.A." Made by the Uneeda Doll Company of New York,
founded in 1917. Dolls unmarked except for tags on clothing.
Collection of Mrs. Donald J. Marion.

BELOW:
937. QUINTUPLETS BY MADAME ALEXANDER
Period: 1936.
Body: Composition; elastic strung.
Remarks: A complete and original set of Dionne Quintuplet
dolls standing 7½" (19.1cm) in height. Painted hair and features.
Wear original costumes with gold colored name pins. Quintuplet
dolls were made to represent the famous children at various age
levels. Marked on head and shoulders: "Alexander." Made by
Madame Alexander of New York. *Collection of Zelda H.
Cushner.*

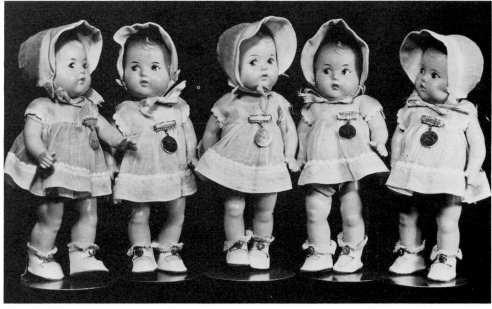

LEFT:
938. SHIRLEY TEMPLE — DOLL IN COMPOSITION
Period: 1934.
Body: Composition; elastic strung.
Remarks: In 1934 the *Shirley Temple* doll first appeared. Made by the Ideal Novelty and Toy Company in likeness of the child actress. The doll was made in various sizes with extensive wardrobe. *Merrill Collection.*

939. SHIRLEY TEMPLE DOLL — JAPANESE COPY
Period: Late 1930s.
Body: Jointed composition; elastic strung.
Remarks: 7½" (19.1cm) cheaply made Japanese version of the popular *Shirley Temple* doll. Smiling face has painted features. Note molded and painted hair as opposed to American made *Shirley Temple* which has a wig of mohair. Interesting also is the painting of black slippers over feet with molded toes. Marked on back shoulders (see insert): "Japan" with reversed letter "J" and "N." *Merrill Collection.*

LEFT:
940. "SNOW WHITE" DOLL
Period: 1937.
Body: Jointed composition; elastic strung.
Remarks: 15" (38.1cm) composition character doll of *Snow White*, from the famous movie of that name by Walt Disney. The painted head has expressive brown eyes cast to side; molded blue bow in black hair. Wears original dress of yellow rayon with brown velvet bodice. Underside of hair marked: "© Walt Disney 1937." Back shoulders marked: "Knickerbocker Toy Co. New York."

RIGHT:
941. "WENDY-ANN" DOLLS BY MME. ALEXANDER
Period: Circa 1930.
Body: Jointed composition; elastic strung.
Left: Composition doll with painted blue eyes and molded brown hair. Of lesser quality than doll at right — perhaps of slightly later manufacture.
Right: Well finished composition doll with sleeping eyes; hair lashes; human hair wig.

Both dolls are 13" (33cm) in height, and are marked: "Wendy-Ann//Mme. Alexander//New York." Elaborate costumes were made for the *Wendy-Ann* dolls.

942. PRINCESS ELIZABETH — DOLL IN COMPOSITION
Period: Circa 1937.
Body: Jointed composition; elastic strung.
Remarks: 13½" (34.3cm) composition *Princess Elizabeth* doll. Sleeping eyes; open mouth with teeth; blonde human hair wig. Wears original costume and coronet. Back of head marked: "Pr. Elizabeth Alexander." Tag sewed to dress reads: "Princess Elizabeth by Madame Alexander, N.Y. All rights reserved." Doll made at time of coronation of King George VI.

RIGHT:
943. SONJA HENIE DOLL
Period: 1939-40.
Body: Jointed composition; elastic strung.
Remarks: 21" (53.3cm) all original *Sonja Henie* doll — made in the likeness of the skating and movie star. The swivel-neck head has sleeping eyes; open mouth with teeth; blonde human hair wig. She wears a labeled pink satin costume trimmed with silver lace and flowers. Laced boots have attached metal skates. Made by Madame Alexander of New York, New York.

944. CHARLIE McCARTHY DOLL
Period: 1937.
Body: Cloth body with molded composition hands
and feet.
Remarks: Composition character doll of the famous puppet,
Charlie McCarthy, dressed in evening clothes and wearing
monocle. Made by Fleischaker & Baum, New York.

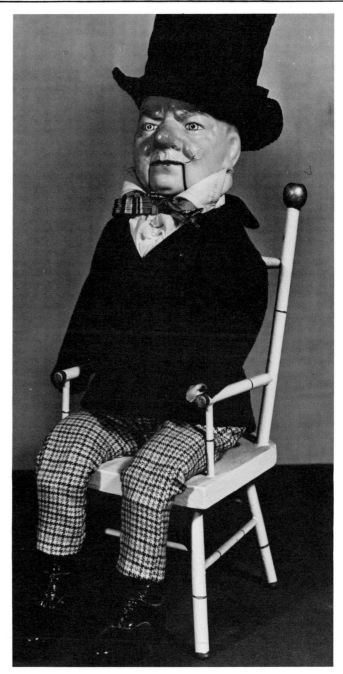

945. W. C. FIELDS DOLL
Period: Second quarter of 20th century.
Body: Cloth with molded composition shoes.
Remarks: Composition character doll (puppet) of the famous
actor, W. C. Fields. Marked on back of shoulders: "W. C. Fields
An Effanbee Product." Made by Fleischaker and Baum, New
York.

LEFT:
946. "BABY SNOOKS" DOLL
Period: 1938.
Body: Composition hands and wooden feet are
attached by flexible wires to wooden torso
allowing doll to assume different postures.
Remarks: *Baby Snooks* as portrayed by famous actress Fanny
Brice. Stands 12" (30.5cm) in height. Composition head with
painted features. Real ribbon bow tied to molded loop atop hair.
Made by Ideal Novelty & Toy Company of New York.

CLOCKWISE:

947. "MAMMY DOLL" BY TONY SARG

Period: 1940.

Body: Brown cloth with brown composition arms and black molded composition shoes; jointed at neck and shoulders.

Remarks: 17" (43.2cm) Black character doll with well modeled laughing face; brown painted eyes; black mohair wig with attached hoop earrings. Wears original red striped dress and white apron. Tag attached to doll reads: "Tony Sarg's Mammy Doll//Sole Distributor Geo. Borgfeldt Corp. New York, N.Y." *Collection of Nancy Shurtleff.*

948. RELIEF DOLL — WORLD WAR II

Period: Circa 1946.

Body: Cloth stuffed with husks; pink crepe de chine covered hands.

Remarks: Handmade, 15" (38.1cm) boy doll in crocheted ethnic costume. Smiling papier mâché head has painted features and brown painted, applied hair. Sent from Germany in appreciation of clothing sent by a woman's group of the Lynn, Massachusetts, Unitarian Church. A common practice following World War II among churches. *Collection of Mrs. Elmer Morley.*

949. KÄTHE KRUSE DOLL MADE IN OCCUPIED GERMANY

Period: Post World War II.

Body: All cloth with stitched-in fingers and toes.

Remarks: A 14" (35.6cm) transitional Käthe Kruse doll with thin composition head on cloth body. Has painted features and human hair wig. Left foot marked: "Kathe Kruse//921659." Right: "Made in Germany//U.S. Zone." Earlier all cloth dolls by Käthe Kruse ceased being made during World War II, and the illustrated doll has been supplanted by an all plastic doll which has sleeping eyes and human hair wig. It is still being marketed. *Merrill Collection.*

397

General Information on Celluloid Dolls

Celluloid is a synthetic material which was invented in 1869 by the Hyatt brothers of Newark, New Jersey. It was used as a substitute for more expensive substances such as bone, ivory, and hard rubber, which it could be made to resemble. A patent to improve dolls of celluloid was granted in the United States to William B. Carpenter in 1880.

Most dolls of celluloid found today were manufactured in Germany and often bear the turtle trademark with the words "Schutz Marke" registered in 1889 by the Rheinische Gummi & Celluloid Fabrik Company who made dolls of celluloid in 1902.

Heads and complete dolls were made of this material, most of them manufactured during the very late 19th and early 20th century.

Heads came on the same type bodies as those used on bisque dolls of the period: strung composition, cloth or leather. In some instances, limbs of celluloid were used when heads of this material topped soft bodies.

Celluloid heads could also have been used as replacements for broken ones of bisque.

950. 19th CENTURY CELLULOID DOLL
Period: Last quarter of 19th century.
Body: Leather.
Remarks: Rare, 9" (48.3cm) celluloid doll with all the appearance of the so-called *French Fashion* dolls of bisque. Made of a heavy celluloid much like ivory in appearance. Doll has swivel-neck; blown blue glass eyes; light mohair wig. *Merrill Collection.*

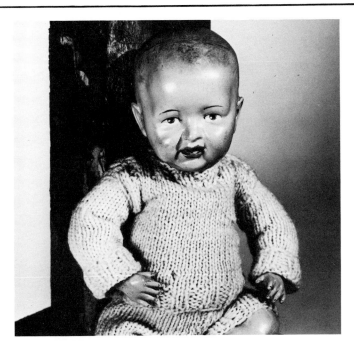

951. PARSONS-JACKSON BABY
Period: Circa 1910.
Body: All celluloid; steel spring jointed.
Remarks: A 10½" (26.7cm) baby doll, with painted features, made entirely of a celluloid-like material advertised as "Bisko-line." Manufactured by the Parsons-Jackson Co. of Cleveland, Ohio, whose name and trademark, of a stork, are carried on the doll's head and back. The typical baby body is jointed with steel springs and, being watertight, will float.

954. CELLULOID BOY DOLL — WITH MECHANISM
Period: First quarter of 20th century.
Body: All celluloid; elastic strung legs only.
Remarks: 19" (48.3cm) all celluloid boy doll with painted features; stationary glass eyes. Manipulation of lever in center back (see illustration) causes head and arms to move. Trademark on back shoulders: "bird in flight." Origin unknown. *Collection of Miss Ruth E. Whittier.*

952. ALL CELLULOID DOLL —
FRENCH
Period: First quarter of 20th century.
Body: Celluloid with elastic strung arms.
Remarks: 13½" (34.3cm) all celluloid doll with molded hair; painted features; and movable arms only. Marked under Wyvern (Winged Dragon) trademark on back shoulders: "35//France." Made by Societe Industrielle de Celluloid, Paris, France. This firm also used trade name Sicoid. *Collection of Ruth E. Whittier.*

FAR RIGHT:
953. ALL CELLULOID DOLL —
GERMAN
Period: First quarter of 20th century.
Body: Celluloid with elastic strung arms.
Remarks: 9" (22.9cm) all celluloid doll with molded hair; painted features; movable arms strung with elastic. Same type doll may have movable legs as well. Found in various sizes. Bears the turtle trademark and words "Schutz-Marke." Made in Germany.

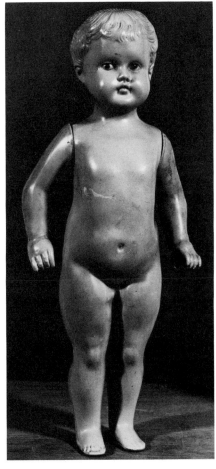

399

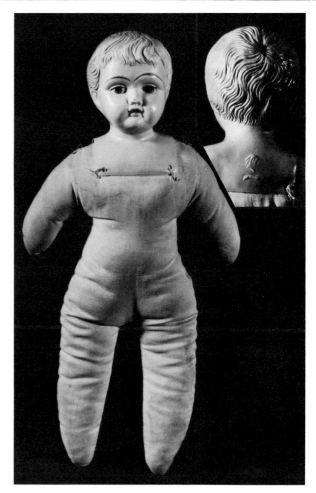

955. CELLULOID MASK DOLL
Period: 1912-1920.
Body: All cloth.
Remarks: 9½" (24.2cm) doll with cloth body showing needle holes where decorative yarns were stitched in lieu of clothing. Doll has bells in place of hands, and came with a peaked cap with bell attached. Frequent references in Sears, Roebuck Co. and Butler Bros. catalogs of the 1912-14 period to their dolls having "full celluloid heads" leads one to suspect the partial celluloid facial masks on this type of doll were of even cheaper price and quality. Maker unknown.

ABOVE RIGHT:
956. CELLULOID DOLL HEAD WITH "AMERICAN" TRADEMARK
Period: Circa 1920.
Body: Cloth.
Remarks: 10" (25.4cm) doll with celluloid shoulderhead on homemade cloth body. Molded hair and features, including blue eyes, are painted. Marked on back of shoulders with Indian head over word "American" (see insert). Indian head trademark used on celluloid dolls by Louis Sametz of New York; made dolls in the 1920s. *Merrill Collection.*

RIGHT:
957. BOY HEAD IN CELLULOID
Period: Early 20th century.
Body: Leather or cloth with celluloid limbs.
Remarks: Well modeled celluloid shoulderhead with set-in glass eyes. Bears turtle trademark and words "Schutz-Marke." This German firm, Rheinische Gummi & Celluloid Fabrik Co., was granted a patent in 1905 for a celluloid doll head with glass eyes.

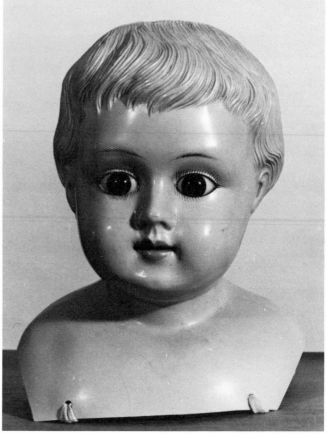

958. CELLULOID HEAD WITH MINERVA TRADEMARK

Period: Early 20th century.
Body: Leather or cloth with celluloid limbs.
Remarks: Celluloid head with molded hair and painted eyes. Marked with "helmet" trademark of the Minerva dolls on front of chest. This trademark more commonly found on metal heads. Made by German firm of Buschow & Beck. This particular head was found on a kid body — a replacement for a broken head of bisque. *Courtesy of Mrs. Philip Wilbur.*

960. BOY DOLL WITH INSECT TRADEMARK

Period: First quarter of 20th century.
Body: Cloth; jointed at shoulders and hips; celluloid arms.
Remarks: 13" (33cm) boy doll whose celluloid head has painted eyes; open-closed mouth with two painted-in teeth and molded brown hair. Head marked with insect trademark plus "30// Germany." Maker uncertain.

959. CELLULOID DOLL HEAD WITH LEHMAN MARK

Period: Early 20th century.
Body: All metal; mechanized.
Remarks: A close-up of a celluloid head from a mechanical doll which bears an unusual mark — that of the Lehman Company of Germany. Dolls by this firm are rare as they made mostly other types of tin wind-up toys. Head shown was probably made by a German doll manufacturer on order of the Lehman Company who, in turn, requested they use the Lehman trademark. For complete doll see page 371, Illustration 860. *Merrill Collection.*

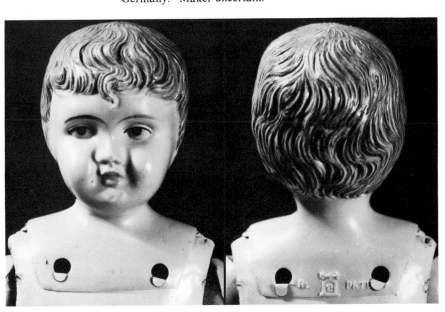

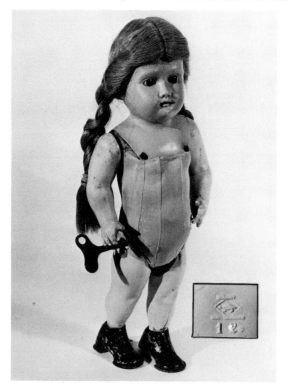

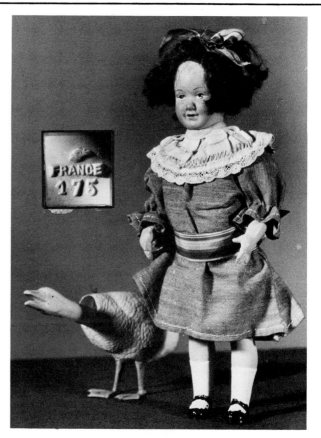

961. CELLULOID WALKING DOLL

Period: Early 20th century.

Body: All composition; cloth-covered torso houses key-wound mechanism.

Remarks: 13" (33cm) key-wound walking doll whose nailed-on celluloid head has set-in glass eyes; open mouth; human hair wig. When set in motion, doll walks on her wide, black metal boots. Head bears tortoise trademark and words: "Germany//Schutz Marke." Size 12 (see insert). *Collection of The Children's Museum, Boston, Massachusetts.*

962. ALL CELLULOID DOLL — MADE IN FRANCE

Period: First quarter of 20th century.

Body: All celluloid; jointed at shoulders and hips.

Remarks: 7" (17.8cm) celluloid doll with painted features and brown mohair wig. Legs have white ribbed socks and black one-strap slippers. The head of an eagle trademark of the factories of Petitcollin with a shop in Paris.

963. CELLULOID DOLL BY J. D. KESTNER

Period: Early 20th century.

Body: Jointed composition; elastic strung.

Remarks: 13" (33cm) doll whose celluloid socket head has sleeping eyes; open mouth with teeth; mohair wig. Made by the German firm of J. D. Kestner. Marked: "J.D.K.//200" plus turtle trademark. Doll heads of the same mold may be found in various materials, including bisque and celluloid. *Collection of Frieda P. Marion.*

964. CELLULOID DOLL BY J. D. KESTNER SHOULDERHEAD

Period: Early 20th century.

Body: Leather with bisque arms.

Remarks: 14½" (36.9cm) doll whose celluloid shoulderhead has sleeping eyes; open mouth with teeth; mohair wig. Head marked: "J.D.K.//201/1." Body bears oval sticker with Kestner trademark plus "JDK//Germany." Made in Germany by the J. D. Kestner Company. *Collection of Melba Brown.*

402

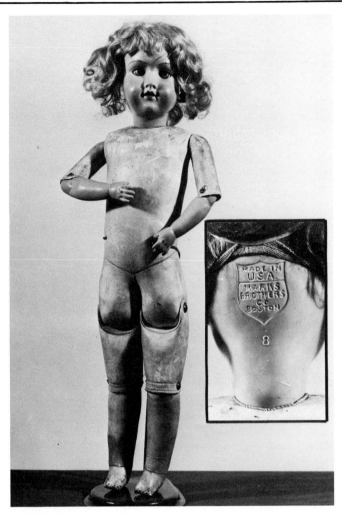

965. CELLULOID DOLL — MADE IN UNITED STATES BY MARKS BROS. OF BOSTON

Period: First quarter of 20th century.

Body: Leather with celluloid forearms and patented joints; arms are elastic-strung through wooden tube in shoulders.

Remarks: 23" (58.4cm) doll whose celluloid head has sleeping eyes; open mouth with teeth; mohair wig. The socket head is spring-mounted on leather covered body — unusual. Head bears the mark: "MADE IN//U.S.A.//MARKS//BROTHERS// CO//BOSTON" (see insert). _Merrill Collection._

BELOW LEFT:
966. FLIRTY-EYED CELLULOID DOLL

Period: Early 20th century.

Body: Composition; elastic strung.

Remarks: Celluloid baby doll whose flirty-eyes have the additional feature of eye lids that open and shut. The lids also have remnants of hair lashes. Wig is blonde mohair. Doll has typical bent limb baby body and is very similar to bisque-headed baby dolls of period. Bears mark: "K & W" within circle. Made in Germany by König & Wernicke.

BELOW:
967. SLEEPING-EYED CELLULOID DOLL

Period: Early 20th century.

Body: Composition; elastic strung.

Remarks: Celluloid head with open and shut eyes; open mouth with teeth; mohair wig. A well proportioned and pleasing doll resembling closely the bisque headed dolls of the period. Bears mark: "K & R" with turtle trademark. Made in Germany.

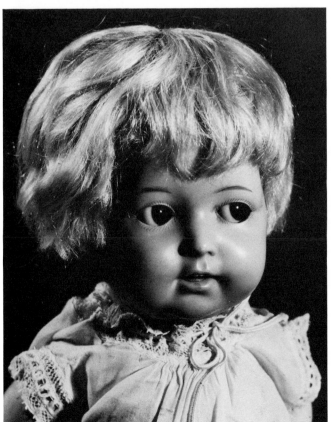

968. CELLULOID BOY DOLL WITH FLIRTING EYES
Period: First quarter of 20th century.
Body: Composition; elastic strung.
Remarks: Good quality, 15" (38.1cm) smiling boy doll in celluloid. Open mouth; molded tongue; two upper teeth; flirting eyes; mohair wig. Marked: "K & R" with star; "1728/4" turtle in diamond. Made by the Kämmer & Reinhardt firm of Germany. *Collection of Mrs. Mildred B. Fink.*

971. CELLULOID BOY DOLL
Period: Second quarter of 20th century.
Body: Celluloid; jointed at hips and shoulders.
Remarks: 20" (50.8cm) boy doll with stationary blue glass eyes; closed mouth; light blonde hair. Bears a crowned mermaid trademark in shield, plus number "50." Made by Celluloidwaren-Fabrik, Babenhausen, Germany. This firm also used "Celba" as a trademark. *Collection of Mrs. Eugenia S. Shorrock.*

969. ALL CELLULOID TODDLER
     WITH FLIRTING EYES
Period: Early 20th century.
Body: All celluloid; elastic strung.
Remarks: 14" (35.6cm) smiling toddler with all celluloid body. Fine quality celluloid head has open mouth with two upper teeth; flirting eyes with hair lashes; light mohair wig. Marked: "K (star) R// 728/5//Germany//38 plus turtle trademark. Made by Kämmer & Reinhardt firm of Germany. *Merrill Collection.*

FAR RIGHT:
970. BOY DOLL — BY MADAME
     HENDREN
Period: First quarter of 20th century.
Body: Cloth with composition limbs.
Remarks: The celluloid head of this 19" (48.3cm) boy has stationary glass eyes; open mouth with teeth; and bears the turtle trademark. Clothing is all original, including black velvet suit and tam-o-shanter. The cloth body, with voice box, is stamped: "Madame Hendren Doll// 1720// Made in U.S.A." Dolls so marked were manufactured in the United States by Averill Manufacturing Company.

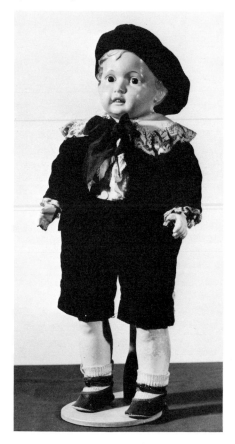

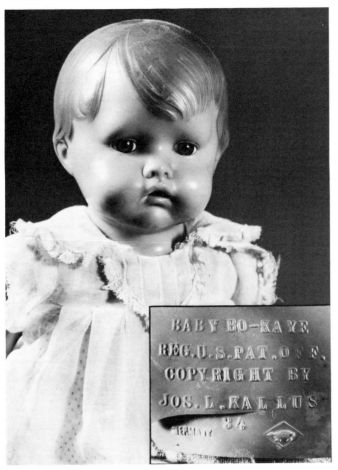

CLOCKWISE:

972. "BABY BO-KAYE" BY KALLUS

Period: Circa 1925.

Body: Cloth with composition arms.

Remarks: The celluloid shoulderhead of this 16" (40.6cm) baby has stationary glass eyes; open mouth with teeth; molded light brown hair. Marked with turtle trademark plus: "BABY BO-KAYE//REG. U.S. PAT. OFF.//COPYRIGHT BY//JOS. L. KALLUS//34//GERMANY" (see insert). This doll was also made in composition and bisque. *Collection of Shirley F. Sanborn.*

973. CELLULOID DOLL MARKED "W Z"

Period: Circa 1925.

Body: Atypical; imitation leather with metal fasteners at knees and hip joints; jointed wooden arms and composition hands are elastic strung through wooden tube in shoulders; voice box in back.

Remarks: The flange-necked celluloid head of this 12" (30.5cm) doll has well modeled and painted head. Open-closed mouth has two painted-in teeth. Marked: "Inge//1//1924//W Z." Probably made by German firm of Wagner & Zetzche.

974. CELLULOID DOLL IN FOREIGN DRESS

Period: Circa 1925-1930.

Body: Imitation leather with patented joints; celluloid arms.

Remarks: 12" (30.5cm) doll whose celluloid shoulderhead has painted blue eyes; rosy cheeks; closed mouth; molded light brown hair. Shown dressed and undressed. Wears original foreign costume. Clothing labelled: "Arbeid Adelt//Keizers-gracht//412." Head marked with turtle trademark. Made in Germany. Foreign dressed dolls of the twentieth century are often found with celluloid heads.

975. CELLULOID CREEPING BABY
Period: Circa 1940.
Body: Key-wound mechanism within metal body shell.
Remarks: 3" (7.6cm) creeping baby with celluloid head and limbs. An inexpensive doll made in Japan. Doll creeps when key-wound mechanism is set in motion.

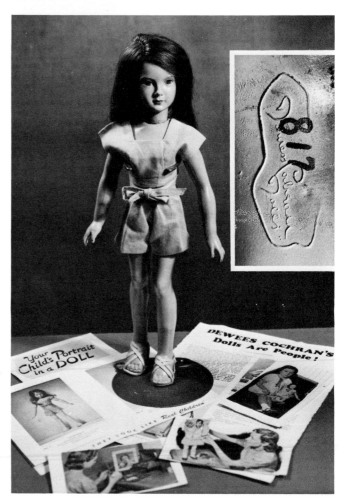

976. ALL RUBBER GIRL DOLL MADE IN ENGLAND
Period: Circa 1940.
Body: All rubber; jointed at hips and shoulders.
Remarks: 18" (45.7cm) all rubber girl doll with painted features; synthetic wig. Original school girl uniform consists of navy blue woolen jacket and skirt; white blouse; straw hat. Blouse labeled: "Clydella//Made in England." Inside jacket labeled: "Beau Brummel Clothing." Pocket embroidered: "Sanford Witherslack." Doll unmarked. Made in England by Sanford Witherslack. *Courtesy of The Margaret Woodbury Strong Museum, Rochester, New York. Photograph by Barbara W. Jendrick.*

977. "CINDY" ALL LATEX DOLL — DESIGNED BY DEWEES COCHRAN
Period: 1947-1948.
Body: All latex; jointed at neck, shoulders and hips.
Remarks: *Cindy* a 15" (38.1cm) quality doll of latex designed by Dewees Cochran. Sold by Dewees Cochran, Inc., Madison Ave., New York. Made by Molded Latex Co. of New Jersey. In production less than one year with only 1000 made. Numbered in order of manufacture (above stamped #817). *Cindy* is the only doll bearing mark of Dewees Cochran (see insert). *Merrill Collection.*

RIGHT:
978. ALL RUBBER BABY DOLL MADE IN JAPAN
Period: Circa 1925-1930.
Body: All rubber; jointed at shoulders and hips;
elastic strung.
Remarks: 8½" (21.6cm) all rubber baby with deeply molded features; painted blue eyes; light brown hair. Marked on back: "85//Perfection//Baby//Japan." *Collection of Miss Ruth E. Whittier.*

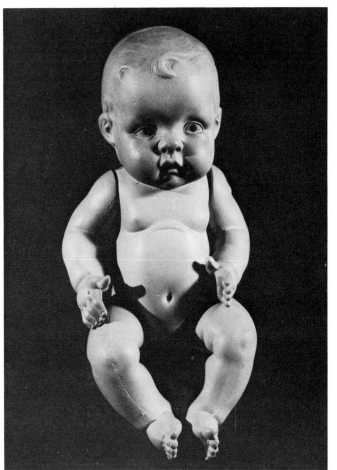

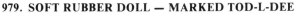

979. SOFT RUBBER DOLL — MARKED TOD-L-DEE
Period: 1925 — pre-vinyl era.
Body: Rubber; set-in plastic eyes.
Remarks: 10½" (26.7cm) soft rubber toddler type doll, with molded underwear, socks, and sandals. The doll has a metal whistle in it's back which whistles when squeezed. Bottom of sandal bears mark: "TOD-L-DEE ©//THE SUN RUBBER CO.//BARBERTON, O. U.S.A.//20." *Merrill Collection.*

RIGHT:
980. CHAD VALLEY RUBBER DOLLS
Period: Second quarter of 20th century.
Body: Rubberized cloth with molded rubber limbs.
Remarks: 12" (30.5cm) (overall) character dolls whose heads, of thin molded rubber, have painted features including hair. Felt clothing is original. Ageing has caused both heads and limbs to become hard and brittle with resultant deterioration. Other character dolls of this type were made by this company who is better known for their fine cloth dolls. Dolls shown are tagged: "Hygienic Toys//Made in England by//The Chad Valley Co. Ltd." *Merrill Collection.*

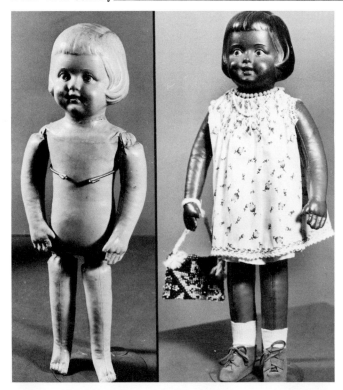

LEFT:
981. VINYL PLAY DOLLS BY M.J. CHASE CO.
Period: 1935+.
Body: Vinyl coated nylon; latex stuffed.
Left: A 16" (40.6cm) doll with a molded and painted vinyl head. Same mold in brown coloring used for Black doll called *Chloe*. Back of shoulders has a circular paper sticker with trademark of The M. J. Chase Company of Pawtucket, Rhode Island. *Collection of Eloise M. Thomas.*
Right: A 17" (43.2cm) Black doll with molded and painted vinyl plastic head. Manufactured by The M. J. Chase Co. of Pawtucket, Rhode Island. This Company was famous for their earlier fine quality, oil painted all cloth dolls. They also made hospital nursing school training models. *Merrill Collection.*

982. "G. I. JOE" CHARACTER DOLL
Period: Circa 1942.
Body: Composition; elastic strung.
Remarks: 15" (38.1cm) smiling character doll representing soldier of World War II. Composition head has painted features and molded on military cap. Wears original khaki uniform. Unmarked. Attached paper label bears title of Frank Loesser's song: "Praise the Lord and Pass the Ammunition." This same doll came dressed as a sailor with molded-on white cap.

983. GENERAL DOUGLAS MacARTHUR
Period: Circa 1942.
Body: Composition; elastic strung; jointed at shoulders and hips.
Remarks: 19" (48.3cm) portrait doll of General Douglas MacArthur. Composition head has painted features and molded-on military cap. Right arm positioned so as to allow saluting. Wears original khaki uniform. Made by Freundlich Novelty Corporation.

408

Metal Dolls - 20th Century

Metal dolls are collectible but currently not of great value.

Heads of this material, frequently found, bear the trademark names "Minerva," "Juno," and "Diana." All made in Germany during the early 20th century and sold in this country through United States distributors.

Metal heads were advertised as combining all the durability of metal with the beauty of bisque but "do not break." They were sold separately as replacements for the easily broken heads of the day. Therefore, metal heads are found on various bodies including those that originally had heads of bisque.

Metal was seldom used in the manufacture of doll bodies.

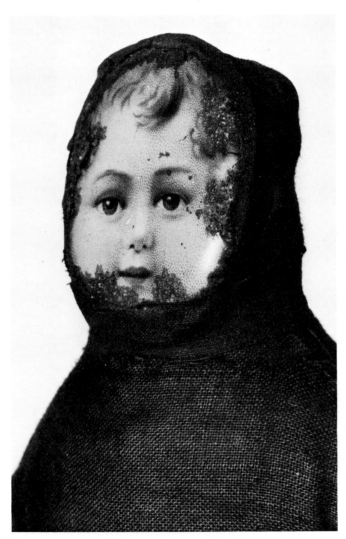

984. DOLL WITH METAL FACE MASK
Period: Early 20th century.
Body: Stuffed cotton; fixed arms and legs.
Remarks: 10" (25.4cm) inexpensive commercially made cloth bodied doll with unique metal facial mask, oval in shape, with features lithographed in bright flesh colors. Bright blue eyes; bright red lips; and brown hair. Body medium blue cotton with dark blue band around waist, and red band around neck line. Unmarked, maker unknown. *Merrill Collection.*

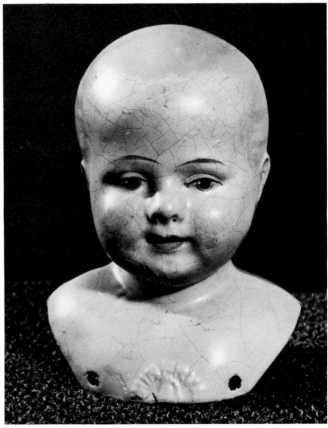

985. BABY HEAD — MARKED "MINERVA"
Period: Early 20th century.
Body: Cloth with composition or leather arms.
Remarks: Marked *Minerva* head of painted metal made in Germany by Buschow & Beck and distributed in United States by A. Vischer & Co. This shoulderhead is of a baby or toddler and has painted blue eyes and blonde hair.

986. METAL DOLL — MARKED "JUNO"
Period: First quarter of 20th century.
Body: Cloth with metal arms.
Remarks: 16" (40.6cm) doll with metal head. Set-in glass eyes; molded blonde hair. Purchased as an entirety on cloth body with metal arms. Metal heads were also advertised and sold as replacements for breakable ones of the period. Marked on chest with a crown trademark and the word "Juno." Made by Karl Standfuss of Germany and distributed by George Borgfeldt & Company of New York.

987. BRASS HEAD MARKED "PATENT"
Period: Early 20th century.
Body: Cloth or leather.
Remarks: 18" (45.7cm) doll whose brass head, mounted on kid body with bisque arms, is a replacement for one of bisque. A common practice as metal heads were made and advertised for this purpose. Has molded blonde hair; inset glass eyes; open mouth with teeth. "Patent" is embossed in metal on front of shoulders; "Deponert//6" on back. Made in Germany. Possibly by Buschow & Beck who made brass doll heads. *Collection of Mrs. Nancy Klix.*

410

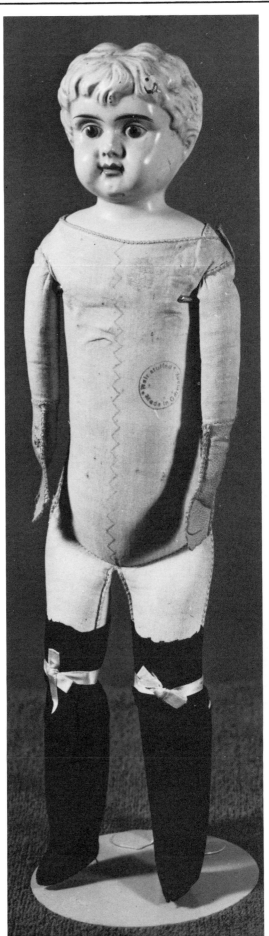

LEFT:
988. "MINERVA" METAL HEADED DOLL
Period: Early 20th century.
Body: Pink muslin with leather forearms.
Remarks: 16" (40.6cm) doll in excellent condition. Brass head has painted features including eyes. Body, original to the doll, is stamped: "Hair Stuffed// Made in Germany." Head marked on front shoulders: "Minerva" over helmet. Made by German firm of Buschow & Beck and distributed in United States by A. Vischer & Company. *Minerva* heads were also sold separately as replacements for damaged heads of the day.

989. WIGGED METAL HEAD — MARKED "MINERVA"
Period: Early 20th century.
Body: Cloth or leather.
Remarks: An excellent example of a trademarked *Minerva* metal doll head with mohair wig and inset glass eyes. This head, made in Germany by Buschow & Beck, was advertised in 1901 by United States distributor, A. Vischer & Co. of New York, as easily adjustable to doll's body, combining all the durability of metal with the beauty of bisque, but "do not break."

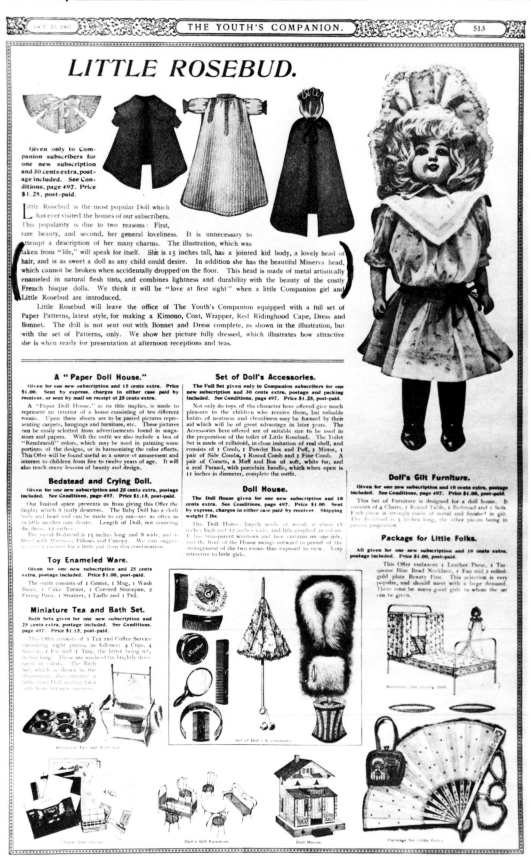

990.
Reproduction of a page from *The Youth's Companion* of
October 19, 1905 advertising *Little Rosebud* doll and accessories.
Section bracketed mentions the use of the "beautiful *Minerva*
head, which cannot be broken---"

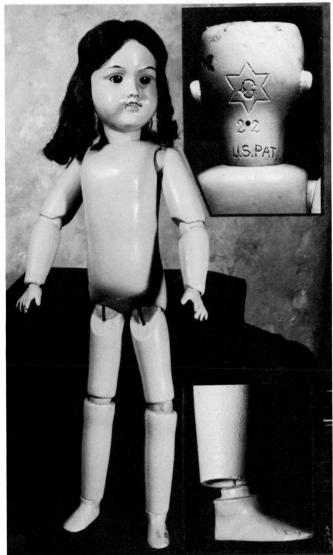

LEFT:
991. SLEEP EYES METAL HEAD — MARKED "MINERVA"
Period: First quarter of 20th century.
Body: All cloth with painted forearms and lower legs.
Remarks: Painted metal head with helmet and Minerva trademark on chest. This head features sleeping glass eyes and remnants of a stitched wig. On page 124 of the 1903 *Montgomery Ward Co. Catalog, Minerva* heads are sold separately to be used as replacements for dolls having broken bisque or china original heads. This 16" (40.6cm) body is obviously older than the date of the *Minerva* head and must have had an older head originally. *Merrill Collection.*

992. METAL DOLL HEAD — MARKED "DIANA"
Period: Circa 1905.
Body: Leather with composition limbs.
Remarks: 15" (38.1cm) doll whose metal head has sleeping glass eyes; open mouth with teeth; applied metal ears; mohair wig. Stamped in red on back shoulders (see insert): "Diana//DEP." A seldom seen mark. Made and distributed by German firm of Alfred Heller. Came on leather body stamped with Columbia trademark of United States distributor Louis Wolf & Company. This company advertised dolls with metal heads in 1904. *Collection of Miss Ruth E. Whittier.*

LEFT:
993. DOLL WITH ALUMINUM HEAD BY GIEBELER-FALK DOLL CORP.
Period: 1918-1921.
Body: Ball-jointed; elastic strung wooden body with aluminum hands and feet.
Remarks: Interesting American made doll. Well painted aluminum head has metal sleeping eyes; open-closed mouth with painted-in teeth; human hair wig. 25" (63.5cm) in height. Marked (see insert): "G (within star) 22//U.S. Pat." Made by Giebeler-Falk Doll Corp. of New York. *Merrill Collection.*

413

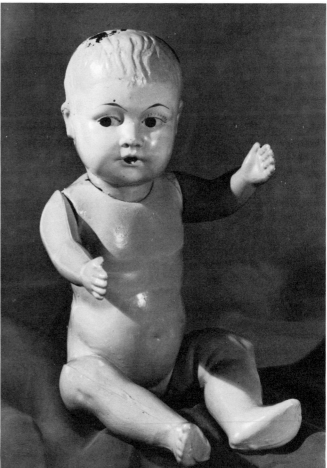

LEFT:

994. "MAMA DOLL" — SQUEEZE BABY

Period: Copyrighted in 1915.

Body: Wooden bellows mounted on circular base; wired-on metal arms; nailed-on head.

Remarks: The flung back metal head of this 9½" (24.2cm) baby is attached to a wooden bellows. Cries: "Mama/Papa." Painted head has blue eyes; open-close mouth; and blonde hair. Wears original cotton dress and bonnet. Label missing from front of dress once read: "Fully Patented//Mama Doll//I Talk!!// Squeeze Me Easy//Made in America//Cop. 1915 by Louis V. Aronson." Made by Art Metal Works of Newark, New Jersey. *Merrill Collection.*

995. ALL METAL BABY DOLL WITH BRASS HEAD

Period: World War I.

Body: All metal; strung with metal springs.

Remarks: 12" (30.5cm) brass headed, all metal doll whose painted features include dark blue eyes cast to side. 5/8" (1.6cm) circular opening in top of head originally held the small hank of mohair used in making wig. A well made doll strung with metal springs instead of the usual elastic — a method used during World War I when elastic was in short supply. Unmarked.

LEFT:

996. BABY DOLL WITH METAL HEAD

Period: Circa 1920.

Body: Cloth with composition limbs.

Remarks: 22" (55.9cm) baby doll whose painted metal head has sleeping eyes and open mouth with four upper teeth. Bears strong resemblance to composition dolls of period. Believed to be dressed in original clothes. Unmarked.

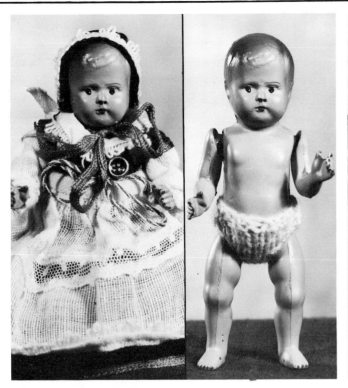

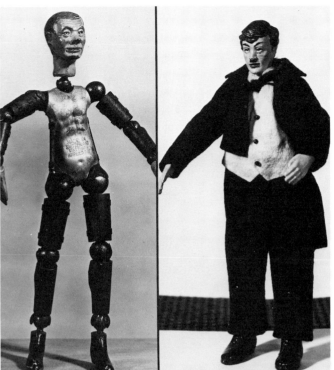

997. ALL METAL DOLL IN DANISH COSTUME
Period: Circa 1949.
Body: All metal; jointed at shoulders and hips.
Remarks: 5" (12.7cm) doll die cast of soft metal. Shown dressed and undressed. Head has painted features and light brown molded hair. Purchased in 1949. Wears original Danish costume.

998. ALL METAL JOINTED DOLLS
Period: 20th century; patented in 1921.
Body: All metal jointed; heads, hands and feet of molded composition.
Remarks: Metal joints of these dolls snap apart. Made in Switzerland. Found in numerous characters. Sold in the 1920s for a few dollars. Quite collectible today. Man on right represents Charlie Chaplin. Also made in comic character likenesses. Both 7½" (19.1cm) tall. A. Bucherer patented these dolls in 1921. *Merrill Collection.*

999. ALL METAL JOINTED DOLLS
Period: 20th century; patented in 1921.
Bodies: All metal jointed; heads arms and feet of molded composition.
Remarks: Swiss-made comic characters 6" (15.2cm) to 10" (25.4cm) in height. **Left to right:** A *Dutch girl, Bugs Bunny, Mrs. Katzenjammer,* and *Maggie.* Made by the firm of A. Bucherer of Switzerland who obtained both German and British patents for metal ball-jointed dolls. *Merrill Collection.*

Cloth Dolls - 20th Century

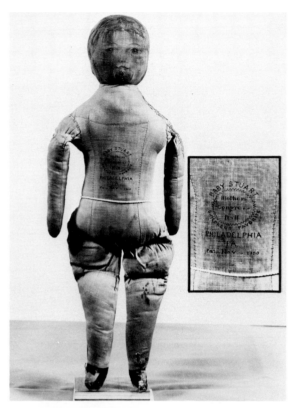

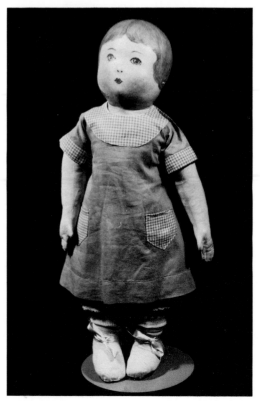

LEFT:
1000. MOTHERS' CONGRESS DOLL
Period: Patented November 6, 1900.
Body: All cloth.
Remarks: 24" (61cm) stuffed rag doll, with printed features, made by Mothers' Congress Doll Co., Philadelphia, Pennsylvania, under patent granted to Madge L. Mead in 1900. Blonde hair with blue bow; blue eyes; black slippers. Marked on body (see insert): "Mothers' Congress Doll//Baby Stuart//Children's Favorite//Philadelphia, Pa.//Pat. Nov. 6, 1900."

1001. FOXY GRANDPA
Period: 1904.
Body: All cloth — stuffed.
Remarks: 20" (50.8cm) stuffed cloth doll in likeness of *Foxy Grandpa*, a lovable old comic strip character created by artist, Charles E. Schultz. With bunny under arm and Masonic emblem on watch fob, he appears exactly as drawn on design patent #36,564, granted to Mr. Schultz on September 22, 1903. The doll was made, under this patent, by the Art Fabric Mills of New York. *Merrill Collection.*

LEFT:
1002. CLOTH DOLL BY NINA BONNER ALBRITTON
Period: 1914 through mid-20th century.
Remarks: 20" (50.8cm) all cloth doll with handpainted features. Designed and made by Nina B. Albritton of Kentucky. These unmarked, individually crafted dolls were generally marketed in the southern United States. Also made as babies, children, Blacks, Indians, Dutch and Japanese. *Collection of Mrs. Elmer Morley.*

416

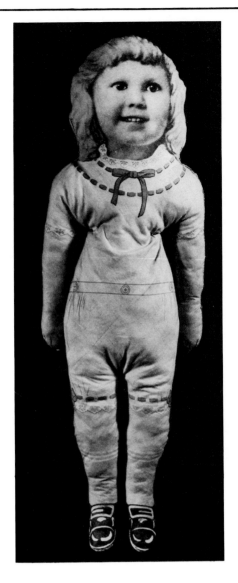

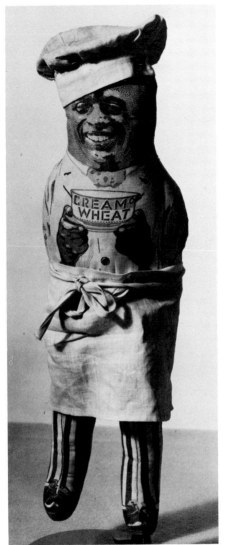

FAR LEFT:
1003. CLOTH DOLL WITH PHOTOGRAPHIC FACE
Period: Circa 1910.
Remarks: 24" (61cm) early 20th century cloth stuffed doll whose colorfully printed face is from a photograph of an actual child. This type doll, with it's alive expression, was made by several manufacturers of cloth dolls. This doll was possibly made by Saalfield Publishing Company of Akron, Ohio. *Merrill Collection.*

1004A. RASTUS, THE CREAM OF WHEAT CHEF
Period: 1920-1930.
Body: All cloth.
Remarks: 18" (45.7cm) premium doll *Rastus, the Cream of Wheat Chef.* Printed in color on cloth, it came ready to cut out, sew and stuff. First appeared in 1922. Obtained by sending a box top and ten cents to manufacturer of cereal. One of many such cut-out dolls produced for advertising purposes.

1004. BLACK CLOTH DOLL
Period: Early 20th century.
Body: Brown cloth with mitten shaped hands.
Remarks: 15" (38.1cm) all cloth Black boy doll with well printed cloth face. Commercially made, but unmarked. Dressed in red jersey shirt; blue cotton pants held up by tan suspenders. Remnants of mohair wig still cling to back of head. *Collection of Mrs. Melba Brown.*

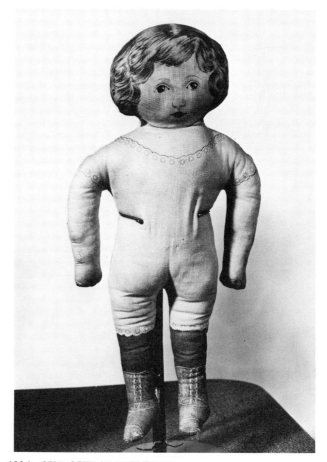

1006. CUT-OUT CLOTH DOLL
Period: Early 20th century.
Body: All cloth.
Remarks: Typical early 20th century 19" (48.3cm) cut-out rag doll. Made by other firms as well as the Art Fabric Mills who made the doll shown. Marked on foot: "Pat. Feb. 13, 1900."

1005. BUSTER BROWN CLOTH DOLL
Period: First quarter of 20th century.
Body: All cloth.
Remarks: 18" (45.7cm) (overall) *Buster Brown* cloth doll made in likeness of the popular cartoon character. A very good commercially made doll with painted features. Fringe of light mohair is sewed to head beneath white tam. Wears dark red linen costume trimmed in white. Unmarked. *Buster Brown* was also printed on cloth to be cut-out and stuffed. *Collection of Mrs. Elmer Morley.*

1007. "SWEETS" — CLOTH DOLLS BY GEORGENE
Period: 1938.
Body: All cloth.
Remarks: Renowned artist, Maude Tousey Fangel, painted one of her famous baby faces for the doll *Sweets* by the Averill Manufacturing Co. of New York, who advertised it as a "cuddly and washable little beauty." Shown dolls, with like faces, were part of a store display for Christmas of 1938.
Left: Baby tagged: "Sweets//A Georgene Doll."
Right: Toddler tagged: "Averill Cloth Doll//An Original Georgene Novelty."

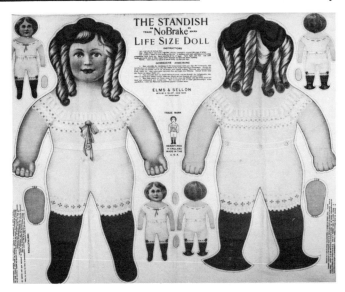

1008. "AMERICAN BEAUTY" CUT-OUT CLOTH DOLL
Period: Copyright 1913.
Remarks: 16" (40.6cm) cloth doll called *American Beauty*. It originally came printed on cloth sold by the yard to be cut out, sewed and stuffed. The same piece of yardage contained a 25½" (64.8cm) version of the same doll plus printed instructions for finishing. She has side parted blonde hair, with red ribbon bow, and printed underwear, socks and shoes. Dolls were printed and sold by the Empire Art Company of Chicago, Illinois. *Merrill Collection.*

1009. UNCUT STANDISH "LIFE SIZE DOLL"
Period: 1918.
Remarks: An uncut Standish *No Brake* cloth doll of little girl in printed underwear, shoes and stockings. Trademark printed "Life Size// Babies Clothes Will Now Fit Dollie// Registered in England// Made in U.S.A." Cloth also printed with full instructions for cutting out, stitching and stuffing. This doll is rarely found in uncut condition.

1010. SCARLETT O'HARA MAMMY DOLL
Period: 1937-1940; believed to be made by WPA workers in Macon, Georgia.
Bodies: 14½" (36.9cm) *Mammy* stuffed black cloth, gray yarn hair, and painted features, 4½" (11.5cm) white baby has fully formed stuffed cloth body. Painted features.
Remarks: *Mammy* dressed in dark brown cotton printed dress. Has pantalettes and petticoat. White apron over dress. Baby dressed in lace trimmed baby clothes. *Mammy* wears high boots made from old imitation leather. *Collection of Mrs. Elmer Morley.*

1011. WORSTED DRESSED CLOWN
Period: Circa 1914.
Body: Cloth.
Remarks: The stockinette face of this 13" (33cm) clown has worsted features and hair, bead eyes. Wears multi-colored worsted figured costume. Advertised in Butler Brothers 1914 catalog as a specialty doll. American made. Also came dressed as boys and girls in various sizes. This type doll was advertised as early as 1889 in Montgomery Ward & Company catalog. *Merrill Collection.*

LEFT:
1012. WHITE DOLL BY BRÜCKNER
Period: Patented July 9, 1901.
Body: All cloth.
Remarks: 14" (35.6cm) white doll made under Brückner patent of 1901. The mask is molded in the white conformation with printed blue eyes; closed mouth with red lips; brown eyes; and mixed brown and yellow hair. Same patent date on right shoulder as seen on Black Brückner doll. *Merrill Collection.*

1013. BLACK DOLL BY BRÜCKNER
Period: Patented July 9, 1901.
Body: All cloth.
Remarks: 14" (35.6cm) Black doll made under Brückner patent of 1901 which covered process for molding fabric faces. The mask face has red shading over large, highlighted eyes, red cheeks and smiling mouth showing two rows of teeth. Black mohair wig is tucked under red kerchief. Right shoulder printed: "Pat'd. July 9, 1901." Made by Albert Brückner of New Jersey. *Merrill Collection.*

LEFT:
1014. TOPSY-TURVY DOLL IN CLOTH BY BRÜCKNER
Period: Patented July 9, 1901.
Body: All cloth.
Remarks: 12½" (31.8cm) upside down cloth doll with one head black, the other white. When in position, the skirt completely covers the unused doll. Both faces are lithographed. The white doll has printed blonde hair; blue eyes; wears red checked dress and bonnet. The black doll has black mohair wig; laughing mouth with teeth; red dress and kerchief. All original, including clothes. Cloth label, sewed to neckband, reads: "Brückner Doll — Made in U.S.A." Made by Albert Brückner of New Jersey under patent of July 9, 1901. This date is also stamped on right front edge of neck — on both dolls.

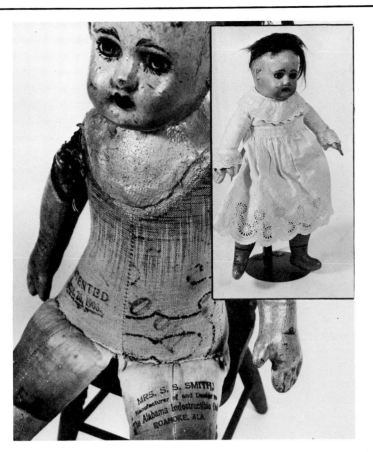

1015. ALABAMA INDESTRUCTIBLE CLOTH DOLL
Period: Patented September 26, 1905.
Body: All cloth.
Remarks: Cloth stuffed doll with painted head, limbs and features; stitched-in fingers; blue legs with shoes outlined in black. Both black and white dolls were made. This doll, shown dressed and undressed (with mark), has hair wig. Uncommon, as most models came with painted hair. Bears maker's stamp on upper leg: "Mrs. S. S. Smith//The Alabama Indestructible Doll//Roanoke, Ala." On the body is printed: "Patented Sept. 26, 1905." *Collection of Mrs. Fidelia Lence.*

1016. BLACK ALABAMA BABY DOLL
Period: Patented September 26, 1905.
Body: All cloth with painted limbs.
Remarks: 19" (48.3cm) Black cloth doll in pristine condition. Hair and features painted. Marked on body: "Patented Sept. 26, 1905//No.1." Marked on leg: "Mrs. S. S. Smith//Manufacturer of and Dealer in The Alabama Indestructible Doll//Roanoke, Ala." *Collection of Mrs. Elmer Morley.*

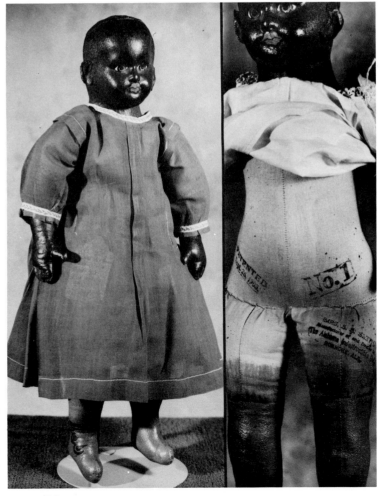

ABOVE LEFT:
1017. CHASE BABY DOLL — STAMPED "SECOND"
Period: Late 19th and early 20th century.
Body: All cloth.
Remarks: 12½" (31.8cm) baby doll by Martha Chase of Pawtucket, Rhode Island. Painted head has brown eyes; blonde hair. Bears paper label on back (see insert). Chase dolls usually marked by stamped trademark. *Interesting note:* "Second" is stamped on body of shown doll. Originally purchased at the M. J. Chase Company factory at Pawtucket, Rhode Island. *Merrill Collection.*

ABOVE:
1018. CHARACTER DOLL BY MARTHA J. CHASE
Period: Early 20th century.
Body: All cloth with oil painted lower limbs.
Remarks: Rare, 16" (40.6cm) character doll by Martha J. Chase of Pawtucket, Rhode Island. An all cloth doll with raised features painted in oil, including brown eyes. Long molded curls are used in styling of upswept hair; cluster of five falling from crown in back and two over each ear on sides. Fringe of painted wispy locks frame face. Stamped with Chase circular trademark as well as paper label. *Collection of Melba Brown.*

LEFT:
1019. BLACK DOLL BY MARTHA J. CHASE
Period: Early 20th century.
Body: All cloth; brown sateen covered.
Remarks: 26" (66cm) Black doll by Martha J. Chase of Pawtucket, Rhode Island. All cloth doll with ethnic features; raised and painted in oils. Wig of black astrakan cloth. Labeled on back (see insert): "The Chase Stockinet Doll//made of stockinet and cloth." Character dolls by Mrs. Chase are scarce. *Collection of Mrs. Elmer Morley.*

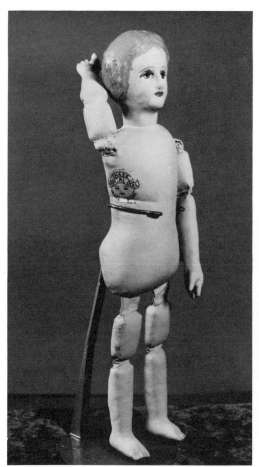

LEFT:
1020. LADY DOLL BY CHASE
Period: Circa 1910.
Body: Waterproof painted cloth; pink in color.
Remarks: 15" (38.1cm) lady doll of cloth with raised features painted in oils, including blue eyes. Light brown painted hair drawn to bun in back. Made to be fully immersed in warm water. Bears circular trademark with words "Chase Hospital Doll" under right arm. Made by M. J. Chase Co., Pawtucket, Rhode Island.

1021. LADY DOLL BY MARTHA CHASE
Period: First quarter of 20th century.
Body: Cloth painted in pink waterproof oil paint.
Remarks: 14½" (39.4cm) lady doll of cloth with raised features painted in oils. Eyes greyish-brown in color. Light brown painted hair is drawn to two buns in back. Made by M. J. Chase Co., Pawtucket, Rhode Island. *Collection of Clara Hobey.*

LEFT:
1022. GEORGE WASHINGTON PORTRAIT DOLL BY MARTHA J. CHASE
Period: Early 20th century.
Body: All cloth.
Remarks: 25" (63.5cm) portrait doll of George Washington by Martha J. Chase of Pawtucket, Rhode Island. An all cloth doll with raised features painted in oils. Wears blue and buff satin costume; lace trimmed. This doll, as well as other character dolls made by Mrs. Chase, is scarce. *Collection of Mrs. Fidelia Lence.*

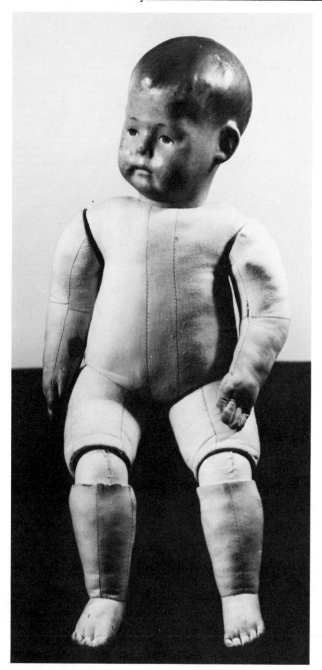

1023. ALL CLOTH DOLL WITH JOINTED, ELASTIC STRUNG BODY

Period: First quarter of 20th century.
Body: All cloth; elastic strung and jointed.
Remarks: Most unusual, unmarked 16" (40.6cm) doll. Cloth stuffed body is jointed and elastic strung. Note cloth covered ball joints at knees. Although head differs, body seams and stitching of hands and toes suggestive of dolls by Käthe Kruse. Mold of painted socket head similar to one in bisque by Simon & Halbig for Kämmer & Reinhardt. *Collection of Miss Zelda Cushner.*

BELOW:
1024. KÄTHE KRUSE ALL CLOTH BOY DOLLS

Period: Early 20th century.
Body: All cloth.
Remarks: 17" (43.2cm) blonde and 16" (40.6cm) brunette boy dolls whose molded and painted cloth heads, on well proportioned toddler bodies, are of highest quality. They bear a number plus the name of their German maker, Käthe Kruse, on the soles of their feet. These early, artistically made, all cloth dolls by this artist are highly collectible. They may be purchased today, but they are of plastic. The all cloth dolls have not been available since World War II. *Merrill Collection.*

1025. FELT DOLL BY STEIFF
Period: Circa 1912.
Body: All felt; jointed at neck, hips and shoulders.
Remarks: 11" (27.9cm) felt doll with seam down center of face characteristic of dolls by Steiff. She has molded features; round blue glass eyes; seamed and stitched-on ears; blonde mohair wig. Given to a child in 1912. Made by Margarete Steiff of Germany. *Merrill Collection.*

1026. FELT DOLL BY STEIFF
Period: First quarter of 20th century.
Body: All felt; jointed at neck, hips and shoulders.
Remarks: 18½" (47cm) felt doll with seamed face; stitched-in features; round blue glass eyes; light mohair wig. Metal button in ear printed with words "Steiff — trademark." Made in Germany. The gray felt elephant pull toy shown is also by Steiff who manufactured a well made line of felt toys and dolls. Doll wears original felt costume; velvet trimmed.

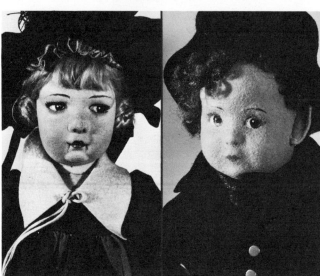

1027. SARDINIAN FOOT SOLDIER BY LENCI
Period: Early 20th century.
Body: All felt.
Remarks: 17" (43.2cm) well made felt doll with painted features; mohair wig. Dressed in dark green-gray uniform of Sardinian foot solider. Feathered, black felt hat is decorated with rosette of Italian national colors. Made in Italy. Trademarked: "Lenci" di E. Scavini (Lenci of E. Scavini). *Collection of Mrs. Elmer Morley.*

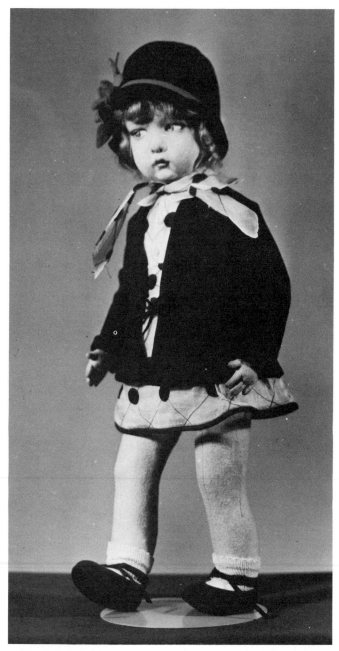

1028. LENCI DOLLS
Period: Early 20th century.
Body: Early ones — felt; later ones — cloth.
Remarks: Artistic and well made felt dolls by Enrico and Elena Scavini. Patented in Turin, Italy, September 8, 1921. Trademarked: "Lenci." Dolls made in many sizes to represent babies, children, and characters.

1029. CHILD DOLL BY LENCI
Period: First quarter of 20th century.
Body: All felt.
Remarks: 22" (55.9cm) all felt doll. Lenci series 109, c.1920-26. Little girl type. Painted features; eyes turned to right. Cotton dress with blue felt polka dots. Blue felt hat; coat; and slippers. Costume and underclothes all original. Stamped "LENCI" on left foot. Made by E. Scavini Co., in Turin, Italy. *Merrill Collection.*

426

1030. CLOTH "PHILADELPHIA BABY"
Period: Early 20th century.
Body: Stockinette covered body with painted cloth
    arms and legs.
Remarks: 22" (55.9cm) cloth doll with molded and painted
features including brown eyes and hair. Called *Sheppard Doll* or
Philadelphia Baby. Made by J. B. Sheppard & Company of
Philadelphia, Pennsylvania. *Merrill Collection.*

1031. CLOTH "PHILADELPHIA BABY"
Period: Early 20th century.
Body: Stockinette covered body with painted cloth
    arms and legs.
Remarks: 22" (55.9cm) cloth doll with molded and painted
features including brown eyes and hair. Called *Sheppard Doll* or
Philadelphia Baby. Made by J. B. Sheppard & Company of
Philadelphia, Pennsylvania. *Collection of Mrs. Elmer Morley.*

427

1032. ALL CLOTH DOLL — MARKED ROLLINSON
Period: 1917-1919.
Body: All cloth; sateen covered; painted lower
limbs.
Remarks: A 22" (55.9cm) all cloth doll with painted face and features. This doll has the Rollinson Doll, Holyoke, Massachusetts, trademark stamped on the back of the body. The handwritten number 8226 can be seen at the upper back neckline. The doll is fitted with a wig. *Collection of Nancy Shurtleff.*

BELOW:
1033. ALL CLOTH DOLL — MARKED ROLLINSON
Period: 1917-1919.
Body: All cloth; sateen covered; painted lower
limbs.
Remarks: 22" (55.9cm) cloth doll with painted head and features; closed mouth; pierced nostrils. "Rollinson Doll//Holyoke, Mass." is printed within border of stamped-on trademark on stomach. These dolls also came with hair wigs and painted-in teeth. New information (1977) plus more legible trademarks, proves designer was Gertrude F. Rollinson. Manufacturer was Utley Doll Co., listed in Holyoke, Massachusetts directories from 1917-1919. *Collection of Mrs. John E. Clark.*

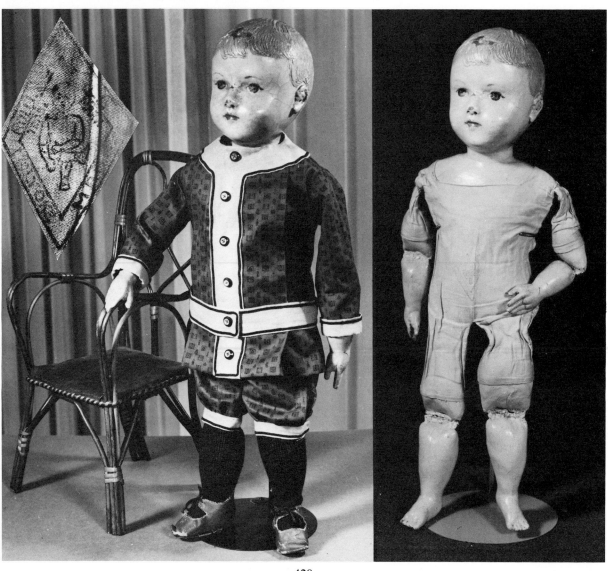

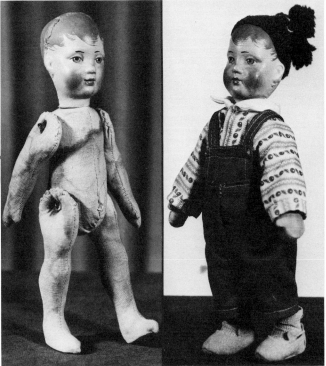

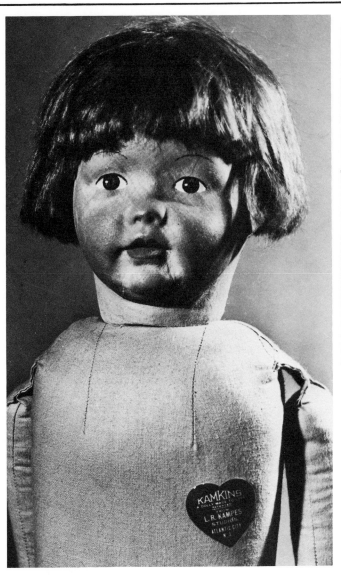

1035. CLOTH BOY DOLL
Period: First quarter of 20th century.
Body: All cloth.
Remarks: 8" (20.3cm) boy doll whose cloth stuffed head has sewed-on facial mask of pressed cloth. Features, including blue eyes, are well painted and his hair is reddish brown in color. Wears printed shirt, overalls, cap and felt shoes. Unmarked.

1034. KAMKINS DOLL
Period: Second quarter of 20th century.
Body: All cloth.
Remarks: 19" (48.3cm) Kamkins doll was made in Atlantic City, New Jersey, by the Kampes family. Well made and expensive doll of the day. New outfits for the dolls were designed each spring and fall. Dolls were also refinished and repaired. They were made to order to resemble their new owners as to coloring, hairstyle, etc. In 1928 listed: L. B. Kampes Studio, 1031 Board Walk, also 6 Central Pier. Out of business in 1934. *Collection of Miss Ruth Whittier.*

1036. CLOTH DOLL WITH GLASS EYES
Period: Circa 1924.
Body: Stockinette.
Remarks: 16" (40.6cm) soft play doll with face of stiffened stockinette; set-in glass eyes; painted features; brown mohair wig. Wears original pink velvet costume. One of a series of dolls designed by English artist Mabel Lucie-Attwell. Made by Chad Valley, Ltd. (formerly Johnson Brothers, Ltd.) by appointment, toymakers to the Queen. In 1938 made portrait dolls of Royal family. Doll shown bears trademark button which reads: "Chad Valley - British - Hygienic Toys." *Collection of Eugenia Shorrock.*

1038. CHARACTER DOLLS BY NORAH WELLINGS
Period: First half of 20th century.
Body: All cloth.
Remarks: Four all cloth dolls 9½" (24.2cm) to 12½" (31.8cm) in height. Features are oil painted on faces of velvet or felt. These inexpensive but well made character dolls were popular items with children as well as tourists. Each doll has label on foot reading: "Made in England//by//Norah Wellings."

1037. CLOTH "FLAPPER" — MADE IN FRANCE
Period: 1920.
Body: Cloth stuffed; chiffon covered head, shoulders and arms.
Remarks: All original, 14½" (36.9cm) flapper. Reinforced, molded cloth head is covered with layers of chiffon upon which features are painted. Overly large glass eyes look sideward. Wears tan crepe dress, blue felt cloche. Chiffon petticoat labelled "Made in France." Probably made by Mme. la Baronne de Laumonth of Paris who, in 1914, began making rag dolls of chiffon. *Collection of Miss Ruth Whittier.*

1039. LIBERTY OF LONDON ROYAL DOLLS
Period: Second quarter of 20th century.
Body: All cloth.
Remarks: Royal portrait dolls by Liberty of London. Flesh colored cloth faces with stitched-in and painted features. Approximately 8¼" (21cm) to 10" (25.4cm) in height. From left to right: *Queen Mary, George VI, Queen Elizabeth* and *Queen Victoria.* Liberty dolls may be found representing many other personages as well as royal and coronation figures.

1040. KING GEORGE VI IN VARIOUS UNIFORMS AND CORONATION ROBES

Period: 1937.
Body: Cloth; jointed at neck, shoulders and hips.
Remarks: 14" (35.6cm) tall. Made for his coronation in 1937. Robes and regalia are complete and authentic. The head is of molded felt with painted features. Labeled on sole of foot: "Farnell's Alpha Toys// Made in England." Coronation robe tagged: "H. M. The King." Made in England by J. K. Farnell & Co. Ltd., Acton, London W3. Dressed in several costumes. Shown also in the uniform of the Royal Air Force and dressed as The Royal Highlanders. *Merrill Collection.*

1041. DUKE OF KENT BY CHAD VALLEY, LTD.

Period: Circa 1940.
Body: Felt torso, velvet limbs.
Remarks: 15" (38.1cm) cloth doll, representing Prince Edward, Duke of Kent. Felt head has painted features; set-in glass eyes; mohair wig. One of four portrait dolls of British royal children by Chad Valley Co., Ltd. Duke of Windsor was also made. 1941 advertisement read: "The Royal Children — Life-like reproductions convoyed by the British Navy." Priced from $12.00 to $15.00 *Princess Elizabeth, Princess Margaret Rose, Prince Edward, Princess Alexandria* were made in this series.

1042. FRENCH PEASANTS BY BERNARD RAVCA
Period: 1945.
Body: Cloth; silk stockinette drawn over faces and
  arms.
Remarks: 10" (25.4cm) all original handmade cloth dolls representing French peasants from Anjou and Auvergne provinces. Needle sculptured faces have painted features. Wear original Paris tags with artist's signature. Two of the many accurately detailed character and portrait dolls by French artist Bernard Ravca who became a United States citizen in 1947.

ABOVE:
1043. RELIEF DOLL — WORLD WAR II
Period: Circa 1946.
Body: Cloth with stockinette limbs.
Remarks: Handmade, 10" (25.4cm) girl doll in ethnic dress. Sent from Germany to a women's group of the Lynnhurst, Massachusetts Methodist Church in appreciation of clothing packages — a common practice in churches following World War II. The features of the stitch-molded stockinette head are embroidered with the exception of painted lashes and brows. Wig of flax. *Merrill Collection.*

1044. CLOTH CHARACTER DOLLS
Period: 1927+.
Body: Wire armatures, fabric covered.
Remarks: The 1927 catalog of the Kämmer & Reinhardt Co., of Waltershausen, Germany, in addition to showing their regular line of bisque headed dolls, contained a page displaying about 25 male character dolls with molded cloth faces. The characters represented various stations in male life, such as *Dude, Bum, Porter, Clerk, Bellhop, Professor, Chauffer, Elderly Gentlemen,* etc. Dolls from 12" (30.5cm) to 16" (40.6cm) in height. Very rare. *Collection of Eugenia Shorrock.*

Index - General _____

M

Mabel; 300, 301, 368
Mae Starr Phonograph Doll; 390
Magic Skin Baby Doll; 393
Maid; 271
Makepeace, B.L. Inc.; 380
Mama Doll; 414
Mammy; 419
Mammy Doll; 397
Marcus, Samuel; 352, 384
Margie; 390
Marquerite; 300, 301, 307
Marie; 287
Marion; 368
Marks Brothers; 403
Marotte; 261
Marque, A.; 280, 281
Marseille, Armand; 243, 298-304, 349-353, 370, 388
Marsh, Charles; 53
Martha Washington; 375
Martin, Frank D.; 17
Martinique; 149
Mary-Anne-Georgian; 3
Mason & Taylor; 17, 18
Massachusetts Organ Company; 68
McAboy, Mary; 334, 374
Mead, Madge L.; 416
Meakin & Ridgeway; 313
Mechanical doll; 237, 248-263, 276, 315, 320, 338, 351, 370-373, 399, 406
Meissen; 96
Metal dolls; 409-415
Metro Doll; 382
Metro Doll Co.; 382
Mibs; 387
Michton, Morris; 381
Milliners Models; 22
Milton Emporium; 149
Milton, Portsmouth; 149
Minerva; 409, 411-413
Minerva dolls; 401
Mrs. Katzenjammer; 415
Molded Latex Co.; 406
Montanari; 47, 51
Montanari type; 52, 54, 55
Montgomery Ward Company; 419
Moon Mullins; 366
Morimura Brothers; 343
Morse, Ozias; 46
Mother; 271
Mother's Congress Doll Co.; 416
Motschmann type; 30, 55, 62, 110
Musical doll; 68
Music box; 369
My Dream Baby; 388
My Playmate; 299

N

Nathan Hale; 376
Nell Gwynne; 376
New Born Babe; 345
New Hampshire Grandma; 375
New Hampshire Grandpa; 375
New York Rubber Company; 156

Nottingham Toy Industry, Ltd.; 313
Nursing Bru; 213

O

Ohlaver, Gebrüder; 313, 364
Ohrdruf, Thüringia, Germany; 176
O'Neill, Rose; 360, 361
Oriental dolls; 240, 279, 343, 344, 349, 375
Orsini, Jeanne I.; 357
Our Darling; 355
Our Fairy; 359

P

Pansy; 300, 301
Papier mâché; 19-37, 39, 41, 44, 46, 75-78, 90, 104, 128, 148, 338, 397
Parian dolls; 158-181, 185-190
Paris-Bébé; 225
Parisienne; 202, 203
Parsons-Jackson Baby; 399
Parsons-Jackson Co.; 399
Patricia; 389
Patsy Baby; 392
Patsyette; 389
Pauline; 368
Peck, E.S.; 144
Pedlar; 50, 79, 108, 149
Peter; 287
Petitcollin; 402
Petite Sally; 389
Petit, Jacob; 88
Petzold, Dora; 385
Philadelphia Baby; 399, 427
Philadelphia Centennial; 252
Phillips, Content; 73
Photographic face doll; 417
Pierrotti; 47, 53
Pillar; 133, 134, 267
Pincushion dolls; 367
Policeman; 144
Porter; 432
Portrait dolls; 341, 375, 376, 379, 408, 415, 423, 430, 431
Portrait Jumeau; 214
Poulbot; 278
Pre-Greiner type dolls; 30, 31
President McKinley; 274
Primitive dolls; 137, 142, 184
Prince Edward; 431
Princess Alexandria; 431
Princess Elizabeth; 393, 395, 431
Pr. Elizabeth Alexander; 395
Princess Margaret Rose; 431
Princess Victoria; 9
Professor; 432
Pumpkin head; 57
Putnam, Grace Storey; 347, 348

Q

Queen Anne doll; 3-6
Queen Anne-type doll; 4, 6, 7, 71
Queen Elizabeth; 430
Queen Louise; 177, 303
Queen Mary; 430
Queen Victoria; 9, 51, 430

Quintuplets; 393

R

Rabery & Delphieu; 224
Rag dolls; 137, 142
Raleigh, Jessie McCutcheon; 384
Rastus, the Cream of Wheat Chef; 417
Ravca, Bernard; 432
Red Riding Hood; 242, 262, 263, 330, 331
Reinecke, Otto; 325
Reliable; 376
Relief Doll - World War II; 397, 432
Revalo; 313, 364
Revere, Paul Pottery; 311
Rheinische Gummi & Celluloid Fabrik Company; 398-400, 402
Robinson, Sarah; 37
Robinson-type body; 37
Rockwell, Grace Corry; 313, 387
Rohmer; 119, 120, 201, 204
Rollinson Doll; 428
Rollinson, Gertrude F.; 428
Rolly-Dolly; 378
Romper Boy; 387
Royal; 239
Royal Copenhagen Manufactory; 82, 88, 90, 94, 110
Rubber dolls; 152-157, 184, 406, 407
Ruth; 300, 301

S

Saalfield Publishing Company; 417
Sailor; 144, 145
St. Nicholas; 144
Sametz, Louis; 400
Sanders; 18
Santa; 307
Santa Claus; 144
Sardinian Foot Soldier; 426
Sarg, Tony; 397
Scarlett O'Hara Mammy Doll; 419
Scavini, E. Co.; 426
Scavini, Elena; 426
Scavini, Enrico; 426
Schilling, F.M. Co.; 43
Schmidt, Franz; 326
Schmidt, Franz & Company; 326
Schmidt, Paul; 310, 325
Schmitt; 64
Schmitt & Fils; 219
Schoenau & Hoffmeister; 310
Schoenhut, A. & Company; 336, 337, 378, 379
Schultz, Charles E.; 416
Schutz Marke; see Rheinische Gummi & Celluloid Fabrik Company
Schwarz, F.A.O.; 242
Scootles; 360
Sears, Roebuck Co.; 400
Seminole Indian doll; 374
S.F.B.J.; 247, 275-279, 384
Shaker doll; 243
Shell doll; 10, 20, 73, 93
Sheppard Doll; 427
Sheppard, J.B. & Company; 339, 427
Shirley Temple; 337, 394

Dates